D1555880

£ 6-50

ART

c 1/20

KA 0227537 6

ENGLISH NATIONAL OPERA GUIDES

Volume One

H.F. Garten
Wagner the Dramatist

Giulio Gatti Casazza
Memories of the Opera

James Harding
Jacques Offenbach — A Biography

Angus Heriot
The Castrati in Opera

Janos Liebner
Mozart on the Stage

Alfred Loewenberg
Annals of Opera 1597-1940

Stendhal
Life of Rossini
Lives of Haydn, Mozart and Metastasio

ENGLISH NATIONAL OPERA GUIDES

Volume One

La Cenerentola

Aida

The Magic Flute

Fidelio

Edited by Nicholas John
with a foreword by Lord Harewood

John Calder • London
Riverrun Press • New York

First published as one volume of four Guides 1980 by
John Calder (Publishers) Ltd.,
18 Brewer Street,
London W1R 4AS
and in the U.S.A. 1981 by
Riverrun Press Inc.,
175 Fifth Avenue,
New York NY10010

The individual *English National Opera Guides* were first published in 1980 as separate volumes by John Calder (Publishers) Ltd. in the U.K. and by Riverrun Press Inc. in the U.S.A.
© English National Opera 1980

'Fairytale and opera buffa: the genre of Rossini's *La Cenerentola*' © Philip Gossett 1980

'*La Cenerentola (Cinderella)*: a musical commentary' © Arthur Jacobs 1980

'*Cinderella* in performance: conversations with Mark Elder and Colin Graham' © English National Opera 1980

English translation of *La Cenerentola* by Arthur Jacobs
© G. Ricordi & Co. Printed by arrangement

Verdi's 'Egyptian business' © Michael Rose 1980

'*Aida*: Text and Music' © William Mann 1980

'The Genesis of *Aida*' © Roger Parker 1980

Extracts from the translations by Hans Busch reproduced by courtesy of the University of Minnesota Press 1979

English version of *Aida* © Edmund Tracey 1980

'Singspiel and symbolism' © Rodney Milnes 1980

'A vision of reconciliation' © David Cairns 1980

'A public for Mozart's last opera' © Nicholas John 1980

The Magic Flute English version
© Lyrics: Michael Geliot 1980
© Dialogue: Anthony Besch 1980

'Introduction' to *Fidelio* © Elizabeth Forbes 1980

'*Fidelio*: an operatic marriage' © Basil Deane 1980

'An extract from *Beethoven the Creator*' © John Calder (Publishers) Ltd. 1980

Fidelio English translation
© Lyrics revised: Tom Hammond 1980
© Dialogue: Rodney Blumer 1980

BRITISH LIBRARY CATALOGUING IN PUBLICATION DATA
English National Opera guides
    Vol. 1
    1. Operas-Librettos
    I. John, Nicholas
    782.1'2   ML50.48   80-41487

    ISBN 0-7145-3805-1 Casebound

Typeset in Plantin by Alan Sutton Publishing Limited, Gloucester.
Printed by Whitstable Litho Limited, Kent
Bound by G. & J. Kitcat Limited, London.

CONTENTS

Foreword

I have for years been a believer in opera in the vernacular — that is to say in the language of the audience. This is no new doctrine because initially every great operatic composer with the exception of Handel has wanted his audience to understand immediately the dramatic purpose for which he wrote his music. Mozart wrote court operas in Italian it is true, but he chose a German text to set if the audience was a more popular one. Almost everyone since has accepted translation as a necessity and has worked to get the translations right, as witness Verdi in Paris and Benjamin Britten everywhere. They all set tremendous store by an immediate audience understanding and reaction, and it is a fact that a well known Viennese composer recently refused to allow his opera to be done in England in German and threatened to withdraw it unless it was translated into English. It was.

We think of English National Opera as a platform of the composer's insistence on his opera providing the audience with a dramatic experience, and an understanding of the libretto is plainly an important part of this process.

There is a long tradition, going back in England at least as far as Handel's day, for librettos of operas to be on sale in the theatre. People used to read them beforehand, sometimes also during the performance (because the lights remained up), and quantities of them have come down to posterity singly or in collections.

The tradition still continues in the United States of America and on the Continent, but it is not nearly so much in evidence in England. I have never quite known why this should be so, since any of us accustomed to taking people to operatic performances will know that there is an invariable rule that your guest, if he or she does not know the work, will ask for a run-down on the story. Just occasionally, if they have the right reference books, they will have looked it all up ahead and it is the purpose of these English National Opera Guides to make this process easy and agreeable.

I know that I am always unhappy if I see a new work and have not had a chance of reading through the libretto or at least the story, and I know too that key verbal phrases will stick in one's mind and, given ordinary luck, have precisely the effect when heard in the theatre which the composer intended. Certainly, this is the kind of effect we hope these Guides will have and I am delighted to see them in a hard back volume.

Lord Harewood

English
National
Opera
Guide

1

La
Cenerentola
(Cinderella)
Rossini

Anna Pollak (Tisbe) and Denis Dowling (Dandini) in the celebrated 1959 Sadler's Wells production (photo: Houston Rogers)

Preface

English National Opera Guides are intended to be companions to opera in performance. They contain articles and illustrations relevant to any production and not only those mounted by English National Opera. Of general interest, also, is the inclusion of the complete original libretto of the opera, side by side with an English translation. There are many reasons why sung words may not be clearly distinguishable, whatever the language and however excellent the performance. The composer may have set several lines of text together, for instance, or he may have demanded an orchestral sound through which no voice can clearly articulate. ENO Guides supply English readers with an opportunity to know a libretto in advance and so greatly increase their understanding and enjoyment of performances whether live, broadcast or recorded.

We hope the Guides will prove useful to new and experienced opera-lovers alike. An audience which knows what to look and listen for — one that demands a high standard of performance and recognises it when it is achieved — is our best support and, of course, an assurance for the future of opera in the English-speaking world.

Nicholas John
Editor

1

La Cenerentola
(Cinderella)

Gioachino Rossini

English National Opera Guides Series Editor:
Nicholas John

John Calder ● London
Riverrun Press ● New York

First published in Great Britain, 1980, by
John Calder (Publishers) Ltd., 18 Brewer Street,
London W1R 4AS
and
First published in the U.S.A., 1980, by
Riverrun Press Inc.,
175 Fifth Avenue,
New York, NY 10010

ISBN 0 7145 3819 1 paperback edition

BRITISH LIBRARY CATALOGUING DATA

Ferretti, Jacopo
  La cenerentola — (English National Opera guides; 1).
  1. Operas — Librettos
  I. Title   II. John, Nicholas   III. Jacobs, Arthur
  IV. Rossini, Gioachino Antonio   V. Series
  782.1'2   ML50.R835

Typeset in Plantin by Alan Sutton Publishing Limited, Gloucester.
Printed by Whitstable Litho Limited in Great Britain.

Contents

List of Illustrations

Fairy–tale and opera buffa: the genre of Rossini's 'La Cenerentola'

Philip Gossett

The *Cinderella* story exists in various guises among the folktales of people throughout the world. Its most characteristic version in the European tradition is that of Charles Perrault, published in his *Contes* of 1697 as *Cendrillon ou La petite pantoufle de verre* (*Cinderella or The little glass slipper*). From Perrault derive the fairy godmother, the wicked step-mother, the Prince's ball, the midnight deadline, and the lost slipper, as well as the pumpkin, mice, rat, and lizards which become, respectively, the coach, horses, driver, and footmen, all indelibly associated with the story children still enjoy. Practically none of these elements, however, figure in the libretto by Giacomo Ferretti, *La Cenerentola, ossia La bontà in trionfo* (*Cinderella, or Goodness triumphant*), set to music by Gioachino Rossini and first performed at the Teatro Valle of Rome on January 25, 1817. The absence of magical elements has frequently been ascribed to Rossini's presumptive dislike of supernatural events in opera and his consequent insistence that Ferretti avoid them. But this explanation rings false, for just ten months later the composer produced his *Armida* in Naples, with spectacular magical effects and scenic extravagance. To understand the genre of *La Cenerentola* and the particular way Rossini and Ferretti handle the story, we must examine the social milieu of operatic composition in early-nineteenth-century Italy, the actual literary sources of Ferretti's libretto, and a significant artistic trend in contemporary Italian operatic librettos: the emergence of the so-called 'mixed genre', *opera semiseria*.

The pressures under which a successful composer was expected to work in Italy during the first decades of the nineteenth century were staggering: three, four, or even five new operas a year were commonplace. Between October 1815 and the première of *La Cenerentola* in January 1817, Rossini, shuttling between Rome and Naples, mounted the first performances of no fewer than six operas: *Elisabetta, regina d'Inghilterra, Torvaldo e Dorliska, Il barbiere di Siviglia, La gazzetta, Otello*, and *La Cenerentola*. The well-documented case of *Il barbiere* is notorious. A month before its first performance, Rossini began to receive the poetry from his librettist, Cesare Sterbini. A month before the première of *La Cenerentola* the subject had barely been chosen. Nor did the composer really have a month to work. Orchestral parts had to be copied, singers had to learn their roles by memory, and the entire

Maria Malibran, who, at the age of 17, created a sensation as Angelina in the first American performances, while her father's company visited New York. In a drawing by Hayter, 1829 (Opera Rara Collection)

Giuseppe de Begnis (in 1822), the creator of the role of Dandini (Opera Rara Collection)

work had to be staged. With Rossini producing masterpieces such as *Il barbiere*, *Otello*, and *La Cenerentola* under these conditions, it is less astonishing that he occasionally borrowed music from earlier operas than that he did not have recourse to this expedient more frequently.

Ever since *La cambiale di matrimonio* by the eighteen-year-old novice had its première at the Teatro San Mosé of Venice in 1810, Rossini was both master and victim of these extraordinary artistic conditions. Commissions poured in from theatres throughout northern Italy: *La pietra del paragone* and *Il Turco in Italia* for

Milan, *Tancredi* and *L'Italiana in Algeri* for Venice, and other works for Bologna and Ferrara. But in 1815 an event profoundly altered Rossini's career: Domenico Barbaja, impresario of the Teatro San Carlo in Naples, invited Rossini to establish residence there and to become musical director of the Neapolitan theatres. This proposal offered Rossini a permanent post and an escape from the excesses of his early career. Barbaja was crafty enough to allow Rossini freedom to compose for other cities, a temptation that at first proved appealing. From 1815 through 1817 he lived much as before, travelling from Naples to Rome and Milan, but from 1818 through 1822 Naples became his artistic home. Rossini could control his own schedule, allowing sufficient time for careful composition and production. His sojourn in Naples and the nature of the artists available there, however, were at least partly responsible for Rossini's abandoning altogether *opera buffa* to concentrate his efforts in the field of *opera seria*.

The composition of *La Cenerentola*, then, came at a crossroads in Rossini's career. He had begun to establish roots in Naples, but was still accepting commissions from other cities. His contract with the Teatro Valle for the Carnival season of 1817 had been signed the year before, on February 29, 1816, after the Roman première of *Il barbiere di Siviglia*. Rossini was supposed to write the opening opera of the season (December 26, 1816), and the theatre agreed to provide him with a libretto by October. Under the best of circumstances, then, Rossini would have been allowed little time, but in fact matters were much worse. Rossini's *Otello* did not have its Neapolitan première until December 4, 1816, so that the composer did not reach Rome until mid-December. The impresario, Pietro Cartoni, had presumably agreed that Rossini would write the second opera of the season instead of the opening one. We learn from the memoirs of Ferretti that the chosen libretto was entitled *Ninetta alla corte,* and was prepared by (Gaetano?) Rossi. Ferretti adds that the subject was actually *Francesca di Foix*, 'one of the least moral comedies of the French theatre in an epoch in which it was beginning to be known as an infamous school of libertinism . . . '* The ecclesiastical censors consequently insisted on so many changes that the libretto became incoherent, and Rossini, two days before Christmas, decided a new subject had to be found.

* Ferretti's report seems strange here and not completely reliable. *Ninetta alla corte* was presumably based on the libretto by Charles-Simon Favart, *Ninette à la cour*, first set to music in 1755, but better known at that time in the version adapted by August Creuzé de Lesser for Henri-François Berton. Berton's opera was first performed in Paris at the Opéra-Comique on December 21, 1811. *Francesca di Foix* is quite a different subject, based on a libretto by Jean-Nicolas Bouilly and Louis-Emmanuel Mercier-Dupaty, *Françoise de Foix*, set to music by Henri-Mouton Berton, father of Henri-François, and first performed at the Opéra-Comique on January 28, 1809. While both stories emphasize the dangers of court life for innocent young ladies, they are quite independent and it is difficult to imagine how they could have been combined into a single drama. *Françoise de Foix* ultimately did become an Italian opera, *Francesca di Foix* by Gaetano Donizetti, with a libretto by Domenico Gilardoni (Naples, Teatro San Carlo, May 30, 1831).

Gioachino Rossini

Pauline Viardot-Garcia, Maria Malibran's sister, who was a celebrated interpreter of La Cenerentola, singing it all over Europe and in St. Petersburg between 1830 and 1850 (Opera Rara Collection)

Ferretti was asked to provide the new libretto, and he and Rossini chose the subject of *Cinderella*. 'On Christmas day Rossini had the Introduzione. The cavatina of Don Magnifico on Saint Stephen's day (December 26); the duet for the tenor and soprano on San Giovanni (December 27). In short: I wrote the verses in *22* days and Rossini the music in *24.*' Rossini did have some assistance. Two arias (Alidoro's and Clorinda's) and a short chorus which opened Act II were the work of Luca Agolini, a Roman musician known mostly for his church music.* The secco recitative was also the work of another musician. But there is very little borrowed music in *La Cenerentola*: only the concluding section of the heroine's final rondò, '*Non più mesta accanto al fuoco,*' derived from the tenor aria in *Il barbiere di Siviglia*, '*Cessa di più resistere,*' and the Sinfonia, taken without change from *La gazzetta*. Rossini composed the remainder of this remarkable score in three weeks.

While Rossini's muse needed little external prodding in this collaboration, Ferretti's was another matter. In the author's preface to the original printing of his libretto, Ferretti excuses the quality of his verses, explaining that he had been compelled to write the text in a very short time. He then adds some words of explanation about the particular content of his version of the *Cinderella* story:

> If Cinderella does not appear in the company of a wizard who works fantastic miracles or a talking cat, and does not lose a slipper at the ball (but instead gives away a bracelet), as in the French theatre or in some vast Italian theatre, it should not be considered a *crimenalesae* (an act of lese majesty) but rather a necessity of staging at the Teatro Valle and a gesture of respect for the delicacy of Roman taste which does not permit on the stage what might please in a fairy-tale beside the fire.

Ferretti omits, except by implication, a fundamental fact. His text is in large part derived from the libretto by Charles-Guillaume Etienne for Nicolò Isouard's *Cendrillon* (Paris, Opéra-Comique, February 22, 1810), as further filtered through the libretto that Felice Romani prepared for Stefano Pavesi's opera *Agatina o La virtù premiata*, which had its première in Milan at the Teatro alla Scala ('some vast Italian theatre') in April 1814.

Cendrillon is an *opéra comique*, the musical numbers separated not by recitative but by spoken dialogue. Etienne's libretto already has most of the characteristic elements of Ferretti's: the step-father and two step-sisters; the Prince's trusted councilor, Alidor; the masquerade in which the Prince exchanges positions with his servant, Dandini. Emphases are different, to be sure. The Baron of Montefiascone is not Rossini's buffoon, for such characters are foreign to the French tradition. The roles of the two sisters are

---

* For a revival of the opera at the Teatro Apollo of Rome during the Carnival season of 1821, Rossini himself composed a new aria for Alidoro, frequently performed today in place of Agolini's.

Luigi Lablache, a famous Dandini (Opera Rara Collection).

more fully developed by Etienne. But already in Isouard's opera the role of the supernatural is minimal. An enchanted sleep is used to plant the elegantly clothed Cendrillon at the ball. Otherwise the story is essentially as in Rossini and Ferretti. Cendrillon does lose a slipper (following Perrault) instead of handing over a bracelet, but Ferretti's substitution is surely due to the offended modesty of the Roman censors. There are many precise parallels. The opening scenes of the operas are, for example, essentially identical, with the two sisters admiring themselves, Cinderella singing a little ballad ('*Il était un p'tit homme*' or '*Una volta c'era un re*'), Alidoro asking for charity, which only Cinderella will give, etc.. Romani's libretto for Pavesi draws directly on Etienne, and Ferretti uses them both. Thus, to speak of Ferretti's having eliminated the magical effects of the *Cinderella* story makes no sense, for he worked not with Perrault's tale but with earlier operatic adaptations. Since the magical effects were absent from his sources, they were absent too in Ferretti.

The nature of its libretto makes this *Cenerentola* of Ferretti and Rossini significantly different from the comic operas Rossini had prepared before. The madcap hilarity of *L'Italiana in Algeri* and the wily, even raucous ways of Rosina in *Il barbiere di Siviglia* are no longer present in *La Cenerentola*. Don Magnifico and Dandini are, of course, comic characters in the great Italian tradition, with their solo buffo arias and their superb Act Two duet, '*Un segreto d'importanza*,' one of the finest buffo numbers in the entire repertory. But the principal characters, Cinderella herself and Don Ramiro, are sentimental, not comic characters. They are heirs of Richardson's *Pamela*, the virtuous servant girl loved and finally married by a noble patron (*Virtue rewarded* is Richardson's alternate title, *Goodness triumphant* is Ferretti's). And the earliest significant appearance of the sentimental genre in Italian opera is Nicolò Piccini's setting of Goldoni's *Pamela* imitation, *La buona figliola* (1760). From there through the remainder of the century *opera buffa* more and more frequently became the home for sentimental and pathetic heroines, expressing their sorrows and pleasures in a musically more simple and popular style.

This style characterizes much of Cenerentola's music, from her opening canzona, '*Una volta c'era un re*,' to her delightfully tentative and naive duet with Don Ramiro, '*Un soave non so che*.' Even when surrounded by the pure buffo declamation of others, as at the close of the *Introduzione*, Cenerentola emerges singing a beautifully soaring vocal line, '*Questo è proprio uno strapazzo!*,' which casts a radiance over the entire ensemble. But Rossini goes beyond even this style, until his heroine is hardly distinguishable from the protagonist of *Elisabetta, regina d'Inghilterra* (listen particularly to Cinderella's beautiful solo within the Act Two Quintet, '*Ah signor, s'è ver che in petto*,' and the *primo tempo* of her concluding *rondò*, '*Nacqui all'affanno e al pianto*'). *Opera buffa* here adapts for its own

15

purposes not only the popular world of the sentimental *semiseria* genre but even the exalted vocal style of *opera seria* itself.

La Cenerentola, then, is far from the simple world of comic opera. In his next work, *La gazza ladra*, Rossini would carry *opera semiseria* beyond the comic sphere altogether. This change in genre, though partly related to the composer's Neapolitan experiences, was inherent in Italian opera of the period. Even in extra-Neapolitan commissions, Rossini did not choose comic plots; only in Paris would he again do so, but *Le Comte Ory* is far from the style of Italian *opera buffa*. Of all Rossini's operas, *La Cenerentola* is the most 'mixed' in genre, the broadest range of musical sources contributing to its rich style: the wealth and greatness of the opera is a direct function of that very diversity.

Because of the rapid preparation of *La Cenerentola*, there was little time for rehearsal, and the first performances were not well received. But, according to Ferretti, Rossini was undisturbed. The day after the fiasco, he told his depressed librettist:

> Fool! Before Carnival is done, everyone will be in love with it, before a year is up it will be sung from Lilibeo to Dora, and in two years it will please in France and astound the English. Impresarios will fight over it and, even more, so will prima donnas.

La Cenerentola did indeed have remarkable success during the nineteenth century. Although performed infrequently in the first decades of this century it never completely disappeared. In the Rossini revival since the war it has triumphantly reestablished itself as a repertory opera: a fairy story come true.

Concerning Christian-names

Dr Gossett has drawn attention to the common mis-spelling of Rossini's Christian name with two 'c's instead of the one 'c' (Gioachino) that he himself always used, and to the alternative Christian names of Giacomo and Jacopo attributed to the librettist, Ferretti, who used both on occasion. - Ed.

'La Cenerentola' (Cinderella)
A musical commentary

Arthur Jacobs

To tell the story clearly, to bring out the characters by musical means, and to please the listener by a succession of immediately attractive solos and ensembles — this combination was the required operatic formula of Rossini's time, and nowhere is it more brilliantly accomplished than in *La Cenerentola*. Not only brilliantly but subtly too. Here is not the pure comedy of *Il Barbiere di Siviglia*, founded on a traditional range of characters: in *La Cenerentola* pathos has its part as well.

Indeed the transformation of Cinderella from cruelly-used servant to triumphant princess is musically shown — she begins with a pathetic little ditty, sung to herself, and moves towards the brilliant 'public' coloratura of the aria with chorus which concludes the work. The heroine's real name in the opera, by the way, is Angelina. 'La Cenerentola', her nickname, derives from *cenere* (ashes), in the same way as Cinderella does from *cinders*; and the same is true of the French form *Cendrillon*, in the story by Perrault from which they both spring. The opening ditty is called a *canzone*, meaning in operatic terms a song that is 'really' sung by one of the characters (that is, it would be a song in real life or in a spoken play).

Cinderella's cruel stepsisters, though vain and silly, are different from the 'ugly sisters' of English pantomime. Other differences will be noted, particularly the absence of magic and the replacement of the fairy godmother by a prudent elderly adviser of the Prince's. The bibulous disposition of Cinderella's stepfather is hinted at in the title of his barony — 'Montefiascone' (Mountflagon). The use of only a *male* chorus was an economy which Italian theatres of the time appreciated.

Before the curtain rises Rossini provides his usual type of overture, a slow section followed by a faster [1, 2, 3] rising to a final climax: for the musical material of the climax, in this case, he borrows from the ensemble which ends the first act of the opera itself. Following the form favoured by Italian composers of that time for comic opera, the opera is in two acts — the first leading at curtain-fall to a situation of maximum complexity, musically involving all the main characters, and the second providing literally the *dénouement*, an 'un-knotting' of the tangle.

The libretto is a brilliant piece of work, and a tribute to its author, Jacopo Ferretti, is due from the present as translator of the English text used by the English National Opera. Such a libretto is written *for* music — not merely for setting line-by-line, but to fit

17

the successive types of musical form which the composer will wish to use. Ferretti accomplishes this neatly *and* writes clear, singable text free from inversions and stiffness — except where Dandini in disguise as the prince deliberately and comically pays court to Cinderella's step-sisters in absurdly high-flown style, comparing himself to the bee seeking the 'one sweetest flower' and then imploring them to release him, 'disarmed by Cupid's dart'.

The translator finds himself, indeed, constantly stimulated by the witty asides and ironies of the text. The only divergence in style which is to be found in the English version is this: Rossini ruthlessly repeats the Italian lines (for musical reasons), but where repetition blunts a comic point I have permitted myself to write new lines to sustain the fun — I hope.

The headings (e.g. 'Introduction', 'Aria') are those of the score, at this period always divided into separate numbers. Characters are named in order of singing within that number.

Act One

Scene One: The Baron's Mansion

Introduction. CLORINDA, TISBE, CINDERELLA, ALIDORO, CAVALIERS

No 'opening chorus', so often favoured in comic opera, is possible within the Baron's impoverished establishment. Cinderella's vain stepsisters are seen trying on some headgear and practising a dance-step [4]. They reprimand Cinderella for singing to herself her favourite song [5] about a king who chooses a true-hearted bride rather than a rich or beautiful one. A beggar (Alidoro, the prince's tutor, in disguise) enters, begging for alms. Spurned by the others, he is pitied by Cinderella, who gives him refreshment.

Now the chorus enters — cavaliers attached to the court of Prince Ramiro, who is staying at a palace nearby. They announce that the prince himself is to arrive to issue invitations to his grand ball[6]. Expressing their separate thoughts the four characters sing *with* the chorus to convey musically the sense of excitement and anticipation.

Recitative and cavatina: Don Magnifico. CLORINDA, CINDERELLA, ALIDORO, TISBE, DON MAGNIFICO

The invitation sets the stepsisters in a whirl[7]. They dismiss the 'beggar' rudely: before leaving he gives Cinderella a mysterious assurance that hers may yet be a happy fate. Cinderella goes to prepare her stepsisters' finery for the ball. The stepsisters quarrel as to which of them should have the right to tell the news to their father, the baron — when, unbidden and annoyed, he enters.

The following *cavatina* (in this sense an entrance aria) in one section without change of tempo, is the first big solo number of the opera. Don Magnifico, Baron Montefiascone, is a run-down aristocrat whose manners match those of his daughters, Clorinda and

18

Tisbe. Awakened from sleep by their chatter, he now narrates the dream he had, and his interpretation. The music begins with heavy repetitious phrases (*'Miei rampolli feminini'* — 'Why the devil did I get you as my offspring?') which mirror his annoyance and general boorishness; but by the end of the aria his prognostications of a change of fortune move him to fast, exhilarating music. In his dream he became an ass with feathers, flying to the top of a belfry — which he interprets as high promotion with each of the daughters marrying a prince. Excitedly, he imagines their royal babies prancing for the delight of their grandpa.

Recitative. CLORINDA, TISBE, DON MAGNIFICO

Informed of the prince's coming, Don Magnifico sees it as verification of his dream and primes his daughters for their royal encounter.

Scena and Duet: Cinderella and Don Ramiro. RAMIRO, CINDERELLA; OFF STAGE: CLORINDA, TISBE

Composers used the expression 'scena and . . . ' to cover the introductory conversational recitative to a formal solo, duet, etc.. Here Don Ramiro, Prince of Salerno (to give him his full title) enters in disguise as one of his own courtiers. Ordered by his father to marry, he has come to spy out the territory where he is to find his ideal bride in a daughter of the house — or so he has been assured by Alidoro, his tutor. Entering alone he first soliloquizes — speaking, in effect, to the audience. When at length Cinderella enters, bringing a cup of coffee for the baron, he takes her for a maid. Startled, she drops the cup.

The two are enchanted with each other [8a]. Finding it impossible to say so openly, they employ the operatic convention of the 'aside' (addressing the audience) — singing first in turn, then in harmony [8b]. The slow tempo breaks into fast as Ramiro finally asks the 'maid' where the Baron's daughters are, and receives a confused reply. The stepsisters' voices are heard. Cinderella must go to attend them, so she and the prince reluctantly bid each other farewell. (The change from slow to fast tempo, with a psychological change between — in this case, breaking from the 'asides' of love to routine conversation — forms one of the chief means by which such an opera as this progresses naturally within a scene.)

Recitative. RAMIRO, DON MAGNIFICO

Cinderella leaves. The baron enters briefly in haste and confusion. Ramiro now awaits the fulfilment of the 'other half' of the disguising: his confidential servant Dandini is to arrive and to pretend to be the prince.

The sextet — Act One

The sextet — Act Two

Chorus and Cavatina: Dandini. COURTIERS, DANDINI, CLORINDA,
TISBE, DON MAGNIFICO, RAMIRO

Preceded by the courtiers, Dandini enters in princely dress and
hugely enjoys his pose. He sings in stately florid style [9] of his
royal quest for perfect beauty and then — as the stepsisters present
themselves, dressed up to kill — makes each of them believe he
adores her, with comic 'asides' to Ramiro.

Here occurs one of those masterly key-changes which Rossini
applies perfectly to the dramatic situation. Ignoring Ramiro's whispered caution not to carry the deception too far, Dandini moves
with mock-sentimental passion from F to A flat to launch an appeal
to the girls: (*'Per pietà, quelle ciglia abbassate'* — 'Ah, have pity, oh,
spare those fatal glances . . . ').

All this is in the same rather slow tempo. Then a faster tempo
and a new tune take over as Dandini grows still more confident
(*'Ma al finir della nostra commedia'* — 'Oh, how easy I find them to
flatter') and the girls likewise feel sure of their conquest. All join
expressing their feelings. But it is still Dandini's number and he
remains the centre of attraction.

Recitative and Quintet. DANDINI, CLORINDA, DON MAGNIFICO,
RAMIRO, TISBE, CINDERELLA, ALIDORO.

One way in which the composer can make a scene progress has
already been indicated in this commentary: within an aria, a change
in mood or dramatic situation (even if it occurs only in the mind of
the character) can prompt a change of tempo from slow to fast, and
so increase the excitement. In this number the same procedure is
used but on a larger scale. A recitative involving six characters
leads (with the disappearance of two) to a formal quartet, in which
Cinderella pleads with Don Magnifico to let her as well as her stepsisters go to the ball (Dandini and Ramiro overhearing and commenting). Then Alidoro in a new guise enters, changing the
dramatic situation and prompting a new strain of music (a quintet)
— itself having a slow, then a fast section. The whole number has,
moreover, a unified key-structure just as would be found in an instrumental movement of comparable length.

We may now describe this number in more detail. In an introductory recitative, Dandini in disguise as the prince narrates (in
comic multiple rhyme) his father's command that he should marry.
To that end he has invited all the unmarried ladies of the district to
a ball. Clorinda and Tisbe, escorted by the cavaliers, leave for the
palace. But as Don Magnifico prepares to go with him, Cinderella
detains him imploringly — will he not take her as well, even for an
hour, half an hour, a quarter of an hour [10]? He pushes her away
and threatens her with his cane, to the disgust of Ramiro and
Dandini — these four voices being displayed in a formal quartet.
Cinderella's vocal line is both pleading and (as she thinks of the

21

dazzle of the ball) florid and excited: even within the demands of the ensemble, Rossini provides a touching musical portrayal of her character.

The quartet ends with apparent finality. Cinderella is *not* to be taken to the ball. With three heavy unison strokes of the keynote C the orchestra confirms it — when suddenly an unprepared change of key (chord of E flat) marks the unexpected appearance of Alidoro. He comes as an official bearing a register, from which it appears that *three* sisters, and not two, inhabit this dwelling. His measured questioning demands a slower pace. The third sister 'died', says Don Magnifico, while Cinderella can scarcely stammer a protest.

A further change of key (to A flat) brings the formal quintet in which Don Magnifico, Cinderella and Dandini in turn remark in slow time on how the face of each one present reveals the doubts within [11]. Then a more active mood seizes them (Don Magnifico sarcastically bullying Cinderella) — a mood expressed with a change of rhythm, a suddenly faster tempo, *and* a return to the opening key (C major). The spectator is perhaps conscious only of the developing story and the succession of agreeable, contrasting musical strains — but this 'works' only because Rossini's mastery as composer has found the technical means to articulate a long musical structure which covers all the expression needed by all the characters. Finally Don Magnifico leaves for the royal palace, as do Dandini and Ramiro.

Recitative. ALIDORO, CINDERELLA.

Left behind with Cinderella, Alidoro gently surprises her. He will bring her to the ball and supply her costume and jewels. 'What's this, a play?' she asks, bewildered. Alidoro's reply is one that the translator cannot resist adapting into: 'Yes, my daughter, all the world's a stage, and all the men and women merely players'.*

Scene Two: The Prince's Palace

First Finale. COURTIERS, DON MAGNIFICO, RAMIRO, DANDINI, CLORINDA, TISBE, ALIDORO, CINDERELLA.

The 'first finale' (i.e. finale to Act One) is, in this type of comic opera, the longest and most complex single item of the score, presenting all the main characters in various vocal combinations. Don Magnifico has amazed the courtiers (or they pretend to amazement) by his drinking capacity, in token of which he is apparently

---

* For a performance in 1821, Rossini wrote a fine aria for Alidoro. This is sometimes performed, so the alternative words have been included in the libretto (page 66), and Colin Graham's comments upon them may be read on page 38. Agolini composed an aria to follow the recitative for the first performance. Entitled '*Vasto teatro è il mondo*', it is still included in the Ricordi vocal score. (Ed.)

to be made the prince's steward. He dictates — while the courtiers write it down — an absurd proclamation against mixing wine with water. Rossini uses here with particular aptness the device of giving a catchy tune not to the singer but to the orchestra, while the 'dictation' goes for long periods on a monotone [17].*

In another room, Prince Ramiro and Dandini meet in haste. Dandini, still dressed as the prince, and pursued by the stepsisters, snatches a word with Ramiro to warn him of how odious the girls are. The musical point of this comic duet is not only its 'scampering' but its confidential whispering, with many repetitions of '*zitto*' ('quiet!'), '*piano*' ('sofly!') and '*sotto voce*'. The scampering pace is maintained not only by the voices but by the orchestral violins [13].

The same scampering music continues when the stepsisters 'catch' Dandini. He protests that he cannot marry two, so he will choose one and bestow the other on . . . his squire (pointing to the real prince). The stepsisters reject such a 'low-class' alliance with scorn, even when Ramiro now begs them to marry him. This is the supremely ironic moment of the plot — and one which is recalled towards the end of the opera.

The ball proper is about to begin when the mood (and the key) changes. An off-stage chorus (from the entrance hall of the palace) announces the arrival of a beauty. Alidoro's announcement that she is veiled deepens the suspense. The stepsisters, suspecting a beautiful rival for the prince's affections, are alarmed. It is, of course, Cinderella — dazzling in appearance and unrecognized. Matching this dazzle she introduces herself with a florid declamation '*Sprezzo quei don che versa fortuna capricciosa*', literally 'I set no value on those gifts which fickle fortune bestows', operatically translated 'All is not gold that glitters'[14].

Then she unveils. Moment of astonishment (and change of key! — E flat to G). In the succeeding ensemble Rossini re-employs, as in the earlier quintet, the device of successive characters entering with the same expression of perplexity: '*Parlar, pensar vorrei . . .* ' — 'I'd like to speak my feelings, but words will not be found' [15]. Don Magnifico, till now absent (in the wine-cellar!) enters and joins the astonishment. *Can* it be Cinderella? Dandini rallies his guests — time to go within for supper and dancing.

But before they do so, a mood of wonder again strikes the company. In a hushed unison, each speaking for himself or herself, they compare their situation to being in an idyllic garden suddenly hit by a tempest [16]. This 'poetic' fancy has a strictly musical point — after a quiet beginning, the gathering 'tempest' is represented in a *crescendo* over an insistent rhythm. The music sinks

---

* Don Magnifico's recitative and aria [17] are sometimes (as at ENO) used to open the second act, instead of a chorus '*Ah della bella incognita*' of which only a manuscript survives, written by Agolini for the first performance, and which is not generally performed at all, or Rossini's own aria written for Magnifico at that point. (Ed.)

down but revives, repeated and extended, as an exhilarating end to the act.

Act Two

Scene One: The Prince's Palace

Recitative and aria*: Don Magnifico. DON MAGNIFICO, TISBE, CLORINDA.

The baron and his daughters review the situation. Upset as they are by the appearance of the unknown beauty, they are still confident of capturing the prince. Whichever of the two wins him, the baron will be sure of a powerful position as go-between at court, with handsome bribes (in money or food) from those anxious to procure a royal favour. He imagines an interview between himself and a female petitioner (imitating her in falsetto) and then, in rapid patter, sees himself as so surrounded by other petitioners that he has to shut the door on them.

Recitative, scena and aria: Don Ramiro. TISBE, CLORINDA, RAMIRO, DANDINI, CINDERELLA, ALIDORO, COURTIERS.

Dandini, still acting as Prince Ramiro, has himself been smitten by Cinderella's charms. But she turns his compliments aside, confessing that she is in love with his 'squire' (that is, the real prince). But when Ramiro appears she turns aside his declaration too: she gives him a bracelet and says that when he finds its companion-piece, *then* she will be his. She leaves. Alidoro encourages the prince to pursue the prompting of his heart. Suddenly resolute, Ramiro tells Dandini the charade of impersonation is over: he orders his coach and prepares to set out and find her.

An aria in three sections, with chorus of his courtiers, expresses his new mood: first expressing determination, in almost martial music [18a], then passing to a gentler strain as he contemplates the bracelet and thinks of its owner, then again resolute [18b]. (The tenor's top C is strongly used in both first and third sections.) Ramiro and his courtiers depart.

Recitative and duet: Dandini and Don Magnifico. ALIDORO, DANDINI, DON MAGNIFICO.

Alidoro, intending to promote his plan by making the prince's coach break down near the baron's house, hastens off. Dandini remains behind, peevishly fretting that he is now an 'ex-prince'. The baron enters, pressing the 'prince' (as he still assumes Dandini to be) for a decision on whether Clorinda or Tisbe is to be the lucky bride. Dandini, affecting an air of tremendous secrecy, promises to tell him what has happened [19]. (The Italian librettist, with the English translator following, uses what must be an old joke. DON

---

* This piece is not always performed. Don Magnifico's 'dictation' aria is used to open the second act instead. It is not included in the libretto. (Ed.)

MAGNIFICO: 'I stand on tip-toe!' DANDINI: 'Then take a seat, I beg you'.)

The air of comic confidences is repeated musically in duet, with short, detached vocal ejaculations. Dandini asks him what comforts his daughter would expect — the baron demands the highest honours — and Dandini explains that far from this, as his wife she would live only on the sevants' level, for he himself is only a valet and what has passed was only a masquerade. As the baron's incredulity gives way to outrage, the music changes from a moderately quick 4/4 to a quicker 6/8. The baron's indignation is in vain and Dandini teases him: 'I'll have my rights!' — 'Right through the door!'

Recitative: ALIDORO.

It is a stormy night — which will aid the plan for the breakdown of the carriage, and the eagerness of the prince for departure was another happy portent. (This recitative is a useful 'cover' for a scene-change rather than dramatically vital.)

Scene Two: The Baron's Residence

Song: Cinderella

The Italian word 'canzone' (see above, p.17) is now used by the composer to denote Cinderella's little ditty, previously heard within the opening number [5]. Its repetition here is a simple, touching way of indicating that superficially Cinderella's situation is as before — her clothes, the setting, and her apparent mood are again those of the downtrodden servant, as at the opening of the opera.

Recitative and Storm. CINDERELLA, CLORINDA, DON MAGNIFICO, TISBE.

But all is *not* the same. She looks lovingly at the bracelet and thinks of the attractive suitor (the prince's squire, as she still supposes) who possesses its companion. Her stepsisters and the baron enter crossly. She pretends not to know why, and goes at their bidding to prepare a meal. Outside a storm is brewing and the orchestra depicts it — fast, loud, agitated music rising to a climax, then subsiding to gentleness (and the minor turning into a 'smiling' major key) as the elements become peaceful again.

Recitative and Sextet. DANDINI, DON MAGNIFICO, DON RAMIRO, CLORINDA, CINDERELLA, TISBE.

The royal carriage has broken down. Dandini, as part of the prince's escort, stumbles into this as the nearest house — not realizing for a moment, that it is the baron's. Despite the embarrassment of this further meeting with Dandini, the Baron is sure it betokens an interest in his daughters' prospects. Astonished to learn that the 'attendant' Ramiro is the true prince, Don Magnifico and the girls are even more astonished when — noticing the

25

matched bracelets — the prince claims Cinderella.

The sextet begins with the same phrase from Dandini, Ramiro, Don Magnifico and Cinderella in succession. Detached notes seem to represent the distracted, surprised thoughts of each [20]. On top of this Clorinda and Tisbe, who have been silent, suddenly make *their* puzzlement heard. The slow, measured pace (the indication is *maestoso*, 'majestically') allows the unrolling of florid coloratura by one character at a time, paralleling the verbal emphasis on the feeling that one's head is spinning.

Abruptly, the suspense is broken (and the tempo is changed to a faster one) as Clorinda turns accusingly on Cinderella, followed by Don Magnifico. With superior weight Ramiro now turns on them. In slower tempo and with a shift of key, as though to establish a reconciliation, Cinderella asks Ramiro [21] to have mercy on her tormentors — but they call her a hypocrite and Don Magnifico tries to re-establish the claims of his daughters. Ramiro sarcastically quotes back at them (in music and words!) the disparagement they flung at him in Act One when he offered himself to them. He formally invites Cinderella to be his consort; she tries once again to gain her stepfather's and stepsisters' good-will and is once again repulsed. The sustained tension is manifested in an insistent strain [22] for all six characters, itself in that 'doubled dynamic' form (soft to loud, sinking down, then rising again to an even greater climax) which forms a cherished constructive device of Rossini's.

Recitative. TISBE, CLORINDA, ALIDORO

The stepsisters realize the game is up. Alidoro enters and reveals that he was the 'beggar' whom they repulsed and Cinderella pitied. (In the Italian he now refers to her by her real name, Angelina.) The baron's property will have to be sold, as he has squandered Cinderella's dowry. He and his daughters will be impoverished unless they beg Cinderella's pardon. Clorinda flounces off, but Tisbe resolves to apologize: 'I prefer humble pie to plain starvation'. Alidoro, who has already made all the arrangements for an immediate wedding, is well content.

Scene Three: A Room with a Throne

Chorus, Scena and Rondò-Finale: Cinderella. COURTIERS, RAMIRO, CINDERELLA, DON MAGNIFICO, DANDINI, CLORINDA, TISBE [AND ALIDORO].

Fortune's wheel has turned, as the chorus of courtiers proclaim, assembling to welcome their new princess. All are to witness 'the triumph of goodness' — which, as 'il trionfo della bontà,' is the subtitle of the opera. Cinderella, led in by Don Ramiro, is 'stupefied by joy' (in the words of the stage direction). The baron and his daughters have by this time *all* realized the prudence of apology. Cinderella asks her consort to allow her the royal privilege of 'revenge' (with a big, 'menacing' flourish in the vocal line) — but her 'revenge' is 'to grant them pardon'.

26

The final item of the opera now follows. It is a long, brilliant aria with chorus — that is, with the unified support of all the other characters as well as the chorus proper. (By an apparent oversight, no part for Alidoro is given in the score, but he would naturally join in the line of his fellow-bass, Don Magnifico.)

For reasons that are obscure, the term *rondò* (we reproduce the correct Italian spelling, with accent on the second syllable) is applied by composers of Italian opera at this and an earlier period to a certain type of compound aria-form without reference to the usual significance of the term in instrumental music. Instrumentally, the form implies the recurrence of one main strain with diverse episodes between. Operatically, as in Fiordiligi's *'Per pietà'* from Mozart's *Così fan tutte*, no such recurrence is found: instead, a spacious slow section is followed by an equally imposing fast section. So here Cinderella begins with a slow 6/8, *'Nacqui all'affanno e al pianto'*, 'Born to a life that was lonely' [23a] — where, with a coloratura flourish, she compares her transformation to a stroke of lightning [23b]. Then, *allegro*, she asks the baron and his daughters not to cry ('No, no, no, no'). She wants only to embrace, to forgive, to be reconciled. The reaction of the courtiers to her kindness prepares for her second strain within the *allegro* tempo. This is the principal part of the aria, beginning *'Non più mesta accanto al fuoco'*, 'Now no longer by the cinders' [23c]. Starting as a simple catchy tune, it proceeds to elaborate vocal variations with choral accompaniment.

The demands on the mezzo-soprano voice include the just-over-two-octave run from high A to low G sharp, and (as a climax) a top B above this. Such brilliant display makes its own appeal but Rossini's feat is — here as in the rest of the opera — to have placed and timed his music perfectly for the realization of story and character.

Della Jones as Cinderella at English National Opera (photo: Reg Wilson)

'Cinderella' in perfomance

There is much debate as to how Rossini's operas should be performed. I took the opportunity of the ENO production of 'Cinderella' to talk to the conductor and producer about performing 'Cinderella' in English for today's audience, and about the musical and theatrical conventions on which Rossini relied, as well as those which have since developed. — Ed.

I — A Conversation with Mark Elder

Mark Elder, ENO Music Director, went to his first opera when he was ten years old (and still a choirboy at Canterbury Cathedral) at Glyndebourne where he subsequently began his professional career. Glyndebourne's remarkable standard of ensemble singing was cultivated by Vittorio Gui, Fritz Busch and Jani Strasser in the years after 1945 on the Mozart and Rossini repertory. Mark Elder has since treasured the Rossini masterpieces, and conducted 'The Italian Girl in Algiers', as well as 'Cinderella', at the London Coliseum.

N.J. What would you tell someone coming to *Cinderella* for the first time to look out for?

M.E. Well, for me, the overriding characteristic of a performance of any Rossini score, whether comic or serious, is that it must give the impression of being a spontaneous, improvised entertainment. Rossini's operas do not fall into any preconceived patterns; and this is particularly true of the comic ones. Their most arresting features, which may be called 'Rossinian', are not rooted in the past. They have certain predecessors in the complicated ensembles of Cimarosa and Mozart, yet in masterpieces such as *Cinderella* and *The Barber* Rossini produced a world of his own, an imaginative scheme that is quite without parallel. The performers have to create an atmosphere where anything might happen, and to communicate this fantasy world to the public. An audience can never be sure how Rossini will cope with a situation, but the performers should appear to have no problems, just as though they were artists in a vocal and dramatic circus.

N.J. — In the sense that the coloratura is 'acrobatic' singing?

M.E Yes. Singing is, after all, an athletic exercise. Rossini's music gives singers wonderful opportunities to display technique and to give the audience the impression that they are creating the music and experimenting all the time. I do not, however, believe that singers should add their own virtuoso displays. (It might be worth pointing out here that, apart from three bars added by Rossini to the finale for the sake of extra brilliance, no music has been added in our performance.) A feature of recent performances of *La Cenerentola* has been the existence of Alberto Zedda's edition of the

29

Dandini (Alan Opie) courts both Clorinda (Meryl Drower) and Tisbe (Shelagh Squires) simultaneously while their proud father (Richard Van Allan) looks on. (photo: Reg Wilson)

score, based on Rossini's manuscript, which is itself remarkable for its clarity. Zedda has, so to speak, used a strong detergent to clean it right out, removing a lot of the traditions which used to be accepted without question. Although I was surprised by some of Zedda's decisions, I can now see the reasons for them. There is, for example, no percussion part — one might argue because Rossini was writing for a theatre small enough not to need one. Yet there is a trombone in almost every number, giving a little more definition and spice to the bass part. The string section is that required for Mozart. Zedda's revisions make the texture more transparent, providing, for example, more interesting work for the two piccolos (not just one). He has swept away all later additions, including notes added to the harmonies and parts for instruments which Rossini did not use. This removes a layer of pastry, as it were, from the music which should be light and buoyant.

N.J. Do you think the very quiet opening of the overture, sometimes scarcely audible in a restless auditorium, is effective?

M.E. Rossini's contribution to the operatic overture stems from his desire to stimulate, entertain, surprise and, sometimes, to shock. His musical sense of humour is his most distinctive feature, and it is communicated with the most economic of means. The opening bar of this overture is extraordinarily unexpected: it sounds as though half the orchestra is missing. Then, with the full orchestra chords that follow we realise that the whole effect was intended to intrigue us. In the overture to *Il Signor Bruschino*, a little-known one-act opera, he calls for the violins to tap the music-stands with their bows, in order to attract attention. It created a minor sensation when first done, because the audience felt the composer was laughing at them. These are deliberate musical outrages, trademarks of Rossini's personality.

N.J. The evening is certainly full of musical jokes. One that springs to mind is the curious exclamation of dismay which Clorinda and Tisbe utter in the Act Two sextet: even if we cannot make out the words ('Hear them moan and hear them mutter'), we immediately appreciate their annoyance.

M.E. Rossini's musical imagination stops at nothing. One of the great challenges for performers is to give the impression that his music is the most natural and most suitable for that moment. His ensembles (sometimes for six, seven, eight or even nine singers) produce a wonderful effect, rather like a family team of acrobats contributing to a great tableau. One character may have a lyrical melody, four others may be chattering or whispering and two others may be making love on the quiet: the whole effect is vivacious and exhilarating. Just before the moment you mentioned (which is incidentally very difficult to sing cleanly), he transforms the scene into a bubble of time. Each character, one by one, repeats

'*Questo è un nodo avviluppato*' ('Here's a plot there's no denying'). Each syllable is pronounced separately and softly, and when performers create this *staccato* effect with the right tension, it seems as if time stands still.

N.J. Another such moment is Alidoro's entrance to announce Cinderella's arrival at the ball. The audience seem to grasp what is going on only after he has deflected three urgent questions, such as 'What's her name?'.

M.E. That is a good example of Rossini's treatment of an entirely prosaic text. He is so great an operatic composer because he has transformed words which were not remarkable on the page into an extended sequence of laughter. We sense in a successful performance that the lines seem to be delayed and that the audience cannot wait for the next question, on account of the orchestral 'giggles' between each question and answer.

N.J. Do you set about rehearsing a Rossini score in a different way from Verdi or Puccini?

M.E. Yes. The challenge is to obtain the right combination of fantasy and discipline. The ensembles are obviously very difficult to sing *exactly* together: the music is of sufficient simplicity that it is relatively easy to sing to a certain standard, but the challenge is to rise above that level with spirit and precision. Whether for only a few notes, or for several pages, these ensembles demand weeks of rehearsal. The singers have to work gradually towards a feeling of sharing it both in musical and human terms. They must be humble enough to work selflessly: the ultimate test of a great artist. This ensemble technique is valuable for Mozart and Donizetti also, and, of course, Mozart's scores explore a deeper range of human emotion altogether.

N.J. Are Rossini's operas difficult to cast?

M.E. It is hard to find a perfectly matched team to achieve this all-important unity. It would be no solution to employ two great principals of international class with a couple of days' rehearsal in addition to five company artists. Rossini singers must have, in addition to power and agility, a lightness and fantasy in their voices, so that the music does not sound like overcooked suet!

N.J. Rossini used to complain that singers were increasingly making their voices perform like instruments. It might seem to today's audiences that Rossini asks for singers just with virtuoso technique.

M.E. The challenge for singers is to develop the bravura technique and then to align it with an imaginative concept so that it seems that at any particular moment this is the most *natural* thing to be doing. For instance, when Cinderella and Ramiro meet for the first time, they both have a number of ecstatic embellishments, intended to illustrate their delight and surprise. Mozart would have written this, perhaps, as a more sustained passage; Rossini makes it breathless and gentle. It can easily sound too instrumental. It is, of course, interesting that Rossini wanted to avoid this happening.

N.J. The Act One finale must also be an unusually difficult passage to make seem convincing on the stage.

M.E. It requires on the part of both audience and performers a degree of fantasy that knocks us sideways, because it is so unexpected. We laugh at the sheer pleasure of it: there seems at that point to be magic and tension in the air.

N.J. In performance it still works, even for today's audience unused to Rossini's conventions. Are you aware that it takes us a little time to 'get into' the spirit of the music?

M.E. The theatre's capacity to draw the audience in to share an experience is remarkable. (It always takes me twenty minutes, when I go to see a Western, to understand what anyone is saying!) This is why the role of the overture or prelude is so interesting: if it is well written, it can prepare us for the type of theatre we are about to experience. This introduction need not be only musical. For example, the East German producer, Joachim Herz, placed a broken-down car outside the Komische Oper in East Berlin before his new production of *Mahagonny*, which opens after a car has broken down in the desert. This intrigues an audience. Rossini's operas have a great place in our theatre because they also intrigue viewers to enter another world.

N.J. Would you like to comment on Rossini's characteristic habit of repeating phrases?

M.E. A characteristic of Italian is to repeat phrases not only for emphasis but to convey different shades of meaning. Look at the many examples of repeated phrases in the operas of Verdi or Puccini. Rossini did not repeat words, in my opinion, because there was a lack of text to set but because he wanted to make a specific point or comic effect.

N.J. What sort of orchestral playing do you find is necessary for Rossini?

M.E. It is a tightrope act. The orchestration is of a delicacy that demands a balance of poise and flexibility. For the string players, particularly the violins, it is an evening of *spiccato* — bouncing the bow on the string. The coordination of finger and bow demands great technique, particularly in fast music. It is just as hard as to sing it correctly, and few people understand this, including the players themselves! The woodwind has to combine lyrical beauty and supreme elegance with a sharp wit. So often is the wind called upon to comment on the stage action, that the wind players stand

'Alboni is not an 'artiste' to startle the multitude by dramatic intensity or the outbreak of passion. Her indolence of action, and apathy in the concerted pieces, afford little notion of the excitement of the passing scene, but when once a simple melody is to be breathed forth, with quiet pathos, the ecstasy at her lovely organ is unbounded, and Alboni's triumph is sure'. Or as 'The Times' observed (May 2, 1848) 'her figure is not exactly calculated to represent the gifted favourite of the good fairy'.

out like characters in the drama. This constant alternation between the two colours poses a great challenge to the players.

N.J. I noticed that you called a lot of recitative rehearsals.

M.E. In order to achieve the necessary flow in the recitatives, it is essential for the singers to repeat them often enough for them to become second nature. Performers must enjoy the business of delivering them, responding to each other by a subconscious reflex. Our recitative rehearsals are similar to the way actors may speak through a scene together in a canteen, without any energy or expression; or to the limbering-up of a ballet dancer.

N.J. Do you change the note-values in recitative to suit the words of the translation?

M.E. I believe there should be a clear demarcation between declamation and lyrical expression. (The composers of the late 19th century who merge them make this increasingly difficult but the classic art from Monteverdi onwards was based on this juxta-position of fantasy and precision.) In recitative, by and large, the musical rhythms have no empiric value of their own and exist only as a natural frame-work to the text. The rhythm can be altered to suit the translation. By contrast, in the lyrical passages, nothing must hinder the original music. After all, the reason why the composer did not set the words originally to a melodic arch was because the line was to be recited or declaimed — as opposed to *arioso*, which is 'strung through the air' according to musical values. The combination of the *cantante* and recitative is the crux of the style.

N.J. Do you, yourself, feel exhilarated after a performance?

M.E. After a good performance certainly. The immediate feeling is elation, even inspiration, especially after the last scene of *La Cenerentola*. The tiredness comes some hours later.

N.J. Do you occasionally find yourself restraining the performers in performance — not just keeping them together, but actually main-taining a control with a return to quiet dynamics and a rock steady rhythm for ensembles? These could at first seem abnormally quiet and slow to an audience, which does not know what is to follow.

M.E. An example might be the famous sextet '*Parlar, pensar vorrei*' ('I'd like to speak my feelings'). We have to suggest curiosity and tension in the entries of Clorinda and Ramiro, so that Cinderella's brilliant notes flower naturally and spontaneously. The variation between loud and soft dynamics is also very marked in Rossini; the performance has to be carefully prepared so that in itself it is a liberation. But the audience must not feel that the conductor is holding back the performers. The relationship of rhythm and dy-namics must be perfectly calculated so that the fast and loud sections fit into the general pattern. Sometimes, of course, per-

35

Elizabeth Inverarity, who sang Cinderella in 'The Fairy Queen or The Little Glass Slipper' at Covent Garden in 1831, at the age of seventeen. (Covent Garden Archives)

formers forget and I have to remind them of what we rehearsed. This discipline cannot be devised in performance; it must be firmly fixed, like the foundation of a house; you can't build on sand.

II — A Conversation with Colin Graham

Colin Graham is ENO Director of Productions, Director of Productions at the Opera Theatre of St Louis and founder-director of the English Music Theatre. He first produced 'Cinderella' in this translation for Scottish Opera in 1969, and then directed a new production for EMT, which toured Britain in 1976-8, before it was taken over by ENO for performances at the London Coliseum.

N.J. You once said to me that, in your opinion, *Cinderella* was the most human of Rossini's operas. Would you care to expand on that?

C.G. I am not a great lover of Rossini's operas, although I do love his music, because I find none of them, except Cinderella, particularly amusing; they are brittle and heartless, and about cardboard, artificial people. But *Cinderella* is a very human story, about a tender person with real problems, and the music, like some passages from *Count Ory*, has for me much greater depths than Rossini's other scores.

N.J. Cinderella is a really delightful character, and not just down-trodden.

C.G. She is not merely a household drudge but very much a member of the family and stands up for herself, as for instance, in the opening scene when she insists on singing her song. Also, we can tell from her observations at the ball that she is getting some fun out of the other characters' reactions to her appearance! The question of loving someone 'for himself alone' is also treated in a very sensitive and satisfactory way. And when the family returns to the Baron's mansion, she is delightfully ingenuous, asking 'What have I done?', now that her new-found love strengthens her ability to cope with them more effectively than before.

N.J. Are you attached to the piece essentially because of this central character?

C.G. I love and have always loved the story itself. It's one of those stories that is part of childhood and yet full of eternal truths. It's very important to be true to this aspect in all the characterisation. The sisters, for instance, must not be caricatures. If you strip away pantomime preconceptions about them, and just listen to the music, you find they both have great character. They argue about the one's superiority over the other: Clorinda is the elder, and sharper, while Tisbe is almost as put upon as Cinderella by her sister! They are both vain and silly, but they are believable people.

N.J. Like their father . . . ?

C.G. You could say that Rossini's musical conception of Don Magnifico makes him the most 'buffo' figure of all, but he is actually an extremely complicated character. At face value, he is very unpleasant. His entrance aria has to be examined carefully to discover why he is called Magnifico.

N.J. He has delusions of grandeur —

C.G. Yes, he has an overblown idea of himself, but at the same time he is able to say to his daughters that 'anyone can tell by looking at you two that your father must have been a donkey!' Such a perceptive remark is not at all 'buffo'. The absence of the cruel stepmother of traditional pantomime, where the father is a comically incapable old man, throws the burden here on the father to be the controlling element in the household: he has to be harsh yet, at the same time, absurd.

N.J. What about the other characters?

C.G. Another unusual feature for a comic Italian opera is Ramiro's relationship to his tutor, Alidoro. Ramiro is a boy who actually grows up in the course of the opera. Even Dandini has his profounder moments — when he falls in love with Cinderella at the ball and regrets that he is not a prince, and cannot have her. You might say that this is reminiscent of Beaumarchais. They *can* all be played *buffo*, of course; but the opera is not called *melodramma giocoso* for nothing: *opera buffa* would be quite a different matter.

N.J. Do you find Alidoro rather a disappointing character?

C.G. No. He must be cast from strength. His philosophy is remarkable, and he expands this particularly in the aria, when he comes to take Cinderella to the ball. He constantly refers to the powers which control everyone's destiny, and expands on this pantheistic version in part of the aria which we do not perform at ENO, because the role is taken by a baritone, whereas the omitted section demands a true *basso cantante*. The singer who took the role for ENO (Geoffrey Chard) at first thought of the character as a secondary part but came to appreciate its richness and depth, and the absolute necessity for it to be cast with a performer of stature and a creative acting talent.

N.J. Apart from cutting part of Alidoro's aria, in ENO performances Don Magnifico's drinking aria with chorus, '*Intendente, reggitor?*', is moved from the opening of the first act finale to the beginning of the second act.

C.G. This is a traditional arrangement in this country — Glyndebourne and the old Sadler's Wells production followed it. The first act already lasts for an hour and a half and this number would increase it to almost an hour and three-quarters. At the

Coliseum (though not with EMT) for reasons of length, we also omit the central section from the second act sextet, in which Cinderella pleads with Ramiro not to be too hard on Clorinda, Tisbe and Don Magnifico. This I very much regret because it lessens the effect of her forgiveness in the final scene, making this moment rather more superficial. We also ignore the aria written by Agolini for Clorinda — it is an *aria del sorbetto*, so-called because the audience could take the opportunity of some music of indifferent quality to eat an ice-cream, and it comes much too late in the opera.

N.J. Does the regular repetition of lines create problems for you?

C.G. Not for me really: the producer and singer have to find reasons for the repeats to elucidate the text. It posed a problem initially for the translator, who preferred in many cases to write new lines instead of repetitions, in the style of what he conceived would have been there if the music had been set to an English original. Mark Elder persuaded him to accept, somewhat reluctantly, a verbal repetition instead at some points. Although such a change removed much of the wit of the translation (we *used* that wit in the English Music Theatre production), I understood the conductor's reasoning. However, I don't think we have yet solved the problem: the *first* line of a rhyming couplet nearly always sets up the resolution of the second, which is the *close* of the rhyme. If you merely repeat the first line, you are invariably repeating an unsatisfactory line. Arthur Jacobs, who made this excellent translation many years ago now, might have preferred to have rewritten the lines in question to ensure an elegant and witty line which would be to the point and *bear* the repetition. But I understand that he maintains his original view, and his text has certainly engaged the responses of audiences at productions of the opera by different companies over the years.

N.J. Do you find this sort of artificial comedy has its problems for you?

C.G. As I have already said, although it is a naive story, the characters are not at all artificial. Yet it is not a comedy of manners, and it is difficult to hit the right degree of comedy in the acting. We have to appreciate the difference between real comedy and farce: *Cinderella*, unlike the 'buffo' *Italian Girl* or *Barber*, is not farce. The text has a very steely edge to it.

N.J. Rossini's habit of suspending the action for an ensemble is very striking. How do you ask the cast to play these passages?

C.G. Of course, this kind of moment happens often in opera. And during Shakespeare's soliloquies time stands still while the characters are immersed in reflection. This can be shown on stage (as it is in this production) by a sudden stillness, and a change of

39

lighting. There is, nevertheless, a danger that long ensembles, such as Rossini's, can become dead if the characters are static. A *frisson* must stay in the air, the characters must remain aware of each other thoughout. They should not retreat too far into their 'Stanislavsky bubbles'.

N.J. Mark Elder also mentioned the importance of rehearsing the ensemble.

C.G. It is essential in this genre: there is no room for 'stars'. Every moment is important and each effect must be calculated to the last detail.

N.J. Would you say it is as demanding as, say, Mozart?

C.G. It is definitely more difficult to direct than Mozart, in order to achieve the correct level of comedy. As for the performers, the most severe test is the all-important appearance of spontaneity, which is the product of concentrated rehearsals with a committed ensemble.

N.J. What do you make of the storm?

C.G. Rossini seems to have had a predilection for storms. This one helps the plot along and it is very charming that, when Alidoro says that he has arranged everything, he implies the weather as well! And it is musically much more attractive than the storm in *The Barber* which is, if anything, even more gratuitous. It provides a much-needed orchestral interlude, following the chatter and plot in the act so far. (We play it as an exterior scene: it must seem odd played as an interior of the Baron's house.)

N.J. Would you like to say something about Roger Butlin's set?

C.G. It was conceived in this light way to match the, shall I say, pellucid character of the score. The white set and off-white costumes also balance and counteract the darkness of the plot: the music sparkles throughout, despite the harshness of some of the words. A grim stone kitchen would not be appropriate.

N.J. This set is particularly apt because it is intriguing. Audiences like to see it revolve, pushed by members of the cast.

C.G. That is part of the man-made magic of a show which has no pumpkin turning into a coach and dissolving ball-dress. We wanted a substitute for pantomime magic. The revolve also provides the six necessary scenes in quick succession without a curtain. It depends for its effect on lighting — another aspect of the man-made magic, if you like. For example, when the offstage chorus annouce Cinderella's arrival, all the lights dim to a romantic blue, full of anticipation and mystery. Then the courtiers enter in red velvet coats, and the candelabra are brought in. The contrasts of colour and light are magical in themselves.

N.J. This leads to the curious first act finale.

C.G. This is an extreme case of the 'suspended moment' we talked about earlier. This time the characters are snatched from reality onto Cloud Nine, along with their melting ice-creams, by the extraordinary situation in which they find themselves. It is one of the most magical moments in Rossini's score: it leads into one of his famous *crescendo* ensembles and it is only at the fall of the curtain that everyone is hurled back to Earth. For me, it also sums up the extraordinary treatment Rossini gives this eternal tale: it is a work of genius and gives us all constant pleasure, however often we find ourselves involved with it.

N.J. You and Mark Elder seem to agree on so many points: what about your work with each other on this opera? As this was the third time you have directed the opera (and the fourth year of the production), how did you react to his opinions?

C.G. He is a conductor who is as much concerned with the total dramatic effect as the musical result. Far from resenting what he often would call his interference, I found this collaboration stimulating and rewarding. All too often a conductor turns up at the last moment and seems to be entirely unconcerned with what happens on stage: this is totally frustrating for a director. I know that the 'original' cast members of this production (Della Jones and Meryl Drower) agree with me that Mark's insight and commitment helped us all to build anew and develop an existing production into something fresh and exciting.

M'elle Cinti d'Amoreau, after Grevedon, an early performer of Angelina (Opera Rara Collection)

41

Thematic Guide

Many of the themes from the opera have been identified in the articles by numbers in square brackets, which refer to the themes set out on these pages. The themes are also identified by the numbers in brackets at the corresponding points in the libretto, so that the words can be related to the musical themes.

[1] OVERTURE

Allegro vivace

p leggiero

[2]

[3]

[4] CLORINDA

Allegro con brio

No, no, no, no: there's none, there's none
No, no, no, no: non v'è,   non   v'è.

[5] CINDERELLA *(in a tone of resignation)*

Andantino

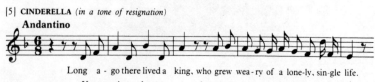

Long   a - go there lived a   king, who grew wea - ry of a lone-ly, sin-gle life.
U - na vol - ta c'era_un   re,   che_a star so-lo, che_a star so-lo s'anno-io;

42

[6] CHORUS

Allegro con brio

Oh, gra-cious daugh-ters of Don Ma-gni-fi-co, our Prince Ra-mi — ro will soon be here.
O fi-glie a-ma-bi-li di Don Ma-gni-fi-co, Ramiro il princi-pe or or ver-rà.

[7] TISBE, CLORINDA

Allegro

T { Cin-der-el-la, here to me. { Cin-der-el-la, here to me.
Ce-ne-ren-to-la vien quà. C { Ce-ne-ren-to-la vien quà.

[8a] RAMIRO (*to himself*)

Maestoso

Oh, so ar-dently I gaze on her eyes, so clear, so —————— bright.
Un so - a - ve non so che in que-gli oc-chi scin-til —————— lò.

[8b] DON RAMIRO

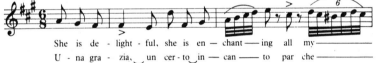

She is de-light-ful, she is en — chant——ing all my——
U - na gra-zia, un cer-to in — can —— to par che——

sen — ses ————— now be ————— guiling
bril——li ————— su quel ————— vi - so

[9] DANDINI

Allegro moderato

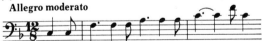

Like the bee, as he roams o'er the bow ————— er
Come un' a - pe ne'gior-ni d'a-pri ————— le

[10] CINDERELLA

Allegro

One hour — all my vi —— sions ex-ceed-ing. Oh—— take me—— to — the—— ball.
Un' o —— ra, un'o —— ra — so—la, por—ta-te—mi a bal——lar.

43

Moderato

It's plain e - nough to see up - on their fa —— ces

Nel volto e - sta - ti - co di questo e quel —— lo

[12] DON MAGNIFICO

Allegro vivace

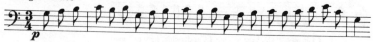

If you let out a word of a - ny - thing you've heard,

you'll pay the pe nal ty, you understand?

Se tu più mormo - ri so - lo una sil - la - ba, un cimi - te - ri - o qui si fa - rà,

[13] RAMIRO

Vivace

sotto voce

Tell me quickly in a whisper, while the o — thers can — not hear us.

Zit - to, zit - to: piano, piano: senza stre - pi - to e ru —— mo — re,

[14] CINDERELLA

Maestoso

(Let) no de - cei

(For) tu - na ca

ver woo me.

pric - cio sa:

[15] CLORINDA

Andante maestoso

I'd like to speak my feel —— ings, but words will not be found.

Par - lar pen sar vor - re —— i, par - lar, pen —— sar non — so.

44

[16] **SEXTET** *(Finale Act One)*

In a dream, I'm in a gar-den, in a gar-den, in a garden. And a—

Mi par d'esser, mi par d'esser-e so—gnando fra giardi-ni, fra giar-

—mong the trees a-mong the trees I wan-der.

— di - ni, fra giardi - ni, fra bo -- schetti.

[17] **DON MAGNIFICO'S ARIA**

[18a] **DON RAMIRO**

Yes, I shall find her, I swear it.

Sì, ri——tro——var——la io giu——ro.

[18b] **DON RAMIRO, CHORUS**

Allegro vivace

R { In ev'—ry dwelling, our pur - pose tell-ing, { In ev'—ry dwell-ing our pur-pose tell-ing.

   { Noi vo-le— re—mo, do-man - de—re—mo. { Noi vo—le— re—mo, do-man-de— re—mo.

[19] **DANDINI**

You'll be staggered, and as—toun—ded,

Un se - gre — to d'impor— tan - za

45

Maestoso

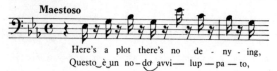

Here's a plot there's no de - ny - ing,
Questo è un no - do avvi — lup — pa — to,

Andantino

Ah, my—— lord, I — pray ex - cuse me.
Ah si——gnor, s'è — ver che in pet - to

Vivace

Hear them moan and hear them mut - ter.
Quel—— lo bron - to— la e bor— bot - ta,

Andante *a piacere*

Born to a life that was lone————ly,
Nac - qui all'a - ffanno e al pian————to,

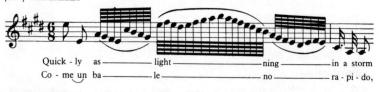

Quick - ly as———— light————ning————in a storm
Co - me un ba————le————— no————ra - pi - do,

Allegro

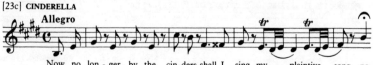

Now no lon - ger by the cin - ders shall I sing my plaintive song, no.
Non più me - sta accanto al fuoco sta—rò so - la a gor - gheg - giar, no.

Like the day————light,
Ah fuun lam————po,

46

La Cenerentola
ossia
La Bontà in Trionfo
(Cinderella or Goodness Triumphant)

Melodramma giocoso in two acts
by Gioachino Rossini

Libretto by Giacomo Ferretti
English translation by Arthur Jacobs

This is the complete Italian libretto written by Ferretti, incorporating his scene descriptions and stage directions. These do not necessarily reflect the current ENO (or any other) production. The Italian text follows old-fashioned spellings and is laid out mainly in rhyming verse. Since the opera is often cut in performance, notes show where scenes are occasionally rearranged. Arthur Jacob's translation was made in 1953 for a television performance and then used in 1959 by Sadler's Wells. Although the performing translation has itself been shortened for English National Opera performances at the London Coliseum, the complete text is reproduced here with the approval of all concerned.

The titles of musical pieces follow the stage directions after an oblique and the numbers in square brackets refer to the thematic guide. The braces in the margin indicate that the characters sing their words together.

La Cenerentola was first performed on January 25, 1817 at the Teatro Valle, in Rome. The first performance in London was at the King's Theatre, Haymarket on January 8, 1820. The first performance in the USA was at the Park Street Theatre, New York on June 27, 1826. It is supposed to have been the first opera produced in Australia (Sydney, February 12, 1844, in English). It was first performed by Sadler's Wells Opera on October 29, 1959 and by English National Opera, in a production originally mounted for English Music Theatre, at the London Coliseum on September 6, 1979.

THE CHARACTERS

Alidoro
philosopher, Don Ramiro's tutor

bass

Clorinda ⎫ *daughters of Don Magnifico*
Tisbe   ⎭

soprano
mezzo-soprano

Angelina
*known as Cinderella, Don Magnifico's
step-daughter*

contralto

Don Magnifico *baron of Monte Fiascone*

bass-baritone buffo

Don Ramiro *prince of Salerno*

tenor

Dandini *his valet*

bass

Courtiers and Servants of the Prince

tenors, basses

The action takes place partly in an old castle belonging to Don Magnifico, and partly in the Prince's country retreat ('un casino di delizie'), about half a mile away.

Act One

Scene One. *An ancient hall in the Baron's castle, with doors. To the right a fireplace, a little table with a mirror, a basket of flowers, and chairs. Clorinda is practising a 'chassée' (a dance step); Tisbe is adorning herself with a flower, now at her bosom, then on her brow; Cinderella is using bellows at the fireplace to brew a pot of coffee. | Introduction*

CLORINDA [4]

No, no, no, no; there's none,
there's none,
None can dance a step so well,
None can dance a step so well.

No, no, no, no; non v'è, non v'è
Chi strisciar sappia così
Leggerissimo *sciassè*.

TISBE

Yes, yes, yes, yes. It suits me so.
Better so? No, better so.
Which is best it's hard to tell.

Sì, sì, sì, sì; va bene quì . . .
Meglio quì . . . nò, meglio quì . . .
Risaltar di più mi fa.

CLORINDA, TISBE

To such beauty, to such art,
Any man must lose his heart.

A quest'arte, a tal beltà,
Sdrucciolar ognun dovrà.

CINDERELLA [5]
(in a resigned tone)

Long ago there lived a king
Who grew weary
Of a lonely, single life.
All around he sought a wife,
But there were three who claimed the
ring. So what then?
He chose not the rich nor fair,
But the one nobody knew.
She was modest, she was simple,
She was simple, kind and true.
Tra la la la, tra la la la, tra la la la.

Una volta c'era un re,
Che a star solo,
Che a star solo s'annoio;
Cerca, cerca, ritrovò:
Ma il volean sposare in tre, cosa fà?
Sprezzò il fasto, e la beltà,
E alla fin sceglie per sè
L'innocenza, l'innocenza,
L'innocenza, e la bontà.
Là là là là, lì lì lì lì, là là là là.

CLORINDA, TISBE

Cinderella, will you hold your tongue?
It's that song you're always singing.
Cinderella, stop that aweful song!
Through our heads it's always ringing.

Cenerentola, finiscila
Con la solita canzone.
(repeat)

CINDERELLA

I must work and have no leisure
But since I've no other pleasure
Surely I may sing my song.
Long ago there lived a king
Long ago . . .

Presso al fuoco in un cantone
(repeat)
Via lasciatemi cantar.
[5] Una volta . . . c'era un re,
Una volta . . .

CLORINDA, TISBE

Yes, quite long enough.

E due, e tre.

CLORINDA

Long enough we've suffered so.

La finisci, sì, o nò?

49

	CLORINDA, TISBE
Will you finish, yes or no?	Se non taci, ti darò . . .

	CINDERELLA [5]
Long ago there . . .	Una volta . . .

There is a knock at the door.

	ALL
Who is there at the door?	Chi sarà? Chi sarà?

Cinderella opens the door. Enter Alidoro, dressed as a beggar.

	ALIDORO
Noble ladies, I am poor.	Un tantin di carità,
Do not turn me from your door.	*(repeat)*

	CLORINDA, TISBE
Off! You beggar, go away.	Accatoni! via di quà.

CINDERELLA
*(pouring out a cup of coffee, and giving it, with some bread, to Alidoro,
so her step-sisters do not see)*

Here's some bread that I've been baking,	Zitto, zitto! su prendete
More I'd gladly see you taking.	Questo pò di colazione.
Oh, alas, that I can never turn	Ah, non reggo alla passione;
Their bitterness away.	Che crudel fatalità!

	ALIDORO
Heaven watches o'er us ever,	Forse il Cielo il guiderdone;
Your reward may come today.	Pria di notte vi darà.

CLORINDA, TISBE
(preening themselves)

For a husband rich and clever	Risvegliar dolce passione
I know just the trick to play.	Più di me nessuna sa.

CLORINDA
(noticing that Alidoro is still there)

What, you rascal, are you still there?	Ma che vedo? . . . Ancora lì!

	TISBE
And drinking coffee, and eating too?	Anche un pane? del caffè?

CLORINDA
(turning on Cinderella)

What a wicked thing to do!	Prendi, questo viene a te.

CINDERELLA
(interposing)

Oh, will no one take my part?	Ah! soccorso chi mi da?

	ALIDORO
Have some pity in your heart.	Vi fermate per pietà!

Enter Courtiers, dressed for riding.

	COURTIERS [6]
Oh, gracious daughters of Don Magnifico,	O figlie amabili di don Magnifico

50

Our Prince Ramiro will soon be here.	Ramiro il principe or or verrà;
And to his palace he'll bid you come,	Al suo palagio vi condurrà!
To dance and sup with royal cheer.	Si canterà, si danzerà;
Then from the company he'll pick the fairest one.	Poi la bellissima fra l'altre femmine
Yes, she, the rarest one, shall be his bride.	Sposa carissima per lui sarà.

CLORINDA

| The Prince himself, you say? | Ma dunque il principe . . . |

COURTIERS

| Soon at your side — | Or or verrà. |

CLORINDA, TISBE, CINDERELLA

| And then the fairest one? | E la bellissima . . . |

COURTIERS

| — Shall be his bride. | Si sceglierà. |

TISBE, CLORINDA [7]

Cinderella, here to me.	Cenerentola vien quà;
Bring my bonnet, bring my shawl.	Le mie scarpe, il mio bonne.
Bring my hat with feathers tall.	Le mie piume, il mio colliè.
I'm already so excited	Nel cervello ho una fucina
What a conquest now for me.	Son più bella, e vo' trionfar.
Just a smile and we are plighted,	A un sorriso, a un'occhiattina
And a princess I shall be.	Don Ramiro ha da cascar.

CINDERELLA

Cinderella, bring my hat	Cenerentola vien quà,
Cinderella this and that.	Cenerentola va là,
Cinderella, bring my shawl.	Cenerentola va su,
Always at their beck and call.	Cenerentola va giù . . .
I must work without an ending,	Questo e proprio uno strapazzo!
Always working, never free.	Mi volete far crepar?
While the others, merry-making,	Chi alla festa, chi al solazzo:
Never think of taking me.	Ed io resto qui a soffiar.

ALIDORO

Though they're getting so excited,	Nel cervello una fucina
Silly girls as I can see,	Sta le pazze a martellar;
When the wrong will soon be righted,	Ma già pronta è la ruina
What a laughing-stock they'll be.	Voglio ridere, e schiattar.

COURTIERS

They are getting so excited,	Già nel capo una fucina
Silly girls, as we can see,	Sta le donne a martellar;
To the great event invited	Il cimento s'avvicina,
For the Prince's bride-to-be.	Il gran punto di trionfar.

Recitative and Cavatina

CLORINDA

(to Cinderella, giving her money for the Courtiers, who retire)

| Give them this money. Thank you! | Date lor mezzo scudo. Grazie. Ai cenni |
| Kindly tell his Highness we've accepted. | Del Principe noi siamo. |

(to Alidoro)

| Still here, you beggar? | Ancor qui siete? |

51

It smells here! Be off, now.　　　　　　　Qual tanfo! andate, o ve ne pentirete.
If you don't, you'll be sorry.

CINDERELLA
(to Alidoro)

That money that I gave them　　　　　　Io poi quel mezzo scudo
I wish I could have giv'n you,　　　　　　A voi l'avrei donato;
But I haven't a farthing. I am so sorry.　　Ma non ho mezzo soldo. (Il core in
　　　　　　　　　　　　　　　　　　　　　　mezzo
I would give anything if I thought I　　　　Mi spaccherei per darlo a un infelice).
could help you.

ALIDORO
(as he leaves, to Cinderella)

Before tomorrow's gone, you may be　　　(Forse al novello dì sarai felice.)
happy.

Exit Alidoro.

TISBE

But we've no time to be dawdling.　　　　Ma non v'è tempo da perdere.

CLORINDA

Don't you think we should go and tell　　　　　　　　　　　　Nostro padre
father?　　　　　　　　　　　　　　　Avvisarne convien.

TISBE
(contending who should go first)

　　　　My dear Clorinda,　　　　　　　　　　　　　　Esser la prima
Pray allow me to tell him.　　　　　　　Voglio a darne la nuova.

CLORINDA

　　　　My dearest Tisbe,　　　　　　　　　　　　　　Oh! mi perdoni,
Remember I'm the elder.　　　　　　　　Io sono la maggiore.

TISBE

No, no, I'll go and tell him.　　　　　　No no, gliel vo'dir io.

CLORINDA

No, no it is my duty.　　　　　　　　　È questo il dover mio.
I'll wake him at once: then you can　　　Io svegliar lo vuo! Venite appresso.
follow.

TISBE

All right, for once I'll let you.　　　　　Oh! non la vincerai.

CLORINDA

Wait now . . . he's coming.　　　　　　　　　　　　　　Ecco egli stesso.

Don Magnifico enters, in a bad temper, in his nightcap and dressing gown.

DON MAGNIFICO

Why the devil did I get you as my　　　　Miei rampolli, miei rampolli femminini
offspring?
I detest you, I renounce you.　　　　　　Vi ripudio; mi vergogno!
Such a dream that I was dreaming　　　　Un magnifico mio sogno
Till you roused me from my bed　　　　　Mi veniste a sconcertar.
(refusing them his hand to kiss)
With a noise to wake the dead!　　　　　*(repeat)*

52

Interrupting all my dreaming,
With your chattering and screaming!
Now attend your noble father,
Pause and ponder on my dream.
In this dream I was no baron,
Not a regal and sedate one,
I was turned into a donkey —
Yes, a donkey, but a great one.
Quick as lightning, and rather fright'ning
I grew feathers, I could spot them,
Though most donkeys haven't got them.
So as graceful as a seagull
And as powerful as an eagle,
Up on high, whoosh!, I flew.
To the summit of a steeple
In a moment I had flown,
And I sat atop the belfry
Like a monarch on a throne.
Then I listened while below me
All the bells began their song.
Ding, dong, ding, dong.
When your silly chitter-chatter
Came and woke me with a fright,
And the dream was lost for ever
Gone for ever from my sight.
And your bickering, bickering, bickering
Went on and on like any pair of dogs
   before a fight.
Yet despite your lack of manners
You shall hear the revelation,
For a dream must have a meaning,
So behold my explanation.
All that chiming of the bells,
A happy wedding it foretells.
And the feathers? You, my daughters.
And the flying? High promotion.
Yes, but what about the donkey?
Why, the donkey, it was I . . .
For I'm certain, when I see you,
That an ass was your papa.
Each of you shall marry princes,
And your children kings shall be;
And a dozen royal babies
I shall dandle on my knee.
With a little monarch there.
Hip hooray, the king's advancing
And a baby monarch there,
Up and down the nursery prancing.
What a family I can see,
And what a glory there for me!
With his Majesty here and his Majesty
   there,
And his Majesty perched on a nursery
   chair.
See his Majesty go and his Majesty come,
And his Majesty sucking his Majesty's
   thumb.

Come son mortificate!
Degne figlie d'un Barone!
Via: silenzio, ed attenzione,
State il sogno a meditar.
Mi sognai tra il fosco, e il chiaro
(repeat)
Un bellissimo somaro;
Un somaro, ma solenne.
Quando a un tratto, oh che portento!
Sulle spalle a cento a cento
(repeat)
Gli spuntavano le penne,
(repeat)
Ed in alto, sen, volò!
Ed in cima a un campanile
Come in trono si fermò
(repeat)

Si sentiano per di sotto
Le campane a sdindonar . . .
Din, don, din, don.
Col ci, ci, ci, ci di botto
Mi faceste risvegliar.
(repeat)

Ma d'un sogno sì intralciato
Ecco il simbolo spiegato.
(repeat)

La campana suona a festa?
Allegria in casa mia.
Quelle penne? Siete voi:
Quel gran volo? Plebe addio.
Resta l'asino di poi?
Ma quell'asino son io,
Chi vi guarda vede chiaro
Che il somaro è il genitor.
Fertilissima Regina
L'una, e l'altra diverrà,
Ed il nonno una dozzina
Di nepoti abbraccierà.
Un re piccolo di quà . . .
Servo , servo, servo, servo;
Un re bambolo di là . . .
E la gloria mia sarà.
(repeat)

Un re piccolo di quà.

(repeat)

I shall love it, I can see,
And what a glory there for me, just for
me.

E la gloria mia sarà.
(repeat)

Recitative

CLORINDA
(interrupting each other)

D'you know that any moment . . .

Sappiate che fra poco . . .

TISBE

D'you know that Prince Ramiro . . .

Il Principe Ramiro . . .

CLORINDA

Now for three days he's been living
near us . . .

Che son tre dì, che nella deliziosa . . .

TISBE

It's about half a mile off,
The palace where he's staying . . .

Vicino mezzo miglio
Venuto è ad abitar . . .

CLORINDA

He's to choose
a bride . . .

Sceglie una sposa . . .

TISBE

And we've had an invitation . . .

Ci mandò ad invitar . . .

CLORINDA

And very shortly . . .

E fra momenti . . .

TISBE

He will be here to call for us . . .

Arriverà per prenderci . . .

CLORINDA

And the fairest one,
He will make her his bride.

E la scelta
La più bella sarà.

DON MAGNIFICO
(with an air of wonder and amazement)

Really, d'you say so?
This mighty Prince (even though I've not
met him)
He's to choose, he's to wed, and you're
invited!
I'm feeling rather dizzy.
Cinderella, come quickly,
Bring me a strong cup of coffee. But
this is awful,
Half of my precious mansion is in ruins,
the rest on the verge.
There's not much for it. We'll do the
best we can, though.
You two, try and talk sensibly.
Be sure to mind your manners, for
heaven's sake!

Figlie, che dite?
Quel Principon! Quantunque io nol
conosca . . .
Sceglierà . . . v'invitò . . . sposa . . .
più bella!
Io cado in svenimento.
Cenerentola, presto,
Portami il mio caffè. Viscere mie,

Metà del mio palazzo è già crollata,
e l'altra e in agonia.
Fatevi onore, mettiamoci un puntello.

Figlie state in vervello,
Parlate in punto, e virgola,

He paces up and down, and brings them back as they are about to leave.

Dress as befits your title.
In this sort of campaign the first shot's
vital.

Per carità: pensate ad abbigliarvi:
Si tratta niente men che imprinciparvi.

54

Exeunt. Enter Don Ramiro, dressed as a squire. He looks around him and advances cautiously.
/Scena and Duet

RAMIRO

The place is deserted. Hello, there!	Tutto è deserto. Amici?
Can no-one hear me? Unsuspected,	Nessun risponde. In questa
In disguise as a servant,	Simulata sembianza . . .
The ladies I shall observe. Is no one coming?	Le belle osserverò. Nè viene alcuno? . . .
But yet I'm told to hope	Eppur mi diè speranza
By my wise Alidoro,	Il sapiente Alidoro,
That here, gracious, full of virtue,	Che quì saggia, e vezzosa
Worthy to share my throne, my bride awaits me.	Degna di me trovar saprò la sposa.
To marry — but not for love! Ah . . . wretched fate . . .	Sposarsi, e non amar! Legge tiranna,
By command of my father, whether I love or no, I must marry!	Che nel fior de' miei giorni A difficile scelta mi condanna!
Ah well, I wonder . . .	Cerchiam, vediamo.

Cinderella returns, singing to herself and abstracted in thought, carrying a coffee cup and saucer.

CINDERELLA [5]

Long ago there lived a . . .	Una volta c'era . . .

(everything falls from her hand)

RAMIRO

What's the matter?	Che cos'è?

CINDERELLA

Oh, how my heart beats!	Che batticuore!

RAMIRO

Do you think I'm a monster?	Forse un mostro son'io?

CINDERELLA

(taken aback, then recovering herself)

Yes . . . no . . . forgive me . . .	Sì . . . no, Signore.

RAMIRO

(to himself) [8a]

Oh, so ardently I gaze	Un soave non so che
On her eyes, so clear, so bright.	In quegli occhi scintillò.

CINDERELLA

(to herself)

How enchanting are his ways,	Io vorrei saper perchè
I am filled with strange delight.	Il mio cor mi palpitò.

RAMIRO

Could I tell her? Oh, no, I dare not.	Le direi, ma non ardisco.

CINDERELLA

Can I tell him, oh no, I may not,	Parlar voglio, e taccio intanto.
I must keep silent.	

CINDERELLA, RAMIRO [8b]

(She) is delightful. (She) is enchanting (He) (He)	Una grazia, un certo incanto

55

All my senses now beguiling.	Par che brilli su quel viso.
Ah, how sweetly now (she's) smiling: (he's)	Quanto caro è quel sorriso!
All my desire I may hope to gain.	Scende all'alma, e fa sperar.

RAMIRO

I'm awaiting the baron's daughters.	Del Barone le figlie io chiedo.
Pray, where are they? For no-one's answered.	Dove son? qui non le vedo.

CINDERELLA

They are in the other rooms, sir,	Stan di là nell'altre stanze.
And must not have heard your knocking.	
Soon they'll be here. (My hopes are dying).	Or verranno. (Addio speranze.)

RAMIRO
(with interest)

But, excuse me, who may you be?	Ma di grazia, voi chi siete?

CINDERELLA

Who may I be? Why, I don't know.	Io chi sono? Eh non lo sò.

RAMIRO

You don't know?	Nol sapete?

CINDERELLA

No, not really.	Quasi no.

RAMIRO

Can't you tell me?	Nol sapete?

CINDERELLA
(rapidly correcting herself and getting muddled)

Well, I'll try.	Quasi no.
Father isn't really father	Quel ch'e padre, non e padre . . .
And the girls are not my sisters,	Onde poi le due sorelle . . .
For a widow was my mother,	Era vedova mia madre . . .
Lost her husband, wed another.	Ma fu madre ancor di quelle . . .
So he isn't really father . . .	Questo padre pien d'orgoglio . . .
I am getting in a muddle.	Sta a vedere che m'imbroglio.
Ah, forgive me, sir, I pray you . . .	Deh scusate, perdonate
I am as lost as I can be.	Alla mia semplicità.

RAMIRO

How delightful, how enchanting	Mi seduce, m'innamora
Are the blushes I can see.	Quella sua semplicità.

CLORINDA, TISBE
(offstage)

Cinderella! Come here!	Cenerentola da me!

RAMIRO

Who is making all that noise?	Quante voci, che cos'è?

CINDERELLA

Not a moment will they leave me.	A ponente, ed a levante,
Always something more to grieve me.	A sirocco, a tramontana,
With my labour I am laden	Non ho calma un solo istante.

56

Ev'ry day and ev'ry hour.
And now goodbye, sir,
If you'll excuse me. Coming! Coming!

Tutto, tutto tocca a me.
Vengo, vengo. Addio signore!
(repeat)

(running first towards one door, and then to the other)

(Oh, alas, I must be going,

(Ah! ci lascio proprio il core:

(with feeling)

Yet with him I leave my heart.)

Questo cor più mio non è.)

RAMIRO
(rapt, always looking at Cinderella)

With a modesty so charming	Quell'accento, quel sembiante
And a manner so disarming,	È una cosa sovrumana.
This demure and lovely maiden	Io mi perdo in questo istante:
Has me gladly in her power.	Già più me non trovo in me.
Oh, how charming, how disarming.	Che innocenza! che candore!
She has won my love for ever,	Ah! m'invola proprio il core:
Yet alas we're torn apart.	Questo cor più mio non è.

CINDERELLA, RAMIRO

Journeys end in lovers' meeting,
That's a saying worth repeating.
But today our joy is fleeting;
From each other we must part.

Ah! (ci lascio) proprio il core:
    (m'invola)
(repeat)
Questo cor più mio non è.

Exit Cinderella. | Recitative

RAMIRO

I find it strange that in such rags and tatters
Such loveliness should be. But Don Magnifico
Has still not shown his face. He does not know me.
I'll say I am the Prince's squire and servant.
My disguise will protect me.
Dressed like a simple courtier,
No-one will notice me, and I
Can watch the ladies well. Meanwhile Dandini
Will amuse himself in my part . . .

Non so che dir. Come in sì rozze spoglie
Un volto sì gentil! Ma don Magnifico
Non apparisce ancor. Nunziar vorrei
Del mascherato principe l'arrivo.
Fortunato consiglio!
Da semplice scudiero
Il cuore delle femmine
Meglio svelar saprò. Dandini intanto
Recitando da principe . . .

Enter Don Magnifico.

DON MAGNIFICO
Oh, sir,   Domando

I've kept you waiting, pray excuse me.
Tell me, when shall we greet his Highness?

Un milion di perdoni.
Dica: Sua Altezza il Prence . . .

RAMIRO
He's on his way here.   Or or arriva.

DON MAGNIFICO
Then shortly?   E quando?

RAMIRO
Say in five minutes.   Fra tre minuti.

DON MAGNIFICO

In five minutes!	Tre minuti! ah figlie!
My girls are not ready yet.	Sbrigatevi:
(calling)	
Make haste, there!	che serve?
I'd better go and stir them. Excuse me,	Le vado ad affettar. Scusi: con queste
It's not that they're wasting time in prattle.	Ragazze benedette
They're loading ammunition before the battle.	Un secolo è un momento alla toeletta.

Exit Don Magnifico.

RAMIRO

What a donkey! Yet Alidoro, my adviser,	Che buffone! e Alidoro mio maestro
Says kindness, truth and virtue	Sostien che in queste mura
Are found within this dwelling.	Sta la bontà più pura.
Patience, patience, we'll see. In just a moment	Basta, basta vedrem. Alle sue figlie
I'll meet the Baron's daughters.	Convien che m' avvicini . . .
But who's that? Yes, I thought so. Here comes Dandini.	Qualfragor . . . non m'inganno, ecco Dandini.

Enter Dandini with Courtiers; Don Magnifico, Clorinda and Tisbe. | Chorus and Cavatina

COURTIERS

This is the day when presently	Scegli la sposa, affrettati:
Our Prince shall choose a bride.	Sen vola via l'età:
Mother of princes she shall be,	La principesca linea
And Queen of all beside.	Se no, s'estinguerà.

DANDINI [9]

Like the bee, as he roams o'er the bower,	Come un'ape ne' giorni d'aprile
Now to rose, now to lily a-straying.	Va volando leggiera, e scherzosa;
All the summer his fancy is playing,	Corre al giglio, poi salta alla rosa,
Seeking always the one sweetest flower—	Dolce un fiore a cercare per se;
So I wander from maiden to maiden,	Tra la belle m'aggiro, e rimiro:
And have marvelled at many a fair one.	Ne ho veduto già tante, e poi tante,
Ah, but never a sufficiently rare one	Ma non trovo un giudizio, un sembiante
Have I found where my wings I could rest,	Un boccone squisito per me.
Where at last there's an end to my quest.	*(repeat)*

Clorinda and Tisbe come forward, and are presented to Dandini by Don Magnifico.

CLORINDA

Highness . . .	Prence . . .

TISBE

Highness . . .	Sire . . .

CLORINDA, TISBE

Your Highness, so gracious!	Ma quanti favori!

DON MAGNIFICO

We're all quite overwhelmed by the honour.	Che diluvio, che abisso di onori.

(first to one, then the other)

Thank you, you are welcome. Nulla, nulla. Vezzosa! graziosa!
How charming! vivacious!

(aside to Ramiro; then to Don Magnifico)

(I pretended. Aren't I splendid?) (Dico bene?) Son tutte papà.
Yes, really, it's true. *(repeat)*
They're exactly like you.

RAMIRO

(Steady, a joke can be carried too far! (Bestia! attento, ti scosta, va là.)
Steady, remember how simple they are.) *(repeat)*

DANDINI
(to the sisters, who are eyeing him passionately)

Ah, have pity, oh, spare those fatal Per pietà quelle ciglia abbassate.
  glances,
Lest I die in an ecstasy of anguish, Galloppando sen va la ragione
For already before you I languish. E fra i colpi d'un doppio cannone
My defences you've shattered apart. Spalancata la brecchia è di già.
Ah, why cause me this exquisite rapture? *(repeat)*
Ah, release me, disarmed by Cupid's
  dart.
At your feet, ah, behold here your
  capture,
Ah, have pity on my heart.
Such beauty! No wonder, with such a Vezzosa! graziosa! son tutte papà.
  papa!
(Oh, how easy I find them to flatter, (Ma al finir della nostra commedia
For the three of them haven't a brain. Che tragedia quì nascer dovrà!)
They give ear to all my stupidest patter, *(repeat)*
And I trick them again and again!
How delightedly all of them chatter
At the prize that they think to obtain.
But if they knew the truth of the matter
Then their pleasure would turn into pain.)

TISBE, CLORINDA

See what longing he shows in his glances (Ei mi guarda, sospira, delira,
I have captured the prize, it is plain. Non v'è dubbio è mio schiavo di già.)
(repeat) *(repeat)*

RAMIRO

Shall I see her again, my enchantress, Ah! perchè qui non viene colei
Or will all expectation be vain? Con quell'aria di grazia, e bontà?

DON MAGNIFICO

They will soon start to call me your (È già cotto, stracotto, spolpato,
  Highness —
That's the title that I shall obtain. L'Eccellenza divien Maestà.)

CHORUS

This is a day of happiness Scegli la sposa, affrettati,
When he his bride shall gain. Sen vola via l'eta.

Recitative and Quintet

DANDINI
(observing Clorinda, Tisbe and Don Magnifico)

Again I compliment you! What fine Allegrissimamente, che bei quadri!
  figures,

59

What an eyelash! What eyes too!	Che bocchino! che ciglia!
Who would have thought it? But seeing is believing.	Siete l'ottava, e nona meraviglia;
This shows the virtue of heredity.	Già *talem Patrem, tales Filias.*

CLORINDA
(curtseying)

| Thank you. | Grazie! |

DON MAGNIFICO
(bowing)

| Oh, most exalted Highness, | Altezza delle Altezze |
| What honour. I've no words left. I'm speechless. | Che dice? mi confonde: debolezze. |

DANDINI

| They're good enough for statues. | Vere figure etrusche. |

(aside to Ramiro)

| (Aren't I splendid?) | (Dico bene?) |

RAMIRO
(aside to Dandini)

| (I think you overdo it.) | (Cominci a dirle grosse.) |

DANDINI
(aside to Ramiro)

| (No, it's what they're expecting. It's the grand manner | (Io recito da grande, e grande essendo, |
| A prince is meant to have.) | Grandi le ho da sparar.) |

DON MAGNIFICO
(aside to his daughters with self-satisfaction)

| (Now there's a prince for you. | (Bel Principotto! |
| He shan't escape, I promise.) | Che non vi fugga: attente.) |

DANDINI

And now may I continue to inform you	Or dunque seguitando quel discorso
What I had not related.	Che non ho cominciato,
I came home from travels, educated,	Dai miei lunghi viaggi ritornato,
And then my ageing father stated	E il mio papà trovato,
That our fam'ly must be perpetuated.	Che fra i quondam è capitombolato,
So a law he had promulgated,	E spirando ha ordinato
That unless I got mated,	Che a vista qual cambiale io sia sposato,
I'd lose the fortune that I'd anticipated.	O son diseredato;
So you are welcome, as I have intimated,	Fatto ho un invito a tutto il vincinato,
To the ball where from the beauties celebrated,	E trovando un boccone delicato,
I'll pick the lucky-fated.	Per me l'ho destinato;
I trust that your mind now is quite illuminated.	Ho detto, ho detto, e adesso prendo fiato.

DON MAGNIFICO
(astonished)

| (What eloquence, what manners!) | (Che eloquenza sublime!) |

CINDERELLA
(comparing Dandini with Ramiro, who is watching her)

| (Oh, how well-dressed he looks! | (Ih! che bell'abito! |
| And there's the one I spoke to.) | E quell'altro mi guarda.) |

RAMIRO

(Again I see her.
How beautiful she is.)

(Ecco colei!
Come palpita il cor.)

DANDINI

Most noble ladies,
If you will kindly accept now as your escorts
These gentlemen who serve me, the coach is ready.

Belle ragazze,
Se volete onorar del vostro braccio
I nostri Cavalieri, il legno è pronto.

CLORINDA

With pleasure.

Andiam.

TISBE

Papa, and your Highness, pray come to join us soon.

Papà, Eccellenza, non tardate a venir

Exeunt Clorinda and Tisbe with the Courtiers.

DON MAGNIFICO
(to Cinderella)

You run along.
Get my hat and cane this minute.

Che fai tu qui?
Il cappello, e il bastone.

CINDERELLA
(leaving)

Oh, yes, at once.

Eh! Signor sì.

DANDINI

Pray, sir, do me the honour
Of gracing my palace
With your baronial and glorious presence.

Perseguitate, presto
Con i piè baronali
I magnifici miei quarti reali.

Exit Dandini.

DON MAGNIFICO
(entering the room into which Cinderella went)

Enter your carriage, I'll follow.

Monti in carrozza, e vengo.

RAMIRO

(If I stay here,
I may see her again.)

(Èppur colei
Vò riveder.)

DON MAGNIFICO
(off stage, angrily)

Don't bother me.

Ma lasciami.

RAMIRO

(He's angry).

(La sgrida?)

CINDERELLA
(returning)

Oh, please, sir!

Sentite.

DON MAGNIFICO
(returns with hat and stick)

Some other time, then.

Il tempo vola.

61

	RAMIRO
(What a brute!)	(Che vorrà?)

	DON MAGNIFICO
Will you stop it?	Vuoi lasciarmi?

	CINDERELLA
Only a word, sir.	Una parola.
Tonight . . . oh, do not turn away my pleading,	Signor, una parola:
Tonight give me an hour of happiness,	In casa di quel Principe
One hour, all my visions exceeding.	[10] Un'ora, un'ora sola,
Oh, take me to the ball.	Portatemi a ballar.

	DON MAGNIFICO
Ha, ha! Yes, you'd be wonderful,	Ih! ih! La bella Venere!
So pretty, such a figure.	Vezzosa! pomposetta!
Get back there to your scullery.	Sguajata! covacenere!
Off with you! Let me go!	Lasciami, deggio andar.
A bride-to-be! From the scullery!	(repeat)

	DANDINI
	(returning to see Ramiro standing motionless)
What's this? Why are you standing there?	Cos'è? qui fa la statua?

	RAMIRO
	(to Dandini)
Be quiet, this needs observing.	Silenzio, ed osserviamo.

	DANDINI
But surely we should be going?	Ma andiamo, o non andiamo?

	RAMIRO
My heart commands me stay.	Mi sento lacerar.

	CINDERELLA
For just a half-hour . . . a quarter . . .	Ma una mezz'ora . . . un quarto . . .

	DON MAGNIFICO
	(to Cinderella, brandishing his stick menacingly)
Be off, or you'll be worse for it.	Ma lasciami, o ti stritolo.

	RAMIRO, DANDINI
	(to Don Magnifico)
Have patience.	Fermate.

	DON MAGNIFICO
	(bowing respectfully to Dandini)
Noble Highness!	Serenissima! . . .
(Get out of here!) Sir, you'll pardon me,	(Ma vattene . . .) Altezzissima! . . .
Such trouble servants give today.	Servaccia ignorantissima!
You can't get good ones anywhere.	(repeat)

	RAMIRO, DANDINI
Servant?	Serva?

	CINDERELLA
That is —	Cioè . . .

DON MAGNIFICO

You hold your tongue!	Vilissima,
Her cradle was the scullery.	D'un estrazion bassissima,
She aims at airs and graces,	Vuol far la sufficiente,
And jewels, and fine laces.	La cara, l'avvenente,
I'll show her what her place is!	E non è buona a niente.
Go in at once, go in at once	Va in camera, va in camera
And back to work again.	La polvere a spazzar.

RAMIRO

(My anger at his cruelty	(Or ora la mia collera
I hardly can restrain.)	Non posso più frenar.)

DANDINI
(in an authoritative tone)

I pray you, Don Magnifico,	Ma, caro don Magnifico,
From harshness to refrain.	Via non la strapazzar.

CINDERELLA
(with ingenuous expression)

Ah, lonely by the fireside	Ah! sempre fra la cenere
Must I tonight remain?	Sempre dovrò restar?
One hour all my joys exceeding,	Signor; persuadetelo,
Ah, help me now to gain.	Portatemi a ballar,
Must I remain here all alone?	Star sempre fra la cenere?

Enter Alidoro, bearing a register open in his hand, at the moment when Don Magnifico breaks away from Dandini.

ALIDORO

See in this register	Qui nel mio codice
Words plainly telling,	Delle zitelle,
Three sisters there should be	Con don Magnifico
Here in this dwelling.	Stan tre sorelle;
Now must his Highness see	Or che va il Principe
In their variety,	La sposa a scegliere,
All girls and women	*(repeat)*
Throughout all society.	
So with these daughters,	La terza figlia
Call now the third one.	Io vi domando.

DON MAGNIFICO
(confused)

This is a jest, sir,	Che terza figlia
And an absurd one. What other?	Mi va figliando? Che terza . . .

ALIDORO

Your other daughter . . .	Terza sorella . . .

DON MAGNIFICO
(alarmed)

Yes, but . . . she died.	Ella . . . morì.

ALIDORO

Not in this register,	Eppur nel codice
Pray look inside.	Non v'è così.

(naively interposing)

(Ah, dare I speak to them?)	(Ah! di me parlano: . . .)
No, she's alive.	No, non morì.

DON MAGNIFICO
(thrusting her into a corner)

Now if you want to go on living	Sta zitta lì.
Shut your mouth and hold your breath.	*(repeat)*
Say not a word.	Guardate quì!
You must conceal it,	Se tu respiri,
If you reveal it,	*(repeat)*
You'll meet your death.	Ti scanno quì.

RAMIRO

Sir, your reply?	Ella morì?

DANDINI

Then did she die?	Ella morì.

DON MAGNIFICO

Your Highness, she died.	Altezza, morì.

DON MAGNIFICO, CINDERELLA, DANDINI, RAMIRO, ALIDORO
(looking at each other)

It's plain enough to see	[11] Nel volto estatico
Upon their faces,	Di questo, e quello,
That guile and perfidy,	Si legge il vortice
Have left their traces,	Del lor cervello,
And in perplexity	Che ondeggia e dubita,
All of them stand. Behold them stand!	E incerto stà.

DON MAGNIFICO

If you let out a word	[12] Se tu più mormori
Of anything you've heard,	Solo una sillaba,
You'll pay the penalty,	Un cimiterio
You understand?	Qui si farà.

CINDERELLA

Don't let him bully me,	Deh soccorretemi,
Oh, did you ever see	Deh non lasciatemi,
A more unhappy girl	Ah! di me misera
In all the land?	Che mai sarà?

ALIDORO

Silence, I beg of you,	Via, meno strepito:
This noise will never do.	Fate silenzio,
Prince, 'tis on your behalf	O qualche scandalo
This I command.	Qui nascerà.

RAMIRO

There is no need to fear,	Via consolatevi:
So long as I am here,	Signor, lasciatela.
I'll see that to you	(Già la mia furia
None shall raise his hand.	Crescendo va.)

DANDINI

Am I a prince indeed,	Io sono un Principe,
Or will you pay no heed?	O sono un cavolo?

| Your full obedience | Vi mando al diavolo, |
| I now demand. | Venite quà. |

Dandini forces Don Magnifico to release Cinderella. All follow Dandini. Cinderella runs to her room. Enter Alidoro disguised as a pilgrim. | Recitative

ALIDORO

Beauty, grace, and elegance you'll find	Grazie, vezzi, beltà potrai scontrare
At ev'ry corner. But goodness and virtue	Ad ogni passo; ma bontà, innocenza,
May still escape you, though you search a	Se non si cerca, non si trova mai.
lifetime.	
That's how the world is . . . Daughter!	Gran ruota è il mondo . . . Figlia?

CINDERELLA

Daughter! You call me daughter? You're	Figlia voi mi chiamate? Oh questa è
very kind, sir,	bella!
But the Baron's so haughty,	Il padrigno barone
He won't be called my father. But	Non vuole essermi padre, e voi . . .
you . . .	

ALIDORO

| Get ready. We must be going. | Tacete: venite meco. |

CINDERELLA

| Get ready? | E dove? |

ALIDORO

It's about time	Or or un cocchio
For the coach to arrive. We'll go in it	S'appresserà. Del Principe
To Prince Ramiro's banquet.	Andremo al festino.

CINDERELLA

| What, dressed as we are? In fancy dress | Con questi stracci? Come Paris e Vienna? |
| as beggars? | |

ALIDORO
(throwing off his disguise to reveal his dress as the Prince's tutor)

Say nothing. Just for this evening	Osservate. Silenzio. Abiti, gioje,
You'll have all you desire: richest of	Tutto avrete da me. Fasto, ricchezza
jewels	
And a beautiful gown. You'll be a lady,	Non v'abbaglino il cor. Dama sarete;
But don't reveal your secret. In all your	Scoprirvi non dovrete. Amor soltanto
actions	
Your heart must be your guide.	Tutto v'insegnerà.

CINDERELLA

| Can I be dreaming, | Ma questa è storia; |
| Or is this a play we're acting? | Oppur una commedia? |

ALIDORO

Yes, my daughter,	Figlia mia,
All the world's a stage,	L'allegrezza e la pena
And all the men and women	Son'commedia, e tragedia,
Merely players.	E il mondo è scena.

Music for an aria entitled *'Vasto teatro è il mondo'* to follow this recitative was written by Agolini for the first performance and is still included in the Ricordi vocal score. An alternative scene with recitative and aria was composed by Rossini himself, to

new words, for a production in 1821, when a different singer was engaged; it is reproduced here.

ALIDORO

Yes, ev'rything will change,	Sì, tutto cangerà
And proud presumption	Quel folle orgoglio
Shall decay into dust,	Poca polve sarà
Blown by the breezes;	Gioco del vento;
While tears and lamentation	E al tenero lamento
Will quickly turn into laughter.	Succederà il sorriso.
Daughter . . . daughter . . .	Figlia . . . figlia . . .

CINDERELLA

And do you call me daughter? Oh, yes, I see it;	Figlia voi mi chiamate? O questa è bella!
While my stepfather shuns me and refuses to own me,	Il padrigno Barone non vuol essermi padre
Yet you, a beggar, in all your rags and tatters — as shabby as mine —	E vuoi per altro guardando i stracci vostri — e i stracci miei —
You're a suitable father for such a daughter!	Degna d'un padre tal figlia sarei!

ALIDORO

Hush, my daughter, we must be going.	Taci, figlia, e vieni meco.

CINDERELLA

Going? but where?	Teco; e dove?

ALIDORO

To Prince Ramiro's banquet.	Del Principe al festino.

CINDERELLA

How can you be so cruel?	Ma dimmi, Pellegrino,
Because I gave you only bread and coffee,	Perchè t'ho data poca colazione
Must you mock me and tease me?	Tu mi vieni a burlar?
Be gone, pray! — yes, leave me!	Va via . . . va via!
I must lock the doors	Voglio serrar la porta . . .
To guard against intruders,	Possono entrar de'ladri
Who might — who might —	E allora . . . allora
Who might employ some deception.	Starei fresca d'avvero.

ALIDORO

No! Put such thoughts aside!	No! Sublima il pensiero!
Gone is the life you led!	Tutto cangiò per te!
On paths exalted,	Calpesterai men che
You shall rise above riches,	Fango i tesori,
Making all hearts your capture.	Rapirai tutti i cuori.
So come now, and have no fear.	Vien meco e non temer:
I feel the presence of heav'n above us,	Per te dal l'Alto m'ispira un nume
Of Him whose throne no pow'r can sunder —	A cui non crolla il trono.
And if still you should doubt	E se dubiti ancor
Look, then, and wonder!	Mira chi sono!

(He throws off his cloak, to reveal his proper clothes beneath.)

There on high, 'mid the stars in their splendour,	Là del ciel nell'arcano profondo,
On a throne which endures through the ages,	Del poter sull'altissimo Trono
Reigns our Father, our shield and defender,	Veglia nume signore del mondo,

Whom the tempest obeys in its rages.	Al cui piè basso mormora il tuono.
Knowing all, loving all, he will never	Tutto sa tutto vede e non lascia
Leave his children remote from his love,	Nell'ambascia perir la bontà.
No, no, he redeems then with grace	*(repeat)*
from above	
Though by ashes and weeping surrounded	Fra la cenere, il pianto, l'affanno
From His throne he looks down and	Ei ti vede o fanciulla innocente,
beholds you,	
And as champion of right and of goodness	E cangiando il tuo stato tiranno
With his strength and compassion	Fra l'orror vibra un lampo innocente,
enfolds you.	
So arise, and have no fear.	No, no, no, no, non temer.
All your fortune will alter,	Si è cambiata la scena:
Do not falter but live life anew.	La tua pena cangiando già va.
Have no fear. Be strong, be true.	*(repeat)*
Do you hear a sound approaching,	Un crescente mormorio
Ever louder to the ear?	Non ti sembra d'ascoltar . . .
Then be joyful, it is my carriage	Ah sta lieta: il cocchio mio
Which will take you away from here.	Su cui voli a trionfar!
You look doubtful and unsteady —	Tu mi guardi, ti confondi . . .
Come, young lady, say you're ready!	Ehi, ragazza, non rispondi?
No, your head is in commotion	Sconcertata è la tua testa
All upset by fear and doubt.	E rimbalza qua e là
Like a ship upon the ocean,	Come nave in gran tempesta
Up and down and round about.	Che di sotto in su sen va.
But the cloud has now departed	Ma già il nembo e terminato
And we greet the shining sun.	Scintillò serenità.
For the kindly, for the true and tender-	Il destino, il destino s'è cangiato
hearted,	
Days of gladness, days of gladness have	L'innocenza, l'innocenza brillerà.
begun.	

Scene Two: *A room in the palace of Don Ramiro. Enter Dandini in conversation with Don Magnifico, and Clorinda and Tisbe on either arm. Also Ramiro. | Recitative*

DANDINI

What mastery, what learning!	Ma bravo, bravo, bravo!
You amaze me, Don Magnifico. On	Caro il mio Don Magnifico! Di vigne,
wines and	
Vines and vintages such a discourse	Di vendemmie, e di vino
You've just delivered, I'm lost in	M'avete fatto una dissertazione.
admiration.	
You're an expert, no question.	Lodo il vostro talento.
	(to Ramiro)
And he's fond of his subject.	Si vede che ha studiato.
	(to Don Magnifico)
Pray go this very moment	Si porti sul momento
To the cellar where my wines are stored	Dove sta il nostro vino conservato.
and guarded.	
Taste them all, sir. If you can do	Se sta saldo, e intrepido
That and still walk out sober,	Al trigesimo assaggio,
I'll appoint you as steward of my	Lo promovo all'onor di cantiniero.
household.	
I believe men of talent should be	Io distinguo i talenti, e premio il saggio.
rewarded.	

Highness, your gen'rous heart gives	Prence, l'Altezza vostra
As freely as a well. The more one draws out,	È un pozzo di bontà. Più se ne cava,
The more there's still to come.	Più ne resta a cavar.

(to his daughters)

(Daughters, d'you hear him?	(Figlie! vedete?
He's unable to resist you.	Non regge al vostro merto;
Now I'm to get promotion: that makes it certain.)	N'è la mia promozione indizio certo.)
Now my dear little ducklings,	Clorinduccia, Tisbina,
I'll leave you with the king. I'm for the cellar.	Tenete allegro il Re. Vado in cantina.

RAMIRO

(to Dandini)

(Observe them both with care, watch all their behaviour,	(Esamina, disvela, e fedelmente
And later you shall tell me. Search out their feelings.	Tutto mi narrerai. Anch'io fra poco.
Yes, that's the thing that counts. All charms and beauty	Il cor ne tenterò; del volto i vezzi
Fade as the years come on, but the heart . . .)	Svaniscon con l'età. Ma il core . . .)

DANDINI

(to Ramiro)

(As far as these two go,	Il core
It's clear enough: hearts cold as pebbles,	Credo che sia un melon tagliato a fette:
And a manner like bullocks.	Un torrente l'ingegno,
And as for brains, they've not a thought to share between them.)	E il cervello una casa spigionata.
That will be all, then. Be off about your duty.	Il mio volere ha forza d'un editto.
And whatever I ordered, do to the letter,	Eseguite trottando il cenno mio.
You understand?	Udiste?

RAMIRO

I do, sir.	Udii.

DANDINI

Go, then, my trusty servant.	Fido vassallo, addio.

Exit Ramiro. Dandini turns to the sisters.

Now at last we're alone here. I'd like to wager	Ora sono da voi. Scommetterei
Your pretty heads are whirling,	Che siete fatte al torno,
And if one asks the reason	E che il guercietto amore
The answer lies with Cupid.	È stato il tornitore.

CLORINDA

(drawing Dandini to her)

If you please, sir.	Con permesso:
I am slightly the elder,	La maggiore son io,
So it's to me, sir,	Onde la prego
That you should give your preference.	Darmi la preferenza.

	TISBE
	(similarly)
Sir, pray allow me,	Con sua licenza:
Look at me, I'm the younger,	La minore son io,
I shan't grow up so early.	Invecchierò più tardi.

	CLORINDA
Pardon: she's just a child still.	Scusi: quella è fanciulla,
Look at her awkward manners.	Proprio non sa nulla.

| | **TISBE** |
| Try me . . . | Senta . . . |

| | **CLORINDA** |
| I'm yours for ever . . . | Mi favorisca . . . |

	DANDINI
	(breaking away, a little angrily)
Ladies, allow me,	Anime belle,
Will you split me in two?	Mi volete spaccar?
I'll not deceive you.	Non dubitate.

(to Clorinda)

| (Trust me, I've got good eyesight and | (Ho due occhi reali, e non adopro |
| I've seen what I wanted.) | occhiali.) |

(to Tisbe)

| (Pretty one, think of me, you know my feelings. | (Fidati pur di me, mio caro oggetto, |
| We'll see each other shortly up in the ballroom.) | Arivederci presto al Spedaletto.) |

| | **TISBE** |
| Your Highness is so gracious. | M'inchino a Vostra Altezza. |

| | **CLORINDA** |
| I thank you indeed, your Highness. | Anzi all'Altezza Vostra. |

	TISBE
I'll bring you shortly	Verrò a portarle
Just a little something.	Qualche memoriale.

| | **CLORINDA** |
| Will she! | *Lectum.* |

| | **TISBE** |
| Then to our meeting. | Ce la vedremo. |

| | **CLORINDA** |
| What a nerve! But we'll see. | Forse sì, forse no. |

| | **TISBE** |
| Mightiest Highness! | Poter del mondo! |

| | **CLORINDA** |
| Accept my humble duty. | Le faccio riverenza. |

| | **TISBE** |
| I take my leave, sir. | E mi sprofondo. |

Exeunt at opposite sides.

The following scene is often moved to the opening of the second act, as in ENO performances, so that the Finale opens with the duet '*Zitto, zitto: piano, piano:*'

Enter Don Magnifico, for whom attendants have brought a richly embroidered cloak. There is a table with writing materials. | *Finale: Chorus and Aria*

CHORUS

He is wonderful to see,	Conciosiacosacchè,
Tasting bottles by the score,	Trenta botti già gustò;
He has drunk enough for three,	E bevuto ha già per tre;
But he still calls out for more.	E finor non barcollò;
He's to run the household here,	È piaciuto a Sua Maestà
By the Prince's new command.	Nominarlo cantinier:
He will guide the royal cheer,	Intendente dei bicchier
With his own baronial hand.	Con estesa autorità,
Cellar door is fastened strong,	Presidente al vendemmiar,
But for him it opens wide.	Reggitor dell'evoè;
So we praise him with a song,	Onde tutti intorno a te
And with merry dance beside.	Ci affolliamo qui a saltar.

DON MAGNIFICO

You confirm it? . . . I'm to stay?	Intendente . . . reggitor?
I'm the steward from today?	Presidente . . . cantinier . . .?
Thank you, thank you. Oh, what joy!	Grazie, grazie . . . che piacer!
What delight at last is mine,	Che girandola . . . ho nel cor.
Lord of spirits, Lord of wine!	Si venga a scrivere
Write it down, ev'ryone,	Quel che dettiamo.
As I desire.	
Six thousand copies	Sei mila copie
I shall require.	Poi ne vogliamo.

They seat themselves around a table, and write.

CHORUS

Now we are ready, sir,	Già pronti a scrivere
Waiting for you.	Tutti siam qui.

DON MAGNIFICO
[17] (*overlooking them*)

'We, Don Magnifico . . .'	Noi Don Magnifico . . .
Put that all in capitals.	Questo in majuscole!
Stupid! In capitals!	Bestie! majuscole!
That's right, like that.	Bravi! così.
'We, Don Magnifico,	Noi Don Magnifico,
Duke of this region.	Duca e Barone
He whose magnificent	Dell'antichissimo
Titles are legion:	Montefiascone;
Earl, count and baron,	Grand'intendente,
Lord of the cellar,	Gran presidente,
Butler and chamberlain,	Con gli altri titoli,
Steward etcetera.	Con venti et cetera,
In splendour suitable,	Di nostra propria
This I ordain.	Autorità,
Law indisputable,	Riceva l'ordine,
This shall remain.	Chi leggerà:
Wine is so good a thing,	Di più non mescere
It's not dilutable,	Per anni quindici,
None should put water in,	Nel vino amabile
That's irrefutable.	D'acqua una gocciola,

70

Anyone drinking
Wine that is watered,
I'll have him
Drawn and quartered,
Properly slaughtered.
Yes, properly slaughtered.
In witness, etcetera,
I, the etcetera
Hereby, etcetera,
Wherefore, etcetera,
Dated, etcetera,
Baron, etcetera.'

'Dated, etcetera',
Never a blot.
'Baron, etcetera',
Now that's the lot.

Now post it everywhere,
All through the town.
Let no teetotaller,
Dare pull it down.

Now let's away, for the
Banquet is beckoning.
Liquor will flow and
Our troubles will fly.

I'm feeling bountiful,
I'll give a sovereign
To any man who can
Drink more than I.

Alias capietur
Et stranguletur,
Capietur,
Stranguletur,
Perchè et cetera,
Laonde et cetera,
Nell'anno et cetera,
Barone et cetera
Perchè et cetera,
Laonde et cetera,
Nell'anno et cetera,
Barone et cetera.

CHORUS

Barone et cetera,
È fatto già.
(repeat)

DON MAGNIFICO

Ora affiggettelo
Per la città.
(repeat)

CHORUS

Il pranzo in ordine
Andiamo a mettere:
Vino a diluvio
Si beverà.

DON MAGNIFICO

Premio bellissimo
Di piastre sedici,
A chi più Malaga
Si beverà.

Exeunt, bowing towards Don Magnifico. Enter Dandini and Ramiro, looking cautiously around them. | Duet

RAMIRO [13]

Tell me quickly in a whisper,
While the others cannot hear us.
How did those two girls impress you?
What reaction did you find?
Tell me everything you gathered.
Tell me what is on your mind.

Zitto, zitto: piano, piano:
Senza strepito, e rumore.
Delle due qual'è l'umore?
Esatezza e verità.
(repeat)

DANDINI

Let me tell you *sotto voce*,
For your private information
They're a pair of silly boobies,
Full of vanity and pride,
I am only too delighted,
They're no longer at my side.

Sotto voce a mezzo tuono,
In estrema confidenza,
Sono un misto d'insolenza,
Di capriccio, e vanità.
(repeat)

RAMIRO

Yet my tutor, Alidoro,
Said a daughter of the Baron . . .

E Alidoro mi diceva
Che una figlia del Barone . . .

71

DANDINI	
Oh, Alidoro is a wise one,	Ah! il maestro ha un gran testone;
Or at least pretends to be.	Oca eguale non si dà.

RAMIRO	
Alidoro said a daughter	Alidoro mi diceva
Was the one I ought to marry . . .	Che una figlia del Barone . . .

DANDINI	
Oh, Alidoro is a prize one,	Ah il maestro ha un gran testone;
He's an ass, it seems to me.	Oca eguale non si dà.
(They're two brazen, ogling hussies;	(Son due vere bandverole . . .
If you leave them, you'll be wise).	Ma convien dissimular).

RAMIRO	
But for just a little longer . . .	Se le sposi purchi vuole . . .
We'll go on with our disguise.	Seguitiamo a recitar.

Clorinda runs in from one side, Tisbe from the other.

CLORINDA	
Oh, your Highness, don't forsake me!	Principino, dove siete?

TISBE	
Oh, your Highness, won't you take me?	Principino, dove state?

CLORINDA, TISBE	
Oh, be kind to your beloved.	Ah! perchè mi abbandonate?
Oh, don't leave me in despair.	Mi farete disperar.

TISBE	
I adore you . . .	Io vi voglio . . .

CLORINDA	
I adore you . . .	Vi vogl'io.

DANDINI	
Gracious ladies, wait a moment.	Ma non diamo in bagatelle.
Happy I could be with either,	Maritarsi a due sorelle
But I cannot marry two.	Tutte insieme non si può.
So what shall I say to you?	*(repeat)*
One I'll marry . . .	Una sposo . . .

CLORINDA	
(impatiently)	
And the other?	E l'altra?

DANDINI	
The other . . .	E l' altra . . .
(pointing to Ramiro)	
On my friend I will bèstow.	All'amico la darò.

CLORINDA, TISBE	
No, no, no, no, no,	Nò, nò, nò, nò, nò,
Wed a courtier, oh, no!	È un scudiero! oibò! oibò!

RAMIRO	
(placing himself between them)	
I will be a loving husband.	Sarò docile, amoroso,
I will cherish you for ever.	Tenerissimo di cuore.

72

(with an air of disdain)

No, a courtier's not for me.   Un scudiero! no, signore.
No, his wife I'll never be.   Un scudiero! questo nò.

CLORINDA

I'll not wed below my station.   Con un'anima plebea!

TISBE

You can see he's rather vulgar.   Con un'aria dozzinale!

RAMIRO

I will love you always . . .   Sarò buono . . . Amoroso . . .

CLORINDA, TISBE
(affectedly)

It's revolting, it's revolting,   Mi fa male, mi fa male
Such a notion makes me ill.   Solamente a immaginar.

RAMIRO, DANDINI
(laughing)

I've seen nothing quite so funny,   La scenetta è originale:
And I think I never will.   Veramente da contar.

CHORUS
(offstage)

Room there, make room there. Prepare Venga, inoltri, avanzi il piè:
  the way.
Let there be no more delay.   Anticamera non v'è.

Enter Alidoro.

RAMIRO

Say, what is it, Alidoro?   Sapientissimo Alidoro,

RAMIRO, DANDINI

What's this noise about the place?   Questo strepito cos'è?

ALIDORO

There's a lady just arrived,   Dama incognita quà vien,
With a veil upon her face.   Sopra il volto un velo tien.

CLORINDA, TISBE

Who can this be?   Una dama!

ALIDORO

I don't know.   Signor sì.

CLORINDA, TISBE

What's her name?   Ma chi è?

ALIDORO

She will not say.   Nol palesò.

CLORINDA, TISBE

Is she pretty?   Sarà bella?

ALIDORO

Yes and no.   Sì, e no.

73

	RAMIRO, DANDINI
Who is she?	Chi sarà?

	ALIDORO
No one can tell.	Ma non si sà.

	CLORINDA
Did she speak?	Non parlò?

	ALIDORO
No, not a word.	Signora no.

	TISBE
Tell me why?	E qui vien?

	ALIDORO
I do not know.	Chi sa perchè?

	ALL
Tell me why? What now? Heaven knows.	Chi sarà? chi è? perchè?
Who is she? Shall we see? Yes, indeed.	Non si sà . . . si vedrà.

	CLORINDA, TISBE
(Oh, how jealous this lady's making me.	(Gelosia già già mi lacera,
I'm afraid to see her here.)	Già il cervel più in me non è.)
(repeat)	*(repeat)*

	ALIDORO
Oh, how jealous this lady's making them,	(Gelosia già già le rosica,
They're afraid to see her here.	Più il cervel in lor non è.)

	RAMIRO
Strange emotion now possesses me.	(Un ignoto arcano palpito
Who is this that will appear?	Ora m'agita, perchè?)

	DANDINI
I'm a magnet, no mistaking it,	(Diventato son di zucchero,
Drawing all the ladies here.	Quante mosche intorno a me.)

Dandini makes a sign to Alidoro to bring the stranger in. Enter Cinderella, richly dressed and veiled.

	CHORUS
Never was one more fair,	Ah! se velata ancor
Among all earthly creatures.	Dal seno il cor ci hai tolto,
Will she unveil her features?	Se svelerai quel volto,
Who can say?	Che incanto mai sarà?

	CINDERELLA
All is not gold that glitters.	Sprezzo quei don che versa
Let no deceiver woo me.	[14]Fortuna capricciosa:
My suitor must bring to me	M'offra, chi mi vuol sposa,
A heart that's good and kind.	Rispetto, amor, bontà.

	RAMIRO
Can I mistake that singing	(Di quella voce il suono
That melts my heart's defences?	Ignoto al cor non scende;
Now rapture fills my senses,	Perchè la speme accende?
And hope inspires my mind.	Di me maggior mi fa.)

DANDINI

Oh, lady, veiled in beauty,	Begl'occhi che dal velo
Delightful and radiant being,	Vibrate un raggio acuto,
Unveil, that we in seeing,	Svelatevi un momento
More beauty yet may find.	Almeno per civiltà.

CLORINDA

And now we'll see the miracle	(Vedremo il gran miracolo
You've heard so much about.	Di questa rarità.)

TISBE

Contain yourself, it won't be long	(*repeat*)
Before we find her out!	

Cinderella unveils. A moment of surprise, of recognition, of uncertainty.

ALL EXCEPT CINDERELLA

Ah!	Ah!

CLORINDA THEN RAMIRO, THEN CINDERELLA, THEN ALL TOGETHER [15]

I'd like to speak my feelings,	Parlar . . . pensar . . . vorrei,
But words will not be found.	Parlar . . . pensar non so.
To see this sight before me,	Questo è un $\binom{\text{(inganno)}}{\text{(incanto)}}$ o Dei!
I'm rooted to the ground.	Quel volto m'atterrò.

ALIDORO

I'd like to speak my feelings,	(Parlar . . . pensar . . .vorrei.
But words will not be found.	Parlar . . . pensar non so.
Already he's enraptured.	Amar già la dovrebbe
My plan is proving sound.	Il colpo non sbagliò.)

DON MAGNIFICO
(running in)

Your Highness, supper's ready now . . .	Signor . . . Altezza in tavola
So . . . what . . . but . . . she . . . Good heavens!	Che, che . . . co . . . sì, che bestia!
Why, what a strange coincidence!	Quando si dice i simili!
She's so like Cinderella!	Non sembra Cenerentola?

TISBE, CLORINDA

At first we thought her so, sir.	Pareva ancora a noi.
But look a little closer . . .	Ma a riguardarla poi . . .
Our Cinders has no figure,	La nostra è goffa e attratta,
And this one's surely bigger.	Questa è un po' più ben fatta;
But still she is no Venus,	Ma poi non è una Venere
We've no cause to take alarm.	Da farci spaventar.

DON MAGNIFICO

Surely the thing's impossible.	Sta quella nella cenere,
She's back at home, no clothes to wear.	Ha stracci sol per abiti.

CINDERELLA

(He can't think what to make of it.)	(Il vecchio guarda, e dubita.)

RAMIRO

(She's spotted me, I'm sure of it.)	(Mi guarda e par che palpiti.)

DANDINI

But don't let's stand here motionless,	Ma non facciam le statue.

75

When supper now is beckoning.
Let's all go in to supper now,
And later there'll be dancing.
And then I'll pick the fairest one,
The choicest one, the rarest one,
The loveliest in sight.

Patisce l'individuo.
Andiamo presto a tavola,
Poi balleremo il Taice,
E quindi la bellissima
(repeat)
Con me s'ha da sposar.

ALL EXCEPT DANDINI

Let's all go in to supper now,
Then dance through all the night.

Andiamo, andiamo a tavola,
Si voli a giubilar.

DANDINI

(What an appetite it gives me,
Acting as His Highness for a day.
Royal duties still allow me
Time to tuck a lot of food away.)

(Oggi che fo da Principe
Per quattro vo'mangiar.)
(repeat)

ALL [16]

In a dream I'm in a garden
And among the trees I wander.
I can hear the river playing,
And the linnet singing yonder.
All the scene is so delightful
As I wander free from care.
But I fear a storm is brewing,
Slow to start, but then progressing,
All the atmosphere oppressing.
Then an earthquake sends us falling
Makes the garden look appalling.
Rocks will shiver, houses quiver,
Trees will tumble, stones will crumble,
Leaving all the garden bare.
And I tremble lest my vision
Thus should fade into the air.

Mi par d'esser sognando
Fra giardini, e fra boschetti,
I ruscelli susurrando,
Gorgheggiando gli augelletti;
In un mare di delizie
Fanno l'animo nuotar.
Ma ho timor che sotto terra
Piano piano, a poco a poco,
Si sviluppi un certo fuoco,
E improvviso a tutti ignoto,
Balzi fuori un terremoto,
Che crollando . . . strepitando,
Fracassando . . . sconquassando,
Poi mi venga a risvegliar;
E ho paura, che il mio sogno
Vada in fumo a dileguar.

END OF ACT ONE

Act Two

Scene One. *A room in Don Ramiro's palace.* | *Recitative, Scena and Aria*

RAMIRO

This lovely unknown lady
Has a curious resemblance to that poor servant,
The girl I saw this morning.
And now this unknown lady
Haunts my mind like a vision. I think Dandini
Is in love with her himself.
Here he comes. I'll hide myself and see what happens.

Ah! questa bella incognita
Con quella somiglianza all'infelice,
Che mi colpì stamane,
Mi và destando in petto
Certa ignota premura . . . Anche Dandini
Mi sembra innamorato,
Eccoli: udirli or qui potrò celato.

Ramiro hides, as Cinderella runs in, pursued by Dandini.

DANDINI

Ah, not so fast, one moment! Half an hour
I've been pacing up and down waiting to see you.

Ma non fuggir per bacco! quattro volte
Mi hai fatto misurar la galleria.

CINDERELLA

I am honoured, your Highness, but please excuse me.

O mutate linguaggio o vado via.

DANDINI

But why? I bring my devotion,
And you act as if I'd hit you.

Ma che? il parlar d'amore
È forse una stoccata!

CINDERELLA

But if my heart were already given?

Ma s'io d'un altro sono innamorata!

DANDINI

What impudence to say so!

E me lo dici in faccia?

CINDERELLA

Ah, please believe me,
And don't be angry with me
Just because I'm being honest.

Ah! mio signore,
Deh! non andate in collera
Se vi parlo sincero.

DANDINI

Who is he?

Ed ami?

CINDERELLA

Please, sir . . .

Scusi . . .

DANDINI

Who is he?

Ed ami?

CINDERELLA

Sir, 'tis your servant.

Il suo scudiero.

RAMIRO
(coming out of concealment)

She loves me! Can I believe it?

Oh gioia! anima mia!

77

(showing his satisfaction)

Just as I had planned it.   (Va a meraviglia!)

RAMIRO

What, not even all his fortune	Ma il grado e la ricchezza
Can tempt you any longer?	Non seduce il tuo core?

CINDERELLA

Though riches glitter bright, a loving heart is stronger.	Mio fasto è la virtù, ricchezza è amore.

RAMIRO

Then you'll give me your promise?	Dunque saresti mia?

CINDERELLA

Slowly, remember	Piano, tu devi
You do not know me.	Pria ricercarmi,
First see if I am worthy,	Conoscermi, vedermi,
And get to know my rank and station.	Esaminar la mia fortuna.

RAMIRO

I take you,	Io teco,
Dearest, now and forever.	Cara, verrò volando.

CINDERELLA

Be silent. Let me leave you. This I entreat you.	Fermati: non seguirmi, io tel comando.

RAMIRO

Do you dismiss me?	E come dunque?

CINDERELLA

(giving Ramiro a bracelet)

Take this bracelet, you'll recognise me	Tieni, cercami, e alla mia destra
When you find its companion.	Il compagno vedrai;
On that day, if you still love me, I'm yours for ever.	E allor . . . se non ti spiaccio . . .allor m'avrai.

Cinderella leaves. A pause.

RAMIRO

Dandini, what's your verdict?	Dandini, che ne dici?

DANDINI

My verdict? Well, it's obvious.	Eh! dico che da Principe
She shows contempt of court; I've been devalued.	Sono passato a far da testimonio.

RAMIRO

She said, 'If you still love me, I'm yours for ever'.	E allor . . . se non ti spiaccio . . . allor m'avrai.
But did she really mean it?	Quai misteri son questi?

(seeing Alidoro)

Oh, Alidoro	Ah! mio sapiente
You have always advised me. I have a heart	Venerato maestro. Il cor m'ingombra
That calls to a strange adventure.	Non mai provato amore
What says your wisdom?	Che far degg'io?

78

Do as your heart commands you. Quel che consiglia il core.

RAMIRO
(to Dandini)

You shall be Prince no longer. I'm grateful to you, Principe più non sei: di tante sciocche

But now the joke is over. Come in, attendants! Si vuoti il mio palazzo. Olà, miei fidi!

Give orders to the coachman. In a few minutes Sia pronto il nostro cocchio, e fra

I'll set out on my search and find my treasure. Così potessi aver l'ali dei venti.

[18 a]

Yes, I shall find her, I swear it. Sì, ritrovarla io giuro.
For love, kind love shall guide me. Amor, amor mi muove:
And she, once more beside me, Se fosse in grembo a Giove
Never from me shall part. Io la ritroverò.
I love but her for ever; *(repeat)*
To her command I yield my heart.

(gazing at the bracelet)

This golden bracelet she gave me, Pegno adorato e caro
How dearly now I prize . . . Che mi lusinghi almeno
But brighter than all its glitter, Ah! come al labbro e al seno,
The light that's in her eyes. Come ti stringerò!

CHORUS

Oh, what a change is on him, Ah! qual tumulto ha in seno!
It takes us by surprise. Comprenderlo non so.

RAMIRO, CHORUS [18 b]

In ev'ry dwelling, our purpose telling Noi voleremo, domanderemo,
We'll go and find her, and then remind her. Ricercheremo, ritroveremo.

One moment hoping, Dolce speranza,
Next moment fearing, Freddo timore,

My brain's excited, Dentro al $\genfrac{}{}{0pt}{}{(mio)}{(suo)}$ core

$\genfrac{}{}{0pt}{}{(My)}{(His)}$ heart's on fire Stanno a pugnar;

Love only, love only Amore, amore,

Rules $\genfrac{}{}{0pt}{}{(my)}{(his)}$ desire. $\genfrac{}{}{0pt}{}{(M'ha)}{(L'ha)}$ da guidar.

Exeunt.

ALIDORO

The night is drawing on now, La notte è omai vicina
That makes my plan still easier. Col favor delle tenebre
I'll arrange that the Prince's coach breaks down Rovesciandosi ad arte la carrozza

Just outside the Baron's house. 'Tis perfect. Presso la casa del Baron, potrei . . .

He will go in for shelter Son vicini alla meta
And there he will find her. I desir miei.

Exit Alidoro. Enter Dandini, pacing up and down. | Recitative and Duet

DANDINI

Ex-Prince, that's what I am! Shot in a moment	Ma dunque io sono un *ex*? dal tutto al niente
From the top to the bottom.	Precipito in un tratto?
It had to happen, I see that,	Veramente ci ho fatto
But I look pretty silly.	Una bella figura!

Enter Don Magnifico, with an air of urgency.

DON MAGNIFICO

Pardon me if I press you,	Scusi la mia premura . . .
But these two patient creatures	Ma quelle due ragazze
Are mad with expectation. May I ask, sir,	Stan colla febbre adosso. Si potrebbe
Which one of them you've honoured?	Sollecitar la scelta?

DANDINI

It's all been decided.	È fatta, amico.

DON MAGNIFICO

Decided! What do I hear? Tell me, which is it?	È fatta! ah! per pieta! dite, parlate!
Decided! My little rosebuds . . .	È fatta! e i miei germogli . . .
Are then to ripen in your palace?	In queste stanze a vegetar verranno?

DANDINI

I'll tell ev'rybody shortly,	Tutti poi lo sapranno!
But just now it's a secret.	Per ora è un gran segreto.

DON MAGNIFICO

Just tell me which of them.	E quale, e quale?
Is it Clorry? Is it Tizzy?	Clorindina, o Tisbetta?

DANDINI

Baron, please have some patience.	Non abbiate tal fretta!

DON MAGNIFICO

Oh, won't you tell papa?	Lo dica ad un papà.

DANDINI

In confidence . . .	Ma silenzio.

DON MAGNIFICO

Why, certainly! Now inform me.	Sì sa, via dica presto.

DANDINI

Can no one hear us?	Non ci ode alcuno?

DON MAGNIFICO

Nobody	In aria
But the fly that's on the window.	Non si vede una mosca.

DANDINI

First you must hear of	È un certo arcano
A mysterious event.	Che farà sbalordir.

DON MAGNIFICO
(impatiently)

I stand on tiptoe.	Sto sulle spine.

DANDINI
(bringing a chair)

Then take a seat, I beg you.	Poniamoci a sedere.

DON MAGNIFICO

Tell me, for heaven's sake!	Presto per carità.

DANDINI

You're no stranger	Voi sentirete
To diplomatic matters.	Un caso assai bizzarro.

DON MAGNIFICO

(He's so diffident,	(Che volesse
You would think I'm the bride.)	Maritarsi con me?

DANDINI

So I entreat you.	Mi raccomando.

DON MAGNIFICO
(with growing impatience)

I'll do just as you say.	Ma si lasci servir.

DANDINI

This thing I tell you —	Stia sigillato
You won't divulge it to a single person?	Quanto ora udrete dalla bocca mia.

DON MAGNIFICO

With me a secret is safe as in a strongroom.	Io tengo in corpo una segreteria.

DANDINI [19]

You'll be staggered, and astounded,	Un segreto d'importanza,
And bewildered, and quite confounded,	Un arcano interessante
When I tell you this surprising piece of news.	Io vi devo palesar:
It's a thing beyond believing,	È una cosa stravagante,
All your mind it will confuse.	Vi farà strasecolar.

DON MAGNIFICO

With excitement I am seething.	Senza battere le ciglia,
You can see me hardly breathing.	Senza trar nemmeno il fiato,
I am ready, pray address me as you choose.	Io mi pongo ad ascoltar.
I am standing like a statue.	Starò qui petrificato
I'm directly looking at you.	Ogni sillaba a contar.
I am waiting for your news.	Senza manco trarre il fiato.

DANDINI

For a long time I've been thinking	Uomo saggio e stagionato,
What should be my wife's position.	Sempre meglio ci consiglia;
It's a difficult decision,	Se sposassi una sua figlia,
I'd appreciate your views.	Come mai l'ho da trattar?

DON MAGNIFICO

(I'm his counsellor already.)	(Consiglier son già stampato).
Since you put the question to me,	Ma che eccesso di clemenza!
My advice I won't refuse.	Mi stia dunque sua Eccellenza . . .
(repeat)	Bestia! . . . Altezza, ad ascoltar.
For your wife's respect and honour,	Abbia sempre pronti in sala

81

Thirty men should wait upon her,	Trenta servi in piena gala,
Forty serving-women fear her,	Cento sedici cavalli,
Fifty cavaliers be near her.	*(repeat)*
Dukes in dozens, peers in plenty,	Duchi, conti e marescialli,
And field-marshals up to twenty.	A dozzine convitati,
Then a coach and six to ride in,	Pranzi sempre coi gelati,
And some ice cream ev'ry day.	Poi carrozze e sei lacchè.

DANDINI

If that's how she's used to living,	Vi rispondo senza arcani
It's by no means what I'm giving.	Che noi siamo assai lontani;
She shall have no one in waiting,	*(repeat)*
All her wants anticipating.	Io non uso far de' pranzi,
With the servants she'll be eating,	Mangio sempre degli avanzi,
She'll complain about the heating.	Non m'accosto a gran signori,
That's the atmosphere I thrive on,	Tratto sempre servitori,
That is how I earn my pay.	Me ne vado sempre a piè.

DON MAGNIFICO

You are joking.	Non corbella?

DANDINI

No, I swear it.	Gliel prometto.

DON MAGNIFICO

But this business?	Questo dunque?

DANDINI

The Prince's orders.	È un romanzetto.

DON MAGNIFICO

I can't believe you.	Questo dunque?

DANDINI

I won't deceive you.	È un romanzetto.
I am not a royal Highness,	È una burla il principato,
And my fortune's strictly minus.	Sono un uomo mascherato;
It was just a sort of masquerade,	Ma venuto è il vero Principe,
And the Prince has had enough of it.	M'ha strappato alfin la maschera.
Though a counterfeit I made, sir,	Io ritorno . . . al mio mestiere;
I must now resume my trade.	*(repeat)*
I'm Dandini, just a valet.	Son Dandini il cameriere
Make the bed, sir, brush your overcoat,	Rifar letti, spazzar abiti,
Shave and haircut or manicure!	Far la barba, e pettinar.

DON MAGNIFICO

Shave and haircut or manicure!	Far la barba, e pettinar!
This is an outrage,	Di quest'ingiuria,
This is appalling.	Di quest'affronto
I've been insulted,	*(repeat)*
I'm most offended.	
I'll see the Prince at once.	Il vero principe
I will not stand it.	Mi darà conto.

DANDINI

Pray don't upset yourself,	Oh non s'incomodi,
It's been no trouble.	Non farà niente.
Don't make a fuss of it,	*(repeat)*
Ev'rything's over.	

82

But now get out of here, Now I command it.	Ma parta subito, Immantinente.

I will not budge.	Non partirò.

Need I say more?	Lei partirà.

I'll have my rights.	Non partirò.

Right through the door.	Lei partirà.

Lay off your hand, sir.	Ci rivedremo.

You understand, sir?	Ci rivedremo.

I'll make you pay, sir.	Ci parleremo.

Bid you good-day, sir.	Ci parleremo.

No servant's hand shall threaten me.	Non partirò. *(etc.)*

I'll be the master, you can see. Shall I assist you, Or will you go?	Lei partirà. *(etc.)* Pronto è il bastone Lei partirà.

I will not go. I'll be ridiculous, Now I can see it. Treacherous fate Has trodden me down. Once I was mighty, Now I'm rejected, Just as a wise man, Might have expected. 'Look at him, look at him!' I hear them calling, Shouting and bawling, All through the town.	Non partirò. Tengo nel cerebro Un contrabasso, Che basso basso Frullando và. Da cima a fondo, Poter del mondo! Che scivolata, Che gran cascata! Eccolo, eccolo! Tutti diranno; Mi burleranno Per la città.

Silly old idiot, Now he can see it, Treacherous fate Has trodden him down. Now from this moment, Learn to behave, sir. Better look smarter, Care for a shave, sir?	Povero diavolo! È un gran sconquasso, Che d'alto in basso Piombar lo fa. Vostr'Eccellenza Ah, ah! guardatelo, Se vuol rasoio, Sapone, e pettine,

I'll do your hair, sir,	Saprò arricciarla,
Nails, if you care, sir.	Sbarbificarla.
Here is the silliest	Ah, ah! guardatelo,
Man in the town.	L'allocco è là.

Exeunt. Enter Alidoro, alone. | *Recitative*

ALIDORO

My design is succeeding. Cupid will help me,	Mi seconda il destino, Amor pietoso
And he's certain to conquer. Even the darkness	Favorisce il disegno. Anche la notte
Now points in my favour.	Procellosa ed oscura
I can control this accident more smoothly.	Rende più natural quest'avventura.
I can hear the coach approaching. But where's Dandini?	La carrozza già è in pronto. Ov'è Dandini?
Oh, yes, he's in the Prince's carriage.	Seco le vuol nel suo viaggio.
Oh, how impatiently the Prince wanted to be going.	Oh come indocile si è fatto e impaziente!
Love will find out a way on any showing.	Che lo pizzica amor segno evidente.

Scene Two. *A hall in Don Magnifico's house. Cinderella is in her usual dress by the fireside.* | *Canzone*

CINDERELLA [5]

Long ago there lived a king	Una volta c'era un re,
Who grew weary	Che a star solo,
Of a lonely, single life.	Che a star solo s'annoiò;
All around he sought a wife;	Cerca, cerca, ritrovò:
But there were three who claimed the ring. So what then?	Ma il volean sposare in tre, cosa fa?
He chose not the rich nor fair,	Sprezzo il fasto, e la beltà,
But the one nobody knew.	E alla fin sceglie per sè
She was modest, she was simple,	L'innocenza, l'innocenza,
She was simple, kind and true.	L'innocenza, e la bontà.
Tra la la la, tra la la la, tra la la la la.	Là là là là, lì lì lì lì, là là là là.

Recitative and Storm

CINDERELLA
(looking at the bracelet)

How very charming!	Quanto sei caro!
And he that possesses that other bracelet,	E quegli cui dato ho il tuo compagno,
Is most charming of all . . . Goodness gracious!	È più caro di te . . . Qual rumore!
Oh, it can't be, it can't be! Yes, they're back here.	Uh che vedo! che ceffi! di ritorno!
I never thought they'd come back until the daylight.	Non credea che tornasse avanti giorno.

She opens the door.

CLORINDA
(pointing at Cinderella)

| Exactly as I told you. | Ma! ve l'avevo detto . . . |

It's amazing, amazing!	Ma cospetto, cospetto!
You might say one's a perfect portrait made from the other.	Similissime sono affatto affatto.
They're as like as two peas in a pod.	Quella è l'original, questa è il ritratto.
	(to Cinderella)
Done all I told you?	Hai fatto tutto?

CINDERELLA

Yes, sir.	Tutto.
Pray tell me what's the reason	Perchè quel ceffo brutto
You all stare at me so?	Voi mi fate così?

DON MAGNIFICO

Because, because . . .	Perchè, perchè . . .
Because we've met a stranger	Per una certa strega
Who looks the same as you.	Che rassomiglia a te . . .

CLORINDA

I almost want to strike you	Su le tue spalle
For what has happened.	Quasi mi sfogherei.

CINDERELLA

Surely you are mistaken.	Povere spalle miei!
What have I done to you?	Cosa ci hanno che far?

TISBE

Oh, did you hear it?	Oh fa mal tempo!
It's getting quite a tempest.	Minaccia un temporale.

It thunders and lightens. A carriage is heard to break down.

DON MAGNIFICO

I'll give you quite a tempest.	Altro che temporale!
I wish a stroke of lightning	Un fulmine vorrei
Would shrivel up that saucy valet.	Che incenerisse il cameriere.

CINDERELLA

But tell me	Ma dite:
What really happened.	Cosa è accaduto? avete
Has something suddenly made you angry?	Qualche segreta pena?

DON MAGNIFICO
(furiously)

Stupid, get out. Go and prepare some breakfast.	Sciocca, va là; va a preparar la cena.

CINDERELLA

All right, I'm going. (Certainly it's upset him!	Vado, sì vado. (Ah che cattivo umore!
Ah, but my own beloved, how can I forget him?)	Ah! lo scudiero mio mi sta nel core.)

She leaves. The storm rages outside. Eventually Dandini and Ramiro enter, in their correct clothes. / Recitative and Sextet

DANDINI

Sir, please excuse me.	Scusate, amico;

| But his Highness's carriage has overturned . . . | La carrozza del Principe |

(recognising Don Magnifico)

| Oh, good heavens! | Ribaltò . . . ma chi vedo? |

DON MAGNIFICO
(taken aback)

| What, you again, sir? | Ah! siete voi? |
| But, tell me, where's the Prince? | Ma il Principe dov'è? |

DANDINI
(indicating Ramiro)

| D'you recognise him? | Lo conoscete? |

DON MAGNIFICO

| His attendant! I'm bewildered. | Lo scudiero! Uh guardate! |

RAMIRO

| Forgive this intrusion, | Signore, perdonate, |
| It's rather a lengthy story. | Se una combinazione . . . |

DON MAGNIFICO

| Your Highness, it's no matter, you are welcome. | Che dici? Si figuri, mio padrone! |

(to his daughters)

(Look, there must be a reason why he came.	(Eh! non senza perchè venuto è qua.
I'm sure that one of you two will get him yet.)	La sposa, figlie mie, fra voi sarà.)
Hey, listen, Cinderella,	Ehi! presto, Cenerentola,
Bring us the chair of state in here.	Porta la sedia nobile.

RAMIRO

| No, no, don't take the trouble: in a few minutes | No, no: pochi minuti; altra carrozza |
| They'll fetch another coach. | Pronta ritornerà. |

DON MAGNIFICO

| Still, pray allow me. | Ma che! gli pare? |

CLORINDA

| Don't dawdle, Cinderella. | Ti sbriga, Cenerentola. |

Cinderella brings a chair of state for Dandini, whom she imagines to be the Prince.

CINDERELLA

| I'm here. | Son qui. |

DON MAGNIFICO

| For his Highness, you stupid, he's standing there. | Dalla al Principe, bestia, eccolo li. |

CINDERELLA

| This one? No, it can't be. He's the Prince? | Questo . . . Ah! che vedo! Principe! |

She covers her face with her hands and is about to run away.

86

One moment! Yes! It's the bracelet!   T'arresta. Che! lo smaniglio!
I've found her. My searching is over.   È lei! che gioia è questa!
Have I found you?   Siete voi?

CINDERELLA
(looking at the Prince's clothes)
You, then, are his Highness?   Voi Prence siete?

CLORINDE, TISBE
(astonished)
I'm astounded!   Qual sorpresa!

DANDINI
A lucky breakdown.   Il caso è bello.

DON MAGNIFICO
(wishing to interrupt Ramiro)
But . . .   Ma . . .

RAMIRO
Be silent.   Tacete.

DON MAGNIFICO
I must be crazy. But . . .   Addio cervello. Se . . .

RAMIRO
No more, sir.   Silenzio.

ALL
Strange indeed!   Che sarà!

DANDINI THEN **RAMIRO** THEN **CINDERELLA**, THEN **DON MAGNIFICO**,
THEN **CLORINDA** AND **TISBE**

Here's a plot there's no denying,   [20] Questo è un nodo avviluppato,
Here's a knot that needs untying,   Questo è un gruppo rintrecciato,
It's a puzzle mystifying,   Chi sviluppa più inviluppa,
All my thoughts and senses trying.   Chi più sgruppa, più raggruppa;
Round and round my thoughts are   Ed intanto la mia testa
  flying.
Hope and dread together vying.   Vola vola, e poi s'arresta,
Doubting fills me, wonder thrills me.   Vò tenton per l'aria oscura,
And my head is in a whirl.   In comincio a delirar.

CLORINDA
(to Cinderella, pushing her roughly)
Why, how dare you, you stupid creature?   Donna sciocca, alma di fango,
It's the limit – such presumption!   Cosa cerchi? che pretendi?
Standing here among your betters.   Fra noi gente d'alto rango
Won't you ever learn your place?   L'arrestarsi è inciviltà.

DON MAGNIFICO
Brazen hussy, I won't allow it,   Serva audace! e chi t'insegna
Coming here and pushing forward.   Di star qui fra tanti oroi?
Go at once into the kitchen   Va in cucina, serva indegna,
I don't want to see your face.   Non tornar mai più di quà.

RAMIRO
Keep your distance, you bunch of   Alme vili! invan tentate
  schemers,

And respect the one I treasure.
Or I'll let you feel my anger,
You'll be quickly in disgrace.

Insultar colei che adoro.
Alme vili! paventate,
Il mio fulmine cadrà.

DANDINI

Now the comedy is ended
And the tragedy's beginning.
It is just as I intended,
I'm delighted with the case.

Già sapea, che la commedia
Si cangiava al second'atto:
Ecco aperta la tragedia,
Me la godo in verità.

CLORINDA, TISBE

I'm bewildered.

Son di gelo.

DON MAGNIFICO

I've been cheated.

Son di stucco.

DANDINI

I should say that he's defeated.

Diventato è un mamalucco.

CLORINDA, TISBE, DON MAGNIFICO

But a servant . . .

Ma una serva . . .

RAMIRO

Enough, you heard me.
Hold your tongues or you will pay.
Do what I say, or you will pay.

Olà, tacete:
L'ira mia più fren non ha.
(repeat)

CINDERELLA [21]

Ah, my lord, I pray excuse me.
One request you'll not refuse me.
Pay their blindness back with kindness,
And let mercy crown the day.

Ah signor, s'è ver che in petto
Qualche amor per me serbate,
Compatite, perdonate,
E trionfi la bontà.

DANDINI

She is weeping, ah, how gen'rous,
Such compassion to display.

Quelle lagrime mirate:
Qual candore, qual bontà!

DON MAGNIFICO, CLORINDA, TISBE

Oh the hypocrite, just listen!
In the long run she will pay.
(repeat)

Ah! l'ipocrita guardate!
Oh che bile che mi fa!
Oh che rabbia che mi fa!

DON MAGNIFICO

But now let's all be sensible,
I'm sure you'll understand me.

Ma in somma della somme.
Altezza, cosa vuole?

RAMIRO

Well, then, here's news you've not
expected.
This one's the bride I've selected.

Piano: non più parole,

Questa sarà mia sposa.

He takes Cinderella's hand.

CLORINDA

Oh, he's just making fun, that's all.

Ah! ah! dirà per ridere.

TISBE

A trick that he has done, that's all.

(repeat)

(to Cinderella)

See what a trick he's playing now.	Non vedi che ti burlano?
Such funny things he's saying now.	*(repeat)*

RAMIRO

I swear it. She shall be mine.	Lo giuro: mia sarà.

DON MAGNIFICO

I thought it was my daughters	Ma fra i rampolli miei,
I rather thought your Highness . . .	Mi par che a creder mio . . .

RAMIRO
(contemptuously)

I don't think they could love me,	Per loro non son io.
They've shown themselves above me.	*(repeat)*
'You see, he's rather vulgar,	Ho l'anima plebea,
A lack of proper breeding!'	Ho l'aria dozzinale.

DANDINI

Now faithful love may have its way.	Alfine sul bracciale,
	Ecco il pallon tornò;
(repeat)	E il giocator maestro
	In aria il ribalzò.

RAMIRO
(to Cinderella)

Come now, I command! Come now, my own one!	Vieni a regnar: vieni, l'impongo.

CINDERELLA

Firstly, my father's blessing,	Su questa mano almeno,
And let me embrace you, sisters.	E prima a questo seno . . .

She tries to kiss Don Magnifico's hand, and to embrace her step-sisters. They energetically repulse her advances.

DON MAGNIFICO

To blazes!	Ti scosta.

CLORINDA, TISBE

And good riddance!	Ti allontana.

RAMIRO

Who could be so ungrateful?	Perfida gente insana!
They will regret it soon.	Io vi farò tremar.
Wait till I show my anger,	*(repeat)*
They'll sing another tune.	

CINDERELLA

Where am I? What is this magic?	Dove son? che incanto è questo?
Oh, how joyful this must make me.	Io felice, o quale evento!
Is it real, or am I dreaming?	È un inganno? ah se mi desto!
And will someone shortly wake me?	Che improvviso cangiamento!
Such a thing is past believing.	Sta in tempesta il mio cervello,
Such a wonder can't be true.	Posso appena respirar.

THE OTHERS

Hear them moan and hear them mutter. [22]	Quello brontola e barbotta,

Hear them stammer, hear them stutter.	Questo strepita e s'adira,
Hear them murmur, hear them mumble.	Quello freme, questo fiotta,
Hear them grouse and hear them grumble.	Chi minaccia, chi sospira,
No one but themselves deceiving.	Va a finir, che a'pazzarelli
They behave as children do.	Ci dovranno strascinar.

RAMIRO, DANDINI

| Come now, for happiness awaits | Vieni, amor ti guiderà |
| And love is calling you. | A regnar, a trionfar. |

Ramiro leaves with Cinderella, followed by Dandini and Don Magnifico. | Recitative and Aria

TISBE

| We've been deceived and cheated! | Dunque noi siam burlate? |

CLORINDA

| I'm so furious, I can hardly speak calmly. | Dalla rabbia io non vedo più lume. |

TISBE

| It's quite beyond belief . . . that Cinderella . . . | Mi pare di sognar . . . la Cenerentola . . . |

Enter Alidoro.

ALIDORO

| . . . Is to be a Princess. | . . . Principessa sarà. |

CLORINDA

| Who are you? | Chi siete? |

ALIDORO

I came among you begging for alms:	Io vi cercai la carità,
You both repulsed me. But, Cinderella,	Voi mi scacciaste. E l'Angiolina, quella
Who saw that I was wretched, and pitied me,	Che non fu sorda ai miseri,
And whom you treated as a beast of burden,	Che voi teneste come vile ancella,
Now shall rise from her kitchen	Fra la cenere, e i cenci,
And reign in royal splendour. Yes, and your father	Or salirà sul trono. Il padre vostro
Will have to raise a tidy fortune,	Le è debitor d'immense somme. Tutta
For it seems he's squandered her dowry.	Si mangiò la sua dote,
It's very likely that this old ruin of a palace	E forse forse questa reliquia di palazzo,
And all this rather faded furniture	Questi non troppo ricchi mobili
Will shortly find themselves put up for auction.	Saranno posti al publico incanto.

TISBE

| What will become of us then? | Che fia di noi frattanto? |

ALIDORO

Well, make your minds up.	Il bivio è questo.
You can decide on poverty for ever,	O terminar fra la miseria i giorni,
Or you can beg for pardon.	O pure a piè del trono
If you are humble, the Princess may forgive you.	Implorar grazia ed impetrar perdono.

90

In a few minutes, I warn you,	Nel vicin atrio io stesso,
They'll be having the wedding.	Presago dell'evento,
I thought it as well to make all	La festa nuziale ho preparato:
arrangements.	
So, now go in and see her.	Questo, questo è il momento.

CLORINDA

Must I bow to that baggage? Why it's	Abbassarmi con lei? Son disperata!
outrageous!	

Exit Clorinda.

ALIDORO

You see the pill is bitter,	La pillola è un po dura:
But you must swallow it.	Ma inghiottir la dovrà;
There's no escape. Have you reached	Non v'è rimedio. E voi cosa pensate?
your decision?	

TISBE

My decision? Seems to me that I've no	Cosa penso? Mi raccomando alla sorte:
option.	
I prefer humble pie to plain starvation.	Se mi umilio alla fin, non vado a morte.

Exit Tisbe.

ALIDORO

Now, at last, all is settled;	Giusto ciel! ti ringrazio!
Justice is done, and my hopes are	I voli miei non han più che sperar.
fulfilled.	
The proud have fallen, and my dear	L'orgoglio è oppresso, sarà felice
pupil	
Can't but be happy. Kind actions have	Il caro alunno. In trono trionfa la bontà:
met their due reward.	
I'm quite contented.	Contento io sono.

Scene Three. *A hall with a throne. Ramiro and Cinderella enter, with Dandini and Courtiers. Don Magnifico stands in a corner, with Clorinda and Tisbe hiding their faces in vexation. | Chorus, Scena and Rondo Finale*

CHORUS

Fortune's a wheel that turns and turns,	Della fortuna istabile
Ruling our joy and our sadness.	La revolubil ruota,
Now it has brought our fair Princess	Mentre ne giunge al vertice,
And brought a time of gladness.	Per te s'arresta immota;
Pride now has gone before a fall,	Cadde l'orgoglio in polvere,
And love has found a way.	Trionfa la bontà.

RAMIRO
(rousing Cinderella)

Dearest . . .	Sposa . . .

CINDERELLA
(almost transfixed with joy)

Forgive me,	Signore, perdona,
If happiness still blinds me.	La tenera incertezza
I still hardly know where to turn. Just	Che mi confonde ancor. Poch'anzi,
lately, remember,	il sai,
I was slaving at the fireside,	Fra la cenere immonda . . .

---

* For the first performance, Agolini composed an aria for Clorinda, 'Sventurata mi credea', at this point.

91

And now to heaven I find myself transported.	Ed or sul Trono . . . e un serto mi circonda.

DON MAGNIFICO
(kneeling)

Your Highness . . . let me entreat you . . .	Altezza . . . a voi si prostra . . .

CINDERELLA

As a daughter at last now let me greet you.	Nè mai m'udrò chiamar la figlia vostra?

RAMIRO
(indicating the sisters)

And your proud sisters?	Quelle orgogliose . . .

CINDERELLA

Your Highness,		Ah Prence,
One favour you won't refuse.		Io cado ai vostri piè.
All my misfortunes in this hour are forgotten.		Le antiche ingiurie mi svanir dalla mente.
I gain a throne . . . and as a Princess I do my duty.		Sul Trono io salgo, e voglio starvi maggior del Trono;
Now let this be my vengeance — to grant them pardon.		E sarà mia vendetta il lor perdono.
Born to a life that was lonely,	[23a]	Nacqui all'affanno e al pianto,
I knew no moment of pleasure.		Soffrì tacendo il core;
It was through love, love only,		Ma per soave incanto
I found my joy and treasure.		Dell'età mia nel fiore,
Quickly as lightning in a storm,	[23b]	Come un baleno rapido
Love raised me up, and gave me one to be my own.		La sorte mia, la sorte mia cangiò.
Love raised me up to a throne.		*(repeat)*

(to Don Magnifico and her sisters)

No, no, I'll have no weeping.	No, no! tergete il ciglio:
Don't be afraid of me.	Perchè tremar, perchè?
Give me your hands, and let me now embrace you.	A questo sen volate,
Daughter, companion, and sister,	Figlia, sorella, amica,
Daughter, sister, and	Tutto, tutto, tutto,
Companion before you, you see.	Tutto trovate in me.

(embracing her step-sisters)

ALL
(except Cinderella)

She shames us all, so merciful,	M'intenerisce e m'agita,
So ready to forgive.	È un nume agli occhi miei.
Long may you reign and live . . .	Degna del Tron tu sei,
We share your happiness	Ma è poco un Trono a te.
We greet you, our own Princess.	

CINDERELLA

Father, husband, companions, I greet you.		Padre . . . Sposo . . . Amico . . . oh istante!
	[23c]	
Now no longer by the cinders		Non più mesta accanto al fuoco
Shall I sing my plaintive song, no!		Starò sola a gorgheggiar, no!
Like the daylight joy has risen	[23d]	Ah fu un lampo, un sogno, un gioco

On a night so sad and long.

(repeat)

Il mio lungo palpitar.

ALL THE OTHERS AND **CHORUS**

Long the lane that has no turning

Love and kindness can't go wrong.

Tutto cangia a poco a poco

Cessa alfin di sospirar.

THE END

The rondo finale, illustrating some of Cinderella's two octave runs, in Rossini's autograph score. (Accademia Filarmonica, Bologna)

MAJESTY'S THEATRE,

ITALIAN OPERA HOUSE.

THIS EVENING,
THURSDAY, May 17, 1849,

Will be performed Rossini's Opera,

LA CENERENTOLA

Angelina,	Madlle ALBONI.
Clorinda,	Made. GRIMALDI,
Thisbe,	Madlle S. HOWSON,
Dandini,	Sig. BELLETTI,
Don Magnifico,	Sig. LABLACHE,
Alidoro,	Sig. ARNOLDI,
Don Ramiro,	Sig. CALZOLARI.

After which, a Selection from

FIORITA.

Principal parts by **Madlle C. ROSATI. &c.**

To be followed by the last Act of BELLINI'S Opera

NORMA.

Norma,	Madlle PARODI,
Adalgisa,	Made GIULIANI,
Pollione,	Sig. BORDAS,
Oroveso,	Sig. LABLACHE.

NOTICE!—The Nobility, Gentry, and the Frequenters of the Opera are respectfully cautioned in purchasing the Libretto. They will do well in taking notice of the Printer's Name, as an imposition is practised by the vending of a spurious and incorrect Book. The editions printed by G. STUART, 38, Rupert Street, Haymarket, may be strictly relied upon, as the text is particularly attended to.

Director of the Music, and Conductor,   **M. BALFE.**

To conclude with, a New Ballet, in Five Tableaux, entitled

ELECTRA:
Or, the Lost Pleiade.

Electra,		Madlle C. GRISI,
Queen of Stars,		Madlle P. STEPHAN.
Edda,	[betrothed to Ehrick]	Madlle M. TAGLINOI.
Ehrick,	[a Hunter, betrothed to Edda]	M. P. TAGLIONI.
Alcyone.		Madlle MARRA,
Maia,		Madlle TOMMASSINI,

Doors open at 7 o'clock; the Opera to commence at half-past 7.

STUART, Printer, 38, Rupert-street, Haymarket.

A London playbill from 1849 (Theatre Museum)

Bibliography

A selective list of books in English about Rossini

The most recent biography is by Weinstock (*Rossini,* Oxford University Press 1968) but Francis Toye's biography (*Rossini: A study in tragi-comedy,* Heinemann 1934) is eminently readable. Earlier still is the amusing *Rossini and Some Forgotten Nightingales* by G H Johnstone (Lord Derwent) which contains many amusing anecdotes. By far the greatest commentator to write about this subject, however, was Stendhal. His *Life of Rossini* (trans. Richard Coe, Calder & Boyars, 1970) is a classic of musical criticism, overflowing with enthusiasm for the subject and perpetually stimulating.

The full score of the edition made by Alberto Zedda is published by Ricordi & Co.

Discography All performances are in Italian, and in stereo, but Abbado conducts the score revised by Alberto Zedda.

Conductor Company/Orchestra	*Fabritiis* Maggio Musicale Fiorentino	*Abbado* LSO
Cenerentola	G. Simionato	T. Berganza
Magnifico	P. Montarsolo	P. Montarsolo
Ramiro	U. Benelli	L. Alva
Dandini	S. Bruscantini	R. Capecchi
Clorinda	D. Carral	M. Guglielmi
Tisbe	M. Truccato Pace	L. Zannini
Alidoro	G. Foiani	U. Trama

UK Disc Number	GOS631 - 3	2709/039
US Disc Number	LON1376	DG2709 039
Excerpts only	SET345	2538 324 (coupled with excerpts from *The Barber of Seville*)

Excerpts

Number	Artists	UK Numbers only Disc Number	Tape Number
overture	NBC SO/Toscanini	AT 108 ★	
	LSO/Gamba	ECS 531	
	Philharmonia/Giulini	SXLP 30143	
	ECO/Asensio	LGD 023	ZCNEL2005 (cassette) Y8NEL2005 (cartridge)
	RPO/Paita	PFS4386	
	Academy of St Martin's/ Marriner	9500 349	
	LSO/Abbado	2530 559	3300 497
	Chicago SO/Reiner	C45020	
Nacqui all'affanno; Non più mesta	M. Horne	SXL 6149	
	T. Berganza	SDD 224	
	F. von Stade	9500 098	7300 571

★ Mono

English
National
Opera
Guide

2

Aida Verdi

Giuseppe Verdi 1813 — 1901

Preface

English National Opera Guides are intended to be companions to opera in performance. They contain articles and illustrations relevant to any production and not only those mounted by English National Opera. Of general interest, also, is the inclusion of the complete original libretto of the opera, side by side with an English translation. There are many reasons why sung words may not be clearly distinguishable, whatever the language and however excellent the performance. The composer may have set several lines of text together, for instance, or he may have demanded an orchestral sound through which no voice can clearly articulate. ENO Guides supply English readers with an opportunity to know a libretto in advance and so greatly increase their understanding and enjoyment of performances whether live, broadcast or recorded.

We hope the Guides prove useful to new and experienced opera-lovers alike. An audience which knows what to look and listen for — one that demands a high standard of performance and recognises it when it is achieved — is our best support and, of course, an assurance for the future of opera in the English-speaking world.

Nicholas John
Editor

2

AIDA

Giuseppe Verdi

English National Opera Guides Series Editor:
Nicholas John

John Calder ● London
Riverrun Press ● New York

First published in Great Britain, 1980, by
John Calder (Publishers) Ltd., 18 Brewer Street,
London W1R 4AS
and
in the U.S.A., 1980, by
Riverrun Press Inc.,
175 Fifth Avenue,
New York, NY 10010

ISBN 0 7145 3770 5   Paperback edition

BRITISH LIBRARY CATALOGUING DATA

Ghislanzoni, Antonio
   Aida. — (English National Opera guides; 2).
   1. Operas — Librettos
   I. Title   II. John, Nicholas   III. Tracey, Edmund
   IV. Verdi, Giuseppe   V. Series
   782.1'2   ML50.V484

Typeset in Plantin by Alan Sutton Publishing Limited, Gloucester
Printed by Whitstable Litho Ltd in Great Britain.

Contents

List of Illustrations

Verdi's 'Egyptian Business'

Michael Rose

"If anyone had said to me two years ago 'You are going to write an opera for Cairo', I'd have said he was mad — but now I see it's me who is mad. . . ."

You can look at *Aida* as an Egyptian opera, a French opera or an Italian opera. For most people, perhaps, it is the Egyptian aspect that predominates. *Aida* is the Grand Opera of all Grand Operas, *the* great operatic spectacular: tunes, choruses, trumpets; vast crowds, monumental sets; armies, temples, Egyptian priests, Ethiopian slaves, horses, camels, elephants — the lot. And all written, incredibly, to open the Suez Canal. . . .

The interior of the Cairo Opera House showing the box on the left reserved for the Khedive's harem. Although the première (and indeed the dress rehearsal) of 'Aida' were received with the greatest enthusiasm by a packed house, which included the Khedive, the audience comprised chiefly Europeans. A fez was a rare sight in the opera house.

That, at least, is the legend. And it is true that, ever since the celebrations which surrounded the opening of the Canal in 1869, the Khedive of Egypt had been anxious to secure Verdi's co-operation in writing a work especially for Cairo. But the draft of a letter written by Verdi's wife in August of that year makes it clear that the original request was for a 'hymn' and not for an opera, and that the occasion was to be the inauguration of the Cairo Opera House, built to celebrate the opening of the Suez Canal, rather than the opening of the Canal itself. In any case, Verdi refused and the Opera House opened with *Rigoletto* on November 1, 1869. It was not till nearly three weeks later that a French ship, bearing the Empress Eugénie, steamed into Suez at the head of a cortège of sixty-eight vessels of various nationalities, and the Canal was formally opened to traffic.

Nevertheless, the Khedive's hopes of getting an opera out of his favourite composer were by no means dashed, though to begin with he met with no more luck than any of the other friends, acquaintances and interested parties who, ever since *Don Carlos*, had been plying Verdi with suggestions for a new libretto. Chief among these was Camille du Locle, the Director of the Paris Opéra-Comique, who now acted as intermediary in the Egyptian negotiations: to him wrote Mariette Bey, the great French Egyptologist and founder of the Cairo Museum, expressing the disappointment of the Khedive who was 'greatly vexed at the idea of giving up the collaboration of M. Verdi, whose talents he holds in immense esteem', and adding: 'A last word. If M. Verdi still does not accept, His Highness requests you to try knocking at another door. . . . There are ideas of Gounod, even Wagner. If the latter would do it he might produce something *grandiose*'. It is tempting to wonder whether the last phrase of this letter, which Du Locle astutely sent on to Verdi, may have had something to do with the composer's change of heart. But Du Locle enclosed at the same time a scenario of the proposed opera actually written by Mariette Bey (though at this stage, rather naively, Verdi was encouraged to believe that the Khedive himself had had a hand in it) — and in the end what undoubtedly drew Verdi's interest was, as always, the quality of the story itself.

The Egyptian aspect of the opera is one that has loomed very large in the development of the *Aida* legend, and indeed the popular idea of ancient Egypt is to a great extent encapsulated for us in this most successful of all Verdi's works. Clearly the archeological framework of the subject was one of the things which first tickled Verdi's imagination: it was something new, something different, which he felt would get him out of the rut of the usual operatic settings, and from the beginning he was much concerned about the historical details of the scenario. He pestered his publisher, Giulio Ricordi, with demands for information — was ancient Egyptian worship reserved exclusively for men? was Ethiopia the same as Abyssinia? which of the Rameses might correspond to the King in the opera? where and how were the mysteries of Isis celebrated? He extracted from a friend who had lived in Egypt three closely written pages about the ancient Egyptian

Costume design by Mariette Bey (courtesy of the Bibliothèque de l'Opéra, Paris) for an Ethiopian prisoner

religion, its beliefs, prayers, music and dances, and through Du Locle kept closely in touch with Mariette Bey, to whose original scenic ideas he clung through all the changes in the text as being far more authentic than anything he or Ghislanzoni could think up. Mariette was helpful about the music too. The sacred dance, he wrote, was probably accompanied by a kind of chant, forming the bass to a very high chant above it which was executed by young sopranos: the instruments accompanying it would have been harps with twenty-four strings, double flutes, trumpets, drums, large castanets and cymbals. Verdi actually went to Florence to examine an Egyptian flute in the museum there — but was disappointed to find that it was 'just a reed with holes in it, like our shepherds have'. And the details of staging and costumes were supervised by Mariette with scrupulous care: he was even worried about the personal appearance of the Italian singers, and wrote to the Director of the Cairo Opera, 'I really must speak to you seriously about this question of the actors and their moustaches and beards. . . . I know from experience that in Italy they don't trouble to get everything exactly right, and in *Aida* it is absolutely essential that there are no beards or moustaches. . . . I consider this a matter of life and death for the opera. . . .'

It is in the first two acts, with their religious and triumphal ceremonials, that the historical details are most in evidence, reaching a climax in the visual and musical splendours of the Triumph Scene, the biggest and best of many such scenes in nineteenth-century French and Italian opera. For Mariette, with his romantic vision of the grandeur of the Kingdom of the Pharaohs, this was an essential scene, in which all the elements of ancient Egyptian greatness could be paraded in a monumental setting with glittering ceremonial and a vast panoply of musical effect. For Verdi, however, once he had worked himself into his subject, the archeological trappings began to assume less importance, and became simply a background against which he was able to concentrate on the human situations which were the real stuff of the drama. (As he said in another context: 'To copy reality can be a good thing, but to invent reality is better, much better'.) Nevertheless, he had recognised from the beginning that this was a work which, if it was to live up to the spirit of its commission, must be 'of vast proportions, as if it were for that great barn of an opera house in Paris', and there is no doubt that the whole musical and scenic conception of *Aida* owed a lot to the traditions of Parisian Grand Opera.

Paris, with its sophisticated, cosmopolitan attitude to music and the theatre, was the recognised operatic centre of Europe, the magnet which attracted all the major nineteenth-century opera composers at some time or other, not always with the happiest results. Verdi had twice attempted a work there on the grandiose scale demanded by French operatic taste, but *Les Vêpres siciliennes*, in 1855, was dogged by libretto trouble, production difficulties and recurring threats of cancellation, and even *Don Carlos*, for all its great qualities, had somehow missed a real success. Verdi had therefore already decided that he would not again write an opera for the 'Grande Boutique'. But however unsatisfactory his personal experience in Paris may have been, he was far too good a composer not to have gained some positive advantage from the French connection, and what in fact emerged in *Aida* was a Grand Opera with some of the attributes of its Parisian model but without the complexities and conventions that were the bugbear of the Parisian style.

To a great extent this was due to the simplicity of the plot. The story of *Aida* is far more direct and single-minded than the complicated series of episodes and characters which make up the libretto of *Don Carlos* — indeed, it has often been criticized for going too far in the opposite direction. But the change was deliberate, and the result a quicker, clearer and more continuous articulation of the drama, and a more immediate identification with the characters and their feelings. At first glance it may seem that this is confined to the more intimate, personal episodes of the opera: the first scene of Act Two, the Nile Scene, or the final duet. But this is not really the case. The same consistency of dramatic intention lies behind the big spectaculars, into which the dramatic conflict is woven with unfailing care and consistency. Take the Triumph Scene again: as spectacle it is magnificent, and perfectly adapted both to the occasion for which it was written and to its position in the opera. It is the kind of thing that Meyerbeer did, only not quite so well. But its very success in these respects has tended to obscure not only its extraordinary melodic vitality and cumulative musical invention (Meyerbeer, in all his glory, never came near to this), but also its place in the drama. And the crucial dramatic point on which the triumph scene turns is the entry of Amonasro, father of Aida and King of the defeated Ethiopian people.

Amonasro is patriotism incarnate, and it is only with his appearance on the scene that we realise that patriotism is really what *Aida* is about. All his life, Verdi had been a passionate supporter of the cause of Italian nationalism: the success of *Nabucco* and the overwhelming popular reaction to the chorus '*Va pensiero*' were only the first indications of a vein of patriotic sentiment which burst out again and again in his earlier operas and made him, as his fame increased, into one of the figureheads of the *Risorgimento*. By the time *Aida* was written the situation had naturally moved with the years: Verdi was a national figure, a great admirer of Cavour, and after the unification of Italy under Victor Emanuel II of Piedmont in 1861 he had been persuaded, much against his will, to act as a deputy in the first Italian parliament. But the role never suited him, and his political views remained always instinctive and human, rather than in any way professional. And so in *Aida*, where the conflict is between Radamès's love for Aida and love for his country on the one hand, and Aida's similar emotional struggle on the other, the question is: whose side was Verdi really on?

From one point of view it is easy enough to see the tremendous parade of ancient Egyptian nationalism which runs through the earlier scenes of the opera as a very thinly disguised celebration of the spirit of the new Italy. The setting and subject of the Triumph Scene may be Egyptian, its theatrical conception Parisian, but its musical content remains obstinately Italian and the Grand March, for all those gorgeous 'Egyptian' trumpets which Verdi invented specially for the occasion, would be (and frequently has been) perfectly at home in the piazzas of Rome, Milan or Turin. The nobility of the King and the repressive conservatism of the High Priest are absolutely in line with such a view — indeed the sanctimonious attitude of the priesthood is a specially Verdian touch. He wrote to Ghislanzoni about a point in the libretto for this scene: 'You must alter the first eight lines of the chorus and add eight more for the priests to the effect that "we have conquered with the help of divine providence. The enemy is delivered into our hands. God is henceforward on our side". (See King William's telegram).' The reference is, of course, to the famous message sent by the King of Prussia to his queen after the victory of Sedan, news of which reached Italy as the Triumph Scene was being written. Although it didn't work out quite as blatantly as that in the final libretto, it is amusing to see the words of the German King being attributed to the priests rather than to the titular head of ancient Egypt. To Italians of Verdi's generation France had always been considered the natural ally of Italy, and when the Franco-Prussian war broke out in 1870 Verdi's sympathies were with the French: in spite of his distrust of Napoleon III he saw a powerful German Empire, united under the iron control of Bismarck, as just as serious a threat to Europe and Italy as ever Austria had been, and it is characteristic that he should have identified this aspect of European politics with the group that, in his own country, he had always seen as the main opponent of Italian progress.

Nevertheless, whatever the implications of Egyptian nationalism as an allegory of the contemporary situation in Italy, there is no doubt that the true drama of *Aida* originates in quite another quarter. To this drama the display of Egyptian power and state-consciousness is an essential adjunct, because it gives concrete, visual expression to one side of Radamès's predicament. But the entry of Amonasro makes it perfectly clear where Verdi's sympathies lie: whatever the musical seductions of Pharaonic grandeur, the emotional impetus of the opera comes from Ethiopia, and its ultimate protagonist is not Radamès, or Amneris, or Ramfis, or the King, but Aida herself. In the end, Verdi was nearly always on the side of the underdog: 'Va pensiero' is the song of the underdog in exile, and the patriotic nostalgia of the Jews during the Babylonian captivity is not much different in kind from the patriotic nostalgia of Aida and Amonasro in Egyptian servitude. In the days of Nabucco, Italy was herself the underdog: by the time of Aida, however, the new Italian state no longer saw itself like that and Verdi, who was proud of his country and its achievement, was prepared to celebrate the new spirit. Yet — Bismarck, Napoleon III, wars and aggression and displays of strength — these were manifestations of a national obsessiveness that were a far cry from the human patriotism of the Risorgimento, and so there is in Aida a confusion of patriotic feeling, a double tug at the national heart strings, which reflects something very real in Verdi's state of mind and provides at the same time the background, and even to some extent the motivation, for Radamès's tragic dilemma.

Now in all this there is, in the end, very little that is Egyptian and not much that is French. Yet there is a lot that is Italian, and not only from a political point of view. All through the opera, and in the last scenes particularly, there is a concentration on the essence of the drama, and an insistence on the direct dramatic impact of the singing line, that is profoundly Italian. Verdi refines yet again on the continuity of musical texture which he has been developing ever since Rigoletto, through Simon Boccanegra, Un Ballo in Maschera, La Forza del Destino and even Don Carlos, but here the simplicity of the story allows him to bring together all his mature experience, the Parisian part not forgotten, in a parallel simplicity of human dramatic treatment. His letters to Ghislanzoni are filled with warnings to write directly, naturally, without the clichés of the typical opera libretto, with an overall result that is poles apart from the elaborate theatricality of the Parisian manner and the novelty-seeking ingenuities of Meyerbeerian Grand Opera.

In a letter to Du Locle, written after the production of Don Carlos, Verdi had expressed his feelings as an Italian composer in Paris: 'In your musical theatre there are too many connoisseurs! Everybody wants to judge for himself, according to his own tastes and, what is worse, according to a system, without taking account of the character and individuality of the composer. Everyone wants to give an opinion, express a doubt, and a composer, living for long in this atmosphere of uncertainty, can hardly help being shaken in his convictions and ends by correcting and adjusting, which really means spoiling his work. In this way the final product is never an opera created in a single jet, but a mosaic — as beautiful as you like, but still a mosaic. . . .'

13

It is because *Aida*, for all its monumental framework and archeological paraphernalia, is fundamentally an opera 'created in a single jet' that it has outlived, and will continue to outlive, so many of its Grand Operatic fellows. For all the refinement of method and richness of musical idiom, it is an opera in the same tradition as *Nabucco* or *Trovatore*, transformed by a master into something which takes it even beyond a narrow national idiom and into a world of its own. 'I believe in inspiration, you believe in construction', he wrote in the same letter; 'I want the enthusiasm that you lack, both in feeling and judgement. . . . For me, true success is not possible unless I write as I feel, free from any outside influence whatever, without thinking whether I write for Paris or for the moon. . . .'

Aida a lunar opera? That would perhaps be going too far. But to let it get stuck at the Egyptian level is certainly not going far enough.

Eva Turner as Aida, Chicago Civic Opera, 1928 (by courtesy of the Covent Garden Archives)

'Aida': Text and Music

William Mann

Ever since its Cairo première in December 1871, followed a month later by the Italian première at La Scala, Milan (for which Verdi composed an Overture which was not played, though it survives), *Aida** has been acclaimed as a non-pareil spectacular opera, an almost automatic choice for a grand operatic occasion, the epitome of Grand Opera in the French tradition of the Rossini of *Moïse* or *Guillaume Tell* and Spontini. Very splendid it looks in the monumental open-air productions at the Caracalla Baths in Rome or the Arena of Verona; Mariette Bey (he had been ennobled by the Khedive) noted initially that the first scene would show a distant view of the Pyramids at Memphis, and Ghislanzoni's final stage directions specify unusual stage effects in every scene. Both scenes of the last act, for example, involve action, although not necessarily visible, on two levels.

Verdi's score, nevertheless, concentrates on a private drama between three principal characters, Radamès and the two women who love him. The fourth principal character is the Egyptian priesthood, whose spokesman is the High Priest, Ramfis, rather than the Ethiopian King, Amonasro, whose demands precipitate the tragic dénouement but whose role is otherwise almost subsidiary to the plot. Verdi used certain characteristic themes (similar to Wagner's *Leitmotiven* except that they are hardly developed symphonically) principally in order to draw attention to a particular identity or emotion — Aida [1] and the Priests [2] have one each, Amneris has two [4, 5]. They are sparingly reintroduced, each time to cogent purpose. By the time that Verdi came to compose *Aida* he had, like most of his operatic contemporaries, abandoned separate musical numbers and was writing virtually uninterrupted scenes to maintain dramatic continuity, though he did, in some cases (for example, after *'Celeste Aida'*, but not after *'O patria mia'*), end a set piece with a tactful pause during which the audience could express appreciation, or otherwise, of the singing.

The musical structure of *Aida* is both refined and diversified in proportions, pace, and mood, above all in texture, whether orchestral, vocal, or both together. Because the score is melodically profuse, and contains those spectacular mass ensembles, some past commentators, when only a few operas by Verdi were well known, used to regard *Aida* as the end of the 'middle period' which began with *Rigoletto*, and was succeeded by the succinct 'late period' of

---

* In Italian the first two letters of her name ('ai') are always pronounced separately, as in 'naïve' not as the dipthong in English 'plaice', German 'Hain', or French 'Laine'.

Otello and *Falstaff*. Now that all of Verdi's music can be heard, thanks to radio, records, and a much expanded stage repertory, we are likely to reject the 'three periods' view of Verdi, and set *Aida* where it belongs, in the continuous chain of Verdi's musical development, every work looking forwards and backwards at once.

The old-fashioned operatic overture, which began and ended noisily, was necessary in theatres where the auditorium lights were never extinguished, late-comers an occupational hazard, and the composer's duty was to alert the attention of every listener. The *Preludio* to *Aida* begins softly with muted strings by themselves, violins divided two and two; the third act will also begin softly, a reminder that by 1871 it was physically possible and aesthetically desirable to extinguish the house lights before the music began, so that the audience would, with any luck, be silent and able to attend to 'soft music and sweet harmony'.

Aida begins with the theme [1] for that lady held as a prisoner of war and ranked as a slave, though her Egyptian captors are unaware that she is the daughter of the Ethiopian King. She is, for the moment, kindly treated by the Egyptian princess Amneris to whose handmaidens she has been assigned. Her theme is wayward and desolate, regal pride subsumed by her unpromising fate: Ethiopians and Egyptians have long been at war (it is perhaps about 1000 BC, the time of the Trojan War), Egypt numerically superior, Ethiopia plucky and persistent. The key of the Prelude is D major, but more melancholy D minor is quickly suggested, and the theme comes to rest in F sharp major, the key in which the opera will end. This appealing tune grows and expands, with soft added flute and clarinet, rousing emotions of pity and love for Aida. Still very softly, muted cellos introduce the stubborn theme of the Egyptian priests, [2], taken up in contrapuntal imitation by higher strings, then woodwind. Almost at once Aida's theme is combined with it, loudly: it is the dramatic confrontation of the opera, Ethiopia against Egypt, one powerless, lovable woman against another nation's might. The full orchestra is involved. The confrontation fades away, leaving divided first violins with Aida's melody, cadenced, cushioned by wind, rising aloft.

The curtain rises on Pharaoh's palace in Memphis. Radamès, the captain of the Pharaoh's Guard, and the high priest Ramfis are conversing about the new invasion of Egypt by Ethiopian troops. The key has changed to G major, one step away on the flat side, conveying relaxation (key progressions in tonal music, whether flat or sharp, always have a clear emotional effect). Ramfis's opening remarks are sagely accompanied by imitative priestly counterpoint for three groups of cellos, sometimes joined discreetly by violas, all dark in tone. Ramfis leaves to tell Pharaoh the name of the chosen general, and Radamès, an ambitious dreamer, wishes that he might

16

be the divinely selected leader. Brassy fanfares echo his wish and bring maximum contrast to the preceding soft music. When he thinks of Aida, in whose name he would fight and conquer (though against her own kinsmen!), gentler strings support his utterance and when he launches into his first aria, after a further fanfare, two muted violins gently breathe a high sustained F to inspire his amorous reverie.

'Celeste Aida' [3] is placed close to the beginning of the opera as if to make an immediate declaration of intent by Verdi: *Aida* will abound in long melody and *bel canto*, gratifying and challenging the greatest Italianate voices of every generation to sing with as much subtlety and discretion as the orchestra which accompanies them. Twice in his *Romanza* Radamès rises to a *forte* top B flat but he begins and ends softly (though few modern tenors respect the *pianissimo morendo*, presumably indicating head-voice, attached to his last high B flat). His melody is delicately, elegantly phrased, doubled at first by low flute, actually a sixth above him, though effectively a third below, since the tenor voice gives the illusion of sounding an octave above its real pitch (except in concerted vocal ensemble). The scoring of this solo is a miracle of delicacy: lower strings are plucked, with a buoyant rhythmical pattern for cellos; violins are among them, except for six soloists who shimmer aloft (Verdi, marked them *a parte*, ' separately disposed'). After the fourth line, before '*Il tuo bel cielo*', both flutes begin to undulate, still in their low register, below oboe and bassoon in tenths who introduce the singer's new melody for those words. At '*un regal serto*' the pace slightly quickens, and the texture is enriched towards the first climax at '*un trono vicino al sol*' whence the music returns to the opening, '*Celeste Aida*', newly and more elaborately accompanied until '*sei lo splendor*'. Here a variant of the oboe-bassoon tenths persists while Radamès repeats '*Il tuo bel cielo*' to a soft low monotone, breaking out into melody at '*un regal serto*', and returning quickly to *pppp* after his second high B flat. The ending, darkly luminous, should sound wondrously tender with hidden depths of sincerity beneath his gentle ardour.

As the solo ends (without the conventional quicker second section, now repudiated by Verdi 'unless there is dramatic motivation for it'), the Egyptian princess Amneris enters, introduced by her theme of smooth, stately graciousness (first violins on their lowest string) [4]. She remarks teasingly on his eager expression of joy, following but not doubling her theme, and is unconvinced by his talk of military aspiration. Does he not cherish dreams of love ('*Ne un altro sogno mai*')? — and violins slide into a wheedling phrase, concerned with *her* secret passion. Typical of the late Verdi's methods are the oboe's openly quizzical *acciaccature* at '*Non hai tu in Menfi*', and the clarinet's echoes of the music for those words. This moment of intensity marks the approach to a Duettino, *Allegro agitato presto* in E minor (*'Forse l'arcano amore'*), which will eventually become a Terzetto after Aida's entrance. The duet begins the second of Amneris's recurrent themes, subdued and anxious, representing Radamès's guilty secret as much as Amneris's desperate jealousy [5]; it is another long, expanding melody. As it peters out, Aida enters *Andante mosso* to her theme [1], frail and pensive on clarinet. Amneris scents a possible rival and the Duettino is resumed with its scurrying tune. Amneris controls her jealousy and, *Andante* in C major, turns graciously to Aida, with another stately tune, calling her sister rather than slave. Flute and oboe — *acciaccature* again — show that Aida is in tears, as Amneris observes in a cadencing phrase which looks forward to Desdemona pleading for Cassio in the second act of *Otello*. Aida blames the fearful rumours of war, *più mosso* with grand expansion at *'per voi pavento'*. In a deadly hush Amneris asks if that is the whole truth. Aida casts down her gaze to hide her real anxiety, and the Duettino is resumed for the third time, becoming a Trio in E major, around the suspicion *motiv* [5], as Aida's voice is joined with the alternate mutterings of the others in a broad melody which confesses aside her tearful, hopeless love for Radamès; softly, in the background, timpani depict the uneasy pounding of their three hearts.

The trio ends with a hectic return to E minor, and a diplomatic pause for audience participation, before trumpets and other brass dispel those three conflicting and private disquiets with loud fanfares of public pomp, dark and savage — the noisy string trills anticipate Verdi's music for Iago (in *Otello*). Pharaoh, with his captains, ministers, and priests led by Ramfis, arrives to proclaim the renewal of war against Ethiopia, calling on a Messenger to disclose his news (a doleful E minor phrase for oboe, clarinet and bassoon, then loud explosive leaps for the amazement of the listening crowd). The Messenger announces that the invaders are led by an indomitable warrior, Amonasro: the crowd knows him as the Ethiopian king but, we now discover from her aside, he is also Aida's father. 'Battle' is the inexorable cry (*'Guerra'* — full chorus and orchestra). In recitative, Pharaoh announces the goddess Isis's choice of Radamès to lead the Egyptian army — joy for him and Amneris, despair for Aida, surprise for the rest. He is sent by Pharaoh to be armed and consecrated in the temple of Ptah (the king uses the god's classical Italian name of Vulcano), and a pompous march-ensemble is launched (*'Sù! del cor prorompa il grido'*) [6] with much xenophobic declaration of *'morte allo stranier'* (lit. 'Death to foreigners')! It ends with Amneris's call to Radamès, repeated by all, of *'Ritorna vincitor'!* Then Aida is left alone, asking herself how she could bear to wish anyone victory over her own father, family and compatriots.

This is her extremely famous and beloved *Scena e Romanza* [7], known by the opening words of its introductory recitative, those with which Amneris and the Memphides have just sent Radamès off to war, namely, *'Ritorna vincitor!'* (whereas most operatic solos are called by the first words of the subsequent aria). As a musical entity it has begun, not with Aida's first words, nor with the march reprise preceding them (usually used as prelude when the solo is performed by itself), but with Amneris's cry before that, an example of Verdi's drastic break with the conventional 'number-opera'. The traditional form of the solo aria was in two sections, slow and quicker, but *'Ritorna vincitor'* is in five sections. First comes a recitative, *Allegro agitato*, with orchestral comments about Egypt's might and the doleful fate foreseen by Aida for her family. Then, after a pause, a faster passage, *'L'insana parola'*, urgently melodious with prominent bassoon backing, comes to an alarmed climax (*'Ah! sventurata!'*). The third section brings back Aida's *motiv* [1] from the Prelude, *Andante* ('slower than the first time', said Verdi), and edges between aria and recitative; it is followed by a fast, agitated, melodious section, *'I sacri nomi'* [8] in A flat minor full of triplet movement and easing into the *cantabile* final section, *'Numi, pietà'* [9], infinitely touching with its tremulous string background. *'Numi, pietà'* will be heard again, though it is not a true *Leitmotiv*.

It ends with cellos descending to their bottom C, thence climbing the arpeggio of A flat major to pause on its fifth, E flat, whose major mode begins the next scene. The music continues without a break for the scene change. It would be a thrilling surprise to hear the E flat major harp chords break into the cellos' last note, if only because operagoers have learned to accept a wait while the set changes. The temple of Ptah in Memphis is another grand setting with columns stretching back out of sight, and statues, and tripods exuding incense around the central altar of the divinity. The High Priestess (identified as Termouthis by Mariette Bey), invisible to us, is invoking *'Possente Fthà, del mondo spirito animator'* to a designedly exotic melody, almost in the Phrygian mode [10]. She is answered by Priests gathered on stage. Three times the hymn is heard, with off-stage priestesses to join Termouthis. Then comes a Sacred Dance of Priestesses [11], somewhat faster, in E flat major, featuring three flutes (a hallmark of this score), elements of the Phrygian mode, and those biting *acciaccature* which Verdi must have have likewise thought Egyptian-sounding. The dance must be extremely solemn and rather mysterious to accord with its music: this is, after all, a sacred rite. Halfway through it, the strings move purposefully and Radamès, unarmed, is brought to the altar to be invested. The Dance ends with a brief choral antiphony of priestesses and priests.

Ramfis, in a new section of recitative, consecrates Radamès (*'Mortal, diletto ai numi'*) as leader of the Egyptian army, investing him with the sacred sword; heavy brass and chorus confirm the solemnity of the ceremony. Strings softly slide into solemn G minor for a broad-phrased prayer to Ptah (*'Nume, custode e vindice'*) [12] in which he is joined gravely by Radamès and the priests, and which acquires brilliance as well as weight as its melody is combined with the Priestesses' hymn. Just before the close of the scene, and act, there is a sublime, unaccompanied cry of *'Immenso Fthà!'*

Act Two takes place in Thebes, some 400 miles upstream from Memphis, and begins in Amneris's apartments where she is being ceremoniously attired for the triumphal return of Radamès from the wars. Loud strumming in G minor upon the harp, distantly punctuated by a solo trumpet, suggests the martial occasion. A chorus of female slaves hymns the victorious hero (*'Chi mai fra gl'inni'*) [13] who will be rewarded (refrain of rising scales at *'Vieni: sul crin ti piovano'*) with floral tributes. Amneris adds her own love-call in G major, rather chromatic and totally haunting, marked 'expansively' so that the most can be made of these amorous phrases (*'Ah! vieni, amor mio'*) [14]. A second, similar verse follows, then a jolly G minor Dance of Moorish slave-boys, [15] with triangle and cymbals and piccolo (relics of 18th century Turkish music!); lastly a third repeat of the double refrain from Amneris's handmaidens and herself (*'Vieni: sul crin'*, etc.).

Aida's theme [1] (now in the bass) indicates her approach. The other slaves are dismissed so that their mistress may unfathom Aida's secret (a telling unaccompanied signal on solo horn indicates her intention with characteristic brevity — throughout *Aida* Verdi unconventionally marks dramatic turning-points without making a meal of them). *Moderato* in A major, Amneris solicitously begins her great Scena and Duet with Aida by feigning consolation for the other's grief in the defeat of her compatriots, and protesting her love for her slave. Aida's hectic protestations (bassoons and lower strings hint at Amonasro to come) do not disturb Amneris's condescending sweetness: Aida must find consolation in love. She touches a raw spot, as throbbing string bass triplets and woodwind counterpoint, surrounding Aida's animated asides (*'Amore! gaudio, tormento'*) [1], leave no doubt. In the same triplets Amneris welcomes her breakthrough (*'Ah, quel pallore'*) and proceeds to her subterfuge.

To a new, slower melody [16] that by now seems familiar because so characteristic of Verdi's music for Amneris, extravagantly gracious, almost toadying, on oboes, clarinets and first violins in B flat major, she asks (*'Ebben: qual nuovo fremito'*) for Aida's confidence as to whether she has a lover in the Egyptian army. Her carefully restrained quizzing is reflected by gentle clarinets in consoling thirds and sixths over bassoons, which somehow suggest raised eyebrows. After all, she hints, the army's leader has been slain. There are sounds of agitation on strings as Aida learns Amneris's false report of Radamès's death. Aida is plunged into grief. Amneris suspects the worst and confirms it by then declaring that Radamès still lives — news which brings Aida to her knees in gratitude, and lifts her to an exultant top A calling, for a moment, on the full orchestra's force. A sinister, brusque slither for bassoons and lower strings gazes deep into Amneris's scheming soul, and shows the fatal blunder of Aida's outburst. Like a cat who has cornered a mouse, Amneris gloats: 'with maximum fury' writes Verdi over her words *'Si . . . tu l'ami'* ('you love him? I love him too . . . you understand? You see your rival . . . I who am Pharaoh's daughter'), but he partners them sarcastically with soft clarinets in smiling thirds, and the bassoon and horn who underpin *'son tua rivale'* sound anything but enraged.

Aida's heart beats wildly, and she retorts, with passion until she reaches *'tal'* (implying that she and Amneris are 'alike' of royal blood), when the orchestra holds its peace, and we appreciate her timely embarrassment. Her confusion brings back full orchestra, again for only an instant, as she realizes how nearly she implicated the rest of her family, as well as herself, perhaps all Ethiopia, in this private quarrel. Her only recourse can be apologetic self-abasement, which we hear in abject F minor, *Adagio cantabile* [17], her supple melodic line coloured by low flutes (later clarinets, for more warmth) and put in focus by the bassoon's harmonic outlines — how often, in this opera, Verdi shows us the physical aspect of his characters, as well as their emotions. Amneris knows that she has won this match, and she could afford, after this handsome apology, to react with kindness but she needs to savour her triumph, even over a slave. She explodes with scorn (*'trema, vil schiava'*) [18] and unbecoming brusqueness. Aida resumes her self-abasement, this time as a duet.

Amneris's private triumph is mirrored publicly by the offstage military band's fanfares, and the distant choral salutation in A flat major [6] to Radamès on his victorious return from the wars. We might have assumed that the duet was over, and that the off-stage chorus and band were preparing for the scene-change, but they have motivated a quicker closing section. Aida bewails her misery in A flat minor and willingness to placate her rival by dying. Amneris's reply in fulsome A flat major is that of a domineering schoolmistress dragging her errant pupil off to be seen by the Head, but it reaches a massive climax, dispelled as Amneris leaves. Before the curtain falls, Verdi makes Aida repeat her prayer *de profundis* from the end of '*Ritorna vincitor*.' It was a melodic moment worthy of reprise, and justified by the turn of events: then Aida feared for her lover and her country, now her compatriots are vanquished, her lover apparently lost to her not through death but through power politics. This time '*Numi, pietà*' [9] has no closing cello solo but an even more forlorn fade-away on shuddering strings with plucked bass.

Verdi seems to have intended a pause until the curtain is ready to rise again for the *Gran Finale secondo* with the military band in position on stage. Producers can keep the music running, by using a narrow stage for the first scene, and removing its furniture during the fanfares and dark-toned expectant music on the verge of E flat major, gradually brightening with the trumpet entry, so that the brightly lit stage, filled with people, is seen when that key arrives. The score does show that Pharaoh, Amneris with Aida and others enter just before that, and dramatically it is best if the curtain can rise as soon as possible. The choral outburst of '*Gloria all'Egitto*' [19] with stage band and full orchestra is like a sudden flood of brilliant sunlight, tempting to the producer seeking a dramatic *coup*. Experiencing it at the first performance, the Khedive wished it might be adopted as the Egyptian National Anthem — or did he mean the March trio section [20] in A flat with massed trumpets (which is more melodious)? The E flat part of this March is quite subtle for public purposes, with essential dynamic contrast and shading, including a very refined, almost fragile turn into the second subject for female chorus, followed by the Priests [2], and then both choruses in fervent unison. Now comes the most famous tune of all, the Trio section [20], specifically for Egyptian trumpets — the long ones, which used to be called Bach trumpets, pitched in A flat and subsequently in B natural. The melody deserves its fame, being muscular and vivacious in gait, its fanfare character enhanced by the insistence of the prolonged first cadence, declaring as it were, 'This is the conqueror, yes he's the one, it's him, he's the one we're saluting'. The trumpets are crooked in two keys because, when the tune has been played, it is at once repeated in another key, and then, most effectively, both groups play together.

A Ballabile, that is a dance, follows in C minor [21], rather faster, during which the captured treasures of the Ethiopians are displayed. Its music is also of great subtlety: staccato flute triplets over a chugging bass, with a melodious countersubject for bassoon and violas, the whole sounding gaunt and official, yet animated. The chirpy grace-notes, in the F minor trio-section, [22] excuse the usual gollywog disguise of the dancers, though the text does not specify a return of the Moorish boys. The dance is gleeful and exotic, perhaps even a little conspiratorial. Afterwards comes a choral reprise [19] of the salute to Radamès, again involving the Priestly theme, then a coda with the female chorus, extended to include everybody.

Pharaoh descends from his throne to welcome Radamès: the stage band responds enthusiastically. Amneris is called to lay on his head the victor's laurel wreath, a signal for her solemn, regal theme, heard in the first scene [4], sumptuously set for violins on their rich G string, with undulating clarinet arpeggios, and pale flutes: we 'hear' pallor and grandeur at once, because Amneris knows that Radamès loves another. Now Pharaoh offers to fulfil Radamès's greatest wish. He ought to ask for the hand of Aida but he presumably thinks the moment is inappropriate, since he asks instead that the Ethiopian prisoners be brought in. They are led on while the Priests chant a variant of their *motiv*, which is singularly gloomy for a hymn of thanksgiving to the gods. Among them is Amonasro, dressed as an army officer. Aida's cry of recognition is echoed with surprise by everyone else: 'Her father!' Quietly he tells her not to betray him; bassoons, cimbasso (preferred by Verdi to the modern tuba), and lower strings thunder out a *motiv* of majestic size whose rhythm and shape persist into his solo *'Anch' io pugnai'*. Familiarly known as the *'Sortita d'Amonasro'* or 'Entrance of Amonasro', this is a marvellous piece of character-portrayal through music with its dark, sturdy colours and grand melodic line at *'Al mio piè'* (Amonasro pretends that he saw the Ethiopian king dead on the battlefield). It culminates in the serene cantilena of

'*Ma tu, Re, tu signore possente*' [23], which is repeated by Aida and the other Ethiopians, with delicate wind accompaniment. Contrast comes with the vigorous objections of Ramfis and the other priests to any thought of mercy for these prisoners [24]; and from here Verdi builds up a grand ensemble, with a softer contrapuntal centre and a cadenza-like flourish for Aida before the reprise of '*Ma tu, Re*', and an energetic coda. There is a pause for admiration after the final cadence (and amid all the eloquence, we may still have missed Radamès's amorous asides as he watches Aida, and Amneris's rage as she observes him).

Radamès, as his favour, asks Pharaoh to release the Ethiopians and send them home ('What? All of them?', is Amneris's typical comment). Ramfis counsels against such unwisdom and finally persuades Pharaoh at least to keep Aida and her father in Egypt as hostages. The King then gives Radamès the hand of Amneris in marriage, and the promise of eventual succession — which draws another gloating aside from the bride-to-be, to a phrase which may come to mind during her ordeal in Act Four. Band and Chorus resume their hymn [19], '*Gloria all' Egitto*', with a separate vocal part for Pharaoh. The Priests add a new melody, Aida and Radamès a third one, all in enthusiastic style (though the new material is marked down to pianissimo) and in E flat major. Much faster, and in the minor, Amonasro whispers to Aida that they will soon be revenged on Egypt, and the soloists all indulge private reflexions in counterpoint while the choruses prepare for a return to the Triumphal Hymn now combined with its two succeeding tunes. A faster reprise of the Priests' *motiv* [2] leads to a grand coda incorporating the massed trumpets' March Trio tune [20].

Act Three is subtitled *The Banks of the Nile*. Camille du Locle's scenario specifies palmtrees growing amongst granite rocks upon the summit of which stands the temple of Isis, half-hidden by leafy branches. It is a starry, brightly moonlit night. Verdi's orchestral introduction depicts all this with flute solo and strings, a miracle of atmospheric loveliness, and of restraint: four octaves of staccato G, *molto pianissimo*, on muted first violins, then sustained Gs for cellos in glassy harmonics, three octaves of slower staccato Gs on muted violas, and a shimmering tremolo for muted second violins on G and D, yielding a mere sensation of open fifths in G upon which the flute dips and sways exotically. From the temple the priests and their priestesses are heard invoking the mother-bride of Osiris. As they chant, a boat glides down the river, bringing Amneris and Ramfis, with guards and veiled handmaidens, to the temple. Gentle strings accompany Ramfis as he invites the princess to pray in the temple until dawn for the blessing of Isis on her marriage to Radamès next day. Her agreement brings a new mood for Amneris, simple and girlish, slightly hesitant and with a magically benign cadence. As they enter the temple the introductory music is resumed, now combined with the chorus and two priestesses. As it dwindles to two solo violins on high G, three flutes bring back Aida's *motiv* [1], violas murmuring below. Aida enters cautiously, wondering why Radamès has asked her to meet him here; if it is to say farewell, she will drown herself in the Nile (a short but vivid orchestral tempest). That would mean that she would never again see her native land, as she reflects in the Romanza, 'O patria mia', which Verdi added at the last minute with Theresa Stolz, the first Aida at La Scala, in mind. It is difficult to imagine the opera, let alone the third act, without it. The oboe solo's introductory bars pursue the curiously exotic vein which was Verdi's vision of African music (I have drawn attention to other examples). Aida's first two lines are in arioso style but the Romanza begins, melodically, at the third line, 'O cieli azzurri' [25], with prominent flute trio again, and a memorable reshaping of her first phrase ('O patria mia') at 'O verdi colli'. Throughout the Romanza, Verdi's F major has tendencies towards D minor which contributes to the exotic effect and, at the end of the first verse (there are two), her top A is unexpectedly but affectingly harmonised as a first inversion A minor chord, another modal effect. Her second verse adds to the three flutes some active solo strings to enhance the chamber-musical intimacy. The verse now ascends to a soft top C, and ends with an exquisite (and testing) long, phrase beginning on her top A, climbing down to middle C, then back again with oboe and flute as Aida's partners. We can find precedents for the musical refinement of this Romanza in *Simon Boccanegra* and *Don Carlos*, for instance, and still it seems unmatched in Verdi's work.

A solo clarinet muses gently on the 'O patria mia' theme, then breaks off. Aida sees her father approaching. The shock is reflected by loud strings in E flat major, an abrupt drop of a whole tone. Amonasro's first sentences of recitative seem to look back thematically to his *Sortita*, perhaps only inasmuch as Verdi was composing consistently in character. At 'E patria, e trono', Amonasro eases with dignity into melodiousness, in preparation for the first of the two duets, side by side, which carry the weight of the act after the Romanza. This first duet, 'Rivedrai le foreste imbalsamate' [26], is formally tripartite: a wooing, cantabile *Allegro giusto* in D flat major, with a tougher episode at 'Pur rammenti', and a return to lyricism at Aida's 'Ah! ben rammento' (a glance at the libretto will explain this), after which the section turns towards recitative, until Amonasro reveals Aida's task. When she refuses, the second, more dramatic section begins, Allegro in C minor, 'Su, dunque! sorgete, egizie coorti' [27] (almost unnecessarily marked 'with savage impetus', so mordant are the brilliant trumpet parts). Amonasro's music of conspiracy ('Flutti di sangue scorrono'), scare-mongering

('*Una larva orribile*'), and open threat ('*Non sei mia figlia*') look forward to Verdi's Iago but are recognizably in the character of the warrior who sang the *Sortita*. Soft cello arpeggios again suggest Aida's abject distress. It is the bassoon, with low strings, which sets the tone for the final section of the duet, *Andante assai sostenuto* in D flat, '*Padre a costoro schiava non sono*', expanding from near recitative into noble melody at Amonasro's '*Pensa che un popolo*' [28], during which the violins rise steadily and momentously through Aida's reply to an apex at '*Quanto mi costi*'. Then darkness descends again and Amonasro leaves Aida alone to deceive the man she adores.

Radamès hurries to meet Aida. Anxious exchanges for violins and cellos suggest the lovers hailing one another. The second of the two duets begins with a swaggering, confident tune for Radamès's '*Pur ti riveggo*' [29], all careless C major extraversion, like himself. Each of his joyous exclamations is doused by Aida's assumed coolness and scorn, while the melody continues darkly in the orchestra. Radamès stands up for his optimism ('*Nel fiero anelito*') with another martial theme for trumpet duet, which is distinctly likable; in his confidence he returns to complete his enthusiastic opening tune. Aida reminds him of jealous Amneris, and Verdi reverts to

Nellie Melba as Aida
(Philadelphia, 1898)

the scurrying theme [5] of the duet (*'Forse l'arcano amore'*) upon which she intruded in the first scene. He uses this technique of thematic back-reference quite seldom but always with particular cogency — once in most of the mature operas, and several times in *Aida*. She assures Radamès that his optimism is hopeless, and proposes that their only future together lies in escape to Ethiopia. His shocked astonishment allows her to launch a new section, a wheedling pastoral which opens with an oboe solo (more exotic chromaticism), and truly begins at *'Là, tra foreste vergine'* [30], again blessed with three prominent flutes (once too often, one might fear, but the charm still works). Radamès's answer is more frankly melodious in character (*'Il suol dov' io raccolsi'*) while the willowy pleading of her melody is now resumed as a simultaneous duet which repeats both melodic halves. In semi-recitative Aida goads Radamès until he agrees to run away with her: the third section of the duet, *'Sì: fuggiam da queste mura'* [31], now begins, impetuously but for the most part softly, with a generous yet rather stiff tune, sung by both, and leading to a reprise in unison of the duet's intitial melody [29].

It breaks off as Aida turns to ask, in recitative, where the Egyptian army is posted. Amonasro leaves his hiding-place to repeat the words triumphantly. Radamès is appalled that he has been overheard and to discover Amonasro's real identity. The resultant Trio begins in semi-recitative, turning to memorable melody at Aida's *'Ah no! ti calma'* (consoling in D flat minor) answered in proud despairing D flat major by Radamès, and benignly by Amonasro, a rich complex of three splendid tunes, worthy of ample development were it not that the drama must press forward. Before the Trio can expatiate, Amneris appears outside the temple and precipitates the dénouement, not with an aria, or even a vocal quartet, but with the one word *'Traditor!'*. Amonasro, prevented from stabbing her, escapes with Aida in a coda of confusion and high drama, broken for Radamès's characteristically heroic gesture of self-sacrifice, before the final rush of D minor. The third act of *Aida* stands up to the closest scrutiny. It is the finest scene in the opera, and for some ardent Verdians excels anything even in *Otello* and *Falstaff* to come — though among such exalted company it is idle to pick favourites.

Act Four has two scenes. The first shows a hall in Pharaoh's palace connecting the cell, where Radamès is imprisoned, with the subterranean vault where he is to be tried. Woodwind stride softly down the arpeggio of G minor, notably the eerie voice of the piccolo. We may imagine Amneris swooping down some large staircase to this hall, where she paces anxiously to and fro as her nervous jealousy theme [5] (from the first act duet) suggests — it is soon deployed in contrapuntal imitation by strings, and is

27

accompanied by undulating flutes, with soft yet distinct cries on piccolo (those *acciaccature* which have featured earlier in the score). Her movements may be deduced from the music; the stage directions merely place her 'sadly crouched in front of the door of the vault'. She is enraged that her rival has escaped while her bridegroom is incarcerated on a charge of treason. She was his accuser, yet she still loves him — a return to her stately theme from the Triumph Scene. She decides to save him, even now. Verdi lets us hear her ponder how to do it, then sense her decision, as she orders the guards to bring him to her.

The music for his entrance is woeful with cor anglais prominent, then bass clarinet whose drooping arpeggios launch their big duet, *'Già i sacerdoti adunansi'* [32]. It is marked *Andante sostenuto* in the dark key of E flat minor, and is relieved, as though by a shaft of sunlight, when the last two lines of the verse move into the relative major and a warmer orchestral texture. It is at such moments of transition from one mood to another and back that a composer reveals mastery: the move to G flat major enables Radamès to repeat the music in the second verse, and in a key (F sharp minor, enharmonic with G flat) better suited to his vocal compass, ordinary clarinet replacing bass clarinet. After some tense exchanges in A major, the key reached at the end of Radamès's verse, Verdi screws the music up another third to D flat major for Amneris's next entreaty, *'Ah! tu dêi vivere!'* [33], a confession of love and longing, and therefore a melody of brighter, aspiring cast. Radamès repeats its last phrases with reference to his love for Aida. Mention of her rival inflames Amneris, and Radamès quickly returns to the key and melody of *'Già i sacerdoti'* [32], rounding off this section of the duet. The approach to the subsequent, faster part is made via agitation: Radamès rejects Amneris's offers, confirms his devotion to Aida, and resolves to pay the extreme penalty. Amneris bursts out in tearful C minor, *Allegro agitato vivo*, *'Chi ti salva, sciagurato'*, doing her best to harden her heart, the music declares, against him. Radamès answers calmly in C major (though the orchestral background remains agitated) but they end their interview to her C minor tune, and an inconclusive coda as he returns to his cell. The orchestral postlude gives a shattering glimpse of her utter despair (whether by accident or design, it repeats the rising-third key-switches from the start of the duet).

Crashing full chords, with pauses in between, draw attention not only to her loneliness and misery but to realization of the fatal consequences of her jealousy. Promptly enter the orchestral double basses with the Priests' theme, [2], its periods pointed by three soft trombones, until it becomes the gloomy march to which they process across the stage and down to the vault, while Amneris mutters helplessly her guilt in delivering him into their jurisdiction

28

('*Io stessa lo gettai*' — her woebegone reiterations stamp the phrase on the memory). From below, the Priests are heard in unaccompanied unison. Amneris answers it with her own distraught A minor prayer. They resume their chant as Radamès is led below. Amneris is left whimpering alone.

The trial begins in the vault. Three times Ramfis, assisted by four trumpets, four trombones, and bass drum, all sounding from the judgement chamber, calls on Radamès to answer the charges. Each time he remains silent, and Amneris hysterically entreats the gods to save him: the musical effect is as if the spotlight on her during her exclamations were extinguished whenever the drama moves to the vault below (visible in some productions). After Amneris's third plea, Ramfis and all the Priests announce their verdict in loud, strongly rhythmical unison with full orchestral punctuation: to be buried alive beneath the altar of Ptah. Amneris rails against the unyielding judges as they return [2], inveighing against the traitor. She pleads with them once, reviles them in an ensemble, and finally curses them. The scene ends with a raging orchestral coda that includes a stern unison figure which will be heard again. The last note of the coda involves the crash of a tam-tam (a rimless gong with a fine resonance).

Verdi particularly requested that the final scene should take place on two levels, the upper stage showing the brightly lit and gorgeous interior of the temple of Ptah, the lower part the vault in which Radamès is left to die. During the introductory bars, two priests are supervising the closure of the stone at the top of the steps by which the victim has entered his execution-chamber. This is the temple in which Radamès was consecrated during the second scene of Act One. The kinship of the loud string phrases at the end of the preceding scene, and the wan echoes which begin this last scene, will be clear if the scene-change has been rapid. Radamès muses on his dismal fate. Then, as he thinks happily of Aida, a faint radiance falls from the string harmonies. Flute and oboe sigh a falling octave on Aida's behalf, for she has hidden here to be with Radamès at the last. The impassioned descending string chords (first inversions) after her opening words perfectly convey Radamès's amazement. Her explanation ('*Presago il core*') is sepulchrally scored for low clarinet, bassoon, bass drum and low strings with plucked double-basses, a timbre looking forward to the last act of *Otello*.

Her decision to die with him seems to banish Radamès's gloom, for his response in A flat major, '*Morir! si pura e bella!*' [34], is not only tender but buoyant with its plucked strings, comments for flute and oboes, and cosy chains of clarinet thirds. This is the introduction to the final Duet, arguably the most magical in the opera's rich series of duets. Aida's reply, [35], in delirious D flat major ecstasy, has an elaborate and luminous accompaniment, first violins divided into four groups, as if one were watching a starry galaxy through a telescope. Their euphoria is interrupted by the prayers of priests and priestesses in the temple above (with a harp on stage) [10]. Radamès, bravely but in vain, attempts to lift the seal-stone. Flutes recall part of the Priestesses' Dance, from Act One, scene two, as the lovers resign themselves to fate.

Aida begins the final duet proper, 'O terra, addio' [36], with another, paler, luminous string texture, a melody in G flat major that hauntingly rises an octave via the seventh degree, again and again. When Radamès repeats the melody, with comments from her, the luminous strings are a little more animated. Again the Priests in the temple invoke Ptah (in a different part of their hymn). Amneris enters the temple and kneels in prayer upon the 'fatal stone', as Radamès and Aida in unison approach the third and last verse of their duet, this time with a simpler shimmering orchestral background, and with intervening orisons from Amneris. The lovers add a last, crowning line to their melody, then embrace as Aida dies. A solo violin recalls their melody above the chanted prayers in the temple. Aida ends quietly, as it began. To investigate its score, even as cursorily as here, is to marvel at the profusion of delicate, restrained, highly subtle effects, including soft, elegantly nuanced singing. They far outnumber the grand, full-throated climaxes which probably brought us to Aida in the first place. Verdi had been commissioned to supply a stirring nationalistic spectacle, and he obliged where necessary, but he expended his genius on what is most touching and durable in Mariette Bey's story, the secret places of human hearts.

The Genesis of 'Aida'
Roger Parker

It is well known that the pace of Verdi's creative output slowed considerably as he became older. The steady stream of new operas which had appeared in the 1840's and 1850's gradually dwindled, and the composer's violent, energetic imagination seemed to lose its confident voice. There are many explanations for this decline in productivity. One is undoubtedly that Verdi's inherent pessimism, fuelled by the deaths of many of his friends and by chaotic developments in the international political situation, led him to distrust the usefulness of composing as a way of life. Another is his increasingly firm financial position: earlier in his career, during the so-called 'galley years', his activity seemed fired by a frenetic desire to achieve financial independence. There is also evidence to suggest that he was undergoing an artistic crisis. Possible operatic subjects were picked over endlessly, only to be rejected for vague reasons of 'coldness' or 'lack of power' — the comparison with Puccini's unproductive maturity is unmistakable—; there is not the same dynamic enthusiasm which characterised his earlier years. This apparent diffidence had much to do with the direction in which Verdi saw his career moving. The triumphant successes of the early 1850's (*Rigoletto*, *Il trovatore* and *La traviata*) gain much of their effect from a strong unity of conception, while the operas which follow are painted on a broader canvas, with a greater variety of style and effect. This gradual change certainly brought Verdi nearer to the French grand opera tradition, but advance in one direction caused problems in another: the unity which characterised the finest early works was lost. Verdi expressed this in a letter to Camille du Locle, his co-librettist for *Don Carlos*, the opera written immediately before *Aida* (Paris Opéra, March 1867). Du Locle's attempts to interest the composer in further French projects stimulated a lengthy reply, which has been partly quoted on page 13. Although on the surface it is an attack levelled at the *mores* of the Paris Opéra, it seems in context to contain an implicit self-criticism by Verdi of his more recent works:

> [. . .] *Hélas*, it is neither the labour of writing an opera nor the judgement of the Parisian public that holds me back but rather the certainty of not being able to have my music performed in Paris the way I want it. It is quite singular that an author must always see his ideas frustrated and his conceptions distorted!
> . . . You will argue that the *Opéra* has produced a string of masterpieces in this manner. You may call them masterpieces all you want, but permit me to say that they would be much more perfect if the *patchwork* and the adjustments were not felt

all the time. Certainly no one will deny genius to Rossini. Nevertheless, in spite of all his genius, in *Guillaume Tell* one detects this fatal atmosphere of the *Opéra*; and several times, although less frequently than with other authors, one feels that there is too much here, too little there, and that the musical flow is not as free and secure as in the *Barbiere*.[. . .] (December 8, 1869)

It is against the background of this statement of policy, this passionate concern with the unity of a dramatic statement, that the music of *Aida* gradually evolved.

In spite of the apparent rebuff, du Locle continued to discuss possible, operatic subjects with Verdi. Finally, in May 1870, a breakthrough occurred. Du Locle sent the outline of an Egyptian plot for approval. It was greeted with genuine, if guarded, enthusiasm:

> [. . .] I have read the Egyptian outline. It is well done; it offers a splendid *mise-en-scène*, and there are two or three situations which, if not very new, are certainly very beautiful. But who did it? There is a very expert hand in it, one accustomed to writing and one who knows the theatre very well. Now let's hear the financial conditions from Egypt, and then we shall decide. Who would have the Italian libretto made? Of course it would be necessary that I myself have it made. [. . .] (May 26, 1870)

As soon as Verdi showed an interest, matters moved very quickly. The composer's demanding terms, which included a fee of 150,000 lire, were immediately accepted on condition that the opera be ready for the following January. Verdi's enormous fee seems to have caused him a little embarrassment. As he wrote to du Locle:

> We must at least keep the fee secret, since it would serve as a pretext to disturb so many poor dead men. Someone would be sure to point out the *400 scudi* for the *Barbiere di Siviglia*, *Beethoven's* poverty, *Schubert's* misery, *Mozart's* roaming about just to make a living, etc., etc. [. . .] (June 18, 1870)

For his librettist, Verdi chose Antonio Ghislanzoni, who had already helped with the revisions to *La forza del destino*, performed at La Scala in February 1869. The composer and his wife first made an Italian translation of Mariette's French outline and then, between June 19 and 26, Verdi and du Locle prepared a scenario which shaped the already detailed situations into dialogue form. Except in a few minor cases, the scenario keeps very close to the outline, again demonstrating Verdi's faith in Mariette's theatrical sense. A brief quotation from Mariette's first scene will demonstrate the detail he included, and how much of it was incorporated into the final text:

[. . .] Amneris is assailed by cruel doubts at Rhadames's coldness. A rival is certainly contending for Rhadames's heart. Who is it? Aïda, the Ethiopian slave who fell into the hands of the Egyptians after a recent victory, appears at the rear of the stage. An ardent look from Rhadames, a long sigh from Aïda threaten to reveal everything. Some instinct tells the princess that her rival is the slave she sees before her. At the moment when they, to themselves, are expressing their love, their lamentations, their displeasures, their sorrows, an officer of the king's household announces that his majesty is coming to the hall to receive a messenger sent by the governor of the Egyptian provinces bordering on Ethiopia. [. . .]

After Verdi and Ghislanzoni had met in mid-July, the librettist was sent away with du Locle's scenario to begin work. As a draft libretto gradually arrived by post, Verdi replied to Ghislanzoni with an almost line by line commentary, frequently requesting revisions, cuts and additions. Between August 12, 1870 and January 13, 1871, there survive no less than thirty-four letters from composer to librettist, constituting one of the most detailed documentary sources we have for the genesis of a Verdi (or indeed, any) opera. Before examining some of the major themes presented in this invaluable correspondence, a note of warning should be sounded. If read out of context, the letters may give the impression that once Verdi had established the text of a passage, his process of composition was virtually complete.

This impression is strengthened by the extreme speed with which he passed from one scene to the next. There was, however, another side to his work on which he collaborated with nobody. Once he had defined the drama verbally, a task which was, as we shall see, of vital importance, he had to confront the musical decisions and problems. Of these we (naturally) hear little in the letters. Their documentation lies in the sketches Verdi made for his opera, which unfortunately have either been destroyed or remain unavailable.

One point which emerges with great force from the Verdi Ghislanzoni correspondence is the extent to which Verdi actually composed the libretto. At times, Ghislanzoni seems to have been little more than a versifying secretary, putting the final touches of poetic credibility to the text.

This situation was by no means unusual for Verdi. Although he never took complete responsibility for a libretto — in Italy the librettist was still referred to, and regarded as, 'il poeta' and Verdi would never have presumed to usurp this basic literary pride — his most fruitful collaborations (with Piave, Somma, Cammarano, even Boito) were on the firm understanding of 'prima la musica, dopo le parole'. The following example is quite representative of the manner in which Verdi commanded the shape of the final text. He is commenting on the final scene of Act Four:

[. . .] Yesterday I told you to write eight seven-syllable lines for Radamès before the eight for Aida. These two *soli*, even with two different *cantilene*, would have more or less the same form, the same character; and here we are back to the commonplace. The French, even in their poetry set to music, sometimes use longer or shorter lines. Why couldn't we do the same? This entire scene cannot, and must not, be anything more than a scene of singing, pure and simple. A somewhat unusual verse form for Radamès would oblige me to find a melody different from those usually set to lines of seven and eight syllables and would also oblige me to change the tempo and metre in order to write Aida's *solo* (a kind of *half-aria*). Thus with a

> somewhat unusual *cantabile* for Radamès,
> another *half-aria* for Aida,
> the *dirge* of the priests,
> the *dance* of the priestesses,
> the *farewell to life* of the lovers,
> the *in pace* of Amneris,

we would form a varied and well-developed ensemble; and if I am able, musically, to tie it all together as a whole, we shall have done something good, or at least something that will not be common. Take heart then, Signor Ghislanzoni, we are approaching the harvest; or at least you are.

Now see if you can make good verses out of this jumble of rhymeless words I am sending you, as you have done with so many others.

AIDA

And here, far from any human gaze	E qui, lontana da ogni sguardo umano
. . . To die on your heart	. . . Sul tuo cor morire (A very emotional line)

RADAMÈS

To die! Innocent?	Morire! Tu innocente?
To die! So beautiful?	Morire! . . . Tu sì bella?
You, in the April of your years	Tu, negli april degli anni
To depart from life?	Lasciar la vita?
How much I loved you, no, it cannot be told!	Quant'io t'amai, no, nol può dir favella!
But my love was fatal for you.	Ma fù mortale l'amor mio per te.
To die! Innocent?	Morire! Tu innocente?
To die! So beautiful?	Morire! Tu sì bella?
See? The angel of death	Vedi? di morte l'angelo
etc. etc.	etc. etc.

34

Antonio Ghislanzoni 1824 — 1893 (courtesy of Ricordi & Co., Milan)

You cannot imagine what a beautiful melody can be made out of so strange a form, and how much grace is given to it by the five-syllable line coming after the three of seven, and how much variety is lent by the two twelve-syllable lines that follow. Nevertheless, it would be good for both to be either truncated or even. See if you can knock some lines out of it and preserve the . . . *tu sì bella?*, which fits the cadence so well. [. . .] (?November 13, 1870)

Ghislanzoni dutifully 'knocked some lines' together out of the unusual syllabic pattern, and sent them off to Verdi. But he had wasted his time. The composer replied:

I received the verses, which are beautiful but not at all right for me. To avoid losing time, since you took so long sending them to me, I had already written the piece to the monstrous verses I sent you. [. . .] (undated, probably second half of November 1870)

The definitive rhyming form was presumably arranged during another personal meeting. A glance at the libretto shows that it follows Verdi's 'monstrous verses' very closely.

As we can see from this, Verdi was anxious to avoid a mechanical adherence to traditional operatic verse forms; he wanted a text which was intimately linked to the dramatic situations and words which would stimulate him towards musical forms which were similarly free of conventional formulae. To express his intentions more clearly, Verdi coined the term *parola scenica*, the 'theatrical word' or 'scenic utterance'. In another letter to Ghislanzoni, commenting on the Act Two Aida-Amneris duet, he explains the term's practical application:

In the duet, there are some excellent things at the beginning and at the end, but it is too long and drawn out. It seems to me that the recitative could be said in fewer lines. The strophes are good until *a te in cor destò*. But then, when the action warms up, it seems to me that the *theatrical word* is missing. I don't know if I make myself clear when I say "*theatrical word*" but I mean the word that clarifies and presents the situation neatly and plainly.

For example, the lines:

Look straight into my eyes	*In volto gli occhi affisami*
And lie again if you dare:	*E menti ancor se l'osi:*
Radamès lives . . .	*Radamès vive . . .*

This is less theatrical than the words (ugly, if you wish):

. . . with one word	*. . . con una parola*
I will tear out your secret.	*stapperò il tuo segreto.*
Look at me, I have deceived you:	*Guardami, t'ho ingannata:*
Radamès lives . . .	*Radamès vive . . .*

[. . .] I know very well that you will ask: "And the verse, the rhyme, the strophe?" I don't know what to say. But when the action demands it, I would quickly abandon rhythm, rhyme, strophe; I would write unrhymed verse to say clearly and distinctly whatever the action requires. Unfortunately, it is sometimes necessary in the theatre for poets and composers to have the talent *not* to write poetry or music, [. . .] (August 17, 1870)

It seems that, at least in some ways, Verdi saw the 'theatrical word' as a reaction against the more conventional 'number opera' where the drama was rigidly partitioned into self contained musical units. In another letter to Ghislanzoni he remarks of one passage that 'the *theatrical word* is missing, or if it is there, it is buried under the rhyme or under the verse and doesn't jump out as neatly and plainly as it should' (August 14, 1870). Typically Verdi stresses the device during dramatic outbursts in recitative or arioso: in 'unrhymed' sections of text, where the music is free of any strict formal constraint. While the structuring of long passages in this 'unrhymed' style was by no means new — we need think no further than Rigoletto's *'Cortigiani, vil razza dannata'* — never before *Aida* had it formed the cornerstone of Verdi's musical composition.

If the 'theatrical word' was intimately bound up with a new, freer form of dramatic expression, we should not imagine that Verdi deliberately avoided the older operatic forms when they seemed appropriate. On the problematical question of the *cabaletta* (the fast closing section of an aria or duet frequently criticised for its dramatic irrelevance and musical banality) he had this to say to Ghislanzoni:

[. . .]Have no doubt, I do not abhor *cabalettas*, but I want a subject and a pretext for them. In the duet in *Ballo in maschera* [Amelia-Riccardo, Act Two] there was a magnificent pretext. After that whole scene, if I may say so, an outburst of love was necessary . . . (August 22, 1870)

He was, however aware that only rarely could the old style mix successfully with the new. In this context, the third act, which is by far the most conventional in formal terms, worried him the most. The so-called 'closed forms', the slow *cantabiles*, the fast *cabalettas*, imposed a unity of their own, and once employed could not easily be discarded. Concerning this act, Verdi wrote: 'since we have taken the path of *cantabiles* and *cabalettas*, we must continue on that path' (October 16, 1870). Even after the first performances, he was still unsure of their final effect. While making arrangements for a revival of *Aida* in Parma, the composer wrote to his friend and publisher Giulio Ricordi:

[. . .] Once again, I believe the third act is best in terms of *drama.* I only want to rework the instrumentation of that horrible *cabaletta*, which has attracted so much advice, so much wisdom, and so much benevolence from your critics!! Therefore send me the original of the *cabaletta.* [. . .] (April 6, 1872)

In spite of all the problems he raised with Ghislanzoni, Verdi composed the opera at a remarkable speed. Act One was written between late July and mid-August 1870, Act Two was finished in late September, Act Three in mid-October. By mid-November he wrote to Giulio Ricordi that he had 'finished the opera', and soon after that he began making enquiries about how to obtain the balance of his fee. It then became obvious that international events would interfere with the *Aida* timetable. On July 19, 1870 France declared war on Prussia, and exactly two months later Prussian forces began the Siege of Paris. Verdi took up a firmly partisan attitude:

> This disaster in France brings despair to my heart as it does to yours! It's true that the humbug, the impertinence, the arrogance of the French was — and continues to be — insupportable, despite all their misfortunes; nevertheless France has given liberty and civilization to the modern world. If she falls, let's not deceive ourselves; all our liberties and our civilization will fall. Let our scholars and politicians glorify the knowledge, the sciences, and even — God forgive them — the arts of these victors. But if one looked a little deeper, one would see that the old Gothic blood still runs through their veins; that they are immensely proud, harsh, intolerant of anything that is not German, and rapacious without limit. Men with heads but without hearts. A strong but not a civil race. And that King who always chatters about God and providence, with those help he is destroying the better part of Europe. He thinks himself ordained to reform the manners and to cleanse the vices of the modern world!! Some missionary! [. . .] (to Clarina Maffei, September 30, 1870)

The siege froze preparations for the Cairo première of *Aida*. All the scenery and costumes were being made in Paris, where they were now trapped. It became clear that the première would have to be postponed. Verdi accepted the delay reluctantly, deciding to orchestrate his score at leisure during the winter. It is very likely that its unprecedented wealth of orchestral detail owes a good deal to this enforced delay and unhurried completion. Verdi did not deliver the full score to Ricordi until the end of August 1871, shortly after having made a last minute addition of the aria 'O patria mia'.

Another advantage of the long gap between composition and first performance was that it allowed Verdi to spend much more than usual time and effort preparing the opera for the stage. He decided very early on not to go to Cairo for the world première (he was 'afraid of being mummified'), and concentrated his energies on the Italian première at La Scala, which was scheduled to take place very soon after. As usual, there were endless problems about the exact choice of singers. In particular the role of Amneris caused trouble, as Verdi wrote to Giulio Ricordi: 'the voice alone, no matter how beautiful [. . .], is not enough for that role. So-called *polished singing* matters little to me' (July 10, 1871), demands which were strikingly similar to those he requested of the first Lady Macbeth, some twenty-four years earlier. The composer also concerned himself with details of the *mise-en-scène*, and even offered his advice on how the orchestra ought to be arranged:

[. . .] The seating arrangement of the orchestra is of much greater importance than is commonly believed — for the *blending* of the instruments, for the sonority, and for the effect. These small improvements will afterward open the way for other innovations, which will surely come one day; among them, taking the spectators' boxes off the stage, bringing the curtain to the footlights; another, making the *orchestra invisible*. This is not my idea but Wagner's. It's excellent. It seems impossible that today we tolerate the sight of shabby *tails* and white ties, for example, mixed with Egyptian, Assyrian, and Druidic costumes, etc., etc., and, even more, the sight of the entire orchestra, which is part of the fictitious world, almost in the middle of the floor, among the whistling or applauding crowd. Add to all this the indecency of seeing the tops of the harps, the necks of the double basses, and the baton of the conductor all up in the air. [. . .] (July 10, 1871)

Verdi took an active interest in the production of his operas almost from the first, and after his experiences at the Paris Opéra in the late 1840's, never again tolerated the absurdities so common in Italian opera houses.

The Siege of Paris was lifted on January 28, 1871, but it was not until December 24 of that year that *Aida* finally received its world première at the Cairo Opera House.

On February 8, 1872, performances began at La Scala, Milan. Both productions were immediately hailed as triumphant successes, and the opera soon began the round of major European opera houses. The day after the Milanese première, Verdi summed up his achievement with characteristically blunt modesty:

[. . .] The audience reacted favourably. I don't want to affect modesty with you, but this opera is certainly not one of my worst. Time will afterward give it the place it deserves . . .
(Letter to Opprandino Arrivabene, February 9, 1872)

Gratified as he was by the enormous public success, it was not sufficient to halt his increasing disenchantment with the ways of the operatic world. The silence which had threatened after *Don Carlos* now closed in around him, apart from the *Requiem*, and no new opera came from Verdi's pen for sixteen years. In many ways, then, *Aida* marks the close of a definite period in Verdi's creative life, and for this and many other reasons, the opera is an essential experience for any who wish to understand fully the composer's artistic development.

(All the letters quoted here, and the extract from Mariette's outline, are taken from Hans Busch: Verdi's 'Aida'. The History of an Opera in Letters and Documents, *Minneapolis, 1978. This fascinating book, one of the most complete collections of documents related to the history of an opera, is warmly recommended to those wishing to find out more about the genesis of* Aida.*)*

Thematic Guide

Many of the themes from the opera have been identified in the articles by numbers in square brackets, which refer to the themes set out on these pages. The themes are also identified by the numbers in brackets at the corresponding points in the libretto, so that the words can be related to the musical themes.

[1] AIDA
Andante mosso

[2] THE PRIESTS
Andante mosso

[3] RADAMÈS
Andantino

God - dess A - i - da, —— fair as — a vi - sion, —
Ce - le - ste A - i - da, —— for - ma — di - vi - na, —

[4] AMNERIS
Allegro assai moderato

[5] AMNERIS
Allegro agitato e presto

41

[6] **KING**

Allegro maestoso

Now go for-ward no-ble ar-my, guard the shores of sa-cred Nile;
Su! del Ni-lo al sa-cro lido ac-cor-re-te, Egi-zii e-roi,

[7] **AIDA**

Allegro agitato

A con-que-ror re-turn!
Ri-tor-na vin-ci-tor!

[8] **AIDA**

Allegro giusto poco agitato

pp The sa-cred names of a fa-ther and lov-er
triste e dolce I sa-cri no-mi di pa-dre, d'a-mante

[9] **AIDA**

Cantabile

pp Hear me ye Gods, pi — ty my cry!
Nu — mi, pie-tà del mio sof-frir!

[10] **HIGH PRIESTESS**

Andante

mf Al — migh — ty, al-migh-ty Phthà!
Pos- sen- te, pos-sen-te Fthà!

[11] **DANCE OF THE PRIESTESSES**

Allegretto

p
dolcissimo

[12] **RAMFIS**

Grave *cantabile*

p
Great God-head we pe-ti-tion thee,
Nu- me, cus-to-de e vin-di-ce

42

[13] **CHORUS**
Allegro giusto

We hear, ———————— the hymns and cheering
Chi mai, ———————— fra gl'inni e i plau - si

We hear, the hymns, we hear the cheer - ing,
Chi mai, chi mai fra gl'in - ni e i plau - si

[14] **AMNERIS**
Allegro giusto *con espansione*

Ah come — — to me, ah come my love, en - slave me
Ah! vie - — — ni, vie - ni a - mor mio, m'i - neb - bria

[15] **DANCE OF THE MOORISH SLAVES**

Molto allegro

pp legerissimo

[16]
Andante espressivo

f

[17] **AIDA**
Adagio cantabile

But look with pi - ty on my dis - tress
Pie - tà ti pren - da del mio do - lor

[18] **AMNERIS**
Adagio

f I will des - troy you, I'll break your heart ———
Tre - ma, vil schia - — — va! spez - za il tuo co - re

[19] **CHORUS**
Maestoso

Glo - ry to I - sis, god - dess fair,
Glo - ria all' Eg - it - to ad I - si - de

[20] TRIUMPHAL MARCH AND DANCES

Maestoso

[21] Mosso

[22] Mosso

[23] AMONASRO
Andante

Migh - ty   King,   you   are   no -   ble   and   glo - rious,
Ma   tu,   Re,   tu   si -   gno -   re   pos - sen -   te,

[24] PRIESTS
Andante mosso

Death, O   King,———   to   these   sav - age   in - vad - ers,
Strug - gi, O   Re,———   que -   ste   ciur - me   fe - ro - ci,

[25] AIDA
Andante cantabile

Oh, skies of   blue, oh   soft   car - ess - ing   bree——   zes,
O   cie- li az -   zur - ri, o dol -   ci au -   re   na - ti -   ve,

[26] AMONASRO
Allegro giusto   cantabile dolcissimo

Once a -   gain   you   will   see   our   lof - ty   for - ests,
Ri - ve -   drai   le   fo -   re - ste im- bal -   sa -   ma - te,

44

[27] AMONASRO

Allegro con impeto selvaggio

Des - troy _____ us, you ar - mies of E - gypt,
Su dun - _____ que! sor - get - te e - gi - zie co -

des - troy us! re - duce all our cities to ash - es and dust.
or - ti! col fuo - co strug - ge - te le no - stre cit - tà.

[28] AMONASRO

Andante sostenuto

Think — how your peo - ple all have been sub - jec - ted,
Pen - sa che un po - - po - lo, vin - to, stra - zia - to,

[29] RADAMÈS

Allegro giusto con trasporto

At last I see _____ you, swee - test A - i - da
Pur ti ri - veg - - go, mia dol - ce A - i - da

[30] AIDA

Andantino dolcissimo

There, where _____ the vir - gin for - ests rise
Là, tra _____ fo - re - ste ver - gi - ni

[31] RADAMÈS

Allegro assai vivo

Hand in hand we'll fly to geth - er, find a path - way a - cross the de - sert:
Sì: fug - giam da que - ste mu - ra, al de - ser - to in - siem fug - gia - mo:

[32] AMNERIS

Andante sostenuto

Soon — all the priests will ga - ther here,
Già i — sa - cer - do - ti a - du - nan - si

45

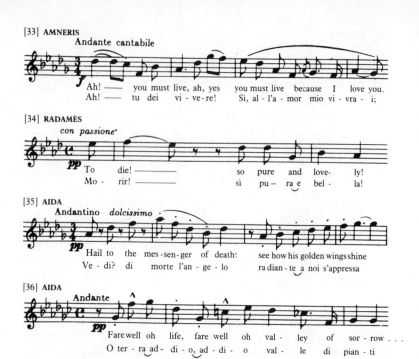

[33] **AMNERIS**
Andante cantabile

Ah! — you must live, ah, yes you must live because I love you.
Ah! — tu dei vi - ve - re! Sì, al - l'a - mor mio vi - vra - i;

[34] **RADAMÈS**
con passione

pp
To die! — so pure and love - ly!
Mo - rir! — sì pu — ra e bel - la!

[35] **AIDA**
Andantino dolcissimo

pp
Hail to the mes - sen - ger of death: see how his golden wings shine
Ve - di? di morte l'an - ge - lo ra dian - te a noi s'appressa

[36] **AIDA**
Andante

pp
Farewell oh life, fare well oh val - ley of sor - row . . .
O ter - ra ad - di - o, ad - di - o val - le di pian - ti

46

Aida

an opera in four acts by Giuseppe Verdi

Libretto by Antonio Ghislanzoni based on a story
by Auguste Mariette
English version by Edmund Tracey

This is the performing version used by English National Opera at the London Coliseum. Ghislanzoni's libretto is written in verse, laid out here correctly as far as possibly; in several cases, this was altered by Verdi in the course of composing the opera, and so these amendments interrupt the original scheme of alignment. Where choruses and ensembles repeat lines, this has been indicated also, to make it easy to follow the text as it is sung.

The stage directions and character descriptions are those in the original full score and do not necessarily represent the ENO (or any other) production. They have been followed because they were sanctioned by the composer and consequently illustrate his intentions, and form a more or less integral part of the text. The titles of musical pieces follow the relevant scene descriptions after an oblique and the numbers in square brackets refer to the thematic guide.

The first performance of *Aida* was given at the Cairo Opera House on December 24, 1871. The first performance in London was at Covent Garden on June 22, 1876. The first performance in the USA was at the New York Academy of Music on November 26, 1873. It was first performed by Sadler's Wells Opera on March 20, 1931, and by English National Opera at the London Coliseum on September 26, 1979.

THE CHARACTERS

Ramfis *high priest* — bass

Radamès *captain of the guard* — tenor

Amneris *princess of Egypt* — mezzo-soprano

Aida *an Ethiopian slave* — soprano

The King of Egypt — bass

Messenger — tenor

High priestess — soprano

Amonasro *Aida's father, king of Ethiopia* — baritone

Priests, priestesses, ministers, officers, guards, courtiers, Nubians, populace, slaves, prisoners

The action takes place in Memphis and Thebes at the time of the Pharaohs.

Act One

Scene One. *Hall in the palace of the King at Memphis. To the right and left a colonnade with statues and flowering shrubs. At the back a grand gate from which may be seen the temples and palaces of Memphis and the Pyramids. | Introduction. Radames and Ramfis in consultation*

RAMFIS

Yes, Ethiopia once again has dared to
Defy our power: On the Nile we are
  threaten'd
And in the state of Thebes. I sent a
  messenger
To find the truth.

Sì: corre voce che l'Etiope ardisca
Sfidarci ancora, e del Nilo la valle

E Tebe minacciar. Fra breve un messo

Recherà il ver.

RADAMES

　　　　The will of
Isis has been consulted?

　　　　La sacra
Iside consultasti?

RAMFIS

　　　　She has decided
Who will take the supreme
Command of all our armies.

　　　　Ella ha nomato
Dell'Egizie falangi
Il condottier supremo.

RADAMES

　　Ah, what an honour!

　　　　　　Oh lui felice!

RAMFIS

(meaningfully, looking fixedly at Radamès)

Nobly born, he's young and valiant. The
  god has spoken:
Now I must tell the King.

Giovane e prode è desso. Ora, del Nume

Reco i decreti al Re.

Ramfis leaves. | Romanza

RADAMES

　　　　I pray that I
Be chosen and achieve my
Dream of Glory!
With a glorious valiant army
And I as leader . . .
Egypt victorious, . . acclaimed
By the whole of Memphis!
To you my sweet Aida
I'd enter crown'd with laurel . . .
Saying: 'for you I battled, for you I
  conquer'd!'

Goddess Aida, fair as a vision,　　　[3]
Magic in beauty, glowing with light,
Like some fair planet you shine above
  me,
You are the ruler of my whole life.
Home to your country I would return
  you,

　　　　Se quel guerrier
Io fossi! se il mio sogno
Si avverasse! Un esercito di prodi
Da me guidato . . . e la vittoria, e il plauso
Di Menfi tutta!

E a te, mia dolce Aida,
Tornar di lauri cinto . . .
Dirti: 'per te ho pugnato, per te ho
  vinto!'

Celeste Aida, forma divina,
Mistico serto di luce e fior,
Del mio pensiero tu sei regina,

Tu di mia vita sei lo splendor.
Il tuo bel cielo vorrei ridarti,

Back to the sweet-scented land you love:
Then with a garland I would adorn you,
Build you a throne near to the sun!

Le dolci brezze del patrio suol;
Un regal serto sul crin posarti,
Ergerti un trono vicino al sol!

Amneris enters | Duet and Trio

AMNERIS [4]

Have you just heard a joyful
Tale that stirs you? A valiant
Noble elation seems to glow inside you!
How all the world would envy
And honour the woman who merely by
  her presence
And her beauty could waken in you such
  ardour!

Quale insolita gioia
Nel tuo sguardo! Di quale
Nobil fierezza ti balena il volto!
Degna d'invidia oh! quanto,
Saria la donna il cui bramato aspetto

Tanta luce di gaudio in te destasse!

RADAMÈS

A soldier's heart beats faster
When he's dreaming of glory. Isis today
Has named the man who will command
  our army
And lead them forth to face the foe . . .
  Ah! if only
I might achieve that honour!

D'un sogno avventuroso
Si beava il mio cuore. Oggi, la Diva
Profferse il nome del guerrier che al
  campo
Le schiere egizie condurrà . . . Ah! s'io
  fossi
A tal' onor prescelto . . .

AMNERIS

Another dream may charm you,
Still more sweet, still more lovely,
To captivate your heart. A secret
  longing . . .
A devotion . . . more tender?

Nè un altro sogno mai
Più gentil, più soave
Al core ti parlò? Non hai tu in Menfi

Desiderii, speranze?

RADAMÈS [5]

      I? (A devotion?
Surely she can't discover
the love that burns within me?)

      Io! (Quale inchiesta!
Forse l'arcano amore
Scoprì che m'arde in core . . .)

AMNERIS [5]

(I'll die if there's another . . .
A rival holding him as lover!)

(Oh! guai se un altro amore
Ardesse a lui nel core!)

RADAMÈS

(Can she have guess'd Aida
By looking in my eyes?)

(Della sua schiava il nome
Mi lesse nel pensier!

AMNERIS

(I will die if I have found a
Darkly hidden secret love!)

(Guai se il mio sguardo penetra
Questo fatal mister!)

Aida enters [1]

RADAMÈS
(seeing Aida)

    Aida!

              Dessa!

AMNERIS
(to herself; watching)

(He is troubled . . . Ah, what a
Look of devotion there!

(Ei si turba, e quale
Sguardo rivolse a lei!

50

Aida! Is she my rival?   [5] Aida! A me rivale . . .
Is he in love with her?)   Forse saria costei?)

(turning to Aida)

Come my dear, come close to me . . . Vieni, o diletta appressati,
Never a slave I find you!   Schiava non sei nè ancella,
You are a sister dear to me,   Qui, dove in dolce fascino
With sweetest ties I bind you . . . Io ti chiamai sorella . . .
Weeping? And will you share   Piangi? delle tue lacrime
With a sister the sorrow,   Svela il segreto a me.
Causing you tears of woe?

AIDA

Alas, I hear the cries of war,   Ohimè! di guerra fremere
The fearful shouts re-echo . . .   L'atroce grido io sento,
What will befall my countrymen? Per l'infelice patria,
For them, for you, I fear so.   Per me, per voi pavento.

AMNERIS

Is this the truth? No deeper reason Favelli il ver? Nè s'agita
Causes your dismay?   Più grave cura in te?
(Aida! Beware my anger!)   (Trema, o rea schiava!)

(Aida casts down her eyes and tries to hide her emotion)

RADAMÈS
(watching Amneris)

(I see her eyes are flashing . . . (Nel volto a lei balena . . .

AMNERIS
(aside, regarding Aida)
Aida, beware my anger!   Ah! Trema, rea schiava, trema!

RADAMÈS

With anger and suspicion . . .) Lo sdegno ed il sospetto)

AMNERIS

In your heart I'll find the secret! Ch'io nel tuo cor discenda!

RADAMÈS

Can she have read the secret   Guai se l'arcano affetto
Our hearts have sweetly hidden? . . A noi leggesse in cor!

AMNERIS

I mean to know the truth   Trema che il ver m'apprenda
Of your blushes and of your tears! Quel pianto e quel rossor!

RADAMÈS

Hidden inside our hearts?   Guai se leggesse in cor!

AIDA

Ah! no, sighs for my country   Ah! — no, sulla mia patria
Now vie in my heart with other sorrows, Non geme il cor soltanto;
These tears fast flowing are mourning Quello ch'io verso è pianto
A sad, unlucky love!   Di sventurato amor!

RADAMÈS

I see in her eyes an angry flash Nel volto a lei balena

An angry flash, suspecting our love!
She reads the tender passion,
That's hidden in our hearts!

Lo sdegno ed il sospetto.
Guai se l'arcano affetto
A noi leggesse in cor!

AMNERIS

Oh slave, beware my anger,
For in your heart I'll find the truth!
I mean to know the truth about your
blushes,
Your blushes and all your tears!

Rea schiava, trema!
Ch'io nel tuo cor discenda!
Ah! trema che il ver m'apprenda
Quel pianto e quel rossor!

The King enters, preceded by his guard and followed by Ramfis, ministers, priests, officers, etc. | Scena and Concerted Piece

THE KING

Grave is the cause that
Summons round their King the faithful
men of Egypt.
From the Ethiopian front a messenger
Has just been admitted. Grave is the
news he brings us.
So we must hear him . . .

Alta cagion v'aduna,
O fidi Egizii, al vostro Re d'intorno.
Dai confin d'Etiopia un messaggiero
Dianzi giungea, gravi novelle ei reca.
Vi piaccia udirlo . . .

(to an official)

Now bring him here before us!

Il messaggier s'avanzi!

The Messenger enters.

THE MESSENGER

Our sacred land has been defiled by
fierce
Ethiopian invaders . . . They ravaged all
our
Fields and our farmsteads, burnt all our
harvests . . . embolden'd
By so easy a triumph, the savage troops
Are advancing on the city.

Il sacro suolo dell'Egitto è invaso
Dai barbari Etiopi. I nostri campi
Fur devastati, arse le messi, e baldi
Della facil vittoria, i predatori
Già marciano su Tebe.

ALL

They would not dare to!

Ed osan tanto!

THE MESSENGER

They are led by a warrior as savage
As a tiger — Amonasro.

Un guerriero indomabile, feroce,
Li conduce — Amonasro.

ALL

The King!

Il Re!

AIDA
(aside)

(My father!)

(Mio padre!)

THE MESSENGER

Now Thebes has risen; from ev'ry door
and gateway
Our men are rushing forth hurling
Fire and sword upon the wild invader.

Già Tebe è in armi e dalle cento porte
Sul barbaro invasore
Proromperà, guerra recando e morte.

Let death and battle be our only warcry!	Sì, guerra e morte il nostro grido sia!

ALL

Battle! Battle!	Guerra! guerra!
Destruction, no quarter given!	Tremenda, inesorata!

THE KING

(addressing Radamès)

Holiest Goddess Isis	Iside venerata
Has chosen her commander,	Di nostre schiere invitte
The man to lead our glorious troops to battle.	Già designava il condottier supremo:
Radamès!	Radamès!

ALL

Radamès!	Radamès!

RADAMÈS

Ah! My thanks to Heaven.	Ah! sien grazie ai Numi!
My prayers have been heard!	Son paghi i voti miei!

AMNERIS

Our leader! our leader!	Ei duce! ei duce!

AIDA

I'm frightened, I'm frightened!	Io tremo! Io tremo!

THE KING

Go now to Vulcan's temple	Or di Vulcano al tempio
Brave Radamès, to gird	Muovi, O guerrier; le sacre
On the armour of victorious Egypt!	Armi ti cingi e alla vittoria vola.

Now go forward noble army,	[6]	Su! del Nilo al sacro lido
Guard the shores of sacred Nile;		Accorrete, Egizii eroi;
Ev'ry voice proclaim our warcry:		D'ogni cor prorompa il grido:
Death and destruction fall upon the foe!		Guerra e morte, morte allo stranier!

RAMFIS

Glory to Isis! All bow before her!	Gloria ai Numi! ognun rammenti
She it is who guides our fortunes.	Ch'essi reggono gli eventi,
Great her might high in the heavens;	Che in poter dei Numi solo
Isis rules the world below.	Stan le sorti del guerrier.

Bow down in homage! Great the might of Isis.	Ognun rammenti
She guides our fortune,	Che in poter dei Numi, dei Numi solo
Isis rules the world below!	Stan le sorti del guerrier!

MINISTERS, CAPTAINS

Now go forward noble army	Su! del Nilo al sacro lido
We shall form a human barrier;	Sien barriera i nostri petti;
Ev'ry voice proclaim our warcry:	Non echeggi che un sol grido;
Death and destruction fall upon the foe!	Guerra, guerra e morte allo stranier!

THE KING

Yes, now go forward noble army,	Su! su! del Nilo al sacro lido
Hasten forward to the river.	Accorrete, Egizii eroi;

Let ev'ry voice proclaim the cry	Da ogni cor prorompa un grido:
Destruction fall upon the foe!	Guerra e morte allo stranier!

AIDA
(to herself)

Who can tell me who I weep for, who I pray for?	Per chi piango? Per chi prego?
Ah this fatal pow'r that binds me!	Qual poter m'avvince a lui!
Dare I love him, yes, love him	Deggio amarlo ed è costui
Both a stranger and a foe!	Un nemico, uno stranier!

RADAMÈS

I can feel the flame of glory	Sacro fremito di gloria
Fire my mind and quite consume me!	Tutta l'anima m'investe.
We will fight and we will conquer:	Su! corriamo alla vittoria!
Death and destruction fall upon the foe!	Guerra e morte allo stranier!

AMNERIS
(handing a standard to Radamès)

From my hand, oh noble leader,	Di mia man ricevi, o duce,
Take this standard bright with glory;	Il vessillo glorioso;
May it guide you, long may it light you	Ti sia guida, ti sia luce
On the valiant path you go!	Della gloria sul sentier.

THE KING [6]

Now go forward, noble army *(etc.)*	Su! del Nilo al sacro lido, *(etc.)*

RAMFIS

Bow in homage men of Egypt!	Gloria ai Numi, e ognun rammenti
Mighty Isis guides our fortunes:	Ch'essi regono gli eventi,
Hers the might and hers the glory!	Che in poter de' Numi solo
Holy Isis rules the world below!	Stan le sorti, le sorti del guerrier!

RADAMÈS, MESSENGER

Fight and conquer!	Su! corriamo,
Fight and we will be victorious!	Su! corriamo alla vittoria!

MINISTERS, CAPTAINS

Now go forward, noble army,	Su! del Nilo al sacro lido
We shall form a human barrier *(etc.)*	Sien barriera i nostri petti, *(etc.)*

AMNERIS

I pray it guide you	. . . ti sia guida
May it guide you, may it light you,	Ti sia guida, ti sia luce
Yes, may it light you on the valiant path you go.	Della gloria sul sentier.

AIDA

(Who can tell me who I weep for, *(etc.)*	(Per chi piango? Per chi prego?, *(etc.)*

ALL
(except Aida)

Battle! Battle! Battle!	Guerra! guerra! guerra!
Destroy them! Death and vengeance on the foe!	Sterminio all'invasor!

AIDA

Dare I give him my heart and love	Deggio amarlo, e veggio in lui
Both a stranger and a foe? Ah!	Un nemico, uno stranier! Ah!

A conqueror return!   Ritorna vincitor!

ALL

A conqueror return!   Ritorna vincitor!

Exeunt all but Aida.| Scena and Romanza

AIDA [7]

A conqueror return! How can I utter   Ritorna vincitor! E dal mio labbro
Words full of betrayal? Do I wish   Uscì l'empia parola! Vincitor
My father conquer'd, a man who wages   Del padre mio, di lui che impugna l'armi
     war just
For me, just to restore me   Per me, per ridonarmi
My homeland, my palace, the royal name Una patria, una reggia, e il nome illustre
I am forc'd to keep unspoken? Do I pray Che qui celar m'è forza! Vincitor
He kill my brothers? . . I think I see De' miei fratelli . . . ond'io lo vegga,
     him, stain'd   tinto
With the blood I cherish, hoisted high in Del sangue amato, trionfar nel plauso
     triumph
By Egyptian battalions. Behind his   Dell'Egizie coorti! E dietro il carro,
     chariot,
A King, my father, led in chains of   Un Re, mio padre, di catene avvinto!
     bondage!

Oh Heaven, forgive all   L'insana parola,
The mad words I utter!   O Numi, sperdete!
Restore to a loving   Al seno d'un padre
Father his daughter;   La figlia rendete;
And slaughter the armies   Struggete le squadre
That so oppress our land! Ah! —   Dei nostri oppressor! Ah! —
Wretched folly to say so! My own   Sventurata! che dissi? E l'amor mio?
     beloved!
How could I turn against him,   Dunque scordar poss'io
With his fervent devotion when all   Questo fervido amore che, oppressa e
     turn'd from me: schiava,
His smile was like the sun shining upon Come raggio di sol qui mi beava?
     me.
Shall I invoke the death   Imprecherò la morte
Of Radamès, the man I love so dearly? A Radamès, a lui ch'amo pur tanto!
Ah, shall I ever bear   Ah! non fu in terra mai
This cruel, deadly weight of burning   Da più crudeli angoscie un core affranto!
     sorrow?

The sacred names of a father and   [8] I sacri nomi di padre, d'amante
     lover
Are what I must not cherish nor even   Nè profferir poss'io, nè ricordar . . .
     say . . .
Confused and trembling . . . the one and Per l'un, per l'altro . . . confusa e
     the other . . .   tremante . . .
I only want to weep . . . I want to pray. Io piangere vorrei, vorrei pregar.
Is it a crime now to own such a feeling,   Ma la mia prece in bestemmia si
                                           muta . . .

And am I wrong to weep and wrong to   Delitto e il pianto a me, colpa il sospir . . .
     sigh?
In darkest night all my senses are reeling, In notte cupa la mente e perduta,
In aching distress I long to die!   E nell'ansia crudel vorrei morir.

55

Hear me ye Gods, pity my cry!	[9]	Numi, pietà del mio soffrir!
All hope is gone, joy comes no more.		Speme non v'ha pel mio dolor.
Ah, fatal love, ah, mighty love,		Amor fatal, tremendo amor,
Come, break my heart, leave me to die!		Spezzami il cor, fammi morir!

Scene Two. *Interior of the Temple of Vulcan at Memphis. A mysterious light from above. A long row of columns, one behind the other, vanishing in darkness. Statues of various deities. In the middle of the stage, above a platform covered with carpet, rises the altar surmounted with sacred emblems. Golden tripods emitting fumes of incense.| Grand Scene of the Consecration and First Finale*

HIGH PRIESTESS

[10] *alone*

Almighty, almighty Phtha, the breathing	Possente, possente Ftha, del mondo
Spirit of life in us all, ah!	Spirito animator, ah!

(with chorus of priestesses from within)

We here implore thee!	Noi t'invochiamo!

RAMFIS, PRIESTS

Who, from the void, created	Tu che dal nulla hai tratto
Sea, air and earth and sky,	L'onde, la terra, il ciel,
We here implore thee!	Noi t'invochiamo!

HIGH PRIESTESS

Almighty, almighty Phtha, the fruitful	Immenso, immenso Fthà, del mondo
Spirit of life in us all, ah! ah!	Spirito fecondator, ah! ah!

(with priestesses)

We here implore thee!	Noi t'invochiamo!

RAMFIS, PRIESTS

Lord God of ancient mystery,	Nume che del tuo spirito
Who art both son and sire,	Sei figlio e genitor,
We here implore thee!	Noi t'invochiamo!

HIGH PRIESTESS

Fire uncreated beyond all time,	Fuoco increato, eterno,
Whence came the light and sun! ah, ah!	Onde ebbe luce il sol, ah, ah!

(with Priestesses)

We here implore thee!	Noi t'invochiamo!

RAMFIS, PRIESTS

Life spirit universal,	Vita dell'universo,
Great fount of deathless love,	Mito d'eterno amor,
We here implore!	Noi t'invochiam!

PRIESTESSES

Almighty Phtha!	Immenso Ftha!

RAMFIS, PRIESTS

We here implore!	Noi t'invochiam!

Sacred Dance of the Priestesses [11]. *Radamès, unarmed, is brought into the Temple and conducted to the altar. A silver veil is placed on his head.*

PRIESTESSES

Almighty Phtha!	Immenso Fthà!

We here implore! Noi t'invochiam!

RAMFIS
(to Radamès)

The gods have shown you favour: to you they now Mortal, diletto ai Numi, a te fidate

Entrust the future of Egypt. The sacred sword Son d'Egitto le sorti. Il sacro brando

Of the god will serve you, striking the invaders Dal Dio temprato, per tua man diventi

And spreading dismay, massacre, carnage. Ai nemici terror, folgore, morte.

PRIESTS

The sacred sword Il sacro brando

Of the god will serve you, striking the invaders Dal Dio temprato, per tua man diventi

And spreading dismay, massacre, carnage. Ai nemici terror, folgore, morte.

RAMFIS

Massacre, carnage. Folgore, morte.
(to the god)

Great Godhead we petition thee, [12] Nume, custode e vindice

Great guardian and avenger, Di questa sacra terra,

Come, raise thy hand in blessing, La mano tua distendi

Blessing over Egyptian soil. Sovra l'egizio suol.

RADAMÈS

Great Godhead we petition thee, Nume, che duce ed arbitro

Great judge and holy leader. Sei d'ogni umana guerra,

Come grant us thy protection, Proteggi tu, difendi

Save us, protect Egyptian soil. D'Egitto il sacro suol.

RAMFIS

Grant us they blessing. La mano tua,

Come raise thy hand in blessing La mano tua distendi

Over our holy Egyptian soil. Sovra l'egizio suol.

PRIESTS

Great Godhead we petition thee, Nume, custode e vindice

Our guardian and avenger, Di questa sacra terra,

Come raise thy hand in blessing La mano tua distendi

Blessing over Egyptian soil! Sovra l'egizio suol!

RAMFIS

Great Godhead we petition thee, Nume, custode ed arbitro

Our guardian and avenger, Di questa sacra terra,

Come raise thy hand in blessing La mano tua distendi

Blessing over Egyptian soil! Sovra l'egizio suol!

RADAMÈS

Come, grant us aid, protect us and defend us. Proteggi tu, difendi

Protect our holy Egyptian soil! D'Egitto il sacro suol!

PRIESTESSES

Almighty, almighty Phtha. Possente, possente Fthà.

57

RAMFIS, RADAMÈS, PRIESTS, PRIESTESSES
Almighty Phtha.   Possente Fthà.

PRIESTESSES

Life spirit in us all.   Del mondo creator.

RAMFIS, RADAMÈS, PRIESTS, PRIESTESSES

Life spirit in us all,	Spirto fecondator
Who hast from nothing the world	Tu che dal nulla hai tratto
Created,	Il mondo,
Thou who from nothing waves hast	Tu che dal nulla hai tratto
Created, earth, air and Heaven,	L'onde, la terra, il cielo,
We here implore thee!	Noi t'invochiamo!

PRIESTESSES

Ah! — Ah!	Ah! — Ah!
Almighty Phtha!	Possente Fthà!
Breathing spirit of life in all,	Spirito animator,
Fruitful spirit of life in all.	Spirito fecondator.

ALL THE OTHERS

We here implore!   Noi t'invochiam!

PRIESTESSES

Almighty Phtha!   Immenso Fthà!

ALL THE OTHERS

We here implore!   Noi t'invochiam!

RADAMÈS, RAMFIS

Almighty Phtha!   Immenso Fthà!

ALL

Almighty Phtha!   Immenso Fthà!

Act Two

Scene One. *A hall in the apartments of Amneris. Amneris surrounded by female slaves who attire her for the triumphal feast. Tripods emitting perfumed vapours. Young Moorish slaves waving feather fans.| Introduction . Scena, Chorus of Women and Dance of Moorish slaves.*

SLAVE-GIRLS [13]

We hear the hymns and cheering,	Chi mai fra gl'inni e i plausi
Praising all his glory and fame;	Erge alla gloria il vol,
His gaze is fierce and terrible,	Al par d'un Dio terribile,
He shines in our acclaim.	Fulgente al par del sol!
Let sweetest flowers rain on you,	Vieni, sul crin ti piovano
Competing with laurels around your brow;	Contesti ai lauri i fior;
Let songs of glory celebrate	Suonin di gloria i cantici
Your lover's tender vow.	Coi cantici d'amor.

AMNERIS [14]

Ah come to me, ah come my love, enslave me,	(Ah! Vieni, vieni amor mio, m'inebbria,
Inflame my heart with love.	Fammi beato il cor.)

SLAVE-GIRLS [13]

The hordes of fierce barbarians,	Or, dove son le barbare
All have vanished away.	Orde dello stranier?
Like sunlight melting winter snows,	Siccome nebbia sparvero
Our armies won the day.	Al soffio del guerrier.
A victory resounding	Vieni: di gloria il premio
Has won our hero fame and glorious high reward.	Raccogli, o vincitor;
And after deeds of glory	T'arrise la vittoria,
The voice of love is heard.	T'arriderà l'amor.

AMNERIS [14]

Ah come to me, ah come, my love awaken me	(Ah! Vieni, vieni amor mio, ravvivami
And speak a tender word!	D'un caro accento ancor!)

Dance of the young Moorish slaves [15]. *The slaves continue attiring Amneris.*

SLAVE-GIRLS [13]

Let sweetest flowers rain on you *(etc.)*	Vieni: sul crin ti piovano *(etc.)*

AMNERIS [14]

Ah come to me, ah come my love, enslave me, *(etc.)*	Ah! Vieni, vieni amor mio m'inebbria, *(etc.)*
No more now! Aida makes her way toward us . . .	Silenzio! Aida verso noi s'avanza . . .
Child of the conquer'd, to me her grief is sacred.	Figlia de' vinti, il suo dolor m'e sacro.

At a sign from Amneris, the slaves retire. Aida enters, carrying the crown.

But when I see her, suspicious	Nel rivederla, il dubbio
Fears come back to plague me . . .	Atroce in me si desta . . .
I'll discover the secret she is hiding!	Il mistero fatal si squarci alfine!

Scena and Duet

(to Aida with feigned affection)

Now the battle is over your people suffer,	Fu la sorte dell'armi a' tuoi funesta,
Wretched Aida! The sorrow	Povera Aida! Il lutto
That oppresses your heart may I not share it?	Che ti pesa sul cor teco divido.
Accept the hand of friendship . . .	Io son l'amica tua . . .
Nothing shall be denied you . . . Live and be happy!	Tutto da me tu avrai . . . Vivrai felice!

AIDA

Be happy! Ah, how can I,	Felice esser poss'io
So far from all my people, hearing no word about	Lungi dal suol natio, qui dove ignota
The fate of my father and my brothers?	M'è la sorte del padre e dei fratelli?

AMNERIS

Ah, how you grieve me! All human misfortune	Ben ti compiango! pure hanno un confine
Must sometime have an end . . . Time will bring comfort	I mali di quaggiù . . . Sanerà il tempo
And heal your present misery . . .	Le angoscie del tuo core . . .
Greater than time too, a god more mighty . . . the god of love.	E più che il tempo, un Dio possente . . . amore!

AIDA [1]
(much moved, aside)

Ah, love, ah, love, oh, joy and torment . . .	Amore, amore! gaudio, tormento . . .
Sweetest elation, burning despair . . .	Soave ebbrezza, ansia crudel . . .
In your affliction I feel life quicken . . .	Ne' tuoi dolori la vita io sento,
A smile from you can open Heaven's gate.	Un tuo sorriso mi schiude il ciel.

AMNERIS
(to herself)

Ev'ry expression . . . all this excitement	Ah, quel pallore, quel turbamento
Tell of the secret fever of love . . .	Svelan l'arcana febbre d'amor . . .
Have I the courage? Dare I still ask her?	D'interrogarla quasi ho sgomento,
I share the torments of all her alarm.	Divido l'ansie del suo terror.

[16] *(to Aida, eyeing her fixedly)*

But now a new anxiety	Ebben: qual nuovo fremito
Assails you, sweet Aida?	T'assal, gentil Aida?
Come share your secret thoughts with me,	I tuoi segreti svelami,
Trust in my friendship, my love and understanding.	All'amor mio t'affida.
Among the men who went to war	Tra i forti che pugnarono
Fighting against your country . . .	Della tua patria a danno . . .
It may be that one has kindled	Qualcuno un dolce affanno
Longing in your secret heart?	Forse a te in cor destò?

A longing?   Che parli?

AMNERIS [16]

A cruel destiny   A tutti barbara
Came only to a few men . . .   Non si mostrò la sorte
For though our glorious Radamès   Se in campo il duce impavido
Has met his death in battle . . .   Cadde trafitto a morte . . .

AIDA

You cannot mean it! Radamès!   Che mai dicesti! misera!

AMNERIS

Yes, Radamès was killed   Sì, Radamès da' tuoi
In battle . . .   Fu spento . . .

AIDA

Wretched fate!   Misera!

AMNERIS

How can you mourn him?   E pianger puoi?

AIDA

I'll mourn him for evermore!   Per sempre io piangerò!

AMNERIS

The gods now have avenged you . . .   Gli Dei t'han vendicata . . .

AIDA

The gods have always   Avversi sempre
Denied me what I wanted . . .   A me furo i Numi . . .

AMNERIS
(breaking out in anger)

Fear me! I know your secret . . .   Trema! in cor ti lessi . . .
You love him . . .   Tu l'ami . . .

AIDA

Love him!   Io!

AMNERIS

Don't deny it!   Non mentire!
But one word further: the truth will   Un detto ancora e il vero
Be clear . . . Look in my eyes now . . .   Saprò. Fissami in volto . . .
I meant to trap you . . . Radamès is   Io t'ingannavo . . . Radamès vive . . .
   living . . .

AIDA
(falling to her knees, in exaltation)

Living!   Vive!
Gods I thank you!   Ah, grazie o Numi!

AMNERIS

And still you would deceive me?   E ancor mentir tu speri?
Yes . . . you love him . . . I love him   Sì, tu l'ami . . . Ma l'amo . . .
   too . . .
(with utmost fury)

You understand? You see your rival . . .	Anch'io, intendi tu? son tua rivale,
I who am Pharaoh's daughter.	Figlia de' Faraoni!

AIDA

(drawing herself up with pride)

You my rival . . .	Mia rivale!
Well then so be it . . . I too . . . could be . . .	Ebben sia pure . . . anch'io . . . son tal . . .

(checking herself and falling at the feet of Amneris)

What have I said? Forgive! Forgive me! Ah!	Ah! che dissi mai? pietà! perdono! ah!

[17]

But look with pity on my distress . . .	Pietà ti prenda del mio dolor . . .
It's true I adore him with all my heart . . .	E vero, io l'amo d'immenso amor . . .
Ah, you are happy and you are mighty,	Tu sei felice, tu sei possente,
I live alone for one glance of love!	Io vivo solo per questo amor!

AMNERIS [18]

I will destroy you, I'll break your heart . . .	Trema, vil schiava! spezza il tuo core . . .
Daring to love him could mean your downfall.	Segnar tua morte puo quest'amore.
Mine is the power ruling your future,	Del tuo destino arbitra sono,
Hatred and vengeance now rule in my heart.	D'odio e vendetta le furie ho in cor!

AIDA

Ah! you are happy and you are mighty . . .	Tu sei felice, tu sei possente,
I live alone for one glance of love!	Io vivo solo per quest'amor!
Ah look with pity on my distress . . . *(etc.)*	Pietà ti prenda del mio dolor! *(etc.)*

AMNERIS

Fear me Aida!	Trema, vil schiava!
I'll break your heart in pieces, you slave girl!	Spezza il tuo cor, trema vil schiava!
I hold your future in my hand	Del tuo destino arbitra io son,
And hate and vengeance now rule in my heart *(etc.)*	D'odio e vendetta le furie ho in cor! *(etc.)*

CHORUS

(outside)

Now go forward noble army,	Su! del Nilo al sacro lido
Guard the Nile, our sacred river;	Sien barriera i nostri petti;
Ev'ry voice proclaim our warcry:	Non echeggi che un sol grido:
Death and destruction fall upon the foe!	Guerra e morte allo stranier!

AMNERIS

To the triumph now preparing	Alla pompa che s'appresta,
You, Aida, will attend me;	Meco, o schiava, assisterai;
You prostrated in the dust and I,	Tu prostrata nella polvere,
I enthron'd beside the King.	Io sul trono accanto al Re.

AIDA

Ah, have pity, what is left me,	Ah, pieta! che piu mi resta?
My whole life is now a desert;	Un deserto è la mia vita;
Live and reign in highest glory,	Vivi e regna, il tuo furore

I will learn to calm your rage.	Io tra breve placherò.
This fond love that so annoys you	Quest'amore che t'irrita
Soon will perish in the grave.	Nella tomba spegnerò.

AMNERIS

Follow behind me and I will show you	Vien . . . mi segui, apprenderai
What it means —	Se lottar –

AIDA

Ah, no more!	Ah! pietà!

AMNERIS

— to compete with me.	— tu puoi con me,
What it means to compete with me.	Se lottar tu puoi con me.

AIDA

Ah, no more,	Quest'amor
This love will perish within the grave.	Nella tomba io spegnerò.
No more! no more!	Pietà! Pietà!

AMNERIS

Ah, what it means	Apprenderai
To compete with me.	Se lottar tu puoi con me,
Come, attend me —	Vieni, mi segui —

CHORUS
(outside) [6]

Let destruction strike the foe!	Guerra e morte allo stranier!

AMNERIS

— and I will show you	— e apprenderai
What it means to compete with me.	Se lottar tu puoi con me.

CHORUS

Let destruction strike the foe!	Guerra e morte allo stranier!

Exit Amneris.

AIDA [9]

Hear me, ye gods, pity my cry!	Numi, pietà del mio martir,
All hope is gone and joy comes no more.	Speme non v'ha pel mio dolor . . .
Hear me ye gods, ah, hear my prayer!	Numi, pietà del mio soffrir,
Ah, hear my prayer, ah, hear my prayer!	Numi, pietà! Pietà! Pietà!

Scene Two. *An avenue to the City of Thebes. In front a clump of palms. On the right a temple dedicated to Ammon. On the left a throne with a purple canopy. At the back a triumphal arch. The stage is crowded with people. | Grand Finale Two.*

Enter the King followed by the Court — officers, priests, captains, fan bearers, standard bearers. Afterwards Amneris with Aida and slaves. The King takes his seat on the throne. Amneris places herself at his left hand.

POPULACE [19]

Glory to Isis, goddess fair,	Gloria al'Egitto, ad Iside
You who protect and shelter.	Che il sacro suol protegge!
Our King who rules the Delta,	Al Re che il Delta regge
Praise we in festive song!	Inni festosi alziam!

Glory! Glory! Glory!	Gloria! gloria! gloria!
Glory oh King!	Gloria al Re!

WOMEN

The lotus buds and laurel	S'intrecci il loto al lauro
Entwine in fragrant bowers!	Sul crin dei vincitori!
A cloud of summer flowers	Nembo gentil di fiori
Hides all the swords in a veil.	Stenda sull'armi un vel.
Now dance Egyptian maidens	Danziam, fanciulle egizie,
To music sweet and holy,	Le mistiche carole,
Dance fervently and slowly,	Come d'intorno al sole
Honour the leader we hail.	Danzano gli astri in ciel.

PRIESTS [2]

All praise and glory to mighty gods	Della vittoria agl'arbitri
In Heaven; now bow down before them;	Supremi il guardo ergete;
Worship and adore them	Grazie agli Dei rendete
On this most blessed day.	Nel fortunato dì.

POPULACE
(women)

Dance fervently and slowly,	Come d'intorno al sole
Honour the leader we hail!	Danzano gli astri in ciel.

(men)

Praise we in festive song,	Inni festosi alziam al Re,
We praise our King in festive song!	Alziamo al Re.

PRIESTS

Worship, bow down before them	Grazie agli Dei rendete
On this most blessed day.	Nel fortunato dì.

The Egyptian troops march past the King [20]; then dancing girls with the spoil captured from the Ethiopians. | Ballabile [21, 22]

POPULACE [19]

Glorious warrior Radamès,	Vieni, o guerriero vindice,
Conqueror of our foes;	Vieni a gioir con noi;
We strew before our heroes,	Sul passo degli eroi
Laurel and fragrant bay!	I lauri, i fior versiam!

PRIESTS

The gods are everlasting,	Agli arbitri supremi
Bow down before them,	Il guardo ergete;
Worship the gods and adore them	Grazie agli Dei rendete
On this most blessed day.	Nel fortunato dì.

Radames enters.

POPULACE
(sopranos)

Hail Radamès!	Vieni, o guerrier,
Praise him, let all rejoice,	Vieni a gioir con noi,
Hail Radamès, victor of all our foes,	Sul passo degl'eroi
We strew before the heroes	I lauri, i fior versiam.
Laurels twin'd with bay.	
Hail glorious warrior, victor of all our	
foes.	

Glory, glory, glory,	Gloria, gloria, gloria,
Hail Radamès! Praise him,	Gloria al guerrier, vieni,
Praise him glorious hero!	Vieni a gioir con noi,
Hail Radamès, victor of all our foes.	Sul passo degl'eroi
We strew before the heroes	I lauri, i fior versiam.
Laurels twin'd with bay.	

PRIESTS

Worship, worship, worship,	Grazie, grazie, grazie,
Worship the gods,	Grazie agli Dei rendete,
Give them praise and glory!	Nel fortunato dì.
Worship the gods and sing their praise.	
Adore them, adore the gods and praise them.	

POPULACE

Glory! glory! glory!	Gloria! gloria! gloria!
Glory to Egypt!	Gloria all'Egitto, gloria!

The King descends from the throne to embrace Radamès.

THE KING

Valiant pride of your country, I here salute you.	Salvator della patria, io ti saluto.
Hero, see, my daughter is at hand to greet you	Vieni, e mia figlia di sua man ti porga
With Egypt's crown of triumph.	Il serto trionfale.

Radamès bows before Amneris, who crowns him. [4]

Your dearest wish	Ora a me chiedi
Today shall be granted. Nothing shall be barred or	Quanto più brami. Nulla a te negato
Denied to you . . . By Egypt's	Sarà in tal dì . . . lo giuro
Glorious crown I swear it: the gods are witness.	Per la corona mia, pei sacri Numi.

RADAMÈS

First bring the captive soldiers forth to stand	Concedi in pria che innanzi a te sien tratti
Before your throne . . .	I prigionier . . .

The Ethiopian prisoners enter, escorted by guards. The last of them is Amonasro, dressed as an officer.

RAMFIS, PRIESTS

Worship and glory to all the gods on high	Grazie agli Dei, grazie rendete
Bow down in worship on this most blessed day.	Nel fortunato dì.

AIDA
(rushing towards Amonasro)

Oh Heaven! Captive! My father!	Che veggo! . . . Egli? . . . Mio padre!

ALL
(except Aida)

Her father!	Suo padre!

65

AMNERIS

And in our power! In poter nostro!

AIDA
(embracing her father)

You! Captive here! Tu! Prigionier!

AMONASRO
(whispering to Aida)

Don't speak my name. Non mi tradir.

THE KING
(to Amonasro)

Come forward . . . T'appressa . . .

Tell me . . . you are . . . Dunque, tu sei?

AMONASRO

Her father. I also fought . . . Suo padre. Anch'io pugnai,

We were defeated . . . all I sought was death. Vinti noi fummo . . . morte invan cercai.

(indicating his uniform)

As you see, I am wearing the colours	Quest'assisa ch'io vesto vi dica
Of my King and my country in battle;	Che il mio Re, la mia patria ho difeso;
Fate was hostile to us and our armies . . .	Fu la sorte a nostr'armi nemica . . .
All our courage and might were in vain.	Tornò vano de' forti l'ardir.
At my feet in the dust of the battle	Al mio piè nella polve disteso
Lay our King sadly mangled and bleeding;	Giacque il Re da più colpi trafitto;
If to fight for your country is an evil,	Se l'amor della patria è delitto
We are guilty, we're ready to die!	Siam rei tutti, siam pronti a morir!

(to the King, in supplication) [23]

Mighty King, you are noble and glorious,	Ma tu, Re, tu signore possente,
Show us mercy, tho' you are victorious.	A costoro ti volgi clemente;
We today have been struck down by fortune,	Oggi noi siam percossi dal fato,
Ah, tomorrow it may be your turn to die.	Ah! doman voi potria il fato colpir.

AIDA

Mighty King, you are noble and glorious, *(etc.)* Ma tu, Re, tu signore possente, *(etc.)*

SLAVE-GIRLS, PRISONERS

We today have been struck down by fortune;	Sì: dai Numi percossi noi siamo;
Here we kneel to implore your compassion;	Tua pietà, tua clemenza imploriamo;
May you never be fated to suffer	Ah! giammai di soffrir vi sia dato
All the shame we have suffer'd today!	Ciò che in oggi n'è dato soffrir!

RAMFIS, PRIESTS [24]

Death, O King, to these savage invaders,	Struggi, o Re, queste ciurme feroci,
Close your heart when they try to persuade us. —	Chiudi il cor alle perfide voci:

AIDA, SLAVE-GIRLS, PRISONERS

Forbear! Pietà!

They are mark'd bv the gods for destruction. —

Fur dai Numi votati alla morte —

AIDA, SLAVE-GIRLS, PRISONERS

Forbear!

Pietà!

RAMFIS, PRIESTS

Let the will of the gods be obey'd.

Or de' Numi si compia il voler!

AIDA, SLAVE-GIRLS, PRISONERS

Forbear!

Pietà!

AIDA [23]

But you O King, are great in glory,
Show us mercy tho' you are
  victorious . . .

Ma tu, o Re, signore possente,
A costoro ti mostra clemente . . .

AMNERIS
(to herself)

How he eyes her, like a doting lover!
How they glow when they see one
  another!

(Quali sguardi sovr'essa ha rivolti!
Di qual fiamma balenano i volti!)

AMONASRO

We today tho' have been struck
  down by fortune
But one day it may be your
  turn to die!

Oggi noi siam percossi
  dal fato,
Voi doman potria il
  fato colpir.

THE KING

Now that fortune smiles in favour on our
  city,
Let us temper justice with mercy . . .

Or che fausti ne arridon gli eventi

A costoro mostriamci clementi . . .

SLAVE-GIRLS, PRISONERS

Here we kneel down to implore pity and
  kindness,
Ah, forbear, forbear!

Tua pietade, tua clemenza imploriamo

Ah, pietà! pietà!

POPULACE

Priests of Isis, your anger dismays us.
Hear the prayer of the vanquish'd.

Sacerdoti, gli sdegni placate,
L'umil prece ascoltate;

RAMFIS, PRIESTS

Destruction! Destruction! Destruction!
O King, these invaders all deserve to die!

A morte! a morte! a morte!
O Re, struggi queste ciurme!

RADAMÈS
(to himself)

Ah, that grief which the Fates send to
  tear her
Seems in my eyes to make her still fairer;
Ev'ry precious lament that she utters
Reawakens my heart's tender love.
Ev'ry precious lament that she utters
Reawakens my longing and love.

Il dolor che in quel volto favella

Al mio sguardo la rende più bella;
Ogni stilla del pianto adorato
Nel mio petto ravviva l'amor.(etc.)

67

(to herself)

How he eyes her, he dotes like a lover!   (Quali sguardi sovr'essa ha rivolti!
How they're glowing to see one another!   Di qual fiamma balenano i volti!
I'm abandon'd, I am sad and rejected,   Ed io sola, avvilita, rejetta?
Bitter vengeance is born in my heart!   La vendetta mi rugge nel cor.)

AMONASRO

Here we kneel: show your pity we beg   Tua pietà, tua clemenza imploriamo,
you *(etc.)*   *(etc.)*

THE KING

Now that fortune has smiled on our city   Or che fausti ne arridon gli eventi,
Let us temper our justice with mercy!   A costoro mostriamci clementi:
Ah, forbear! Mercy rises to Heaven   La pietà sale ai Numi gradita
Reaffirming kingly pow'r.   E rafferma de' prenci il poter.

AIDA

Show pity I beg you . . .   Tua pietà imploro . . .
We have today been struck down by   Oggi noi siam percossi,
fortune
But tomorrow it may be your own turn   Doman voi potria il fato colpir.
to die.

SLAVE-GIRLS, PRISONERS

Forbear, forbear. Ah, forbear!   Pietà, pietà, ah pietà!
Show your pity we implore.   Tua pietade, tua clemenza invochiamo.

POPULACE

Priests of Isis your anger dismays us.   Sacerdoti, gli sdegni placate,
Hear the prayer of the vanquish'd, we beg   L'umil prece de' vinti ascoltate;
you!

RAMFIS, PRIESTS

Let the will of the gods be obey'd!   Si compisca de' Numi il voler!
Death to savage invaders!   Struggi, o Re, queste ciurme feroci,
Let them perish; they are mark'd for   Fur dai Numi votati alla morte,
destruction.
Let the powerful will of the gods be   Si compisca dei Numi il voler!
obey'd.

AIDA [23]

Mighty King, you are noble and glorious   Ma tu, o Re, tu signore possente, *(etc.)*
(etc.)

RADAMÈS

Ah, her grief seems to make her still   Il dolor la rende più bella, *(etc.)*
fairer *(etc.)*

AMONASRO [23]

Mighty King, you are noble and glorious   Ma tu, o Re, tu signore possente, *(etc.)*
(etc.)

THE KING

Ah, forbear! Mercy rises *(etc.)*   La pietà sale ai Numi, *(etc.)*

SLAVE-GIRLS, PRISONERS

We today have been struck down by   Sì, dai Numi percossi noi siamo, *(etc.)*
fortune *(etc.)*

Death to savage invaders *(etc.)*   Struggi, o Re, queste ciurme feroci, *(etc.)*

King most mighty, you O King, are   Re possente, e tu, o Re possente,
  mighty
In power, ah, let mercy disarm you   Tu forte, a clemenza dischiudi il pensier,
  today.   *(etc.)*
Ah, show mercy to our vanquish'd foe.

I'm abandon'd, I, Amneris *(etc.)*   Ed io sola, avvilita, *(etc.)*

O King, by holy Isis   O Re: pei sacri Numi,
And by your crown in its shining   Per lo splendor della tua corona,
  splendour,
You swore to grant me all I wanted . . .   Compier giurasti il voto mio . . .

I swore.   Giurai.

Then hear me: for all prisoners here, I   Ebbene: a te pei prigionieri Etiopi
  beg of you,
Grant them their lives, let them go free.   Vita domando e libertà.

(to herself)
All of them!   (Per tutti!)

Death to our country's hated enemies!   Morte ai nemici della patria!

                        Grant   Grazia
Mercy to the wretched!   Per gl'infelici!

(to the King, then to Radamès)
                Beware O King.   Ascolta, o Re. Tu pure,
  And you our
Glorious hero, yield to the voice of   Giovine eroe, saggio consiglio ascolta:
  wisdom;
They are hardy, valiant fighters.   Son nemici e prodi sono . . .
They have vengeance in their hearts.   La vendetta hanno nel cor,
If you give them all their freedom,   Fatti audaci dal perdono
They will take up arms again!   Correranno all'armi ancor!

With Amonasro, their warrior King, all   Spento Amonasro, il Re guerrier, non
  hope of   resta
Revenge has perish'd.   Speranza ai vinti.

                As pledge of   Almeno,
Peace and security to all, keep   Arra di pace e securtà, fra noi
Aida and hold her father.   Resti col padre Aida.

THE KING

I'll do as you advise me,	Al tuo consiglio io cedo.
But there's a better pledge of peace and safety	Di securtà, di pace un miglior pegno
For the future. Radamès, your country's	Or io vo' darvi. Radamès, la patria
Debt is unbounded. Take in holy marriage	Tutto a te deve. D'Amneris la mano
Princess Amneris; rule over Egypt with her at	Premio ti sia. Sovra l'Egitto un giorno
Your side when I am gone.	Con essa regnerai.

AMNERIS
(to herself)

(Slave, you are nothing!	(Venga la schiava,
Now will you dare to steal away my lover?)	Venga a rapirmi l'amor mio . . . se l'osa!)

THE KING, POPULACE [19, 2, 20]

Glory to Isis, goddess fair,	Gloria all'Egitto, ad Iside,
You who protect and shelter,	Che il sacro suol difende,
The lotus buds and laurel	S'intrecci il loto al lauro
Entwine over the victor's brow.	Sul crin del vincitor.

SLAVE-GIRLS, PRISONERS

Glory to Egypt's clement ways,	Gloria al clemente Egizio
You who have loosed our fetters,	Che i nostri ceppi ha sciolto,
You give us back our liberty	Che ci ridona ai liberi
And in our native land.	Solchi del patrio suol.

RAMFIS, PRIESTS

Offer a hymn to Isis	Inni leviamo ad Iside
Defender of our great country!	Che il sacro suol difende!
And pray that the smile of fortune	Preghiam che i fati arridano
Will always be kind to our land.	Fausti alla patria ognor.

AIDA
(to herself)

Alas what hope is left me now?	(Qual speme omai più restami?
For him a glorious future . . .	A lui la gloria, il trono,
For me oblivion, the bitter tears	A me l'oblio, le lacrime
Of my despairing love.	D'un disperato amor.)

RADAMÈS
(to himself)

The gods have turn'd away from me.	(D'avverso Nume il folgore
Their thunder falls upon me . . .	Sul capo mio discende . . .
Ah no, the throne of Egypt	Ah no! d'Egitto il soglio
Rates low by my Aida's heart.	Non val d'Aida il cor.)

AMNERIS
(to herself)

Ah, how I glow with happiness,	(Dall'inatteso giubilo
Joy never came so suddenly;	Inebbriata io sono;
Here in one day I realise	Tutti in un dì si compiono
The dream I hold so dear.	I sogni del mio cor.)

70

RAMFIS

We pray that fortune always	Preghiam che i fati arridano
Will smile on our holy land.	Fausti alla patria ognor.

THE KING, POPULACE

Glory! We praise the Gods!	Gloria ad Iside!
Glory! Glory!	Gloria! gloria!

AMONASRO
(aside to Aida)

Take heart, a time of comfort	Fa' cor: della tua patria
Is coming for your country;	I lieti eventi aspetta;
For us the day of vengeance	Per noi della vendetta
Now very soon will dawn.	Già prossimo è l'albor.

RADAMÈS

The gods have turned away from me!	Qual inatteso folgore!
Their thunder falls upon me!	Sul capo mio discende!
Ah no! the throne of Egypt	Ah no! d'Egitto il trono
Rates low by my Aida's heart!	Non val d'Aida il cor.

AMNERIS

All in a day I realise	(Tutte in un dì si compiono
The sweet dream I hold so dear.	Le gioje del mio cor.
Ah! now I glow with happiness,	Ah! dall'inatteso gaudio
Joy never came so suddenly.	Inebbriata io sono.)

AMONASRO

Take heart, a time of comfort	Fa' cor: la tua patria
Comes soon for your dear country;	I lieti eventi aspetta;
For us the day of vengeance	Per noi della vendetta
Now very soon will dawn.	Già prossimo è l'albor.

THE KING, POPULACE

Glory to Egypt! Glory to Isis,	Gloria all'Egitto! ad Iside
Goddess fair, you who protect,	Che il sacro suol difende!
The lotus buds and laurel	S'intrecci il loto al lauro
Entwine over the victor's brow!	Sul crin del vincitor!

RAMFIS, PRIESTS

Offer a hymn to Isis	Inni leviamo ad Iside
Defender of our great country.	Che il sacro suol difende!
And pray that fortune always smiles	Preghiam che i fati arridano
On our holy country.	Fausti alla patria ognor.

AIDA
(to herself)

For me oblivion, the bitter tears	A me l'oblio, le lacrime
Of my despairing love.	D'un disperato amor.
Ah! alas what hope is left me now?	Ah! qual speme omai più restami?
For him a glorious future . . .	A lui la gloria, il trono . . .
For me oblivion, the bitter tears	A me l'oblio, le lacrime
Of my despairing love!	D'un disperato amor.

SLAVES, PRISONERS

Glory to Egypt's clement ways,	Gloria al clemente Egizio
You who have loosed our fetters.	Che i nostri ceppi ha sciolto,
You now restore us to freedom	Che ci ridona ai liberi
And also to our native land.	Solchi del patrio suol.

Act Three

The banks of the Nile — granite rocks with palm trees. On the summit of the rocks a temple dedicated to Isis half-hidden in foliage. Starry, moonlit night. | Introduction, Prayer-Chorus, Romanza

CHORUS
(in the temple)

Thou art to great Osiris	O tu che sei d'Osiride
Bride and immortal mother,	Madre immortale e sposa,
Goddess who wakest chaste desire	Diva che i casti palpiti
Deep in the human heart . . .	Desti agli umani in cor;

HIGH PRIESTESS

Have pity on us . . .	Soccorri a noi . . .

CHORUS

Grant us thy aid and pity	Soccorri a noi pietosa
Font of almighty love,	Madre d'immenso amor,
Have pity on us.	Soccorri a noi.

Amneris, Ramfis, attendants and guards alight from a boat that has drawn into the riverbank.

RAMFIS
(to Amneris)

Come to the shrine of Isis, and on the night	Vieni d'Iside al Tempio: alla vigilia
Before you are married invoke	Delle tue nozze, invoca
The holy goddess's favour. To holy Isis	Della Diva il favore. Iside legge
Ev'ry human heart is open; all that is hidden	De' mortali nel core: ogni mistero
Deep inside us is known to Isis.	Degli umani a lei noto.

AMNERIS

Yes, and I will pray that Radamès may truly	Sì; io pregherò che Radamès mi doni
Give me his heart, for truly mine to him	Tutto il suo cor, come il mio cor a lui
Is sacred for ever . . .	Sacro è per sempre . . .

RAMFIS

Now enter.	Andiamo.
You will pray till the sunrise: I shall be with you.	Pregherai fino all'alba; io sarò teco.

All enter the temple.

CHORUS

Grant us thy aid and pity,	Soccorri a noi pietosa,
Font of almighty love,	Madre d'immenso amor,
Have pity on us.	Soccorri a noi.

Aida enters cautiously. [1]

AIDA

Soon Radamès will come! What will he tell me?	Qui Radamès verrà! Che vorrà dirmi?

72

I'm frighten'd. Ah, cruel man,
If you're coming to say farewell for ever,
The dark Nile will surely bury me . . .
Hide me forever . . .
Peace I may find and perhaps oblivion.
Oh, how I long with all my heart, to see
  my home!

[25]

Oh, skies of blue, oh, soft, caressing
  breezes,
Land where my childhood serenely
  passed in joy . . .
Oh fertile meadows . . . scented with
  summer flowers . . .
Ah, gods above me, when shall I see my
  home?
Ah, dearest homeland, ah, my home I
  long for you!

Oh, fragrant valleys, oh, so blessed
  haven!
Once I had hopes of true and faithful
  love . . .
Now that my dream of love vanishes for
  ever . . .
Oh, how I long to be in my native land.
Ah, dearest homeland, *(etc.)*

Io tremo! . . . Ah! se tu vieni
A recarmi, o crudel, l'ultimo addio,
Del Nilo i cupi vortici
Mi daran tomba . . .
E pace forse e oblìo.
O patria mia, mai piu ti rivedro!

O cieli azzurri, o dolci aure native,

Dove sereno il mio mattin brillò,

O verdi colli . . . o profumate rive . . .

O patria mia, mai più ti rivedrò!

O fresche valli, o questo asil beato,

Che un dì promesso dall'amor mi fu;

Or che d'amore il sogno è dileguato,

O patria mia, non ti vedrò mai più!
O patria mia, *(etc.)*

Amonasro enters. | Duet

Heav'n! My father!

Ciel! mio padre!

AMONASRO
I come, full of concern
For you Aida. Not a look has
Escaped me. I realise you
Love Radames . . . he loves you . . . you
  will meet him,
The Pharaoh's only daughter is your
  rival . . .
Curse the Pharaoh! Curse his daughter!
They'd destroy us!

A te grave cagion
M'adduce, Aida. Nulla sfugge al mio
Sguardo. D'amor ti struggi
Per Radames, ei t'ama, qui lo attendi.

Dei Faraon la figlia è tua rivale . . .

Razza infame, abborrita, e a noi
fatale!

AIDA
And I am in her power! I, Amonasro's
Daughter!

E in suo potere io sto! Io d'Amonasro
Figlia!

AMONASRO
You are in her power. No! If
  you wish it
You can fight with Amneris and defeat
  her.
Then homeland and sceptre and love,
  shall all be yours!
Once again you will see our lofty forests,
Our fragrant valleys, our temples bright [26]
  with gold!

In poter di lei! No! se lo brami

La possente rival tu vincerai,

E patria, e trono, e amor, tutto tu avrai.

Rivedrai le foreste imbalsamate,
Le fresche valli, i nostri templi d'or!

73

AIDA

Once again I will see our lofty forests,	Rivedrò le foreste imbalsamate!
Our fragrant valleys, our temples bright with gold!	Le fresche valli, i nostri templi d'òr!

AMONASRO

The happy bride of him you love and treasure,	Sposa felice a lui che amasti tanto,
Your whole existence only to enjoy . . .	Tripudii immensi ivi potrai gioir . . .

AIDA

A single day of such enchanting pleasure . . .	Un giorno solo di sì dolce incanto,
To know an hour of such deep joy, and then to die!	Un'ora di tal gioia, e poi morir!

AMONASRO

Now remember the blasphemous Egyptian	Pur rammenti che a noi l'Egizio immite,
Profaning our temples, our altars and our homes . . .	Le case, i templii, e l'are profano . . .
Hanging fetters on innocent young virgins . . .	Trasse in ceppi le vergini rapite . . .
Mothers . . . children . . . they all were put to death.	Madri, vecchi, fanciulli ei trucidò.

AIDA

Ah, I remember days of bitter grieving!	Ah! ben rammento quegl'infausti giorni!
Weeping, lamenting, we were in despair.	Rammento i lutti che il cor soffrì!
Great gods, oh hear me, show us now your mercy,	Deh! fate, o Numi che per noi ritorni
Grant us a fair season of peace again.	L'alba invocata de' sereni dì.

AMONASRO

Remember.	Rammenta.
I have an army. Our people now are waiting	Non fia che tardi. In armi ora si desta
For my orders; ev'rything's prepared . . .	Il popol nostro; tutto e pronto gia,
Success is sure . . . One single fact is missing.	Vittoria avrem. Solo a saper mi resta,
We must know by what path the foe will march . . .	Qual sentier il nemico seguira.

AIDA

Who could ever discover? Ah, who?	Chi scoprirlo potria? chi mai?

AMONASRO

Aida!	Tu stessa!

AIDA

I!	Io!

AMONASRO

Radamès comes here to meet you . . .	Radamès so che qui attendi . . . Ei
He loves you . . .	t'ama . . .
He commands the Egyptians . . . You follow?	Ei conduci gli Egizii . . . Intendi?

74

Betray him!   Orrore!

Betray the man I love? No, no, ah, no.   Che mi consigli tu? No, no, giammai!

AMONASRO [27]
(with savage fury)

Destroy us, you armies	Su, dunque! sorgete
Of Egypt, destroy us!	Egizie coorti!
Reduce all our cities	Col fuoco struggete
To ashes and dust . . .	Le nostre città . . .
Spread fury and terror,	Spargete il terrore,
Destruction and slaughter,	Le stragi, le morti
For now there is nothing	Al vostro furore
To stand in your way.	Più freno non v'ha.

AIDA

Ah, father, father!   Ah, padre! padre!

AMONASRO
(repulsing her)

My daughter   Mia figlia

No longer!   Ti chiami! . . .

AIDA
(thrown to the ground and begging)

Forbear, forbear, forbear!   Pieta! pieta! pieta!

AMONASRO

Rivers of blood drown all our	Flutti di sangue scorrono
Ruined and beaten cities . . .	Sulle città dei vinti.
Mark me, from gloomy caves below	Vedi? dai negri vortici
Shades of the dead are rising . . .	Si levano gli estinti.
All of them point at you and cry:	Ti additan essi e gridano,
'Destroyer of your land!'	'Per te la patria muor!'

AIDA

Forbear! Forbear! Father, forbear!   Pieta! pieta, padre, pieta!

AMONASRO
(sotto voce)

Now I see a skeleton	Una larva orribile
Rising among the shadows . . .	Fra l'ombre a noi s'affaccia.
Horror! It marks your features —	Trema! le scarne braccia —

AIDA
(with no sound)

Ah!   Ah!

AMONASRO

Pointing a shrivelled arm . . .   Sul capo tuo levò . . .

AIDA

Father! . . .   Padre! . . .

AMONASRO

Do you not see . . .   Tua madre ell'è . . .

No!   No!

AMONASRO

Your mother's hand . . .   Ravvisala . . .

AIDA

Ah!   Ah!

AMONASRO

Raised up to curse you? . . .   Ti maledice . . .

AIDA
(with utmost terror)

Ah no, dear father, spare your child!   Ah! no! ah! no! padre, pietà! pietà!

AMONASRO
(repulsing her)

No more my daughter . . .   Non sei mia figlia!
For you are only a slave of Pharaoh!   Dei Faraoni tu sei la schiava!

AIDA
(with a cry)

Ah! Forgive, forgive, forgive!   Ah! pietà, pietà, pietà!
Father . . . The Egyptians . . have   Padre! a costoro . . . schiava . . . non
    not . . . enslaved me . . .   sono . . .

(dragging herself to her father's feet)

Ah, do not curse me . . . do not revile   Non maledirmi, non imprecarmi;
    me . . .
I am your daughter . . . do not disown   Ancor tua figlia potrai chiamarmi,
    me . . .
I shall be worthy of you and my land.   Della mia patria degna sarò.

AMONASRO [28]

Think how your people all have been   Pensa che un popolo, vinto, straziato,
    subjected
Through you alone they return to life.   Pe te soltanto risorger può . . .

AIDA

Oh dearest country, how much you cost   O patria! o patria quanto mi costi!
    me!

AMONASRO

Have courage, he's coming . . . there I   Coraggio! ei giunge, là tutto udrò . . .
    I shall hide . . .

He hides among the palm trees as Radamès enters. | Duet, Scena — Finale Three

RADAMÈS [29]

At last I see you, sweetest Aida . . .   Pur ti riveggo, mia dolce Aida . . .

AIDA

Don't say that . . . leave me . . . what   T'arresta, vanne, che speri ancor?
    hope is left?

RADAMÈS

A lover's passion has led me here to you.   A te d'appresso l'amor mi guida.

AIDA

Tomorrow's dawn will bring your marriage vows.	Te i riti attendono d'un altro amor.
Amneris loves you . . .	D'Amneris sposo . . .

RADAMÈS

What's that to me?	Che parli mai?
My own Aida, I live for you.	Te sola, Aida, te deggio amar.
The gods above us are witness I love you.	Gli Dei m'ascoltano, tu mia sarai.

AIDA

With such a falsehood you stain your name.	D'uno spergiuro non ti macchiar!
Hero I loved, I cannot love a liar.	Prode t'amai, non t'amerei spergiuro.

RADAMÈS

But do you doubt my love, dear Aida?	Dell'amor mio dubiti, Aida?

AIDA

Do you	E come
Imagine you'll baffle the charms of Amneris	Speri sottrarti d'Amneris ai vezzi,
The will of the King, and the wish of the people,	Del Re al voler, del tuo popolo ai voti,
And all the priests in their fury?	Dei Sacerdoti all'ira?

RADAMÈS

Listen Aida.	Odimi, Aida.
Your people rise again, arming for battle . . .	Nel fiero anelito di nuova guerra
The troops are gathering . . . soon they will march . . .	Il suolo Etiope si ridestò . . .
And when invaders strike across our borders,	I tuoi già invadono la nostra terra,
I will be chosen, I shall command.	Io degli Egizii duce sarò.
And in the triumph, when we're victorious,	Fra il suon, fra i plausi della vittoria,
I'll kneel to Pharaoh, open my heart —	Al Re mi prostro, gli svelo il cor —
Then you will wear the crown of my glory,	Sarai tu il serto della mia gloria,
We will live in the bliss of love.	Vivrem beati d'eterno amore.

AIDA

Do you not fear Amneris —	Nè d'Amneris paventi
The tempest of her rage? Her dreadful vengeance,	Il vindice furor? la sua vendetta,
Like the lightning from heaven,	Come folgor tremenda,
Will fall on me and on my father, my people.	Cadrà su me, sul padre mio, su tutti.

RADAMÈS

I will defend you.	Io vi difendo.

AIDA

In vain! You could not help me . . .	Invan, tu nol potresti . . .
Yet if you love me, there is always a course	Pur, se tu m'ami, ancor s'apre una via

77

For us to take . . .   Di scampo a noi . . .

RADAMÈS
          Tell me!   Quale?

AIDA
               Escape . . .   Fuggir . . .

RADAMÈS
               Escape!   Fuggire!

AIDA
(with impulsive warmth)

We'd leave this white oppressive heat   Fuggiam gli ardori inospiti
And all this barren desert,   Di queste lande ignude;
Turn to another fatherland,   Una novella patria
Where love could blossom truly.   Al nostro amor si schiude.
There where the virgin forests rise, [30]   Là . . . tra foreste vergini,
Perfum'd with fragrant flowers   Di fiori profumate,
In ecstasy of love   In estasi beate
We'll bury all regret.   La terra scorderem.

RADAMÈS
To seek another country   Sovra una terra estrania
And both together fly.   Teco fuggir dovrei!
Abandoning my homeland,   Abbandonar la patria,
Leaving my household gods!   L'are de' nostri Dei!
The soil where first I gathered   Il suol dov'io raccolsi
My laurel leaves of glory,   Di gloria i primi allori,
The place of our first loving,   Il ciel de' nostri amori
How could we both forget?   Come scordar potrem?

AIDA
There where the virgin forests rise *(etc.)*   Là . . . tra foreste vergini, *(etc.)*

RADAMÈS
How to forget the place where we   Il ciel de' nostri amori
   declared our love?   Come scordar potrem?

AIDA
Beneath my sky a freer love   Sotto il mio ciel, più libero
Would flourish more than ever   L'amor ne fia concesso;
And there we'd pray together   Ivi nel tempio istesso
Sharing our gods as well.   Gli stessi Numi avrem.

RADAMÈS
Abandon my dear homeland   Abbandonar la patria
And leave my household gods!   L'are dei nostri Dei!
The place of our first loving,   Il ciel de' nostri amori
How could we both forget?   Come scordar potrem?

AIDA
Ah, come, ah come!   Fuggiam, fuggiam . . .

RADAMÈS
Aida!   Aida!

You don't love me . . . Go!   Tu non m'ami . . . Va!

RADAMÈS

Not love you!   Non t'amo!

AIDA

Go!   Va!

RADAMÈS

There never was a man nor   Mortal giammai nè Dio
Even a god who burned with love as I   Arse d'amor al par del mio possente.
  for you.

AIDA

No! no! Amneris waits   Va, va, t'attende all'ara
To take you . . .   Amneris . . .

RADAMÈS

No! I swear . . .   No! giammai!

AIDA

You swear? You mean it?   Giammai, dicesti?
Then let the axe fall swiftly   Allor piombi la scure
On me and on my father.   Su me, sul padre mio . . .

RADAMÈS
(with impassioned resolution)
Ah no! We'll fly then!   Ah no! fuggiamo!
Hand in hand we'll fly together,   [31]Sì: fuggiam da queste mura,
Find a pathway across the desert;   Al deserto insiem fuggiamo:
Here misfortune rules forever;   Qui sol regna la sventura,
There the heavens smile with love.   Là si schiude un ciel d'amor.
Barren deserts will roll around us,   I deserti interminati
The only marriage bed we lie on,   A noi talamo saranno,
In their courses stars will shine on   Su noi gli astri brilleranno
With a limpid light above.   Di più limpido fulgor.

AIDA

Daily heaven smiles to bless us   Nella terra avventurata
In my father's land of plenty;   De' miei padri, il ciel ne attende;
Sweet and balmy airs caress us,   Ivi l'aura è imbalsamata,
Flowers blossom in ev'ry grove.   Ivi il suolo è aromi e fior.
Fragrant valleys and summer meadows,   Fresche valli e verdi prati
The only marriage bed we lie on,   A noi talamo saranno,
In their courses stars will shine on   Su noi gli astri brilleranno
With a limpid light above.   Di più limpido fulgor.

AIDA AND RADAMÈS

Come away, we'll fly together,   [29]Vieni meco, insiem fuggiamo
Leave behind this land of sorrow!   Questa terra di dolor.
How I love you, how I love you!   Vieni meco, t'amo, t'amo!
Come, and love will be our guide.   A noi duce fia l'amor.

They begin to hurry away, when Aida stops.

AIDA

But tell me, by what path
Can we avoid the troops of
Marching soldiers?

Ma dimmi; per qual via
Eviterem le schiere
Degli armati?

RADAMÈS

We have settled that the road
Where my men will attack will be
deserted
Up until morning . . .

Il sentier scelto dai nostri
A piombar sul nemico fia deserto
Fino a domani . . .

AIDA

Say which it is?

E qual sentier?

RADAMÈS

The gorges
Of Napata . . .

Le gole
Di Nàpata.

AMONASRO
(coming forward)

The gorges of Napata!
There I will post my men!

Di Nàpata le gole!
Ivi saranno i miei!

RADAMÈS

But who has
heard us?

Oh! chi ci ascolta?

AMONASRO

Aida's father, Ethiopia's King.

D'Aida il padre e degli Etiopi il Re.

RADAMÈS
(with the utmost agitation and surprise)

You! Amonasro! You! The King?
Heaven! You cannot . . .

Tu! Amonasro! tu! il Re? Numi! che
dissi?

(with a cry)

No . . . it's not true . . . it's not true,
This is a nightmare.

No! non è ver! sogno, delirio è questo.

AIDA

Ah no, be calm, and trust in me —

Ah no! ti calma, ascoltami —

AMONASRO

You need the love of Aida . . .

A te l'amor d'Aida . . .

AIDA

My loving hand will lead you.

All'amor mio t'affida.

AMONASRO

Her love will bring you a throne.

Un soglio innalzerà!

RADAMÈS

My name is now dishonour'd!
For you I've played the traitor and
betrayed my fatherland!

Io son disonorato!
Per te tradii la patria! tradii la patria!

AIDA

Ah, trust me!

Ti calma!

80

AMONASRO

No, no! No guilt can fall on you;
It was the will of fate, it had to
  happen . . .

No: tu non sei colpevole:
Era voler del fato . . .

RADAMÈS

My name is now dishonour'd!

Io son disonorato!

AIDA

Ah no!   Ah no!

AMONASRO

No!   No!

RADAMÈS

For you I played the traitor!
For you I sold my fatherland!

Per te tradii la patria!
Per te tradii la patria!

AMONASRO

No. No guilt can fall on you.

No: tu non sei colpevole.

AIDA

Ah, trust me . . .

Ti calma . . .

AMONASRO

There where the Nile is glittering,
Soldiers of mine are waiting.
Ev'ry desire that your heart has longed
  for
Will soon be crowned in love.
Come then, quickly, quickly.

Vien: oltre il Nil ne attendono
I prodi a noi devoti,
Là del tuo cor i voti

Coronerà l'amor.
Vieni, vieni, vieni.

(dragging Radamès)

AMNERIS
(coming out of the temple, with Ramfis)

We're betrayed!   Traditor!

AIDA

My rival here!   La mia rival!

AMONASRO
(rushing at Amneris with a dagger)

Would you try to spoil my triumph?   L'opra mia a strugger vieni!
Die then!   Muori!

RADAMÈS
(rushing between them)

Don't strike her, you madman!   Arresta, insano!

AMONASRO

Oh, fury!   O rabbia!

RAMFIS

Guards there, come here!   Guardie, olà!

RADAMÈS
(to Aida and Amonasro)

Quickly! Go quickly!   Presto! fuggite!

81

AMONASRO
(dragging Aida)

Quickly my daughter!   Vieni, o figlia!

RAMFIS
(to the guards, who pursue Aida and Amonasro, who have escaped)

Follow closely!   L'inseguite!

RADAMÈS
(to Ramfis)

Priest of Isis, I yield my sword.   Sacerdote, io resto a te.

The last moments of 'Aida' Act Three, at Her Majesty's Theatre, London (1879), with Marie Roze (Aida), Trebelli (Amneris), Frapolli (Radamès), Pantaleoni (Amonasro) and Pinto (Ramfis) (BBC Hulton Picture Library)

Act Four

Scene One. *A hall in the King's palace. On the left a large portal leading to the subterranean hall of justice. A passage on the right leading to the prison of Radamès. | Scena and Duet*

Amneris mournfully crouched before the portal

AMNERIS [5]

The detestable slave escapes my vengeance . . .	L'abborrita rivale a me sfuggia . . .
And from the priests now Radamès is waiting	Dai sacerdoti Radamès attende
The punishment of traitors. He is no	Dei traditor la pena . . . Traditor
Traitor, I swear . . . Yet he revealed the mighty	Egli non è . . . Pur rivelò di guerra
Secret of battle . . . Flight was the course he'd chosen . . .	L'alto segreto. Egli fuggir volea,
And with Aida. They're a pair of traitors!	Con lei fuggire! Traditori tutti!
Destroy them! Destroy them!	A morte! A morte!
Oh! Gods forgive me! I love him,	Oh! che mai parlo? io l'amo,
I love him . . . This insane, despairing [4]	Io l'amo sempre. Disperato, insano
Love for him is driving me to madness.	È quest'amor che la mia vita strugge.
Ah! if he only could love me!	Oh! s'ei potesse amarmi!
I long to save him . . . But can I?	Vorrei salvarlo. E come?
I'll see him! Soldiers: Radamès may enter.	Si tenti! Guardie: Radamès qui venga.

Radamès is brought in by the guards. [32]

Soon all the priests will gather here,	Già i sacerdoti adunansi,
Judgement will soon be spoken;	Arbitri del tuo fato;
You are accused of treachery;	Pur dell'accusa orribile
Your silence must be broken;	Scolparti ancor t'è dato;
Defend yourself I beg you;	Ti scolpa, e la tua grazia
I will appeal to Pharaoh	Io pregherò dal trono,
And beg his kingly favour	E nunzia di perdono,
And beg that he will grant	E nunzia di perdono,
Forgiveness and spare your life.	Di vita, a te sarò.

RADAMÈS

The judges will never hear from me	Di mie discolpe i giudici
Any defence or reason;	Mai non udran l'accento;
I call the gods to witness here	Dinanzi ai Numi, agl'uomini,
I never plotted treason.	Nè vil, nè reo mi sento.
In innocence I uttered	Profferse il labbro incauto
The words that have offended,	Fatal segreto, è vero,
But all that I intended	Ma puro il mio pensiero
Was to be true, I swear.	E l'onor mio restò.

AMNERIS

Then save your life, defend yourself.	Salvati dunque e scolpati.

RADAMÈS

No!	No!

You will die . . .   Tu morrai . . .

RADAMÈS

          My life is   La vita
Hateful! Ev'ry pleasure   Abborro; d'ogni gaudio
Is turned to bitter ashes,   La fonte inaridita,
And hope is gone for ever.   Svanita ogni speranza,
I pray that I may die.   Sol bramo di morir.

AMNERIS [33]

No never! Ah! you must live, ah, yes   Morire! ah! tu dei vivere!
You must live because I love you.   Sì, all'amor mio vivrai;
I feel I know the pains of death   Per te le angoscie orribili
And now I want to save you: Di morte io già provai;
I love . . . I suffer torture . . .   T'amai, soffersi tanto,
The nights I spend in weeping . . .   Vegliai le notti in pianto,
My country, my sceptre, my throne and   E patria, e trono, e vita
  my life,
All I'd surrender, all the world I'd   Tutto darei per te.
  surrender for you.

RADAMÈS [33]

A traitor to my country . . .   Per essa anch'io la patria
I am dishonour'd and all for her . . .   E l'onor mio tradia . . .

AMNERIS

No more of her . . .   Di lei non più!

RADAMÈS

       Dishonour   L'infamia
Awaits me, you want me living?   M'attende, e vuoi ch'io viva?
Misery overwhelms me,   Misero appien mi festi,
You've taken Aida from me . . .   Aida a me togliesti,
You may have killed her . . . before   Spenta l'hai forse, e in dono
Offering life to me.   Offri la vita a me?

AMNERIS

Do you think I've murdered her!   Io, di sua morte origine!
No, she is living . . .   No! vive Aida . . .

RADAMÈS

       Living!   Vive!

AMNERIS

Egypt had tasted victory . . .   Nei disperati aneliti
The foe was fleeing blindly . . .   Dell'orde fuggitive
Down went her father . . .   Sol cadde il padre . . .

RADAMÈS

      And she?   Ed ella?

AMNERIS

Vanish'd and no-one here has   Sparve ne piu novella
Seen her . . .   S'ebbe . . .

RADAMÈS

    The gods will lead her to   Gli Dei l'adducano
Safety among her people,   Salva alle patrie mura,

She'll never know the torments
Of one who dies for her!

E ignori la sventura
Di chi per lei morrà!

AMNERIS

But if I save you, swear to me
You won't see her again . . .

Ma, s'io ti salvo, giurami
Che più non la vedrai . . .

RADAMÈS

I cannot!

Nol posso!

AMNERIS

You must renounce her
For ever . . . life will be yours!

A lei rinunzia
Per sempre, e tu vivrai!

RADAMÈS

I cannot!

Nol posso!

AMNERIS

Once more I ask you;
Renounce Aida . . .

Anco una volta:
A lei rinuncia . . .

RADAMÈS

It's useless . . .

È vano.

AMNERIS

You cannot want to perish?

Morir vuoi dunque, insano?

RADAMÈS

I pray that death come soon.

Pronto a morir son già.

AMNERIS

Who will save you, wretched madman,
Who will save you from destruction?
Since you spurn the love I offer,
All my joy is turned to care.
Gods in heaven grant me vengeance;
See my tears of black despair.

Chi ti salva, sciagurato,
Dalla sorte che t'aspetta?
In furore hai tu cangiato
Un amor ch'egual non ha.
De' miei pianti la vendetta
Or dal ciel si compirà.

RADAMÈS

Death I greet you, welcome I give you,
Since I die for her I cherish;

È la morte un ben supremo
Se per lei morir m'è dato;

AMNERIS

Ah, who will save you?

Ah! chi ti salva?

RADAMÈS

Full of joy, knowing I perish,
Full of immense accord with her.

Nel subir l'estremo fato
Gaudii immensi il cor avrà;

AMNERIS

Gods in heaven, grant me vengeance,
See, oh, see my tears of black despair.

De' miei pianti la vendetta
Or dal ciel si compirà.

RADAMÈS

Full of rejoicing I die for her.
Human anger cannot touch me,
Show me pity if you dare.

Gaudii immensi il cor avrà;
L'ira umana più non temo,
Temo sol la tua pietà.

Amneris falls despairingly on a chair, Radamès leaves surrounded by guards. | Scene of the Judgement

AMNERIS
(alone, in the utmost despair)

Alas! I feel I'm dying . . . Ah, who will save him?	Ohimè! morir mi sento! Oh! chi lo salva?
He is now in their power,	E in poter di costoro
(choked with tears)	
I'm guilty . . . he is lost! . . . Oh how I curse the	Io stessa lo gettai! Ora, a te impreco
Jealousy that drove me! His death is certain;	Atroce gelosia, che la sua morte
For me a life of endless grief and mourning!	E il lutto eterno del mio cor segnasti!

The Priests process into the subterranean hall. [2]

Oh, how I fear these stern,	Ecco i fatali,
Cruel judges, the lords of destruction . . .	Gl'inesorati ministri di morte . . .
Ah, I'll not look upon these pallid phantoms!	Oh! ch'io non vegga quelle bianche larve!

(she covers her face with her hands)

He is now in their power . . .	E in poter di costoro
And I have sealed his fate!	Io stessa lo gettai!
I'm guilty! He is lost!	Io stessa lo gettai!

RAMFIS, PRIESTS
(from the hall)

Spirit of Isis on us all descending!	Spirto del Nume sovra noi discendi!
Lighten our darkness with your flame eternal;	Ne avviva al raggio dell'eterna luce;
Now thro' our lips express thy justice unending!	Pel labbro nostro tua giustizia apprendi.

AMNERIS

Ye gods above, I beg, I kneel before you;	Numi, pietà del mio straziato core.
For he is innocent and you must save,	Egli è innocente, lo salvate, o Numi!
You must save him or I shall die of sorrow.	Disperato, tremendo è il mio dolore!

Radamès and the guards cross the stage, and enter the hall.

RAMFIS, PRIESTS

Spirit of Isis —	Spirto del Nume —

AMNERIS
(seeing Radamès, with a cry)

Ah! who will save him?	Oh! chi lo salva?

RAMFIS, PRIESTS

— on us all descending!	— sovra noi discendi!

AMNERIS

Ah, who will save him? I feel I will die!	Oh, chi lo salva? mi sento morir!
Alas! Alas! I feel I will die!	Ohimè! ohimè! mi sento morir!

RAMFIS
(in the crypt)

Radamès! Radamès! Radamès!	Radamès! Radamès! Radamès!

You did betray
Your country's highest secrets to
    Amonasro . . .
Defend yourself!

Tu rivelasti
Della patria i segreti allo straniero . . .

Discolpati!

Defend yourself!

Discolpati!

He is silent . . .

Egli tace . . .

He must die!

Traditor!

Ah, have pity, gods, you must save him,
    oh hear my pray'r!

Ah, pietà! egli e innocente! Numi,
    pietà!

Radamès! Radamès! Radamès! You did
    desert
Egypt's army the day before the start of
    battle . . .
Defend yourself!

Radames! Radames! Radames! tu
    disertasti
Dal campo il dì che precedea la
    pugna . . .
Discolpati!

Defend yourself!

Discolpati!

He is silent . . .

Egli tace . . .

He must die!

Traditor!

Ah, have pity, gods, you must save him,
    ah, hear my pray'r!

Ah, pietà! ah, lo salvate, Numi, pietà!

Radamès! Radamès! Radamès! You
    broke your oath
And were false to your country, your
    King and your word!
Defend yourself!

Radamès! Radamès! Radamès! tua fe
    violasti
Alla patria spergiuro, al Re, all'onor.

Discolpati!

Defend yourself!

Discolpati!

He is silent . . .

Egli tace . . .

He must die!

Traditor!

Ah, have pity, gods, you must save him,
    ah, hear my pray'r!

Ah, pieta! ah, lo salvate, Numi, pieta!

Radamès, our decision is taken;

Radamès, è deciso il tuo fato:

You will suffer the death of a traitor;   Degli infami la morte tu avrai;
By the shrine of the god you've forsaken,   Sotto l'ara del Nume sdegnato,
You'll be buried alive in a tomb.   A te vivo fia schiuso l'avel.

AMNERIS

To be buried alive? Cruel monsters!   A lui vivo . . . la tomba . . . oh,
                                       gl'infami!

You will always be thirsty for blood . . .   Nè di sangue son paghi giammai;
And you say you are servants of God!   E si chiaman ministri del ciel!

RAMFIS, PRIESTS
(returning from the crypt) [2]

He must die! He must die! He must die!   Traditor! traditor! traditor!

AMNERIS

Priests of Isis: you're guilty of murder!   Sacerdoti: compiste un delitto!
Pitiless tigers, you reek of destruction.   Tigri infami di sangue assetate,
All the earth and the gods condemn your   Voi la terra ed i Numi oltraggiate . . .
    verdict . . .
Ah, you punish an innocent man.   Voi punite chi colpe non ha!

RAMFIS, PRIESTS

Sentence of death! Sentence of death! Of   E traditor! e traditor! morra.
    death!

AMNERIS
(to Ramfis)

Priest of Isis, the man you are killing   Sacerdote: quest'uomo che uccidi,
Might have ruled as my heart's dear   Tu lo sai, da me un giorno fu amato,
    beloved . . .
May the curse of a woman broken-   L'anatema d'un core straziato
    hearted,
Fall on your senses, avenging his blood!   Col suo sangue su te ricadrà!

RAMFIS, PRIESTS

Sentence of death! Sentence of death! Of   E traditor! e traditor! morra.
    death!

AMNERIS

All the earth and the gods condemn your   Voi la terra ed i Numi oltraggiate . . .
    verdict . . .

RAMFIS, PRIESTS

Of death!   Morrà!

AMNERIS

Ah, you punish an innocent man.   Voi punite chi colpe non ha!
Ah no, oh no, not he.   Ah, no, ah no, non è,
He must not die, I beg, I implore!   Non e traditor . . . pieta!

RAMFIS, PRIESTS

He has to die!   E traditor! morra! morrà!
Traitor die, traitor die, traitor die!   Traditor! traditor! traditor!

The priests leave.

AMNERIS

Evil priesthood, may you all be accurs'd!   Empia razza! anatema su voi!
May the vengeance of heaven descend   La vendetta del ciel scenderà!

on you
May you all be accurs'd!   Anatema su voi!

Scene two. *The stage is divided into two levels. The upper floor represents the interior of the Temple of Vulcan resplendent with gold and glittering light. The lower floor is a crypt. Long arcades vanishing in the gloom. Colossal statues of Osiris with crossed hands support the pillars of the vault. Radamès is discovered in the crypt on the steps which lead down into the vault. Above, two priests in the act of letting down the stone which closes the subterranean apartment.* | *Scena and Duet. Last Finale*

RADAMÈS

The fatal stone is now in place above   La fatal pietra sovra me si chiuse . . .
me . . .
This is my tomb forever. I'll never see   Ecco la tomba mia. Del dì la luce
The daylight again . . . Never behold   Più non vedrò . . . Non rivedrò più
Aida . . .   Aida . . .
Aida, where are you now? May you at   Aida, ove sei tu? Possa tu almeno
least be
Carefree and happy. Pray that you never   Viver felice e la mia sorte orrenda
learn
My horrible fate! I heard a sound! A   Sempre ignorar! Qual gemito! Una
phantom . . .   larva . . .
It is a ghost . . . No! It's a human   Una vision . . . No! forma umana è
figure . . .   questa . . .
Heav'n! Aida!   Ciel! . . . Aida!

AIDA

Beside you . . .   Son io . . .

RADAMÈS
(with utmost despair)

You . . . in this   Tu, in questa
dark prison!   tomba!

AIDA
(sadly)

My heart foretold this horrifying sentence   Presago il core della tua condanna,
I saw them raise the cover to confine you!   In questa tomba che per te s'apriva
I crept inside to find you . . .   Io penetrai furtiva . . .
And here, away from ev'ry human   E qui lontana da ogni umano sguardo
presence,
Held in your arms, I would like to die!   Nelle tue braccia desiai morire.

RADAMÈS [34]

To die! so pure and lovely!   Morir! sì pura e bella!
To die . . . because you love me . . .   Morir per me d'amore . . .
Delicate, precious flower, so delicate a   Degli anni tuoi nel fiore
flower
To fade for ever!   Fuggir la vita!
The gods created you for love and   T'avea il cielo per l'amor creata,
pleasure,
And now I kill my dearest love and   Ed io t'uccido per averti amata!
treasure!
No, do not die!   No, non morrai!
You must not die, you are too lovely!   Troppo t'amai! troppo sei bella!

AIDA [35]
(in a delirium)

Hail to the messenger of death:	Vedi? di morte l'angelo
See how his golden wings shine . . .	Radiante a noi s'appressa;
He comes to tell us of our joy	Ne adduce a eterni gaudii
And carry us above . . .	Sovra i suoi vanni d'ór.
I see the gates of paradise	Gia veggo il ciel dischiudersi,
And there the smile of the gods	Ivi ogni affanno cessa,
divine . . .	
We two will live in ecstacy,	Ivi comincia l'estasi
Eternally in love.	D'un immortale amor.

PRIESTESSES
(from the temple above)

Almighty Phtha the breathing	Immenso Ftha, del mondo
Spirit of life in us all.	Spirito animator
We here implore thee.	Noi t'invochiam.

PRIESTS

Ah! We here implore thee.	Ah! noi t'invochiamo.

AIDA

Solemn chanting!	Triste canto!

RADAMÈS

Yes, the rites of	Il tripudio	
The priests of Isis . . .	Dei Sacerdoti . . .	

AIDA

Our hymn of death is ascending.	Il nostro inno di morte.

RADAMÈS
(trying to displace the stone closing the vault)

Gods, give my arms the power!	Ne le mie forti braccia
Surely my strength can move this dark,	Smuovere ti potranno, o fatal pietra!
fatal cover!	

AIDA

Alas! All things are over	Invan! tutto e finito
Now for us here on earth.	Sulla terra per noi.

RADAMÈS

All over, all over!	E vero! e vero!

AIDA [36]

Farewell oh life, farewell oh valley of	O terra addio, addio valle di pianti . . .
sorrow . . .	
Our dream of joy has faded far away . . .	Sogno di gaudio che in dolor svanì
But now the beauty of heav'n is open	A noi si schiude il ciel e l'alme erranti
wide and now our souls fly	
Up to the light of our eternal day.	Volano al raggio dell' eterno dì.

RADAMÈS

Farewell oh life, farewell oh valley *(etc.)*	O terra addio, addio valle di pianti, *(etc.)*

AIDA

Oh earth I leave you . . . *(etc.)*	O terra addio *(etc.)*

Almighty Phtha we here implore! Immenso Fthà, noi t'invochiam!

AIDA, RADAMES

Ah! the beauty of heav'n! Ah! — si schiude il ciel.
Farewell oh life, farewell oh valley of O terra addio, addio valle di pianti. *(etc.)*
sorrow. *(etc.)*

AMNERIS
(dressed in mourning, prostrates herself on the stone which seals the vault)
Peace, I implore you . . . beloved hero Pace t'imploro . . . salma adorata
May Isis hear you and pardon you! Isi placata ti schiuda il ciel!

CHORUS

We here implore almighty Phtha! Noi t'invochiam, immenso Fthà!

AIDA, RADAMES
(as she dies)
The light . . . eternal day! Il ciel . . . si schiude il ciel!

AMNERIS

Peace I implore you. Peace, I Pace t'imploro. Pace, pace,
implore you. Peace. pace.

CHORUS
Almighty Phtha! Immenso Fthà!

THE END

91

'Aida' at Her Majesty's Theatre, London (1879), with the American Clara Louise
Kellogg in the title role, Trebelli (Amneris) and Campanini (Radamès)

Bibliography

A selective list of books in English for further reading.

The most comprehensive edition of the documents relating to *Aida* is *Verdi's Aida: The History of an Opera in Letters and Documents*, collected and translated by Hans Busch (University of Minnesota Press, Minneapolis, 1978). Besides all the relevant correspondence, this fascinating volume contains biographies of all the characters who took part in the creation of the work.

An appreciation of the opera is contained in Vincent Godefroy's *The Dramatic Genius of Verdi*, Vol 1 (Gollancz, 1975), and another will be included in the third and final volume of Julian Budden's *The Operas of Verdi* (Vols I & II, Cassell, 1973, 1978).

The Letters of Giuseppe Verdi, translated and edited by Charles Osborne (Gollancz, 1971) make a fascinating introduction to Verdi's life, with fresh insights into his character, methods of composition and the times in which he lived. William Weaver's *Verdi: A Documentary Study* (Thames & Hudson, 1977), supplements a selection of the letters with other documents, including press reviews of the Cairo premiere of *Aida* and some beautiful illustrations.

Two general biographies are of interest: *Verdi: His Life and Works* by Francis Toye (Heinemann, 1931) and *The Man Verdi* by Frank Walker (Dent, 1962). Joseph Wechsberg's *Verdi* (Weidenfeld & Nicholson, 1974) and Charles Osborne's *The Operas of Verdi* (Macmillan, 1978) contain some fascinating illustrations, with lively texts.

The full score is published by Ricordi & Co.

Discography

In order of UK release. All performances are in stereo unless asterisked★ and in Italian.

Complete recordings

Conductor Company/Orchestra	Erede Santa Cecilia	Serafin La Scala, Milan	Toscanini NBC SO & Ch. (rec. 1949)	Karajan Vienna GM & PO	Solti Rome Opera	Serafin Rome Opera (rec. 1946)
Aida	R. Tebaldi	M. Callas	H. Nelli	R. Tebaldi	L. Price	M. Caniglia
Amneris	E. Stignani	F. Barbieri	E. Gustavson	G. Simionato	R. Gorr	E. Stignani
Radamès	M. del Monaco	R. Tucker	R. Tucker	C. Bergonzi	J.Vickers	B. Gigli
Amonasro	A.Protti	T. Gobbi	G. Valdengo	C. MacNeil	R. Merrill	G. Bechi
King of Egypt	F. Corena	N. Zaccaria	D. Harbour	F. Corena	P. Clabassi	I. Tajo
Ramphis	D. Caselli	G. Modesti	N. Scott	A. van Mill	G.Tozzi	T. Pasero
High priestess	—	E. Galassi	T. Stich-Randall	E. Ratti	M. Sighele	M. Huder
Messenger	P. di Palma	F. Ricciardi	V. Assandri	P. di Palma	F. Ricciardi	A. Zagonara
Disc UK Number	D47D3	SLS5108	AT302 ★	SXL2167 - 9	SET427 - 9	SH 153 - 5 ★
Tape UK Number		TC - SLS5108		K2A20	K64K32	
Excerpts (Disc)				SXL 2242		
Excerpts (Tape)				KSXC 2242		
Disc US Number	RS 63002 ★	3525CL ★	VIC 5613	LON 1313	LON 1393	
Tape US Number				5 - 1313	5 - 1393	
Excerpts (Disc)				LON 25206		
Excerpts (Tape				5 - 25206		

Excerpts only

Conductor	Muti	Leinsdorf	Prichard
Company/Orchestra	Covent Garden	Alldis Choir/LSO	Covent Garden
Aida	M. Caballé	L. Price	B. Nilsson
Amneris	F. Cossotto	G. Bumbry	G. Hoffmann
Radamès	P. Domingo	P. Domingo	Ottolini
Amonasro	P. Cappuccilli	S. Milnes	L. Quilico
King of Egypt	L. Roni	H. Sotin	—
Ramphis	N. Ghiaurov	—	—
High priestess	E. Casas	J. Mathis	—
Messenger	N. Martinucci	B. Brewer	—
Disc UK Number	SLS 977	SER 5609-11	SXL 6068
Tape UK Number	TC-SLS 9771 - 3	RK40005	
Excerpts (Disc)	ASD 3292		
Excerpts (Tape)	TC-ASD 3292		
Disc US Number	SX 3815	LSC 6198	LON OS 25798
Tape US Number	4X35 - 3815	ARK3 - 2544	
Excerpts (Disc)	S - 37228 (Q0)		LSC - 3275
Excerpts (Tape)			RK - 1237

Excerpts

	Artist	UK numbers only Disc Number	Tape
Prelude	LSO/Abbado	RL31378	
	Hungarian State Opera/ Erdelyi	SHLX90051	
	Berlin PO/Karajan	2707 090	
	Berlin PO/Karajan	2531 145	3301 145
Se quel guerrier/Celeste Aida	C. Bergonzi	6580 150	7317 160
	E. Caruso	RL11749	RK11749
Celeste Aida	C. Bergonzi	SPA535	KCSP535
	P. Domingo	SXL 6451	
	C. Bergonzi	SDD 391	
	L. Pavarotti	SXL 6649	KSXC 6649
Ritorna Vincitor	L. Welitsch	SH 289 ★	
	L. Price	DPS 2001	
	R. Tebaldi	SET 439 - 40	
	F. Weathers	AG 6 41947	
	S. Sass	SXL 6841	KSXC 6841
	M. Chiara	SXL 6605	
	M. Callas	P48	C48
Dances of the Priestesses/ *Moorish Slaves*	Berlin PO/Karajan	2530 200	
	Berlin PO/Karajan	3300 206	3850 068
Gloria all' Egitto	La Scala/Abbado	2530 549	3300 495
	Santa Cecilia/Franci	SXL 6139	
	Covent Garden/Gardelli	TWO 390	
O patria mia	L. Price	DPS 2001	
	M. Chiara	SXL 6548	KSXC 6548
	M. Callas	SLS 5104	TC-SLS 5104
Pur ti riveggo	J. Hammond, C. Craig	ESD 7033	TC-ESD 703.
L'abborrita rivale/ *Gia i sacerdoti*	R. Tebaldi, F. Corelli	SXL 6585	
L'abborrita rivale	E. Komlossy	SLPX 11329	
La fatale pietra (& duet)	J. Sutherland, L. Pavarotti	SXL 6828	KSXC 6828

English
National
Opera
Guide

3

The Magic
Flute

Mozart

English National Opera
receives financial
assistance from the Arts
Council of Great Britain
and the Greater London
Council.

Backstage at Weimar during one of the twenty performances of the opera under Goethe's management (1794). (Photo: Int. Stiftung Mozarteum, Salzburg).

Preface

English National Opera Guides are intended to be companions to opera in performance. They contain articles and illustrations relevant to any production and not only those mounted by English National Opera. Of general interest, also, is the inclusion of the complete original libretto of the opera, side by side with an English translation. There are many reasons why sung words may not be clearly distinguishable, whatever the language and however excellent the performance. The composer may have set several lines of text together, for instance, or he may have demanded an orchestral sound through which no voice can clearly articulate. ENO Guides supply English readers with an opportunity to know a libretto in advance and so greatly increase their understanding and enjoyment of performances whether live, broadcast or recorded.

ENO is very grateful to The Stock Exchange for sponsoring this Guide to *The Magic Flute*. Such sponsorship is an indication of a steadily growing public interest in opera, and we hope the Guides will prove useful to new and experienced opera-lovers alike. An audience which knows what to look and listen for — one that demands a high standard of performance and recognises it when it is achieved — is our best support and, of course, an assurance for the future of opera in the English-speaking world.

Nicholas John
Editor

3

The Magic Flute

Wolfgang Amadeus Mozart

English National Opera Guides Series Editor:
Nicholas John

This Guide is sponsored by The Stock Exchange

John Calder ● London
Riverrun Press ● New York

First published in Great Britain, 1980, by
John Calder (Publishers) Ltd.,
18 Brewer Street,
London W1R 4AS
and
in the U.S.A., 1980, by
Riverrun Press Inc.,
175 Fifth Avenue,
New York, NY 10010

ISBN 0 7145 3768 3 Paperback edition

BRITISH LIBRARY CATALOGUING DATA

Schikaneder, Emanuel
  The magic flute. — (English National Opera
  guides; 3).
  1. Operas — To 1800 — Librettos
  I. Title   II. Giesecke, Karl Ludwig
  III. John, Nicholas   IV. Geliot, Michael
  V. Besch, Anthony   VI. Mozart, Wolfgang Amadeus
  VII. Series
  782.1'2   ML50.M939

Typeset in Plantin by Alan Sutton Publishing Limited, Gloucester
Printed by Whitstable Litho Ltd in Great Britain.

Contents

List of Illustrations

Introduction

In 1791, Mozart, at the age of 35, found himself with little work, out of favour at the court of the new Emperor, Leopold II, and bound to support a growing family and a pregnant young wife. (Nor was his own health strong, since he suffered, putting a brave face on the matter, from a serious liver complaint.) In the spring, he wrote several curiosities: a piece for a mechanical clock and a Rondo to display the virtuoso talents of a blind girl who played the glass harmonica. Yet, no doubt feeling time hang heavily (for him) on his hands, he also agreed to collaborate on an opera with an old friend, a very experienced man of the theatre, called Emmanuel Schikaneder. Schikaneder had first won a reputation touring the Empire with a troupe who performed low comedy and Shakespeare on alternate nights — he had himself been a celebrated Hamlet.

The subject of the collaboration was to include parts for Schikaneder (Papageno) and his company which included Mozart's friend, Benedict Schack (Tamino), and Josefa Hofer his sister-in-law (The Queen of the Night). It was to please the public with a story using the fashionable theme of magic as a pretext for spectacular stage effects in Schikaneder's little wooden theatre on the outskirts of Vienna. And it was to be cast in the popular form of Viennese entertainment known as *Singspiel*, in which the music was interspersed with dialogue in German.

In July, while composing *The Magic Flute*, Mozart received an anonymous commission for a Requiem. He continued to work on both scores together until August when he had to stop entirely to meet an important and very urgent request. This was for an opera to celebrate the coronation of Leopold as King of Bohemia in early September. The form of opera approved by the court for such an occasion was the *opera seria* and Mozart chose an old libretto by Metastasio, the greatest master of libretti for that genre. He and his wife Constanze had to travel to Prague, where in three weeks he completed, rehearsed and conducted the first performance of *La Clemenza di Tito*. The opera pleased the press, which noted the circumstances of the composition and Mozart's ill health, but was received by the new Empress with the comment *'una porcheria tedesca'* — German boorishness. With the fee of 200 gulden in his pocket, Mozart immediately returned to Vienna to complete his score for Schikaneder. The major part of the work must have been ready by then but the overture and March of the Priests were finished only days before the First Night (September 30). Mozart always composed his overtures last and the March may well have been added to assist the staging.

The First Night audience responded with increasing enthusiasm, and particularly liked the scenic effects. Schikaneder repeated it,

Mozart by Doris Stock

although Mozart only conducted one other performance, and during October and November it became a resounding success.

Mozart was by this time hurrying to complete the Requiem, which he had superstitiously come to believe was due for his own funeral. He also completed an aria, a concert piece for basset horn, a clarinet concerto and a Masonic march for the opening of a new lodge. So, at the same time as he was composing a *Singspiel*, he was also working on an opera in the most conventional and elitist form of the period and, while conceiving scores for several Masonic subjects, he was preparing a Catholic Mass. By the end of November, however, ill health forced him to retire to his bed, from where he desperately followed the continuing success of *The Magic Flute*. Constanze, who had been in Baden taking the waters for her health, rejoined him. On December 4, family and friends rehearsed part of the as yet unfinished Requiem at his bedside. Early the next morning, he died, to be buried in a pauper's grave.

Synopsis

This summary of the plot of *The Magic Flute* may be of help in discussing the opera, and recalling the sequence of scenes.

Act One

Tamino, a prince, is saved from a serpent by Three Ladies, attendant on the Queen of the Night. She promises her daughter,

Schikaneder's production Act One, scene one in a coloured engraving by Josef and Peter Schaffer, 1795. (Historisches Museum der Stadt Wien)

Pamina, to him if he will rescue her from Sarastro, whom she calls a wicked demon. Tamino agrees and sets off in the company of the Queen's birdcatcher, a child of nature called Papageno. They each take a magic present (Tamino has a flute, his companion some bells) and they are to be guided by Three Boys in a flying machine.

Pamina is recaptured by Sarastro's Moorish servant, Monostatos, after she has unsuccessfully tried to escape. Papageno, separated on the journey from Tamino, frightens Monostatos so much that he is able to help Pamina escape successfully.

Tamino is convinced by one of Sarastro's followers that Sarastro's principles are virtuous and wise. Pamina and Papageno are discovered by Sarastro as they flee. Tamino and Papageno are invited to undertake the initiation trials of Sarastro's circle.

Act Two

Sarastro thanks his priests for agreeing to allow the two strangers to undertake the trials.

(*First Trial*) Tamino and Papageno are sworn to silence in a darkened room. They resist the temptation to talk to the Three Ladies. Monostatos, about to embrace Pamina, overhears the Queen of the Night swear vengeance on Sarastro, telling Pamina to kill him and bring back to her the Circle of the Sun, which he was given by Pamina's father. Monostatos threatens Pamina when the Queen has vanished but Sarastro intervenes and dismisses him forever from his service.

(*Second Trial*) Tamino and Papageno are still sworn to silence. An old crone easily attracts Papageno's attention but Tamino refuses to greet Pamina, to her infinite sadness. Sarastro then announces that the Second Trial is overcome and that Tamino must now bid Pamina farewell. Papageno tells the old woman that he loves her truly and she is transformed into his perfect female counterpart, Papagena, before they too are forced to part.

Pamina's grief drives her to contemplate suicide which the Three Boys prevent by telling her that Tamino still loves her. She joins Tamino, and together they pass through the (*Third and Fourth*) *Trials of Fire and Water*, as he plays the flute. They enter Sarastro's temple.

The Three Boys then advise Papageno not to hang himself but to use his bells to recover Papagena. The couple are joyfully reunited.

The Queen, her Ladies and Monostatos plot to infiltrate Sarastro's temple. They vanish before the sunlight of wisdom and truth which shines around Sarastro, the Three Boys, the lovers and the priests.

Note

The numbers which appear in square brackets throughout the text refer to the numbered Thematic Guide on pages 51-58.

'Singspiel' and Symbolism

Rodney Milnes

When first performed in 1791, *The Magic Flute* was described in three different ways. The playbill announced *Eine grosse Oper* — 'a grand opera'; the published libretto referred to it as a *Singspiel*; and in his personal catalogue Mozart entered it as a 'German opera'. It is, of course, all three and more. As the playbill promised, it is grander than the term *Singspiel* would have suggested to prospective audiences, and although the adjective 'German' had special significance for Mozart, who for most of his working life sought to re-create a national school of opera — and here succeeded — the score nevertheless contains elements of Italian operatic form, significantly those associated with the Queen of the Night, a character symbolising reaction. And its universality wholly transcends any nationalist designation.

It is impossible to separate *Singspiel* — literally 'song-play' — from other vernacular nationalist operatic schools in conflict with and reaction to the almost complete dominance of Italian opera in Europe that lasted from the end of the seventeenth century for almost a hundred years. One common feature was, of course, spoken dialogue in place of sung recitative. English ballad operas following in the wake of *The Beggar's Opera* (1728), itself a direct counterblast to Handelian *opera seria*, were translated into German and proved immensely popular. *Opéra-comique* survived the Italianization of French opera by Lully and his successors and became the dominant school following the decline of Rameau. Composers of *Singspiel* studied with profit the techniques of French popular opera rather than those of Italian *opera buffa* (three characteristics, strophic song in place of *da-capo* forms, the rondeau, and the vaudeville finale, found their way into both Mozart's German and Italian operas). The common feature of all three is that they represented popular lyric entertainment as opposed to official, court-based Italian opera.

The ancestors of popular opera are many: fairground entertainments and mystery plays; cantatas in costume (a form that flourished in Leipzig where, confusingly, they were sometimes designated *dramma per musica*); school operas and before them liturgical drama, stretching far back into the middle ages and the Byzantine era; perhaps the English 'Jigg', a sung and danced postlude to, or interlude during, a serious play — for example, the finale to the rustics' 'Pyramus and Thisbe' in *A Midsummer Night's Dream* — at first improvised, later written down; this *commedia dell'arte*-type affair relates backwards to the classical Greek satyr play and forwards to the Italian *intermezzo*, direct ancestor of *opera buffa*.

11

The term *Singspiel* seems first to have been used in 1698 to describe the performance in German of a French opera by the Italian Lully given in Stuttgart, in which recitative was replaced by dialogue. In Hamburg, serious operas were given with dialogue, sometimes with the arias in Italian as a sop to establishment taste, until 1739; the free Hanseatic city was the last bastion of repertory vernacular opera. From then on Italian *opera seria* won the day and popular musical entertainment took to the road. Schikaneder's was just one of many touring companies giving both drama and *Singspiel*. Although *Singspiel* was never exclusively comic — Goethe wrote many librettos, and in the 1770s we find 'serious', even 'tragic' *Singspiele* announced — it was by and large a light-hearted affair.

In Vienna, capital of the Empire and of *opera seria*, it was very light-hearted indeed. Subjects were exotic; while *opera seria* and Gluckian reform opera went to the classical world for their subject matter, *Singspiele* (not to mention *opéra-comique*) went one further, to the East; against the interest in classicism born in the seventeenth century was set the first translation of the *1,001 Nights* in the early 1700s. Indeed, Viennese popular theatre in the 1780s must have looked a little like a London season in which pantomimes lasted the year round, an indigestible diet of *Aladdins* and *Ali Babas*. Joseph II's attempt to found a National, or German, Opera in 1778 failed, though its repertory did include Mozart's *Die Entführung aus dem Serail*, in which a *Singspiel* text was allied to music that aimed rather higher, perhaps justifying the Emperor's famous criticism of 'too many notes, my dear Mozart'. Mozart's involvement with *Singspiel*, or near-*Singspiel*, also produced *Der Schauspieldirektor* (more a play with music), *Thämos, König von Ägypten* (definitely a play with music), and the unfinished *Zaide*, in which he used *mélodrame*, or dialogue spoken over music, a technique exploited by the *Singspiel* composer Benda, much admired by Mozart, later used by Weber (*Der Freischütz*), Beethoven (*Fidelio* and *Egmont*), Schubert (*Zauberharfe*), and thereafter seldom until Strauss (*Die Frau ohne Schatten*) and Britten (*Gloriana*); it was, however, the mainstay of popular nineteenth-century theatre in England and the golden age of Hollywood.

Although the roots of *The Magic Flute* are in *Singspiel*, the score transcended the form. Admired by and influential upon great German opera composers who followed, it spawned such works as *Fidelio* and *Freischütz*, technically speaking 'serious' *Singspiele*, before *Singspiel* reverted to comic subjects and changed its name to *Spieloper*. French *opéra-comique*, the other pollinator of that glorious hybrid *Fidelio*, continued to use dialogue (except that successful examples, like *Faust*, were promptly turned into 'respectable' *grand opéra*) until *Carmen* went as far as the form could go. Opera with dialogue is scarcely written any more, much to opera's loss. Dialogue does save *so* much time.

When *The Magic Flute* was first performed at the Theater auf der Wieden, a temporary wooden theatre in the suburbs of Vienna with a capacity of 1,000, audiences may have been expecting another pantomime-like *Singspiel*, a fairy story with many magic effects, which at one level is what they got. The piece was an instant success, as was Mozart's previous German opera, *Die Entführung*, and as were his Italian comedies when performed anywhere other than Vienna. But there was more to the *Flute* than fairy tale, and Mozart himself became impatient at one performance when a boorish Bavarian visitor laughed in the wrong places and plainly did not understand what was going on. Mozart called him a Papageno. The fact that there obviously was something more to the work has given rise over the years to innumerable theories as to exactly what that something was. In 1866 Moritz Zille told the world that Tamino represented the Emperor Joseph II, Pamina the Austrian people, the Queen the reactionary Empress Maria Theresa, Monostatos the Jesuits, etc. etc.. While it may have been obvious from the beginning that much of the ritual in the second act was that of Freemasonry — obvious, certainly, to Masons — it was only at the beginning of this century that it came to be discussed openly, when it gave rise to the famous theory of the (non-existant) change of plot. To examine this we must return to the sources.

The first, though marginal, source was *Lulu, oder die Zauberflöte*, a story by A.J. Liebeskind, one of a collection of pseudo-oriental fairy tales edited by C.M. Wieland and published in 1786 under the title of *Dschinnistan*. This book was raided for countless *Singspiele* both at Schikaneder's theatre (among them Wranitzky's *Oberon*, 1789) and at his rival Marinelli's Kärntnertortheater. While the *Flute* was being written, Marinelli staged *Kaspar the Bassoon-player, or the Magic Zither*, with music by Wenzel Müller and also loosely based on *Lulu*. It is said that fearful of accusations of plagiarism, Mozart and Schikaneder suddenly changed their *Lulu* plot half way through the first act. Plagiarism hardly entered into it: it was rife in the Viennese theatre of the day, and it would make as much sense to say that a Palladium *Aladdin* plagiarised one at the Players Theatre. Commentators may have felt the need to propose the change-of-plot theory because in the story the good fairy Perifeme gives Prince Lulu (thank heavens the name was changed) a magic flute, amongst other things, to rescue her daughter Sidi from the evil magician Dilsengbuin, which he eventually does. In the opera, theorists maintain, the Queen starts as a good character and Sarastro as a bad one, then suddenly the positions are reversed. Is this really tenable if you listen carefully to the Queen's music? It is as unwise to believe everything people say in the theatre as it is in real life, especially if in the middle of a *Singspiel* they suddenly loose off into a torrent of *opera seria* coloratura. In any event, Mozart saw *Kaspar* and dismissed it as worthless.

13

There is another far more significant source of the *Flute*: the Abbé Terrasson's *Sethos*, published in 1731 as a historic treatise on the mysteries of Isis and Osiris and accepted as such until well into the nineteenth century, but in fact a clever forgery and no more than a novel. Sethos was supposedly an Egyptian Prince, and the Queen in *Flute* has the characteristics of his mother-in-law Daluca rather than of Liebeskind's Perifeme. Also from *Sethos* come the text recited by the Armed Men, the Three Ladies, the serpent, the trials of fire and water, and the ritual of the second act. *Sethos* had already been mined for material for *Thämos*, for *Der Stein der Weisen* (libretto by Schikaneder, music by Benedict Schack, later the first Tamino), and for pieces at Marinelli's theatre. The Three Boys, incidentally, come from another story in *Dschinnistan*, and Papageno, designed primarily as a star role for Schikaneder, is a mixture of Kasperle, a Viennese Mr Punch crossed with Merry Andrew, and the *commedia dell'arte* characters popular at the Kärntnertortheater.

So there is no single source for the *Flute* libretto, and there was probably more than one librettist, although as claimants only emerged after the deaths of Mozart and Schikaneder it is impossible to know the truth of this (I am inclined to disbelieve Giesecke's opportunist claim to authorship made in a Viennese restaurant in 1818). But the main source was *Sethos*, a Masonic text, and the rituals were those of Freemasonry, which gave rise to the second change-of-plot theory. This is based on the official suppression of the sect in Vienna after the death of Joseph II, himself a member, and proposes that half way through composition Mozart and Schikaneder, also both Masons, abandoned the fairy tale and turned the *Flute* into, if not propaganda, then at least a morale-booster for their beleaguered brothers. The turning point is supposed to come with Tamino's encounter with the Speaker, and thence the reversal of the Queen's and Sarastro's roles. This theory seems most unlikely on countless grounds: would Mozart, after all that he had achieved, bother to write a simple fairy-tale, even for ready money? Had there not been enough, if not orthodox Masonic, then at least esoteric entertainments, some written by Mozart himself, for them to count as a sub-genre of *Singspiel*? Is the association of night with good and day with evil likely in eighteenth century terms? The idea crumbles once the Masonic symbolism of the libretto is fully explained.

This has at least been done by Jacques Chailley in his exhaustively researched and presumably massively indiscreet *The Magic Flute, Masonic Opera*. Among his many revelations, and they are no less than that, is the existence of controversy in eighteenth-century Masonic circles over whether or not women should be admitted as full members. There were Lodges of Adoption for women, and female initiates took the name of the Order of Mopsos. Among the items in their ritual were a serpent, veils, and a golden padlock. The libretto is thus bristling with Masonic symbols long before the appearance of the Speaker, and the plot is nothing so simple as a matter of 'good' Masons being threatened by a 'bad' Maria Theresa, or whoever. They are all in the same game, and there is no reason why a 'bad' Queen should not be handing out 'good' symbols like a flute and a chime of bells.

The conflict in the *Flute* between the Queen and Sarastro for control of the Circle of the Sun symbolises the conflict in Masonic lore between the dualism proposed by inscriptions on the twin pillars of Hiram's Temple of Solomon, which list various opposing forces: Masculine/Feminine, Sun/Moon, Day/Night, Fire/Water, Gold/Silver etc. etc.. Note here that the Three Boys carry silver (lunar) palms (solar) at their first entry, suggesting that they are above and beyond the dualism, and thus perfect beings. The Queen seeks to perpetuate the conflict by seizing the Circle of the Sun worn by her late husband, Sarastro's predecessor, and institute her own reign. Sarastro's aim is to resolve the conflict by creating in Tamino and Pamina 'the new pair' he sings of in 'Oh, Isis and Osiris'* (Aria with Chorus No. 10). The synthesis of all the warring elements will herald a new, golden age of peace and wisdom. He does not have the unconditional support of his priests, who voice many of the anti-feminist sentiments that must have been expressed in eighteenth-century Masonic circles. Whether or not Sarastro's plan is orthodox Masonry a non-Mason cannot tell (and it is one of the few beans that Professor Chailley does not spill), but in creating Pamina, a woman who joins Tamino for his most dangerous trials, who 'is not afraid of night or death, is worthy and will be accepted', and who sings 'Wherever you go I will be at your side, I myself will lead you as love leads me', Mozart was definitely on the side of the non-Masonic angels, as he was in *'Bei Männern'*, Duet No. 7 [14], with its promise that 'man and woman, woman and man' (the reversal surely not just in the interests of rhyme) 'together attain divinity'. (Schikaneder, incidentally, was a lapsed Mason. An eighteenth-century constitution excluded 'slaves, women, and immoral men' in that order. Schikaneder fell into the last category.)

Professor Chailley's book is extremely complicated, and like all decipherers he sometimes overstates his case, but he does show that far from being just a pantomine or, in E.J. Dent's magnificently orotund phrase, 'one of the most absurd specimens of that form of literature in which absurdity is regarded as a matter of course', the *Flute* libretto is a tightly organised text, its symbolism logically worked out. He explains the various trials, the 'initial swoon' that Pamina and Tamino both undergo and that Papageno parodies, and such details as why the flute and bells are taken away at the beginning of the second act. It is, for example, perfectly logical that two

---

* Sarastro's reference is arguably to Tamino and Papageno, not Pamina, since they are the two profane ones to be initiated at that stage — Editor.

of the characters, Papageno and Monostatos, start out on the wrong sides and move across during the action. Papageno works in the woman's world, but joins Tamino and the priests — note how often his priest-mentor says 'be a *man*'. Monostatos logically joins the forces of darkness. His blackness, incidentally, is not necessarily of skin. He represents the black-magician Siosiri, the Judas-figure of Masonic lore who assassinated the architect Hiram and is descended from the raven that brought bad news back to the ark; Monostatos refers to Pamina as his 'dove', the bird that brought the good news — again, no coincidence.

Although there is a certain satisfaction in seeing everything in the *Flute* slot neatly into place, full understanding of the relevant ritual is certainly not essential to the appreciation of what remains a Masonic opera. It describes a journey from darkness to light, and celebrates the possibility of progress. 'Soon superstition will vanish and wisdom triumph; come, Peace, and fill the hearts of men, so that earth will become a paradise and mortal men as the gods themselves', sing the Boys with touching optimism at the start of the finale. That in a nutshell is what the *Flute* is about. After nearly two hundred years humanity seems no nearer that goal.

Tamino attracts wild beasts with his flute-playing in Schikaneder's 1795 production. (Historisches Museum der Stadt Wien)

A Vision of Reconciliation

David Cairns

For an opera that the general public took to its heart from the beginning and that great poets from Goethe to Auden have revered, *The Magic Flute* has had a strangely grudging press; critics have often been reluctant to take its message seriously. Even now we may sometimes hear it described as sublime music unhappily married to a foolish and vulgar plot, whose text is mere hot air when it isn't juvenile. The sophisticated may even complain, privately, that the music itself with all its beauties is lacking in the rich ironies and ambiguities of *Don Giovanni* and *Così fan tutte*. According to these critics, the work marks a reversion by Mozart to a more primitive genre of opera, in which the composer is no longer in undisputed control of the dramatic machinery, and the musical numbers regularly give way to the spoken word; a genre, too, in which the complex, living individuals of the great Italian comedies are replaced by the two-dimensional stereotypes of contemporary Viennese pantomime. In this view *The Magic Flute* is great in spite of the libretto and solely because of the music; but not even Mozart's genius can turn it into a serious and coherent work of art.

Thus the very simplicity of the work becomes a barrier to an understanding of it. Our way of looking at Mozart is still tinged, unconsciously, with the nineteenth-century view of him as a purely instinctive genius and child of nature who was not really aware of what he did. As a result we fail to realise the extent to which Mozart was consciously in charge, shaping his material to clearly formulated ends. It is always a mistake to make a lot of the formal sources of his mature compositions. He takes his models from what he finds around him, the conventional art of the day, but uses them to create something personal to himself, unique, and coherent. Nowhere more so than in *The Magic Flute*. The more we study it the more unmistakably it is seen to embody a consistent plan.

The simplicity of the music is indeed remarkable: simplicity of form, style, material. It is Mozart's most transparent operatic score, melodically the most direct, harmonically the most pure and unadorned (its chromatic inflexions being always contained within a clear diatonic framework), in texture the most luminous. Yet it is a positive simplicity, subtle and purposeful, seemingly uncomplicated in its effect, profoundly artful in the means used to achieve it — the musician's super-sensitive response to the drama, which at every turn is articulated by the musical form and expression. To consider only the orchestration: we think of it as plainer than that of Mozart's other operas; yet hardly two out of the forty-odd separate or linked movements that make up the work are scored for the same forces. This is something only slightly connected with the presence of unusual instruments: trombones, basset-horns and glockenspiel (the latter two appearing in only a handful of numbers). The conventional instruments of the operatic orchestra are handled with a marvellous diversity to reflect each shift of mood or feeling or atmosphere.

Mozart's consummate dramatic sense is seen above all in the profound unity-in-diversity of the work's musical style, reflecting that of the action and symbolised by the magic flute itself, the instrument created by Osiris from a shepherd's multiple pipes — the many resolved into the one. There is a single '*Magic Flute* style', a synthesis, like the drama itself, of widely differing elements: Viennese vernacular song, Italian bravura aria and buffo ensemble, chorale, fugue, ritual chorus, extended accompanied recitative; learned and popular, sacred and profane, spirit and earth. It is the musical analogue of the drama's high theme of reconciliation.

The theme of *The Magic Flute*: there can no longer be any doubt as to its seriousness, and its deliberate and systematic Masonic connotations and Mozart's central involvement in the plan. *The Magic Flute* is a conscious document of Freemasonry, an affirmation of faith in its mysteries and its beliefs. But Freemasonry is a language for encoding philosophical ideas and spiritual aspirations that are common to many religions; its forms may be esoteric, their content is open to all and concerns mankind. We do not have to be able to read all the signs in order to receive the message of the work. Its essential meaning is immediately clear (though we may never exhaust its meaningfulness). Mozart does not disdain to use the vulgar medium of popular comedy for his parable of the purification of the human soul. Like Shakespeare, like the men who devised the old miracle plays, he sees no incongruity — rather, a fitness. 'Except ye become as little children . . .'

Overture.

The Overture is in E flat (a key whose three flats gave it special significance for Masons). It prepares us for what is to come, with its solemn, momentous introduction (*Adagio*) [1a] leading through tension and uncertainty — throbbing syncopations, harmonic darkenings — to the jubilant polyphony of the *Allegro* [2]. Half way through, the *Allegro* is interrupted by the three-fold wind chord [1b], which in Act Two will summon the postulants at various stages of the initiation. Its effect, in the Overture, is to check the *Allegro*'s confident energy. The strings discuss it in an anxious *sotto voce*, and the music moves through a dark series of minor keys before — the clarinets leading — the orchestra sees its way ahead once more and, instrument by instrument, rushes with joyful eagerness back to E flat major.

From the outset the glow of trombones colours the orchestral sound. Predominantly ecclesiastical instruments in Mozart's time, here they play not just in a scene or two, for special effect (as they do in *Idomeneo* and *Don Giovanni*), but in fully a quarter of the work — one sign among many that this is not a conventional *Singspiel* but a sacred comedy. If (as Jacques Chailley claims) the note-pattern of the opening bars of the Overture — three resounding chords plus the upbeat to the second and the third chord — is meant to be heard as a group of five, that is only appropriate. Five represents Woman in Masonic number-symbolism (five-note figures are prominent in the work in scenes that take place in or under the influence of the feminine domain); and the regeneration of Woman — who in Freemasonry embodies the emotional, instinctive, unreasoning, 'inferior' half of the human psyche — is central to the work. Her progress, in the person of Pamina, becomes the focal point; in the end it is Pamina who, by her fully awakened love, will lead Tamino on the final stage of their journey. This was a bold step by Mozart and Schikaneder. Women were not admitted by orthodox Masonry to full enlightenment, and it must have caused rumblings among the brotherhood. Indeed there is a suggestion in Act Two scene 21 that the priests are taken aback by the novelty of Sarastro's grand design.

Act One

No. 1 Introduction: TAMINO, THREE LADIES.

A rocky, mountainous terrain, with woods and a temple. Tamino, a prince from foreign lands, is being pursued by a huge serpent. He cannot defend himself: he has a bow but no arrows. In forty graphic bars the music depicts his breathless flight and the heaving coils of the approaching snake: a tense, rushing C minor, with strong contrasts of dynamics, stabbing offbeat accents, and lurid chords on woodwind and horns [3]. As the serpent reaches him, Tamino falls to the ground in a faint; but at the same moment three women, servants of the Queen of the Night, wearing black veils and armed with silver spears, come out of the temple and kill the monster. The music swerves, via A flat major, into E flat as they congratulate themselves on their noble deed. Mock heroic fanfares and violin semiquavers parading up and down the scale betray the Ladies' self-importance, but the key of E flat is significant. Tamino's loss of consciousness is to be the start of a new existence for him. It will be paralleled a few scenes later when Pamina, too, faints after an attack by animal nature. For each of them this symbolic death is the precondition of rebirth into the life of the spirit; though neither of them realises it, it is the beginning of a pilgrimage that will lead them, after many trials, to each other's arms and to the threshold of the golden age.

For the present, Tamino is very much in the land of unenlightenment, the domain of ignorance and unregenerate Woman.

The Three Ladies are frivolous, vain, sensual, and of strictly limited understanding; their musical characterisation is quite explicit. They are smitten with the beauty of Tamino, and each longs to be left alone with him and tries desperately to make the other two go away [4], until they realise that they are all three thinking the same thing, whereupon they become almost hysterical with jealousy and frustration. In the end they bid the still unconscious youth a tender farewell [5] and go back into the temple to tell the Queen about him. The music of this whole Trio is at once irresistibly comic and exquisitely beautiful in a luminous, airy way that we will recognise as characteristic of *The Magic Flute*.

Tamino comes to himself to find the serpent dead at his feet. While he is staring at it in amazement he hears pan-pipes from nearby [6]; and a moment later a strange figure, a man, yet covered in feathers like a bird and carrying on his back a cage full of birds, comes into the clearing.

No. 2 Aria PAPAGENO.

Papageno's first aria, [7] in a bright G major, with flowing semiquavers alternating with hopping, birdlike rhythms and intervals, has the folksong-like freshness and open-hearted good humour which will typify his music throughout the opera. The third verse was apparently an afterthought — a wise one (quite apart from the Masonic associations of the magic number three!):

*An early design for Papageno
(Bibliothèque Nationale,
Music Department, Paris)*

the tune is too good to be heard only twice, and the third verse clinches the effect of the first two. Papageno, ever keen to talk about himself, tells us how he lures birds with his pipes and catches them in traps. If only he had a girl-trap, he would catch girls and the one he liked best would be his wife.

The ensuing conversation between Tamino and Papageno is long and written in traditional 'low' pantomime style. It is drastically shortened in many productions, but it serves several purposes: to impart a good deal of necessary information, to characterise the relationship — a variant of the archetypal master-and-servant — which will link the two men until their parallel but separate destinies diverge in the final scenes of the opera, and to establish the identity of the bird-catcher as uncorrupted Natural Man. Papageno works for the Queen of the Night, receiving food and drink in return for the birds he brings her. In the uncut version of the dialogue he does not actually claim that he slew the serpent, so much as fall in readily with Tamino's assumption that he did. Immediately the Three Ladies return: 'Papageno, no wine for you today, only water, no sugarbread but a stone!' And instead of sweet figs they laughingly present him with a padlock, and lock his mouth as a punishment for lying. Papageno is reduced to doleful dumbshow. Before they go the Ladies give the Prince a present from the Queen — a portrait of her daughter, with which he falls instantly in love.

No. 3 Aria TAMINO [8].

This most beautiful of romantic love-songs — a dream of passion, as yet without a real object — is coloured with the warm, amorous tones of clarinets and horns, and set to a vocal line which, alternately soaring in ecstasy and hesitating in doubt and wonder, conveys to perfection Tamino's love-struck state of mind. His growing ardour is reflected not only in the increasingly expressive phrases of the violins (one of them borrowed from *Così fan tutte*) but in the whole form of the aria: at the return of the home key the opening idea does not recur; instead, new and yet more exalted phrases reflect the excited state of Tamino's imagination. Only then is the music of the first section recalled, by the repetition of its concluding phrase, this time expanded into a great arch of soaring melody.

The Three Ladies reappear and, constantly interrupting one another in their excitement, give Tamino the great news. The Queen has heard all; she has chosen him to be the deliverer of her daughter Pamina, kidnapped by a wicked magician and languishing in his castle not far away. Tamino swears to rescue Pamina and begs the Ladies to lead him to the castle at once. At that moment there is a clap of thunder, then two more, and the mountains part to reveal the Queen herself seated on a glittering throne in the midst of a sumptuous palace, surrounded by darkness.

Marcella Sembrich as the Queen
of the Night in the Met. première, 1900

No. 4 Aria QUEEN OF THE NIGHT.

The imposing orchestral introduction, with insistent violin chords in cross-rhythm over a thrashing bass, suggests a person cast in the heroic mould — and a voice to match: despite the florid runs and dizzy ascents to top F of the aria which follows, the part presupposes not a light coloratura voice but a powerful dramatic soprano with an extended top octave. The music also tells us subtly but unmistakably that the Queen is not what the naive Tamino imagines her to be. Already before the end of the recitative there has been a hint of self-pity as well as self-esteem, and the G minor *Larghetto* [9] confirms it: only contrast the opening phrase — stiffly plaintive, contrived in its pathos — with the similarly shaped but heart-rendingly sincere opening phrase of Pamina's G minor aria in Act Two (No. 17) — example (a).* Half way through, the combination of agitated string accompaniment and long, sinuous bassoon and viola countermelody is reminiscent of Donna Anna's *'Or sai chi l'onore'* in *Don Giovanni* and creates a comparable sensation of suppressed hysteria. The *Allegro* [10], with its brilliantly arrogant flourishes and tense, high horn parts, leaves the same doubts in our minds: this person is not to be taken at face value. As the Queen disappears with a noise of thunder and the mountains close again, Tamino marvels at what he has seen. Was it an illusion? 'Oh kindly gods, do not deceive me! Shield me and strengthen my resolve'. He is about to set out on his quest when Papageno, still padlocked and mumbling pitifully, intercepts him.

No. 5 Quintet TAMINO, PAPAGENO, THREE LADIES.

The Quintet begins with a strutting, skipping unison figure on

* Musical Examples (a), (b) and (c) are on page 39.

22

strings and bassoons, which will be heard again in various forms in the next few scenes, usually in the shape of a trill followed by an arpeggio, and always with a sense of finger-snapping assertiveness — example (b). Papageno, still speechless from the padlock, draws loud attention to his plight, his indignant 'hm's [11] being amusingly combined with Tamino's slightly unctuous expressions of regret at not being able to do anything to help. The Ladies re-appear and remove the padlock. Papageno promises not to tell lies again. After some pious moralising, Tamino is presented with a golden flute which will guard him from harm and bring joy to all who hear it. Papageno is horrified to learn that he is to accompany the Prince on his perilous journey to the castle: Sarastro, the enchanter who rules there, will surely catch him and have him plucked and **roasted**; but he is placated with the gift of some magic silver bells, which will make men laugh — as the flute will make them love. The two companions bid farewell to the Ladies, who tell them that Three Boys will guide them on their way [12].

The Quintet has the virtuosity of Mozart's most masterly comic ensembles, here refined to a perfection that one would call un-earthly if it were not also so human and alive. Humour and beauty merge into one another, and every incident finds its apt expression within a seemingly effortless musical continuity. The final section, however, in which Tamino and Papageno are told of their young guides, is set slightly apart from the rest of the movement, for it marks the beginning of a new stage in the drama; and at once a strange, mild light, not encountered before, invests the music, as a gentle theme for clarinets and high bassoons floats down above an accompaniment of pizzicato violins. Never was a succession of notes simpler, or more heart-searching. It is a presage of the sublime compassion that we shall experience in the finale of Act Two [33], when the wisdom of the Three Boys guides Pamina on her way.

The fact that the Flute and the Bells, magical agencies of good, are the gifts of the Queen is often cited as evidence for a change in the plot. This is a very literal-minded approach. As we learn later, the Flute is in the possession of the Queen for the reason that it belonged to her late husband, the leader of Sarastro's priesthood, who made it. In any case, magical objects in fairy stories are by tradition morally neutral. As for the Three Boys, to object that they belong to the good side — and therefore should not be in any way associated with, let alone recommended by, the enemy — is to mistake the nature and meaning of the allegory. It is not a question of good versus evil but rather of the progress of the human soul from the darkness of ignorance to the light of understanding, in which state all its former contradictions are reconciled and all its parts, having shed their negative aspects, are united into a single harmonious whole. The Three Ladies represent human develop-ment at its lowest. The strict limitation of their understanding is

shown by their inability to do more than set Tamino on the first
stage of his quest: they can take him no further, the Boys must
replace them. All that is 'inconsistent' about the opening scenes is
that in them we see the story from the distorted point of view of the
Queen and her creatures. To them Sarastro is an enchanter; the
change he works in men seems to the Ladies a mere question of
magic. (Similarly the Pamina of the early scenes, being still subject
to the influence of her mother the Queen, believes that Papageno
will be tortured and killed if Sarastro catches him.) They see the
Flute likewise, as a purely magical piece of property, whereas in
reality it is a symbol of the power of man and woman united;
Tamino and Pamina achieve their goal not by supernatural means
but by suffering, self-sacrifice and love.*

In the next scene we are in 'a splendid Egyptian room' in
Sarastro's realm. Three slaves excitedly discuss Pamina's escape
from the clutches of their master Monostatos. (This part of the
work is supposed to have been left over from the original version of
the story, in which Monostatos the evil Moor was naturally the
servant of the wicked magician; but it is notable that Sarastro is
treated sympathetically in the slaves' conversation, in opposition to
Monostatos.) A moment later the Moor's angry voice is heard:
Pamina has been recaptured, and is dragged in by other slaves at
his command.

No. 6 Trio PAMINA, MONOSTATOS, PAPAGENO [13]

A whirlwind *Allegro* in G major. The skipping, finger-snapping
figure is much in evidence as Monosatos dances round Pamina.
While her phrases from the first show a tendency towards melodic
expansion, his are tense and down to earth. His musical idiom is
akin to Papageno's but more brutal. He is Papageno's darker self,
Natural Man corrupted, enslaved to his selfish appetites and incapable of development (as his name suggests). Throughout the
opera his music brilliantly depicts him in a permanent condition of
sexual rage and frustration. Yet Papageno, entering the room at the
moment when Pamina has fainted and Monostatos is about to
satisfy his lust, can without any change of musical style and with
only a slight lightening of touch on Mozart's part take over
Monostatos's last phrase (in dotted rhythm) and be his own chirpy
self. Papageno has just time to comment on the whiteness of
Pamina's face (in a musical phrase that exactly echoes a phrase in
the G major section of the Ladies' trio, complete with little five-
note jingle on the flute — example (c)), before he finds himself face
to face with the fearsome Monostatos. The Moor is equally
appalled by the apparition of Papageno (whom to the end of the
opera he believes to be a huge bird), and each begs the other for
mercy, before they both flee in terror. Their brief duet, accompanied by the dotted rhythm in stealthy string octaves, is richly

* See the illuminating essay by Dorothy Koenigsberger, 'A New Metaphor for
Mozart's *Magic Flute*', in *European Studies Review*, vol. 5, no. 3, July 1975.

absurd; but some of the humour is lost if their final 'Hu!'s are not sung firmly on the note and sustained to their full length.

Papageno recovers his nerve sooner than Monostatos; and returns just as Pamina regains consciousness. Though they are later to follow very different paths, as befits their different capabilities, the two children of nature make friends at once. Papageno tells Pamina about her mother and the Prince's mission. She needs no portrait to fall instantly in love with Tamino. Papageno glumly reflects that if he cannot find a Papagena he might as well pull all his feathers out. Pamina encourages him to be patient: Heaven will see that his desires are answered, and sooner than he imagines.

No. 7 Duet PAMINA, PAPAGENO [14].

The directness and unsophistication of the melody of this hymn to the power of love, and the plainness of the accompaniment,

'*The Magic Flute*' at ENO: Valerie Masterson (Pamina) with Alan Opie (Papageno) in the production by Anthony Besch, designed by John Stoddart. (photo: Andrew March)

reflect not only the simplicity of Pamina and Papageno but also their humanity. Although they do not understand what the love they sing about so fervently involves, instinctively Pamina commits herself to it, and Papageno in his more primitive way (his vocal line significantly less abundant and exalted than hers) follows her. The key is E flat major, the Masonic key. They are on the way to achieving the unselfish love between man and woman which is the source of human happiness and by which they may attain divinity. ('*Reichen an die Gottheit an*').

25

No. 8 Finale.

We return to Tamino, and a crucial moment in the drama. With the first bar, a new sound is heard: a solemn march (*Larghetto*) [15], with soft pulsations of bassoons, trombones and muted trumpets and drums, and the gleam of flutes and clarinets in octaves. Tamino, guided by the Three Boys, has left the domain of Woman. His initiation can begin. Here, the Boys tell him, is his goal, and here, a youth, he must conquer like a man. Will I be able to rescue Pamina, he cries. It is not for them to say. Let him but be steadfast, tolerant, discreet.

Left alone, Tamino looks wonderingly around him. Instead of the frowning walls and embattled turrets of his chivalrous fancies, he sees a pleasant grove, overlooked by three temples inscribed to

David Hockney's design for Act One finale (Glyndebourne, 1978: photo: Guy Gravett)

Nature, Reason and Wisdom — a sanctuary where crime seems to have no place. Very well: he will enter boldly, he has nothing to fear; let the evil-doer tremble, Pamina shall be rescued. Tamino's phrases ring with a fine ardour; but as he advances towards the first of the temples, as though to remind us that he is still confused and ignorant, the violins play the defiant, self-assertive theme (trill followed by arpeggio), which in various forms has been heard several times in the earlier scenes. At the first two temples he is stopped by a voice which cries 'Go back!'. At the third, he knocks on the door and an old priest comes out. Their long dialogue, conducted almost entirely in recitative, is the turning point of the action. If we have understood the allegory of the preceding scenes, the much more elevated tone that now comes over the work is evidence not of any change of intention on the authors' part but rather that the drama has entered a new phase — for which, we can see with hindsight, there have been a number of clear preparatory signs. During their dialogue, under the guidance of the patient, kindly Priest, Tamino takes a decisive step away from ignorance and false values. Yet the ambiguity, the perplexity of his state of mind, is reflected in the fluctuating character of his utterances. At the very beginning, to the Priest's enquiry 'What do you seek in the sanctuary?', he replies like a postulant seeking admission to the rites of initiation, 'The domain of love and virtue', in a serene E flat major with a harmonious accompaniment of clarinets, bassoons and cellos. But that is only a fleeting glimpse of wisdom; Tamino is still breathing fire against Sarastro, and for a long time his phrases have an angry impetuosity, in contrast to the measured calm of the Priest's. (The whole long conversation, with all its weightiness, has a vividness and eloquence that Mozart himself, master of dramatic recitative, never surpassed.) By the end Tamino has come dimly to recognise his error. His aggressiveness has been disarmed; and his final question to the Priest, 'When will the veil be removed?', unconsciously anticipates the moment, now near, when his initiation will begin. The Priest's reply, hopeful but enigmatic, is sung to a noble theme doubled by the cellos. Tamino is left alone: in a desolate A minor, the violins repeat the sad drooping phrase first heard at the point where he had discovered that his enemy Sarastro ruled in the Temple of Wisdom, and all the certainties of his life crumbled to nothing. 'Oh endless night, when will you be gone? When will daylight greet my sight?' He has spoken to himself; but mysterious voices (male), supported by soft trombone chords, answer him from far off, above the Priest's final melody in the cellos, 'Soon, young man, soon or never'. Roused from his dejection, Tamino asks aloud if Pamina still lives. 'Pamina still lives', comes the solemn answer. At that, Tamino in his joy and gratitude to the gods takes out the flute and plays it [16]. At once wild beasts appear, enchanted by its sound. Tamino wonders why it does not also bring Pamina to him; and the music turns to C minor, while oboes memorably add an extra poignancy. He calls Pamina's name; then, when there is no answer, plays a rising scale on the flute. The last five notes are those of Papageno's panpipes, and immediately they answer him from nearby [6]. Tamino's joy overflows, and the music, now an excited *Presto*, flowers into a glorious exaltation: perhaps Papageno has found Pamina and is bringing her to him. He hurries away in search of them.

A moment later the fugitives run in from the opposite side of the stage, to a typically Papageno-like figure in G major [17].(Unlike Tamino, they have not yet learned anything; Papageno, to himself and to Pamina, is still the emissary of the Queen whose task is to rescue Pamina from the evil magician.) A five-note figure promi-

27

nent in the Quintet is again in evidence; and when Pamina gives expression to her joy in an expansive phrase, the cocky trill-and-arpeggio theme accompanies Papageno's 'Sh, I know better'. He plays his pipes [6]. Tamino's flute answers; and they are hurrying in the direction of the sound when Monostatos creeps up on them (his musical idiom, as before, an angry version of Papageno's), and calls his slaves to tie them up. Just in time Papageno remembers the magic bells, and at their first tinkling strains [18] Monostatos and the slaves are enchanted out of themselves and dance away, laughing with delight. Pamina and Papageno moralise to an exquisite folksong-like tune (echoed later by Schubert's song *Heidenröslein*) [19]. Their moment of happiness is cut short by a fanfare of trumpets and drums, followed by an offstage chorus hailing Sarastro. Both Pamina and Papageno are terrified but the difference in their natures and in their destinies, till now concealed by their common interest and mutual sympathy, is clearly reflected in their music: Papageno's earthy and fragmented, with unison accompaniment, Pamina's expansive and exalted even in fear, and simply but warmly harmonised.

A grand processional chorus in C major now heralds the entry of Sarastro, who arrives in a chariot drawn by six lions. Pamina kneels before him, to five firm chords on strings and woodwind (to which for the first time the gleam of Masonic basset-horns is added). Now more than ever the music conveys the sweetness and nobility of her nature. Her conversation with Sarastro is in a style between arioso and recitative; the musical idiom is without formal restriction of any kind and as natural as speech, yet of unparalleled eloquence. Sarastro (in phrases that Beethoven remembered when he composed the Minister's statement about human brotherhood in the final scene of *Fidelio*) bids Pamina rise, and gently rebukes her, seeking to draw her away from her mother's influence. He knows the secret of her heart. Monostatos has no power over her, she is destined for another, but he cannot yet set her free. Had he left her in her mother's hands, her happiness would have been lost for ever. Only a man can guide her heart's passions to their true fulfilment. Monostatos bustles in (*Allegro*), wheedling and assertive; he has caught Tamino, who with the help of this strange bird (pointing to Papageno) was trying to kidnap Pamina. But Tamino and Pamina have seen one another, and for the moment, in each other's arms, are oblivious of everything else. (It is characteristic of this unconventional work that the lovers' first meeting, should be accomplished almost in parenthesis, in fifteen bars of rapid tempo.) Monostatos drags them apart and, kneeling at Sarastro's feet, demands the reward for faithful service. He is granted it — seventy-seven strokes of the bastinado — and taken away. Sarastro orders Tamino and Papageno to be conducted, with heads covered, to the temple of initiation. The chorus, in jubilant C major with drums and trumpets prominent, sings of virtue and justice, the path to mankind's redemption and the kingdom of heaven upon earth.

Act Two

From now on the work takes on openly the character of a religious initiation, while retaining its *Singspiel* form and pantomime style. Even more than Act One, Act Two is made up of short contrasting scenes; and the trials of Tamino and Pamina are continually offset by the comic adventures of Papageno, as he pursues his destiny on a different level of being, towards his own union of male and female. There are those who are offended by this mixture of high and low; and in an attempt to minimise it, cuts are commonly made in the spoken dialogue. The dialogue, however, contains information necessary for an understanding of the story; and so far from being a weakness and a mere concession to popular taste, the mixture of genres is central to the work. And at every stage of the action the music articulates and illuminates the dramatic situation.

No. 9 March of the Priests [20].

A sacred grove of palm-trees, with silvery trunks and golden leaves symbolising woman and man — the gold superior to the silver (as the sun's direct light is superior to the reflected light of the moon) yet issuing from it. Sarastro and the Priests assemble to the music of a serene, flowing march [20]. For the first time since *Idomeneo*, the spirit of Gluck breathes through Mozart's music. The scoring, full yet lucid, has not been heard in the work before: a single flute, basset-horns, bassoons, horns, trombones and quiet strings.

The Priests take their seats on thrones and, raising golden horns to their lips, blow the Threefold Chord (No. 9a) [1b]. The chord is heard several times during the discussion that follows, in which the Priests listen to and endorse Sarastro's plan for Tamino's initiation and the frustration of the Queen of the Night's plots against the brotherhood. Two priests (one of them known as the Speaker) are sent to bring Tamino and his companion to the temple courtyard and to instruct them in the duties of mankind and the power of the gods.

No. 10 Aria with chorus SARASTRO, PRIESTS [21].

Once again, a completely new sonority — basset-horns, trombones, violas in two parts and cellos (no violins or double basses) — to underline the solemnity of this prayer for the safety of the newly admitted pair in the midst of their perilous ordeals; and, again, music of powerful simplicity. The solo part demands a true bass with strong and resonant low notes and the breath-control to deliver it smoothly, in long phrases, not broken up into groups of a few notes. At the end of each half of the aria, the four-part male chorus repeats the final phrase, with varied distribution of parts — a mysterious effect. The three-bar orchestral epilogue conveys, by the simplest means, a total sense of finality.

A courtyard of the temple. Tamino and Papageno are led in, and the covering is taken from their heads. It is night, and thunder is rumbling. Tamino is steadfast, Papageno panic-stricken. In answer to the Speaker, Tamino promises to undertake the ordeals, but the Second Priest is less successful with his companion, even when he hints that Sarastro may have found him a Papagena who is his living image. Papageno would rather stay single and enjoy his familiar creature comforts than face the ordeals, if he can't have her without them. He promises, however, to remain silent if she appears.

No. 11 Duet TWO PRIESTS [22].

The Second Priest and another (the Speaker's is a non-singing role) emphasise the importance of guarding against the wiles of womankind: death and destruction have overtaken all who disobeyed this cardinal law during the ordeals. The advice is timely, as the next scene will show; yet the old-fashioned, rather pompous cut that Mozart has given their duet — underlined by surprisingly full orchestration (including brass and drums in the final bars) — is surely intentional: Sarastro's plan to include a representative woman in the highest rank of the order is certainly beyond the vision of most of the brotherhood.

On the departure of the priests, the two friends are left alone in the darkness.

No. 12 Quintet THREE LADIES, TAMINO, PAPAGENO [23].

Papageno has time only to cry plaintively for light and Tamino to urge him to be patient, before the Three Ladies spring up out of the earth and confront them: the Queen is near at hand, distressed at their apostasy; they will be destroyed if they give further heed to the lies of the priests and remain a moment longer in the temple. The Ladies' music belies the seriousness of their words. From the first phrase (an echo of the finale of Mozart's string quartet in the same key of G major), it is in the comically frivolous, airy vein of their scenes in Act One. Papageno is nervy and disposed to attend to them but Tamino, prudent and unshakeable, manages to restrain him. The Ladies pout and plead, in vain: they are forced to recognise their failure, and make ready to leave, in music that Mozart is able to make both silly and beautiful. The final G major cadence gives way without warning to a roar of indignation in C minor from an offstage chorus of priests at the profanation of the holy precincts; and to flashes of lightning and thunderclaps and repeated diminished sevenths, fortissimo and across the beat, the Ladies sink into the earth and vanish. Papageno, echoing their final cry of horror, falls to the ground. But the Threefold Chord [1b], ringing out, signals that the ordeal has been passed successfully.

The Speaker and the Second Priest return with torches. Tamino has a hood placed over his head and is led off by the Speaker. The Second Priest with difficulty rouses Papageno and takes him away too, protesting as he goes that this endless trekking about is enough to put a man off love for good.

The scene changes to a garden, with a ring of trees in the shape of a horseshoe, and in the foreground a grassy bank. In the middle of the trees is a rose-arbour, in which Pamina is lying asleep, the moonlight shining on her upturned face. Her ordeals, the equivalent of Tamino's, are about to begin. Monostatos creeps up and observes her hungrily.

No. 13 Aria MONOSTATOS [24].

Monostatos's character as *schwarz*-Papageno is again expressed in this whispered, lustful aria in which the Moor complains angrily of his want of a woman, and resolves to satisfy his hunger with Pamina — if the moon will only hide its light. (Monostatos thus affirms his allegiance to the domain of darkness.) Apart from a single *mezzo forte* accent in each verse, the busy, rapid orchestral accompaniment, topped by piccolo, is *pianissimo* throughout; but Mozart has given it a tingling intensity, comic and diabolical, so that the music positively dances with a kind of Priapic frenzy.

Before Monostatos can touch Pamina, with a clap of thunder the Queen of the Night rises out of the earth beside her couch and dismisses him (he does not go, however, but hides and listens). The conversation between mother and daughter tells us certain important things, in particular of the struggle between matriarchy and patriarchy, passion and reason, which underlies the opera. The Queen's husband, Pamina's father, was Sarastro's predecessor as High Priest of the Sun, and before his death entrusted the emblem of his authority, the seven-fold circle of the sun, not to his wife but to Sarastro. The Queen has been driven to attempt to recover by force what she considers to be rightly hers. Her champion Tamino has been seduced by the enemy and now her daughter too, she urges, is in mortal danger. All will be ended unless Pamina is able to bring Tamino, before dawn illumines the earth, to the subterranean vaults that lead to her domain, or unless, failing that, Pamina kills Sarastro with the dagger that she now thrusts into her hand.

No. 14 Aria QUEEN OF THE NIGHT [25a].

The vengeance of hell boils within her, death and despair flame about her: if Pamina does not plunge the dagger into Sarastro's heart, she is her daughter no longer, she is for ever an outcast. Gods of revenge, hear a mother's oath! The whole style of this prodigious aria, and the orchestration (with its thrillingly decisive interventions of trumpets and drums), suggest a dramatic soprano. Even more than in the Queen's aria in Act One (No. 4), the coloratura [25b] should be sung not lightly but with maximum vehemence; the mask that she wore then is stripped from her. The singer must of course have a range of two octaves, up to top F, but no less necessary is the power to project the manic insistence of those repeated Fs and Gs in the middle of the compass, at 'be rejected for ever, abandoned for ever, destroyed for ever!', and the splendour of the terrifying sustained B flat at the end. The music, adequately sung, is as momentous as the grandest things in *Idomeneo* or *Don Giovanni*.*

Left alone, Pamina rejects the thought of murder. Monostatos reappears and again threatens her. Sarastro intervenes and, dismissing the Moor forever from his service, gently explains to the bewildered girl that she will only find happiness away from her mother. Victory depends on Tamino. If he survives his trials, the Queen will leave the vaults of the temple where now she roams, brooding on revenge, and return to the domain of night, her power finally at an end.

No. 15 Aria SARASTRO [26].

But thoughts of revenge are far from those who dwell in this holy place, where friendship and love are the lights that guide all pilgrims worthy to be called men. The serenity of the aria's flowing melodic lines and the warmth of its flute and bassoon colouring are the positive counterpart of the Queen's outburst of hatred, exorcising its malevolence. As before, Sarastro's music calls for the ample legato and powerful low notes of a true basso cantante.

In another part of the temple, Tamino and Papageno, their heads uncovered, are led in to await their next ordeal. Silence is again enjoined. Tamino has constantly to shush his talkative companion. Papageno longs for a drink. An old hag appears and offers him a large beaker of water. He cannot resist talking to her. When she tells him that she is 18 years old and has a sweetheart called Papageno who is standing right beside her, he throws the water in her face. She is about to tell him her name, when there is a roll of thunder and she vanishes.

No. 16 Trio THREE BOYS [27].

The Three Boys come floating down in an aerial car, bringing the Flute and the Bells and a table laid with food and drink. Their music, in a warm, bright A major full of serene, playful gravity, with whimiscal little flourishes for violins, flutes and bassoons, is as bewitching as any in the score.

Papageno, seemingly uninterested in having the bells restored to him, sets to work on the supper and invites Tamino to join him. Without answering, Tamino takes the flute and plays it. The sound

---

* The aria begins, in the voice, with the pattern of notes — D-A-F-E-D — that is found so often in the key of D minor in Mozart's music: e.g., in *Don Giovanni*, 'Fuggi, crudele, fuggi', 'Bisogna aver corraggio' (Act One finale), 'Lascia, lascia alla mia pena' (Sextet). See also the opening of the Piano Concerto K.466 and the Minuet of the Quartet K.421.

brings Pamina running to him but he turns away with a sigh and refuses to speak to her.

No. 17 Aria PAMINA [28].

Pamina gives way to inconsolable grief: never more will her heart know the wonder of love. 'Tamino, see, these tears flow for you alone, beloved. If you feel no answering love, then in death alone will I find peace'. Even by the standards of *The Magic Flute*, the economy and purity of the music are astonishing. The string accompaniment is a simple, almost unvaried succession of short chords in groups of two separated by a rest — a poignant echo of the Act One duet with Papageno (No. 7), where the same pattern of notes in the same metre accompanied her naive declaration of faith in the power of love: here the effect is faltering and piteous. Long-drawn phrases for flute, oboe and bassoon strike sharply across it at moments of harmonic intensification. And the vocal line, in its rise and fall, its keen anguish and utter dejection, is like a musical distillation of suffering itself. After the voice has ceased, the strings, contained till then, well out in a flood of compassion.

The Threefold Chord [1b] now summons Tamino and Papageno. Papageno is in no hurry: he will finish his meal even if Sarastro's lions tried to drag him from it. Immediately the lions appear; and Tamino, hearing his cries, has to hurry back and play the flute to get rid of them. Two further blasts of the Threefold Chord are required before Papageno will join Tamino.

No. 18 Chorus of Priests.

A hall of pyramids. In sonorous D major, with horns, trumpets, and trombones (but no drums) the priests sing a hymn of thanksgiving to the gods [29]. Darkness is in retreat before the brightness of the sun. Tamino is coming into possession of a new life; soon (the word is sung in solemn threefold repetition) he will be an initiate.

Tamino is led in. Sarastro reaffirms the purpose of his mission. Then he calls for Pamina. Amid a profound silence she enters with her head covered. Sarastro removes the covering. He tells her to say goodbye to Tamino.

Emmy Destinn (Pamina), Edward Lankow (Sarastro) and Leo Slezak (Tamino) at the Met.

No. 19 Trio PAMINA, TAMINO, SARASTRO [30].

The music of this hauntingly beautiful piece reflects the ambiguity of the dramatic situation: Pamina and Tamino summoned to bid each other a 'last farewell' yet assured by Sarastro that they will see one another again. The anxious, restless quaver accompaniment on bassoons, violas and cellos is in contrast to the ordered progress of the harmonies and the firm and glowing vocal line of the two men. Pamina sings on her own at first and gives full expression to her feelings in phrase after glorious phrase. Only at Sarastro's words, 'The hour has struck, you must part', do the lovers' voices join, to lament the bitterness of separation and pray for golden peace to fill their hearts. The texture becomes increasingly contrapuntal, the harmonies richer and the emotional expression more passionate, before the quiet, resigned close.*

A moment after they have gone, Papageno runs in, calling for Tamino. Their paths have finally diverged. Papageno tries the doors, only to be driven back each time by a voice crying 'Go back!'. When the Speaker appears and tells him that he will never experience the joys of the initiated, he does not mind, having had more than his fill of the mysteries: there are, as he remarks, plenty of others like him; and he cheers up and forgets his misery when, having told the priest that his greatest and indeed only desire in the world is for a good glass of wine, he sees a great beaker of red wine rise out of the ground. Under its influence he remembers another wish, and plays the magic bells to make it come true.

No. 20 Aria PAPAGENO [31, 32].

A young wife would be bliss for him, he'd be one of the blessed then. If only one of all the lovely girls there are in the world would come to him in his need! If none comes, he'll mope himself to death, he'll burn in his own flame. But a kiss from a little wife would cure everything. The tune is not original to *The Magic Flute*; it was taken from a popular song of the time. The glockenspiel part, increasingly elaborated during the three verses, was played by Mozart at least once, as he described in a letter to his wife Constanze:

During Papageno's aria with the glockenspiel I went behind the scenes, as I felt a sort of impulse today to play it myself.

* It is sometimes said that this scene makes nonsense of Pamina's subsequent suicide attempt, and that the Trio is wrongly placed and should come earlier. One could reply that such a solution creates more problems than it solves; but the truth is that, except to the literal-minded, there is no problem. The griefs and conflicts under which Pamina will nearly break have not been resolved by the Trio; the crucial question of her mother's influence on her remains to be settled, and her reunion with Tamino has been tantalisingly brief and overshadowed by doubt. Both the music and the words breathe a mood of sadness and poignant tenderness that, for Pamina, is only partly qualified by a vague hope: the most vivid reality is her enforced parting from Tamino. The Trio sounds out of place when performed near the beginning of the act, in a different context from that in which Mozart and Schikaneder placed it.

Papageno's aria (No. 20) in the manuscript score

Well, just for fun, at the point where Schikaneder has a pause, I played an arpeggio. He was startled, looked behind the wings and saw me. When he had his next pause, I played no arpeggio. This time he stopped and refused to go on. I guessed what he was thinking and again played a chord. He then struck the glockenspiel [i.e. the magic bells] and said "Shut up". Whereupon everyone laughed. I am inclined to think that this joke taught many of the audience for the first time that Papageno does not play the instrument himself. [*trans.* Emily Anderson]

Papageno's wish is answered instantly, to his alarm, by the reappearance of the old crone, who capers in, leaning on a stick and calling him her angel. Since the alternative, she says, is solitary confinement on bread and water for all eternity, he is forced to swear to be true to her (with reservations). As he does so, she is transformed before his eyes into a young girl with feathers just like himself. He stammers out 'Papagena!' and is on the point of seizing her, when the Speaker whisks her away: Papageno is not yet worthy. As he is vowing to catch her whatever happens to him, the ground gives way beneath him.

No. 21 Finale.

In a small garden, at daybreak, the Three Boys await the rising of the sun which will disperse for ever the dark night of

35

superstition [33]. They pray that peace will enter the hearts of men; then (the words are those of the final chorus of Act One) mankind will achieve the kingdom of heaven on earth. But Pamina still knows no peace. Grief at Tamino's seeming indifference and the final struggle of her soul to free itself from her mother's influence have driven her to the verge of madness, and she has resolved to take her life [34]. The Boys, seeing her wandering about the garden distraught, with the Queen's dagger in her hand, hurry to her and with gentle strength and healing words take charge of her: Tamino loves her and they will lead her to him. Pamina's sorrow is turned to joy. This scene is arguably the loveliest in the score. As in their A major Trio (No. 16), the Boys' music is delicate and airborne, to which the glow of clarinets, bassoons and horns and the key of E flat lend a serene solemnity. The contrast between their flowing, disciplined phrases and Pamina's more and more wild (yet always supremely beautiful) melodic line is marvellously imagined, as is the gradual growth of tension, by means of syncopated upper strings and an increasingly insistent bass, to the moment of truth, where G minor, the key of Pamina's grief, yields decisively to E flat major. Even in the joyful *Allegro* which follows, her line remains wayward at first, as though she can hardly dare to believe what the Boys have told her. Calm returns only gradually to her; when it does, her voice combines with the other three, then breaks free again, to soar up to an exultant high B flat, sustained for four bars, then swooping down nearly two octaves, like a bird released from captivity.

A powerful three-note summons on unison strings and trombones, answered by a plangent phrase for woodwind and cellos, announces the climax of the drama. We are in a harsh landscape, a place where two mountains meet. In one can be seen, through iron grills, a roaring waterfall, in the other a fiery furnace. Between the mountains, a pyramid, with an inscription in transparent letters. Two men in black armour, with flames coming from their helmets, lead in Tamino, lightly dressed and without shoes. They recite the inscription: he who travels this difficult road will be purified by fire, water, air and earth; if he can overcome the terror of death, he will rise to heaven and be received into the mysteries of Isis and Osiris. The music of their chant is a Lutheran chorale ('*Ach Gott, vom Himmel sieh darein*') [35]. Woodwind and trombones play in unison with the two voices, while the strings develop an austere fugue round the chorale, in the manner of Bach [36]. (Mozart had encountered Bach's music, then largely forgotten, at Baron van Swieten's Sunday morning musical gatherings in Vienna, and had also had the opportunity to look through the manuscript parts of some of Bach's motets on his way through Leipzig two years earlier; it may not be mere chance that the rising figure which begins Mozart's fugue subject recalls '*Guter Nacht, o Wesen*' in Bach's motet *Jesu, meine Freude*, where the soul puts the cares and corruptions of worldly life behind it.) The music has generated a formidable tension, and it does not relax when the chorale ends and, to a simple string accompaniment, Tamino steps forward, preparing to enter the gates. The sudden sound of Pamina's voice, calling from near, stops him: 'Tamino, wait — I must see you!' Tamino and the men in armour are shaken out of their solemnity. The music breaks into a surprised and excited *Allegretto*. Now, cries Tamino (and the armed men confirm it), they will never be parted, they will go together into the temple: a woman whom night and death do not frighten is worthy and will be initiated.

The drama has reached its heart. It is now Pamina, refined by suffering, who leads Tamino [37]; and, explaining to him how her father made the Flute, she bids him play it, for its power will carry them through death's dark night. Then they pass into the furnace, and are later seen walking through the waterfall; and when they have passed through, they embrace. A door opens into a temple, brilliantly lit. Pamina and Tamino, 'the noble pair', enter and are welcomed by the brotherhood with shouts of triumph. The sublimity of the '*Magic Flute* style' attains its height in this scene. Nothing could be simpler than the harmonisation of Pamina's vocal line, nothing more obvious than the accompaniment of repeated string chords and long horn and woodwind notes over a rising five-note pizzicato figure in the bass; yet the emotional intensity of this music catches at the listener's heart. It moves with an ease that makes it seem totally natural and unpremeditated; yet when, after Pamina has recounted the origin of the Flute, the tonality regains F major and the four voices combine in an exalted quartet [38], we experience a feeling of concord and perfect fulfilment of which there are few parallels in music. After that there is a pause; and then, as Pamina and Tamino pass through the fire and the water, comes the strangest thing in the score, a climax of mysterious stillness. Without raising his voice, and by means of a quiet march played by a handful of instruments — a slow but florid melody for solo flute [39], punctuated at the end of each phrase by brass chords followed by soft drumbeats (always on the offbeat) — Mozart creates an overwhelming sense of tension, the ordeals of a lifetime compressed into a few bars.

Two more issues remain to be resolved. Papageno, in his search for Papagena, has come to the little garden where the Three Boys saved Pamina from taking her life. He has brought a rope with him, and he attaches it to the branch of a tree. In the intervals of talking he blows his panpipes [6], hoping for an answering bird-call [40], but when none comes his bouncy, irrepressible G major turns to a woebegone G minor (with harmonies that only half-humorously recall Pamina's aria); and, saying goodbye to the perfidious world, he gets ready to hang himself. The Boys, however, are once more at hand, floating down in their aerial car; and just as their influence healed Pamina's grief, so now (in a musical idiom akin to Papageno's earthier chatter) they excitedly remind him of the magic bells, which the silly fellow in his pre-occupation had forgotten: their sound will bring his girl to him. While Papageno, with gleeful solemnity, plays the bells [41], the Boys fetch Papagena from their car. At first, hardly able to believe their good fortune, the two of them can only stare at each other and stammer the syllables of their names [42]. Then, with violins trilling and bassoons gurgling delightedly, they picture the joys of their life together and the endless line of little Papagenos and Papagenas that the gods in their goodness will bless them with. The orchestration is of marvellous freshness and brilliance. Note too the trill-and-arpeggio figure, now innocent and positive, its aggressiveness fruitfully channelled into the begetting of children. Papageno's quest, too, has reached its appointed end.

As they scamper away, the Queen of the Night, Monostatos and the Three Ladies rise from the ground, bent on a last attempt to overthrow the brotherhood. The music [43], in stealthy string staccatos and tremolos, eerie woodwind chords and close vocal harmony, conveys an effect not so much sinister as dreamlike, unreal. The Queen and her creatures, or rather the base appetites and unredeemed attributes they represent, do not have to be defeated by force but can be cast off in one final spasm, to return to the night of illusion to which they belong, for they are by now only shadows, faint memories of former discords in the unenlightened soul, fading for ever in the splendour of the rising sun. There is an elemental roar, with syncopated string chords, a blare of woodwind and brass in diminished seventh harmony, then the sky clears; the stage becomes one radiant sun, with Sarastro on high and Pamina and Tamino in priestly garments, priests on either side of them, and the Three Boys with flowers in their hands. Sarastro, in triumphant recitative, proclaims the passing of night. Then we hear again the C minor music that introduced the scene with the armed men, now transposed into the relative major, a solemn, brilliant E flat, for a hymn of thanksgiving to Isis and Osiris [44]. There follows a jubilant Allegro [45], celebrating the victory of virtue and justice and the everlasting reign of beauty and wisdom.

Perhaps, after all the commentaries that have been lavished on this marvellous work, the wisest words are those uttered by the Three Boys: 'Schweige still' — 'Keep quiet and listen'. Or, as Dent put it, 'The story of the opera is itself a lesson to those who would understand its music; we must prepare ourselves by silence and meditation, we must pass through the fire and water, before we can enter the temple of wisdom'.

Musical Examples

Musical Examples (a), (b) and (c) to which David Cairns refers in the preceding article.

Example (a)

No. 4

No. 17

Example (b)

No. 1

No. 5

No. 5

No. 6

No. 8

No. 8

No. 8

No. 12

No. 21

Example (c)

No. 1

No. 6

No. 8

A Public for Mozart's Last Opera

a review of opinions on 'The Magic Flute',
collected and edited by Nicholas John

Since its opening night, Mozart's last opera has been the centre
of controversy. The team of Imperial Kapellmeister and populist
actor-manager was odd in the first place, and their choice of subject
turned out to be something new for Mozart — though in the conventional *Singspiel* form — and unique for the world. But for his
thriftlessness, Schikaneder would have made a fortune from the
proceeds. In October 1791, there was a performance of it at the
Theater auf der Weiden almost every night and he revived it regularly
by popular request over the next ten years. The Viennese success
was followed by exceptionally well attended productions all over
German-speaking Europe. To establish some reasons for this popularity, we may consider firstly the attraction of the stage spectacle,
then the dialogue, serious and comic, and lastly the score.

Everyone can sympathise with Mozart's rueful comment about
the prospect of taking his mother-in-law to a performance: 'She will
see it but not hear it'. Schikaneder spent lavishly on the first production (and indeed on two subsequent ones) in order to please his
audience. The effects are essential to the opera, that is, to the
music: many commentators have pointed out, for example, how
bare the march through the Trials of Fire and Water would sound
outside its dramatic context. This was demonstrated many years
later, when the impresario of Her Majesty's Theatre in the Haymarket, Benjamin Lumley, gave, at the singer's request, a single
'Grand Classical Performance' of the opera to mark Jenny Lind's
return to the London stage; the result was 'a perfect failure'.

'Could it have been otherwise? Any device to treat a lyrical
drama as if it were not a drama, or, in other words, to cheat a
theatrical representation of its necessary appliances, so as to
evade the "stage", could be nothing but a failure. The great
masterpiece of Mozart, without the essential accessories of
scenery and action, without the illustrative resources which the
composer himself contemplated, was simply rendered dreary
and incomprehensible. Where was the well-known "Jenny
Lind" crush? The house was comparatively empty. Where was
the customary enthusiasm amounting to a mania? The applause
was cold and feeble. The singer who had been accustomed to
hear those same walls ring with plaudits, could not but feel
chilled at the faint and rare echoes of that night, so different
from the noisy demonstrations of the previous year. The
Flauto Magico was accordingly the first and last of these
disappointing "grand classical performances", permission for
which had been with so much difficulty wrung from
Mademoiselle Lind . . .'

The very heavy demands made on the scenic artist are partly due

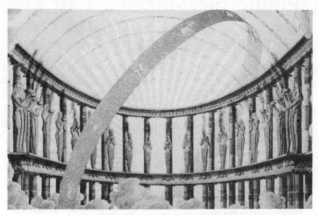

Simon Quaglio's design for Berlin 1816

to the symbolic importance of most of the props and effects. In reply to the enthusiastic recommendation of Frederick William II of Prussia (March 1792), the co-director of the Berlin National Theatre wrote critically,

'It seems to have been the author's intention to crowd together every conceivable difficulty for the stage designer and machinists, and a work has thus been created whose sole merit is visual splendour. At least, it is impossible for an audience which is ignorant of certain mysteries and incapable of seeing through the dark and heavy veil of allegory, to find the slightest interest in it. I regret moreover that the great composer Mozart has had to squander his talent on such unrewarding, mystical and untheatrical material'.

The opera has challenged the imagination of some of the finest theatre designers, notably in our own day Marc Chagall (the Met., 1967) and David Hockney (Glyndebourne, 1978). We are also fortunate that the designs by Schinkel (Berlin, 1816) and Simon Quaglio (Munich, 1818) have been preserved as exquisite examples

Joseph Quaglio's design for Munich 1793

The trials by fire (right) and water (left) in Schikaneder's production, in a coloured engraving by Josef and Peter Schaffer, 1795. Historisches Museum der Stadt Wien)

of neo-classical and early Romantic art. The poet, playwright and composer, E.T.A. Hoffmann, reviewed a performance where Schinkel's designs were used.

'Much has already been said and written about the sets. Suffice it to say that only the so-called *cognoscenti* fail to give due praise to Schinkel's ingenious and subtle creations.

'It was the opinion, in the vicinity of the Reviewer, that the

David Hockney's design for the Trial by Water (Glyndebourne, 1978: photo: Guy Gravett)

moonlight gleaming on the lovely groups of trees in the inner court was entirely natural; to which someone interjected that that was not proper. In his view, the sets should be completely fantastic; for since the characters themselves are not natural, they seem strange and fantastic in a natural setting. He thought it would be a good idea to have red or sky-blue trees. There is an element of truth in this but it is still a fairly strange opinion, from a fairly strange man.'

This articulate approach to *The Magic Flute* leads us to the second controversial element of the opera: just as each of us have a more or less clear personal view about what its fantasy world should look like, we also have decided opinions about how seriously to take Sarastro's pronouncements, and how topical Papageno's jokes should be! The contrast between comedy and solemnity is, in fact, so marked in the dialogue that it lends credit to the claim that it was written by two authors. Giesecke, the actor in Schikaneder's troupe who played the Third Slave and later became Professor of Mineralogy at Dublin University, claimed years later to have written most of it himself, leaving Schikaneder only to write his own comic scenes. We do not know how much Mozart himself contributed to the text. At any rate, subsequent producers have felt free to edit scenes (such as the opening of the second act) and sometimes to omit whole sequences which explain the plot for fear of boring audiences. The result is often no improvement because an audience who cannot understand the action is not in the best position to appreciate the music. The version adopted by ENO recognises this and shortens the scenes without omitting any information necessary to understand the meaning of the opera.

The comic dialogue is very similar to other examples of Viennese *Singspiel*, and Schikaneder himself wrote a sequel (1794) entitled *The Labyrinth or The Struggle for the Elements* in the same vein. (The music was composed by Winter and the project was a failure). Producers have also felt at liberty to update Schikaneder's jokes, so that, for example, Papageno's wine has changed from town to town into a beer from the local brewery. Yet, problematic though the dialogue may be, Mozart's music is unthinkable without it, as anyone who has heard a recording of just the musical numbers will know.

Mozart's score was not, of course, by any means ignored at the time and even Count Zinzendorf (an aristocratic diarist who had no particular sympathy for Mozart's work) noted that the music was 'pretty' — as was the scenery. More importantly, it was greatly admired by Salieri, Mozart's one-time rival for court favour whose musical opinion, after Haydn, he probably valued most, and Madame Cavalieri, the first Constanza in *The Seraglio*. They called it an 'operone' (a grand opera) 'worthy to be performed for the grandest festival and before the greatest monarch'. Another contemporary who took *The Magic Flute* seriously was Goethe, whose mother wrote excitedly to him from Frankfurt about the success of the opera there. (By employing the local children as extras for the animals she noted that even the jobbing gardeners wanted to see the performances!) Goethe himself saw the opera in Weimar in 1795 and the experience inspired him to begin a sequel himself. He never completed *The Magic Flute: Part Two*, possibly because he could not find a composer. It follows the story of Tamino and Pamina's succession to Sarastro, and their parenthood*, and is couched in verse which Einstein found 'full of fairytale radiance, poetic fantasy and profound thought'. Goethe's Tamino, Pamina and the Spirit of their first born child may be seen as models for Faust, Helena and Euphorion in *Faust II*. And in a more far-reaching view, we may trace from the ideals of *The Magic Flute* a recurrent theme of German art — that of a journey, through trials, to enlightenment.

Beethoven revered the ideal (exalted by the French Revolution) of the virtuous love of a man for a woman and enshrined it in *Fidelio*. There are numerous other points of similarity between these operas, notably the brilliant daylight of their triumphant finales, which follow trials in dark prisons. Dent concluded that Beethoven's opera looks back to Mozart more than it looks forward to Weber; and the latter has his own debts to *Die Zauberflöte*. After all, the theme of both *Der Freischütz* and *Euryanthe* is the test of love and fidelity. The fantastic world of *Oberon* is even more familiar because its source is the same book of Oriental tales, the book which was later to furnish Hofmannsthal with the idea for *Die Frau ohne Schatten*.

In these operas, and in *Lohengrin*, *Tannhäuser* and even *Parsifal*, important human spiritual values are expounded in myths and medieval romances. At the core of the fantasy, there is a concern for human virtues, quite distinct from the grand opera popular in France or the Italian *melodramma*.

In a wider sense Liszt and Shaw pointed out that *The Ring Cycle* was *The Magic Flute* of their time. G.B.S. wrote:

> '*Die Zauberflöte* is the ancestor, not only of the 9th Symphony but of the Wagnerian allegorical music-drama, with personified abstractions instead of individualised characters as *dramatis personae*'.

---

* The sequence of serious and comic scenes introduces the first-born son of Tamino and Pamina, over whom the other characters of the original struggle for dominance. Sarastro leaves the temple to spend a year in the world of men. The parents' love in the closing scenes assures them of safe passage through the Trials of Fire and Water to see their son, who has been imprisoned in a golden coffin by the Queen of the Night and Monostatos. The boy's spirit greets them and flies up above.

Wagner, himself, acknowledged the greatness of Mozart's music but said,

'It is possible to regret that this great stride of a musical giant should have laid the foundation for German opera and simultaneously imposed its limits by creating the masterpiece of the genre with a sureness of touch that could never be surpassed, and scarcely equalled. Although German opera flourishes today, it is in fact degenerate and declining as fast — alas! — as it reached its peak with Mozart's masterwork'.

To conclude this brief survey of the public reception of Mozart's last opera, let us return to E.T.A. Hoffmann's account of that Berlin performance. Any opera lends itself to disasters in performance and the technical challenge of *The Magic Flute* makes it more vulnerable than most.

Hoffmann refers to the general practice of adding a ballet to the evening's entertainment, which already lasts nearly three hours. One contemporary English critic asked for indulgence from the public for being too tired to stay at opera performances after 1 am!

'*The Magic Flute* has been frequently revived, and always to full houses. This shows how much it repays the trouble of not letting true masterpieces fall into oblivion. Furthermore, although we Germans are accused of always hankering after something new, it is only because we are spoilt by these masterpieces, and so pay no attention to a great deal of newer, poorer stuff, but wait impatiently for something really good to turn up; this is why we are so keen on novelty.

'The performance at the Theatre was excellent as usual, and Mademoiselle Eunike sang the aria '*Ach, ich fühl's*' in particular, in a most affecting manner. The exquisitely beautiful trio '*Soll ich dich Teurer*' was also superbly sung. The acting in the scene in which Papageno and the Moor see each other for the first time, and terrify each other completely, destroyed any intended effect. Where there is exaggeration, art is lost.

'The orchestral playing on this occasion lacked the precision and coherence which usually gives such a fine finish to their performance. The Allegro in the Overture was played too fast, and at the end especially it lost all its clarity. This kind of tempo will do in the concert hall but not in a large theatre, where the sound is muffled.

'A few other passages dragged, in contrast, especially the Chorus exclamation of '*Triumph, Triumph*', which was ragged from start to finish. The main reason for this, however, lies in the practically insurmountable difficulty of having the Chorus perform off-stage. In the libretto, the words 'Unseen Choirs' create a powerful impression but the effect in performance is as poor as the original impression is great. It is more or less essential to find some excuse for bringing the 'Unseen Choirs' into the open, near the orchestra. In the scenes we are speaking of, the Temple Guardians, priests and boys, could appear at each side at the front of the stage (or perhaps better in the front galleries above), while the two purified lovers are being admitted into the Inner Sanctum. The line *'Kommt — kommt'* would be no more out of place than the Spirits' ingenious reply, 'She's out of her mind' (*Sie ist von Sinnen*), to the question 'Where is she then?' (*Wo ist sie denn?*).

' In this context we should not fail to mention the excellent way in which the Spirits played their difficult role. Only once in the Finale of the Second Act were they slightly out of time with each other.

'What a shame it was that the beautiful passage *'Nur stille'* was completely lost due to a fault in the machinery (at least that is what the tree which moved restlessly backwards and forwards seemed to suggest). The Queen and the Moor had already ascended into the Upper World by a different route by the time the Ladies came on, and they had to hurry to greet their mistress with *'Die grosse Königin der Nacht'*.

'The final Chorus went off to perfection, in the most admirable manner. Our Chorus has improved perceptibly thanks to the tireless and praiseworthy efforts of Herr Leidel.

'The close of *The Magic Flute* is grave, solemn, and noble. If there really has to be a Ballet after it, then it should, in the Reviewer's opinion, be either completely unrelated to the opera, or else be performed in the same set, and be closely connected with the thought of the composer, rather than the librettist. The mysteries of Isis and Osiris, such as the consecration, should be represented symbolically, and the dance conceived in the most elevated sense, rather than as a series of amazing leaps and turns. The expressiveness and the novelty of such a performance would soon win over the mass of the public. There would then be no need for the Egyptian god, who was grave to the point of sullenness, or for him to find the comic pair of false Papagenos or the over-jocular Moors in his inner sanctum (his Boudoir), and he would be able to resist the temptation of having them thrown out by his two bronzed acolytes and his guard . . .'

The performance history of the opera outside those German-speaking countries where it was given regularly has been very curious.

In France, the constraints on the Opéra forbidding the presentation of music set to a foreign librettist's text, prompted an arrangement of the libretto under the title *Les Mystères d'Isis* (1801). This not only involved a wholesale reconstruction of the plot and renaming of the characters (Papagena became Mona, for example), but also, for good measure, a total dismemberment of the score. Excerpts from other Mozart operas and Haydn symphonies were included and the whole mixture served up to great public acclaim for several decades. The press dubbed it *Les misères d'ici* and Berlioz recalled (1837),

'It was thus, dressed up as an ape, got up grotesquely in cheap finery, with one eye gouged out, an arm withered, a leg broken, that they dared to present the greatest musician in the world to this French public, so delicate, so demanding, saying to it: 'Look — Mozart,' etc. O misérable . . . etc.'

Paris heard a German company in the authentic version in 1827 and waited until 1863 for a French translation.

England first heard the opera (as *Il Flauto magico*) at a benefit night for Giuseppe Naldi, the Italian tenor who had opened to immense success in *Così fan tutte*. It was one of the works presented at Covent Garden in the 1833 German season, when Wilhelmine Schroder-Devrient sang Pamina, the role in which she had made her world debut in 1821 in Vienna. A brilliant cast including Grisi (Pamina), Mario (Tamino), Giorgio Ronconi (Papageno), Karl Formes (Sarastro) and Pauline Viardot-Garcìa (Papagena) sang the opera at Covent Garden in 1851, with a Queen of the Night who reminded the critic Chorley 'of a pea-hen masquerading as a lark'.

Later in the century, Shaw took on Ruskin over his dismissal of the opera in a book on music. The passage is quoted fully because it is a splendid argument in which Shaw admits that his antagonist has 'a hundred times more insight in (his) mistakes than in most other men's accuracies'.

'Mr Ruskin is head and ears in love with Music; and so am I; but I am married to her, so to speak, as a professional critic, whereas he is still a wooer, and has the illusions of imperfect knowledge as well as the illuminations of perfect love. Listen to this, for example:
' "True music is the natural expression of a lofty passion for a right cause. In proportion to the kingliness and force of any personality, the expression either of its joy or suffering becomes measured, chastened, calm, and capable of interpretation only by the majesty of ordered, beautiful, and worded sound. Exactly in proportion to the degree in which we become narrow in the cause and conception of our passions, incontinent in the utterance of them, feeble of perseverance in them, sullied or shameful in the indulgence of them, their expression by musical means becomes broken, mean, fatuitous, and at last impossible: the measured waves of heaven will not lend themselves to the expression of ultimate vice: it must be for ever sunk in discordance or silence."
'I entirely agree with Mr Ruskin in this; but it will not hold

water, for all that. "The measured waves of heaven" are not so particular as he thinks. Music will express any emotion, base or lofty. She is absolutely immoral: we find her in Verdi's last work heightening to the utmost the expression of Falstaff's carnal gloating over a cup of sack, just as willingly as she heightened the expression of "a lofty passion for a right cause" for Beethoven in the Ninth Symphony. She mocked and prostituted the Orpheus legend for Offenbach just as keenly and effectively as she ennobled it for Gluck. Mr Ruskin himself has given an instance of this — a signally wrong instance, by the way; but let that pass for a moment:

' "And yonder musician, who used the greatest power which (in the art he knew) the Father of Spirits ever yet breathed into the clay of this world; who used it, I say, to follow and fit with perfect sound the words of the *Zauberflöte* and of *Don Giovanni* — foolishest and most monstrous of conceivable human words and subjects of thought — for the future amusement of his race! No such spectacle of unconscious (and in that unconsciousness all the more fearful) moral degradation of the highest faculty to the lowest purpose can be found in history".

'This is a capital instance of Mr Ruskin's besetting sin — virtuous indignation. If these two operas are examples of "foolishest and most monstrous" words fitted and followed with perfect sound — that is, with true music — what becomes of the definition which limits true music to "the natural expression of a lofty passion for a right cause"? Clearly, that will not do.

'And now may I beg Mr Ruskin to mend his illustration, if not his argument? The generation which could see nothing in *Die Zauberflöte* but a silly extravaganza was one which Mr Ruskin certainly belonged to in point of time; and he has for once sunk to the average level of its thought in this shallow criticism of the work which Mozart deliberately devoted to the expression of his moral sympathies. Everything that is true and vital in his worship of music would be shattered if it were a fact — happily it is not — that the music of Sarastro came from a silly and trivial mood. If I were to assure Mr Ruskin that Bellini's *Madonna with St Ursula*, in Venice, was originally knocked off as a sign for a tavern by the painter, Mr Ruskin would simply refuse to entertain the story, no matter what the evidence might be, knowing that the thing was eternally impossible. Since he sees no such impossibility in the case of *Die Zauberflöte*, I must conclude that he does not know the masterpieces of music as he knows those of painting.'

To bring the history of performances into this century, we should mention the Cambridge production prepared by E.J. Dent in 1907 and Beecham's performances at Drury Lane in 1914 with the incomparable Claire Dux as Pamina. Richard Tauber sang Tamino for Beecham at Covent Garden in 1938. Sadler's Wells Opera gave it during its first season at the Wells (1931) since when there have been regular revivals of 5 new productions.

'More knowledge is required to understand the value of this libretto than to mock it', wrote Goethe, and the extent of its Masonic significance is only now becoming fully appreciated. There will always be those, like Hoffmann's neighbour, who simply want to establish a fantasy world, with regard for neither realism nor symbolism. Allegory or fairy story? The debate continues. In a review such as this we can only touch upon the variety of attitudes which managements, artists and audiences have expressed towards this great work, in the hope that in future there will be evidence of no less imagination but rather more humility.

A scene from the ENO production, designed by John Stoddart. (photo: Donald Southern)

Thematic Guide

Many of the themes from the opera have been identified in the preceding articles by numbers in square brackets, which refer to the themes on these pages. The original numbers of the musical items in the full score have been noted in italics, and should not be confused with the numbers of the thematic guide. The numbers in square brackets also appear at relevant moments in the libretto so that the words can be related to the musical examples in the thematic guide.

[1a] OVERTURE
Adagio

[1b] THE THREEFOLD CHORD
Adagio

[2]
Allegro

[3] TAMINO (*No. 1 Introduction*)
Allegro

Oh help   me!   oh help   me!   can   no -   bo -   dy   hear me?
Zu Hil -   fe!   zu Hil -   fe!   sonst   bin   ich   ver -   lo - ren!

[4] THE THREE LADIES
Allegretto

2nd LADY   I   am   to
Ich soll - te

go? **1st LADY** I am to go?
fort? Ich soll - te fort?

3rd LADY I am to go?
Ich soll - te fort?

[5] THE THREE LADIES
Allegro

Now love - ly boy, I'll say a - dieu,
Du Jüng - ling, schön und lie - be - voll,

[6] PAPAGENO'S PIPES

[7] PAPAGENO (No. 2 Aria)
Andante

My trade is catch - ing birds, you know, I spread my nets and in they go!
Der Vo - gel fäng - er – bin ich ja, stets - lu - stig hei - sa hop - sa - ssa!

[8] TAMINO (No. 3 Aria)
Larghetto

No fi - ner picture I am sure was ev - er seen by man be - fore!
Dies Bild - nis ist be - zau - bernd schön, wie noch kein Au - ge je ge - sehn!

[9] QUEEN OF THE NIGHT (No. 4 Aria)
Larghetto

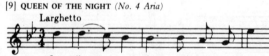

I die —— a thou - sand deaths each mo - ment
Zum Lei - den bin ich aus — er - ko - ren

[10] QUEEN OF THE NIGHT
Allegro moderato

You, you, you, I — choose now to be her sav —— iour
Du, du, du wirst — sie — zu be - frei - en ge - hen

[11] **PAPAGENO** *(No. 5 Quintet)*
Allegro

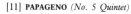

Hm! hm! hm! hm! hm! hm! hm! hm! hm! hm! hm! hm! hm! hm! hm! hm!

[12] **THE THREE LADIES**
Andante *sotto voce*

Three spir - its, young but old in wis - dom will
Drei Knab - en, jung, schön, hold und wei - se, um -

take you to Sa - ras - tro's king - dom
schwe - ben euch auf eu - rer Rei - se.

[13] **MONOSTATOS, PAMINA** *(No. 6 Trio)*
Allegro molto

M {You won't es - cape, do what you can! P {You are a heart - less e - vil man!
  {Du fei - nes Täub - chen, nur her - ein!   {O wel-che Mar - ter! wel - che Pein!

[14] **PAMINA** *(No. 7 Duet)*
Andantino

The gen - tle love of man and wo - man shows hu - mans
Bei Män - nern, wel - che Lie - be füh - len, fehlt auch - ein

are — a race a - part
gu - tes Her - ze nicht.

[15] **THE THREE BOYS** *(No. 8 Finale)*
Larghetto

The road you trod has led you here, ask here you'll find the goal you're seek - ing.
Zum Zie - le führt dich die - se Bahn, doch musst du, Jüng - ling, männ - lich sie - gen.

[16] **THE MAGIC FLUTE**
Andante

[17] **PAMINA, PAPAGENO**
Andante

Walk on tip-toe, cou-rage high. We'll be safe now, you and I.
Schnel-le Füs-se, ra-scher Mut, schützt vor Fein-des List und Wut.

[18] **MONOSTATOS'S DANCE**
Allegro

[19] **PAMINA, PAPAGENO**

How I wish that ev'-ry-man
Könn-te jed-er bra-ve Mann

[20] **MARCH OF THE PRIESTS** (*No. 9*)
Andante

sotto voce

[21] **SARASTRO** (*No. 10 Aria with Chorus*)
Adagio

Oh, Is- is and O-sir- is, hear us, we pray that
O, I- sis und O-si- ris, schen-ket der Weis-heit

you will guide this pair.
Geist dem neu-en Parr!

[22] **TWO PRIESTS** (*No. 11 Duet*)
Andante

Be on your guard for wom- man's hu- mours-
Be-wah-ret euch vor Wei- ber- tüc- ken:

[23] **THE THREE LADIES** (*No. 12 Quintet*)
Allegro

So! So! So! You are in Sa-ras-tro's court?
Wie? wie? wie? ihr an die-sem Schrec-kens-ort?

54

[24] MONOSTATOS (No. 13 Aria)

Allegro

All en - joy the beds of pass - ion, cling, ca - ress and stroke and kiss:
Al - les fühlt der Lie - be Freu-den, schnä-belt, tän-delt, herzt und küsst;

[25a] QUEEN OF THE NIGHT (No. 14 Aria)

Allegro assai

I feel my heart a - flame with hate and mur - der.
Der Höl - le Ra - che kocht in mei - nem Her - zen!

[25b]

Allegro assai

ah

[26] SARASTRO (No. 15 Aria)

Larghetto

To rule by Hate and Ven - geance is not our prac - tice here,
In die - sen heil'gen Hal - len kennt man die Ra - che nicht,

[27] THE THREE BOYS (No. 16 Trio)

Allegretto

now
Twice we've glad - ly come to meet you
Seid uns zum zwei - ten— mal will-kom-men

[28] PAMINA (No. 17 Aria)

Andante

Ah, I know that all is end - ed.
Ach, ich fühl's, es ist ver - schwun-den.

[29] CHORUS (No. 18)

Adagio

Oh Is - is and O - sir - is
O Is - is und O - sir - is

[30] PAMINA, SARASTRO (No. 19 Trio)

Andante moderato

P { My on - ly joy, ah must we part? S { You need not fear, but trust his heart.
  { Soll ich dich, Teu - rer, nicht mehr sehn?   { Ihr wer - det froh euch wie - der sehn.

55

31

PAPAGENO *(No. 20 Aria)*

Andante

I'd like a wife to hug me and keep me warm at night.
Ein Mäd - chen o - der Weib - chen wünscht Pa - pa - ge— no sich.

[32] **PAPAGENO**

Allegro

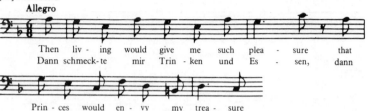

Then liv - ing would give me such plea - sure that
Dann schmeck- te mir Trin - ken und Es - sen, dann

Prin - ces would en - vy my trea - sure
könnt ich mit Für - sten mich mes - sen

[33] **THE THREE BOYS** *(No. 21 Finale)*

Andante

The sun a - ri - ses like a vi - sion and
Bald prangt, den Mor - gen zu ver - kün - den, die

brings a brigh - ter morn;
Sonn' auf gold - ner Bahn.

[34] **PAMINA**

Andante

And so a knife must wed me now?
Du al - so bist mein Bräu - ti - gam!

[35] **THE ARMED MEN**

Man that is born of wo - man walks thro' life in sha - dow.
Der, wel-cher wan-dert die-se Stra-sse voll Be-schwerd-en,

[36] **FUGUE**

Adagio

p

56

[37] PAMINA
Andante

Ta - mi - no   mine!   Oh   what   great   joy!
Ta - mi - no   mein!   O   welch   ein   Glück!

[38] PAMINA
Andante

We'll walk   un - harmed,   through   mu —————
Wir wan ————— deln   durch   des   To —————

TAMINO We'll   walk   un -   harmed   thro'
       Wir   wan -   deln   durch   des

TWO MEN IN ARMOUR They'll walk   un - harm ——— ed
               Ihr   wan - delt   durch ——— des

——— sic's   power
——— nes   Macht

mu   sic's   power
To -   nes   Macht

thro'   mu - sic's   power
To -   nes   Macht

[39] THE TRIALS MARCH
Adagio

[40] PAPAGENO
Allegro

Pa - pa - ge - na!   Pa - pa - ge - na!   Pa - pa - ge -   na!

[41] PAPAGENO
Allegro

Now bells, let your   mu -   sic   bring my sweetheart   here!
Klin-get, Glöck-chen   klin - get!   schafft mein Mäd - chen   her!

[42] PAPAGENO, PAPAGENA

Allegro

P'O Pa— pa— pa- P'A Pa— pa—

—pa P'O Pa— pa— pa— pa— P'A Pa— pa— pa— pa

[43] MONOSTATOS

Allegretto

We must be si - lent, si - lent, si - lent. We're near the
Nur stil - le, stil - le, stil - le, stil - le! Bald drin - gen

in - ner tem - ple now.
wir im Tem - pel ein.

[44] CHORUS

Andante

Hail the two who tri - umphed! Hail the two who tri - umphed!
Heil sei euch Ge -weih - ten! Heil sei euch Ge - weih - ten!

[45]

Allegro

p

The Magic Flute

an opera in two acts

Libretto by Emanuel Schikaneder
and Carl Ludwig Giesecke
English version: Lyrics by Michael Geliot
Dialogue by Anthony Besch

The complete German text of *Die Zauberflöte* is reprinted here. Although the dialogue is now always shortened in performance, there is no definitive performing edition. Over the years many German variations have been evolved, reflecting changing attitudes to 18th century conventions and what Mozart and his librettists intended or wanted. Whole scenes are sometimes omitted, or re-arranged in sequence; many lines are paraphrased, rewritten or cut. It is very rare for two productions to share the same dialogue.

The English text is the one used by English National Opera at the London Coliseum. Anthony Besch's version of the dialogue (made for his ENO production) is fuller and truer to the original than any previous English version. It is, inevitably, shorter than the German printed here beside it. In order to supply readers with an English rendering of all the original, I have supplied literal translations of passages which are omitted or paraphrased in the performing dialogue. These literal translations form no part whatsoever of the Geliot/Besch performing version and were made only for this Guide. They are clearly distinguished in the text from the performing dialogue by square brackets or, where they were too long to be suitably included in the text, in footnotes.

The stage directions follow Schikaneder's 1791 instructions and do not necessarily reflect the ENO (or any other modern) production. The musical numbers which follow the stage directions after an oblique are those given in the full score. The numbers in square brackets refer to the Thematic Guide.

Authorship of the libretto is traditionally attributed to Giesecke as well as Schikaneder, following E J Dent's monograph (1911) which did much to revive interest in the opera. It is not now accepted by all commentators, *vide* Rodney Milnes. - Editor.

Die Zauberflöte was first performed at the Theater auf der Wieden on September 30, 1791. It was first performed (in Italian) in London at the King's Theatre, Haymarket in 1811 and then at Covent Garden (in German) in 1833. It was first performed in the USA at the Park Theatre, New York, on April 17, 1833.

THE CHARACTERS

Sarastro	bass
Tamino	tenor
The Speaker	bass
A second priest	tenor
An old priest	bass
The Queen of the Night	soprano
Pamina, her daughter	soprano
First ⎫	soprano
Second ⎬ Ladies of the Queen	soprano
Third ⎭	mezzo-soprano
First ⎫	treble (soprano)
Second ⎬ Boys	treble (soprano)
Third ⎭	alto
Papageno	baritone
Papagena	soprano
Monostatos, a moor	tenor
First ⎫	tenor
Second ⎭ Men in Armour	bass
First ⎫	
Second ⎬ Slaves	speaking parts
Third ⎭	

Priests, Attendants, Populace, Slaves, Voices, Apparitions

Act One

A rocky scene dotted with a few trees. In the centre stands a temple, to which steep paths lead from either side.

Scene One. *Tamino, dressed in a magnificent Japanese hunting costume, enters over one of the rocks: he carries a bow without arrows; he is pursued by a serpent. | Introduction No. 1.*

TAMINO [3]

Oh help me! oh help me! can nobody hear me?	Zu Hilfe! Zu Hilfe! Sonst bin ich verloren,
The venomous fangs of the serpent are near me.	Der listigen Schlange zum Opfer erkoren!
Oh heaven, protect me! I cannot escape.	Barmherziger Götter! Schon nahet sie sich!
Ah rescue me, help me, save me!	Ach rettet mich! Ach schützet mich!

He falls unconscious. At that moment the door of the temple opens and the Three Ladies, veiled, enter each with a silver javelin.

THE THREE LADIES

Now we are here the beast shall die!	Stirb, Ungeheuer, durch unsere Macht!
He dies! He dies! The deed is done,	Triumph! Triumph! Sie ist vollbracht,
The battle won. We've set him free.	Die Heldentat! Er ist befreit
We've saved him through our bravery.	Durch unsres Armes Tapferkeit.

FIRST LADY
(looking at Tamino)

A handsome stranger, full of grace.	Ein holder Jüngling, sanft und schön!

SECOND LADY

I never saw so fair a face.	So schön, als ich noch nie gesehn!

THIRD LADY

Yes, yes, that's true, a lovely face.	Ja, ja, gewiss, zum Malen schön!

THE THREE LADIES

If I should fall in love one day	Würd ich mein Herz der Liebe weihn,
It will be with this youth I pray.	So müsst es dieser Jüngling sein.
But let us hasten to the Queen now	Lasst uns zu unsrer Fürstin eilen,
And tell her what we've done and seen here.	Ihr diese Nachricht zu erteilen.
Perhaps this good man can restore	Vielleicht, dass dieser schöne Mann
The peace and joy she knew before.	Die vor'ge Ruhe ihr geben kann.

FIRST LADY

So hurry and begone,	So geht and sagt es ihr,
I'll guard him here alone.	Ich bleib indessen hier.

SECOND LADY

No, no, I'd rather stay,	Nein, nein, geht ihr nur hin,
I'll watch him thro' the day.	Ich wache hier für ihn!

THIRD LADY

There's no cause for alarm,	Nein, nein, das kann nicht sein,
I'll keep him safe from harm.	Ich schütze ihn allein.

61

	FIRST LADY
I'll guard him here alone!	Ich bleib indessen hier!
	SECOND LADY
I'll watch him thro' the day!	Ich wache hier für ihn!
	THIRD LADY
I'll keep him safe from harm!	Ich schütze ihn allein!
	FIRST LADY
I'll guard him!	Ich bleibe!
	SECOND LADY
I'll watch him!	Ich wache!
	THIRD LADY
I'll keep him!	Ich schütze!
	ALL THREE
I, I, I.	Ich, ich, ich!

(each one to herself)

I am to go? Oh no, not so.	[4] Ich sollte fort? Ei, ei! Wie fein!
They'd like to be alone	Sie wären gern bei ihm allein.
I know. I shall not go.	Nein, nein, das kann nicht sein.

(one after the other, then all together)

I'd give up all my hopes of heaven	Was wollte ich darum nicht geben,
To live with this young man forever.	Könnt ich mit diesem Jüngling leben!
I know he would be good and kind.	Hätt ich ihn doch so ganz allein!
But they'll not leave, for love is blind!	Doch keine geht, es kann nicht sein.
And so I must be on my way.	Am besten ist es nun, ich geh. —
Now lovely boy, I'll say adieu.	[5] Du Jüngling, schön und liebevoll,
So dear young man, farewell to you.	Du trauter Jüngling, lebe wohl,
We'll meet again I pray.	Bis ich dich wieder seh'!

They go towards the door of the temple, which opens and closes behind them.

TAMINO
(awaking, and looking nervously around)

Where am I? Am I still alive or am I dreaming? The evil serpent lying dead at my feet . . . Have I been protected by Providence?	Wo bin ich? Ist's Phantasie, dass ich noch lebe? Oder hat eine höhere Macht mich gerettet? Wie? — Die bösartige Schlange liegt tot zu meinen Füssen?

He stands up, and looks around. In the distance, panpipes are heard, accompanied quietly by the orchestra. Tamino follows the sound. [6]

What's that I hear? There's a man coming through the trees . . . or something like a man.	Was hör' ich? Wo bin ich? Welch unbekannter Ort? Ha, eine männliche Gestalt nähert sich dem Thale.

He hides behind a tree.

Scene Two. *During the introduction, Papageno comes down a path. On his back he carries a cage of various birds. In his hands he holds the panpipe with which he accompanies his singing. / Aria No. 2*

PAPAGENO [7]

My trade is catching birds, you know,	Der Vogelfänger bin ich ja,
I spread my nets and in they go,	Stets lustig, heissa, hopsassa!

And all men know me as a friend	Ich Vogelfänger bin bekannt
Throughout the land, from end to end.	Bei alt und jung im ganzen Land.
I know what ev'ry cockbird likes	Weiss mit dem Locken umzugehn
So lure the peahen with my pipes.	Und mich aufs Pfeifen zu verstehn.
No wonder that I'm happy then	Drum kann ich froh und lustig sein,
Since I can catch both cock and hen.	Denn alle Vögel sind ja mein.

(He pipes.)

My trade is catching birds, you know,	Der Vogelfänger bin ich ja,
I spread my nets and in they go,	Stets lustig, heissa, hopsassa!
And all men know me as a friend	Ich Vogelfänger bin bekannt
Throughout the land, from end to end.	Bei alt und jung im ganzen Land.
But one thing still I'd like to get	Ein Netz für Mädchen möchte ich,
A dozen ladies in my net.	Ich fing sie dutzendweis für mich;
Yes I would think it very fine,	Dann sperrte ich sie bei mir ein,
If twelve young maidens could be mine.	Und alle Mädchen wären mein.

(He pipes.)

If twelve young maidens could be mine	Wenn alle Mädchen wären mein,
I'd build a cage of fine design,	So tauschte ich brav Zucker ein;
I'd choose the one who loved me best,	Die welche mir am liebsten wär,
We'd hop inside and make our nest.	Der gäb ich gleich den zucker her.
And if she then would be my wife	Und küsste sie mich zärtlich dann,
And kiss and comfort me through life	Wär sie mein Weib und ich ihr Mann.
She'd sleep beside me, snug and warm,	Sie schlief an meiner Seite ein,
And I would keep her safe from harm.	Ich wiegte wie ein Kind sie ein.

He pipes and, when the aria is finished, goes towards the temple door.

TAMINO
(taking him by the hand)

Hey there!	He da!

PAPAGENO

Who's that?	Was da?

TAMINO

You're a lively fellow, my friend . . .	Sag' mir, du lustiger Freund, wer du
Who are you?	bist!

PAPAGENO
(to himself)

That's a silly question —	Wer ich bin? Dumme Frage!

(aloud)

A man like you are. But who are you	Ein Mensch, wie du. Wenn ich dich nun
anyway?	fragte, wer du bist?

TAMINO

Well, to begin with, I'm a prince of royal	So würde ich dir antworten, dass ich aus
blood.	fürstlichem Geblüte bin.

PAPAGENO

Royal blood? Prince? You must speak	Das ist mir zu hoch. Musst dich
more plainly if I'm to understand you.	deutlicher erklären, wenn ich dich
	verstehen soll!

TAMINO

My father is a King who rules over many	Mein Vater ist Fürst, der über viele
countries and many people. [That's why	Länder und Menschen herrscht; darum
I'm called Prince.]	nennt man mich Prinz.

PAPAGENO

[Lands? People? Prince?]

Länder? — Menschen? — Prinz?

TAMINO

[That's why I ask you . . .]

Daher frag ich dich —

PAPAGENO

[Slowly! Let me ask the questions!]
Do you mean to say that beyond these
mountains there are other countries and
other people?

Langsam! Lass mich fragen! Sag'
du mir zuvor: gibt's ausser diesen Bergen
auch noch Länder und Menschen?

TAMINO

Yes! Many thousands.

Viele Tausende!

PAPAGENO

What a market for my parakeets.

Da liess' sich eine Spekulation mit
meinen Vögeln machen.

TAMINO

[Now tell me, in what country are we?]

Nun sag du mir, in welcher Gegend wir
sind?

PAPAGENO
(looking around)

[In what country? Between valleys and
mountains.]

In welcher Gegend? Zwischen Tälern
und Bergen.

TAMINO

[That's right enough.]
And now you must tell me who rules this
country?

Schon recht. Aber . . .
Wie nennt man eigentlich diese Gegend?
Wer beherrscht sie?

PAPAGENO

How would I know? You might as well
ask me how I came to be born.

Das kann ich dir ebenso wenig
beantworten, als ich weiss, wie ich auf
die Welt gekommen bin.

TAMINO
(laughing)

Don't you even know who your parents
were?

Wie? Du wüsstest nicht, wo du geboren,
oder wer deine Eltern waren?

PAPAGENO*

I only know that I was brought up by a
strange old man, and that my mother

---

* This conversation is set out in more detail in the original dialogue as follows:

PAPAGENO

Not a thing! I only know that an old but
very merry man brought me up and fed
me.

Kein Wort! Ich weiss nicht mehr und
nicht weniger, als dass mich ein alter,
aber sehr lustiger Mann auferzogen und
ernährt hat.

TAMINO

He was your father no doubt!

Das war vermutlich dein Vater?

64

was once a servant in the temple of the Starblazing Queen. My straw-hut protects me from rain and cold and I earn my living by catching birds for the Queen and her ladies. They give me food and drink in exchange.

TAMINO

Have you ever seen this Starblazing Queen you speak of?

Original dialogue cont'd

PAPAGENO

I don't know.	Das weiss ich nicht.

TAMINO

Did you never know your mother?	Hattest du denn deine Mutter nicht gekannt?

PAPAGENO

I never knew her. I have been sometimes told that my mother used to serve the starblazing Queen of the Night. But whether she is still alive or what has become of her, I do not know. All I do know is that, not far from here, is my straw hut which protects me from rain and cold.	Gekannt hab ich sie nicht. Erzählen liess ich mir's einigemal, dass meine Mutter einst da in diesem verschlossenen Gebäude bei der nächtlich stern-flammenden Königin gedient hätte. Ob sie noch lebt oder was aus ihr geworden ist, weiss ich nicht. Ich weiss nur so viel, dass nicht weit von hier meine Stroh-hütte steht, die mich vor Regen und Kälte schützt.

TAMINO

But how do you live?	Aber wie lebst du?

PAPAGENO

By eating and drinking, like any other man.	Von Essen und Trinken, wie alle Menschen.

TAMINO

How do you obtain that?	Wodurch erhältst du das?

PAPAGENO

From barter. I catch all sorts of birds for the starblazing Queen and her ladies; in exchange I receive daily food and drink from her.	Durch Tausch. Ich fange für die stern-flammende Königin und ihre Jungfrauen verschiedene Vögel; dafür erhalt ich täglich Speis' und Trank von ihr.

TAMINO
(aside)

Starblazing Queen? Supposing it should be the powerful sovereign of the night!	Sternflammende Königin? Wenn es etwa gar die mächtige Herrscherin der Nacht wäre!

(aloud)

Tell me, my good friend, have you ever been so lucky as to see this goddess of the night?	Sag mir, guter Freund, warst du schon so glücklich, diese Göttin der Nacht zu sehen?

PAPAGENO
(who has been playing his pipes occasionally)

Your last question is so stupid that I can tell that you come from a different country.	Deine letzte alberne Frage überzeugt mich, dass du in einem fremden Land geboren bist.

65

PAPAGENO

Seen her? You must be crazy! There's no
one alive that's ever seen her. Why are
you staring at me so suspiciously?

TAMINO

Because I'm beginning to doubt whether   Weil — weil ich zweifle, ob du Mensch
you're human.   bist.

PAPAGENO

What's that?   Wie war das?

Original dialogue cont'd

TAMINO

Don't be cross, my good friend! I only   Sei darüber nicht ungehalten, lieber
wanted to say —   Freund! Ich dachte nur —

PAPAGENO

See her? See the starblazing Queen? If   Sehen? Die sternflammende Königin
you ask me another such birdbrained   sehen? Wenn du noch mit einer solchen
question, as sure as my name is   albernen Frage an mich kommst, so sperr'
Papageno I shall pop you in my birdcage   ich dich, so wahr ich Papageno heisse,
like a bull finch (*pun: 'Gimpel' also means* wie einen Gimpel in mein Vogel-haus,
'birdbrain') and sell you with my other   verhandle dich dann mit meinen übrigen
birds to the Queen of the Night and her   Vögeln an die nächtliche Königin und
ladies. They could then choose, as far as ihre Jungfrauen; dann mögen sie dich
I'm concerned, between boiling you or   meinetwegen sieden oder braten.
roasting you.

TAMINO
(aside)

What a strange man!   Ein wunderlicher Mann!

PAPAGENO

See her? See the starblazing Queen?   Sehen? Die sternflammende Königin
What mortal could boast of having seen   sehen? Welcher Sterbliche kann sich
her? What human sight could see through   rühmen, sie je gesehen zu haben? Welches
her veil woven from darkness?   Menschen Auge würde durch ihren
                                           schwarzdurchwebten Schleier blicken
                                           können?

TAMINO

Now it is clear! This must indeed be the   Nun ist's klar; es ist eben diese
Queen of the Night of whom my father so   nächtliche Königin, von der mein Vater
often spoke to me. But it is beyond my   mir so oft erzählte. Aber zu fassen,
comprehension how I can have wandered   wie ich mich hierher verirrte, ist ausser
here. This man is no ordinary man.   meiner Macht. Unfehlbar ist auch dieser
Perhaps he is one of her attendant   Mann kein gewöhnlicher Mensch —
spirits.   vielleicht einer ihrer dienstbaren Geister.

PAPAGENO
(aside)

How he stares at me! I am almost afraid   Wie er mich so starr anblickt! Bald
of him.   fang ich an, mich vor ihm zu fürchten.

(aloud)

Why are you staring at me so   Warum siehst du so verdächtig und
suspiciously?   schelmisch nach mir?

Judging by your feathers, you might almost be some kind of bird.

Nach deinen Federn, die dich bedecken, halt' ich dich . . .

PAPAGENO

Don't you insult me! You keep your distance! I'll have you know I've got the strength of a giant.

Doch für keinen Vogel? Bleib zurück, sag' ich, und traue mir nicht; denn ich habe Riesenkraft, wenn ich jemand packe.

(aside)

[If I don't succeed in frightening him, I'll make a hasty exit.]

Wenn er sich nicht bald von mir schrecken lässt, so lauf ich davon.

TAMINO
(He looks at the serpent.)

The strength of a giant? Was it you who rescued me from this serpent?

Riesenkraft? Also warst du wohl gar mein Erretter, der diese giftige Schlange bekämpfte?

PAPAGENO

Serpent? Where?

Schlange? Was da!

(He looks round and suddenly utters a shriek.)

Is it dead or alive?

Ist sie tot oder lebendig?

TAMINO

[You are trying to avoid my thanks with your modest questions.] Thank you for saving my life, I'll always be grateful to you.

Du willst durch deine bescheidene Frage meinen Dank ablehnen. Aber ich muss dir sagen, das ich ewig für deine so tapfere Handlung dankbar sein werde.

PAPAGENO

Think nothing of it — just let's be thankful it's dead.

Schweigen wir davon still. Freuen wir uns, dass sie so glücklich überwunden ist.

TAMINO

But how did you kill it? You have no weapons.

Aber um alles in der Welt, Freund, wie hast du dieses Ungeheuer bekämpft? Du bist ohne Waffen.

PAPAGENO

I don't need them — brute strength.

Brauch keine! Bei mir ist ein starker Druck mit der Hand mehr als Waffen.

TAMINO

You strangled it?

Du hast sie also erdrosselt?

PAPAGENO

Strangled!

Erdrosselt!

(aside)

I've never felt so strong in my life as I do today!

Binin meinem Leben nicht so stark gewesen, als heute.

Enter the Three Ladies.

THE THREE LADIES
(*calling threateningly*)

Papageno!

Papageno!

(That'll be for me.) [Look behind you, friend!]

Aha, das geht mich an! Sieh dich um, Freund!

TAMINO

Who are these ladies?

Wer sind diese Damen?

PAPAGENO

I don't exactly know who they are, but every day I hand over my birds to them and they give me wine, sugar cakes and sweet figs in return.

Wer sie eigentlich sind, weiss ich selbst nicht. Ich weiss nur so viel, dass sie mir täglich meine Vögel abnehmen und mir dafür Wein, Zuckerbrot und süsse Feigen bringen.

TAMINO

Are they very beautiful?

Sie sind vermutlich sehr schön?

PAPAGENO

I shouldn't think so or they wouldn't hide their faces.

Ich denke nicht! Denn wenn sie schön wären, würden sie ihre Gesichter nicht bedecken.

THE THREE LADIES
(menacingly)

Papageno!

Papageno!

PAPAGENO

[Be quiet! Hear how angrily they call me!] Are they beautiful, did you say? I've never seen three such beautiful veiled ladies in my life. (That ought to please them.)

Sei still! Sie drohen mir schon. Du fragst, ob sie schön sind, und ich kann dir darauf nichts antworten, als dass ich in meinem Leben nichts Reizenderes sah. Jetzt werden sie bald wieder gut werden.

THE THREE LADIES

Papageno!

Papageno!

PAPAGENO

(What have I done to make them so angry?) Look, my beauties, here are the birds for your breakfast.

Was muss ich denn heute verbrochen haben, dass sie so aufgebracht wider mich sind? Hier, meine Schönen, übergeb' ich meine Vögel.

FIRST LADY
(handing him a jug of water)

And in return the Queen sends you clear, cold water instead of wine.

Dafür schickt dir unsere Fürstin heute zum ersten Mal statt Wein reines, helles Wasser.

SECOND LADY

And instead of sugar cake she has ordered me to give you this stone. [I hope it does you good.]

Und mir befahl sie, dass ich statt Zuckerbrot diesen Stein dir überbringen soll. Ich wünsche, dass er dir wohl bekommen möge.

PAPAGENO

[What! Must I eat stones?]

Was? Steine soll ich fressen?

THIRD LADY

And instead of ripe figs I have the

Und statt der süssen Feigen hab' ich die

68

pleasure of closing your mouth with this golden lock.	Ehre, dir dies goldene Schloss vor den Mund zu schlagen.

She padlocks his mouth. Papageno protests violently.

FIRST LADY

Do you want to know why the Queen has punished you today?	Du willst vermutlich wissen, warum die Fürstin dich heute so wunderbar bestraft?

Papageno nods.

SECOND LADY

So that in future you will not tell lies to strangers.	Damit du künftig nie mehr Fremde belügst.

THIRD LADY

And so that you will never again boast of heroic deeds which were really performed by others.	Und dass du dich nie der Heldentaten rühmest, die and're vollzogen.

FIRST LADY

Tell me, did you kill this serpent?	Sag' an, hast du diese Schlange bekämpft?

Papageno shakes his head.

SECOND LADY

Who did then?	Wer denn also?

Papageno shakes his head.

THIRD LADY

It was we *three* who came to your rescue, young man, but do not be amazed. Joy and delight await you. Our sovereign lady the Queen sends you this picture of her daughter Pamina which I have painted. If you find that you are not unmoved by the beauty of this portrait, then fortune, honour and glory will be yours. A bientôt, Prince.	Wir waren's Jüngling, die dich befreiten. Zittre nicht, dich erwartet Freude und Entzücken. Hier, dies Gemälde schickt dir die grosse Fürstin; es ist das Bildnis ihrer Tochter. Findest du, sagte sie, dass diese Züge dir nicht gleichgültig sind, dann ist Glück, Ehr' und Ruhm dein Los! Auf Wiedersehen!

Exit.

SECOND LADY

Adieu, Monsieur Papageno!	Adieu, Monsieur Papageno!

Exit.

THIRD LADY

Don't get indigestion!	Fein nicht zu hastig getrunken!

Exit, laughing.

Papageno does not stop gesticulating dumbly. Since he received the portrait, Tamino has gazed at it intently. Deaf to everything he feels his love growing. **Scene Four** / *Aria No. 3*

TAMINO [8]

No finer picture, I am sure Was ever seen by man before!	Dies Bildnis ist bezaubernd schön, Wie noch kein Auge je gesehn!

It moves me, and her pure young face,
Enchants my heart and makes it race.
This strange and unfamiliar yearning,
This fierce and ardent pleasure burning —
What is this sweet and piercing flame?
I know! It must be love alone.
Oh, how I long to see her glory,
I'd tell her . . . tell her . . . pure and
    kind . . .
What would I say? Upon my heart
    would I press her,
Within these loving arms caress her,
And then I know she would be mine.

Ich fühl es, wie dies Götterbild
Mein Herz mit neuer Regung füllt.
Dies Etwas kann ich zwar nicht nennen,
Doch fühl ich's hier wie Feuer brennen.
Soll die Empfindung Liebe sein?
Ja, ja! Die Liebe ist's allein.
O wenn ich sie nur finden Könnte!
O wenn sie doch schon vor mir stände!
Ich würde – würde – warm und rein –
Was würde ich? – Ich würde sie voll
    Entzücken
An diesen heissen Busen drücken,
Und ewig wäre sie dann mein.

He begins to go.

The Three Ladies return. **Scene Five**

FIRST LADY

Noble youth you must summon up your
courage — our Royal Lady . . .

Rüste dich mit Mut und Standhaftigkeit,
schöner Jüngling! Die Fürstin . . .

SECOND LADY

Has ordered me to tell you . . .

Hat mir aufgetragen, dir zu sagen . . .

THIRD LADY

That your future happiness is certain.
She has . . .

Dass der Weg zu deinem künftigen
Glücke nunmehr gebahnt sei.

FIRST LADY

Heard every word you said. She has . . .

Sie hat jedes deiner Worte gehört, so du
sprachst; sie hat . . .

SECOND LADY

Read the expression in your face. Her
loving mother's heart . . .

Jeden Zug in deinem Gesicht gelesen.
Ja noch mehr, ihr mütterliches Herz . . .

THIRD LADY

Has decided to make you really happy. If
this youth, she said, is as brave as he is
tender-hearted, then my daughter is as
good as rescued.

Hat beschlossen, dich ganz glücklich
zu machen. Hat dieser Jüngling, sprach
sie, auch so viel Mut und Tapferkeit,
als er zärtlich ist, o, so ist meine Tochter
ganz gewiss gerettet.

TAMINO

Rescued? What do you mean? [Oh
endless darkness! The girl in the portrait]

Gerettet? was hör' ich? O ewige
Dunkelheit! Das Original –

FIRST LADY

The Princess, Pamina, has been carried
off by a powerful and malicious demon.

Wisse, ein böser Dämon hat Paminen ihr
entrissen!

TAMINO

[Carried off? O ye Gods! Tell me how
this happened.]

Entrissen? O ihr Götter! Sagt, wie
konnte das geschehen.

FIRST LADY

One beautiful May morning she was
sitting all alone in her favourite cypress
grove when the villain sneaked in

Sie sass an einem schönen Maientag
ganz allein in dem alles belebenden
Zypressenwäldchen, welches immer ihr

un-noticed and stole Pamina away.

Lieblingsaufenthalt war. Der Bösewicht
schlich unbemerkt hinein –

TAMINO

Pamina has been abducted? Where does
the tyrant live?

SECOND LADY

Not far from here in a carefully guarded
fortress.

TAMINO

Show me the way! I will rescue Pamina
and destroy the villain. I swear it by all

Komm't, Mädchen, führ't mich! Sie sei
gerettet. Das schwöre ich bei meiner

---

* The Three Ladies have more to say in the original dialogue.

FIRST LADY (cont'd)

The wicked man sneaked in
unnoticed —

Der Bösewicht schlich unbemerkt
hinein —

SECOND LADY

Spied her —

Belauschte sie und —

THIRD LADY

He has, besides an evil heart, the power
to change into any imaginable shape;
in this way, Pamina was —

Er hat nebst seinem bösen Herzen auch
noch die Macht, sich in jede erdenkliche
Gestalt zu verwandeln; auf solche
Weise hat er auch Pamina —

FIRST LADY

Pamina is the name of the Queen's
daughter, the one whom you adore.

Dies ist der Name der königlichen
Tochter, so Ihr anbetet.

TAMINO

Oh, Pamina! You have been torn away
from me – you are in the power of a
wicked voluptuary! You are perhaps at
this moment – horrible thought –

O Pamina! Du mir entrissen — du in
der Gewalt eines üppigen Bösewichts!
Bist vielleicht in diesem Augenblick —
schrecklicher Gedanke —

THE THREE LADIES

Silence youth!

Schweig, Jüngling!

FIRST LADY

Do not slander the virtue of beauty so
gracious. Innocence bears all patiently,
defiant to torture. Neither force nor
flattery would entice her from the paths
of virtue.

Lästere der holden Schönheit Tugend
nicht. Trotz aller Pein, so die Unschuld
duldet, ist sie sich immer gleich. Weder
Zwang noch Schmeichelei ist vermögend,
sie zum Wege des Lasters zu verführen.

TAMINO

Tell me, ladies, tell me where this tyrant
lives?

O sagt, Mädchen, sagt wo ist des
Tyrannen Aufenthalt?

SECOND LADY

He lives very near to our mountains, in
an enticing and delightful valley. His
impregnable castle is closely guarded.

Sehr nahe an unseren Bergen lebt er in
einem angenehmen und reizenden Tal.
Seine Burg ist prachtvoll und sorgsam
bewacht.

71

I hold sacred.	Leibe, bei meinem Herzen!
	(Thunder)
Heavens, what is that?	Ihr Götter, was ist das?

THE THREE LADIES

Be brave!	Fasse dich!

FIRST LADY

It heralds the arrival of our Queen.	Es verkündet die Ankunft unserer Königin.
	(Thunder)

THE THREE LADIES

She comes! She comes! She comes!	Sie kommt! Sie kommt! Sie kommt!
	(Thunder)

The mountains part and the stage is transformed into a magnificent chamber. **Scene Six.**
The Queen is seated on a throne which gleams with sparkling stars. / *Recitative and Aria No. 4*

THE QUEEN

You need not fear, my dearest son,	O zitt're nicht, mein lieber Sohn!
For you are blameless, noble, strong.	Du bist unschuldig, weise, fromm;
A young man like yourself can best imagine	Ein Jüngling, so wie du, vermag am besten
The grief a mother feels, and show compassion.	Dies tiefbetrübte Mutterherz zu trösten.
I die a thousand deaths each moment	[9] Zum Leiden bin ich auserkoren,
Without my daughter by my side,	Denn meine Tochter fehlet mir;
And all my joy is turned to torment —	Durch sie ging all mein Glück verloren,
An evil man took her away.	Ein Bözewicht entfloh mit ihr.
I still see her terror	Noch sehe ich ihr Zittern
When held by her captors,	Mit bangem Erschüttern,
I saw her implore them	Ihr ängstliches Beben,
And tremble before them.	Ihr schüchternes Streben.
I saw the horror all too plainly.	Ich musste sie mir rauben sehen,
'Oh help' I heard her feebly cry.	Ach helft, war alles, was sie sprach;
Alas, I tried but could not save her,	Allein, vergebens ward ihr Flehen,
For all my pow'r was far too weak.	Denn meine Hilfe war zu schwach.
You I choose now to be her saviour,	[10] Du wirst sie zu befreien gehen,
You are the man to set her free.	Du wirst der Tochter Retter sein;
And when you do succeed to save her	Und werd ich dich als Sieger sehen,
I give my word she'll be your bride.	So sei sie dann auf ewig dein.

Exeunt the Queen and Three Ladies. The scene changes back to what it was before. **Scene Seven.**

TAMINO
(after a pause)

Was that vision I saw? [Or are my senses confused?] Oh Gods! Do not deceive me and help me to find Pamina. [Strengthen my arm, uphold my courage, and Tamino's heart will give you eternal thanks.]	Ist's denn auch Wirklichkeit, was ich sah? Oder betäuben mich meine Sinne? O ihr guten Götter, täusch't mich nicht, oder ich unterliege eu'rer Prüfung! Schützet meinen Arm, stählt meinen Mut, und Taminos Herz wird ewigen Dank euch entgegen schlagen.

He begins to leave but Papageno intercepts him. / *Quintet No. 5* [11]

PAPAGENO
(pointing at the padlock on his mouth)

Hm, hm, hm!   Hm, hm, hm!

TAMINO

The poor young man has come to rue it   Der Arme kann von Strafe sagen,
A golden lock has sealed his tongue.   Denn seine Sprache ist dahin.

PAPAGENO

Hm, hm, hm!   Hm, hm, hm!

TAMINO

I'd like to help but can't undo it   Ich kann nichts tun, als dich beklagen,
The magic power is far too strong.   Weil ich zu schwach zu helfen bin.

PAPAGENO

Hm, hm, hm!   Hm, hm, hm!

Scene Eight. *The Three Ladies return.*

FIRST LADY
(taking the lock from Papageno's mouth)

If you will promise you'll repent   Die Königin begnadigt dich,
The Queen will end your punishment.   Erlässt die Strafe dir durch mich.

PAPAGENO

Now hear how Papageno chatters.   Nun plaudert Papageno wieder.

SECOND LADY

But lying is a different matter.   Ja, plaud're! Lüge nur nicht wieder!

PAPAGENO

I'll never tell a lie again!   Ich lüge nimmermehr. Nein! Nein!

THE THREE LADIES

This lock will be your warning then.   Dies Schloss soll deine Warnung sein!

PAPAGENO

The lock shall be my warning then.   Dies Schloss soll meine Warnung sein!

THE THREE LADIES, PAPAGENO

If ev'ry liar were made to wander   Bekämen doch die Lügner alle
With such a lock, for his own good,   Ein solches Schloss vor ihren Mund;
Then hate, destruction, and vile slander   Statt Hass, Verleumdung, schwarzer
                                                    Galle,
Would yield to love and brotherhood.   Bestünde Lieb und Bruderbund.

FIRST LADY
(giving Tamino a golden flute)

Oh Prince, now take this magic flute,   O Prinz, nimm dies Geschenk von mir!
It's given by our Queen's command.   Dies sendet unsre Fürstin dir.
Its pow'r protects thro' ev'ry danger,   Die Zauberflöte wird dich schützen,
In all misfortune it will aid you.   Im grössten Unglück unterstützen.

THE THREE LADIES

You'll rule mankind in godlike fashion,   Hiermit kannst du allmächtig handeln,
It gives power over human passion.   Der Menschen Leidenschaft verwandeln.
It frees the soul of grief and pain   Der Traurige wird freudig sein,

And hardened hearts know love again.	Den Hagestolz nimmt Liebe ein.

ALL

Oh, this holy present is worth far more than crowns of gold	O, so eine Flöte ist mehr als Gold und Kronen wert,
For its power brings human hearts peace and joy throughout the world.	Denn durch sie wird Menschenglück und Zufriedenheit vermehrt.

PAPAGENO

Now you proud and lovely bevy	Nun, ihr schönen Frauenzimmer,
May I take my leave of you?	Darf ich — so empfehl ich mich.

THE THREE LADIES

Papageno, wait a moment.	Dich empfehlen kannst du immer,
Hear the orders of the Queen.	Doch bestimmt die Fürstin dich,
Take the Prince, your task is simple,	Mit dem Prinzen ohn' Verweilen
To Sarastro's secret temple.	Nach Sarastros Burg zu eilen.

PAPAGENO

No, I'm damned if I will go!	Nein, dafür bedank ich mich!
You yourselves have let me know	Von euch selbsten hörte ich,
That he's fiercer than a foe	Dass er wie ein Tigertier!
And, I'm certain, without mercy,	Sicher liess ohn' alle Gnaden
That Sarastro would ill-use me —	Mich Sarastro rupfen, braten,
Chop me, chew me, rip me, pierce me,	Setzte mich den Hunden für.
Then he'd feed me to his dogs.	

THE THREE LADIES

Then trust the Prince, he'll keep you safe	Dich schützt der Prinz, trau ihm allein!
If you will be his willing slave.	Dafür sollst du sein Diener sein.

PAPAGENO
(to himself)

To trust the Prince would be plain silly.	Dass doch der Prinz beim Teufel wäre!
My life is all I've got,	Mein Leben ist mir lieb;
I know he'd run off, willy-nilly,	Am Ende schleicht, bei meiner Ehre,
And he'd leave me to rot.	Er von mir wie ein Dieb.

FIRST LADY
(giving Papageno the magic bells in a little box)

Now take this present, do not hide.	Hier nimm dies Kleinod, es ist dein.

PAPAGENO

Ay, ay, I wonder what's inside!	Ei, ei! Was mag darinnen sein?

THE THREE LADIES

You'll find a chime of bells a-ringing.	Darinnen hörst du Glöckchen tönen.

PAPAGENO

And may I also set them swinging?	Werd ich sie auch wohl spielen können?

THE THREE LADIES

Oh yes, of course, of course you may!	O ganz gewiss! Ja, ja gewiss!

ALL

Bells' enchantment, flute's perfection,	Silberglöckchen, Zauberflöten,
They shall be our sure protection.	Sind zu {eurem / unserm} Schutz vonnöten.
Fare you well, we cannot stay.	Lebet wohl, wir wollen gehn.
So farewell, no more delay.	Lebet wohl, auf Wiedersehn!

They all begin to go.

TAMINO

But lovely ladies, good and wise: Doch schöne Damen, saget an:

PAPAGENO

Tell us which way the temple lies.   Wie man die Burg wohl finden kann?

THE THREE LADIES [12]

Three spirits, young but old in wisdom	Drei Knäblein, jung, schön, hold und weise,
Will take you to Sarastro's kingdom.	Umschweben euch auf eurer Reise;
They'll be your guide in time of need.	Sie werden eure Führer sein,
Take their advice, go where they lead.	Folgt ihrem Rate ganz allein.

TAMINO, PAPAGENO

Three spirits, young, but old in wisdom	Drei Knäblein, jung, schön, hold und weise,
Will take us to Sarastro's kingdom.	Umschweben uns auf unsrer Reise.

ALL

So fare you well, the way is plain.	So lebet wohl! Wir wollen gehn,
Farewell, farewell, we'll meet again.	Lebt wohl, lebt wohl! Auf Wiedersehn!

Exeunt.

Transformation: Scene Nine. *As soon as the scene has changed into a chamber richly furnished in the Egyptian style, two slaves bring on beautiful cushions, and an ornate Turkish table; they roll out carpets. Enter the third slave.*

THIRD SLAVE

Ha, ha, ha!   Hahaha!

SECOND SLAVE

What are you laughing about?   Was soll denn das Lachen?

THIRD SLAVE *

That lascivious Moor, Monostatos, will
certainly either be hanged or else
beheaded! Pamina has escaped!

---

* Original dialogue

THIRD SLAVE

Our tormentor, the Moor who overhears all, will certainly be hanged or beheaded tomorrow.	Unser Peiniger, der alles belauschende Mohr, wird morgen sicherlich gehangen oder gespiesst.

FIRST SLAVE

Well?   Nun?

THIRD SLAVE

The delectable maiden! Hahaha!   Das reizende Mädchen! Hahaha!

SECOND SLAVE

Well?   Nun?

THIRD SLAVE

Has escaped.   Ist entsprungen.

FIRST AND SECOND SLAVES

Escaped?   Entsprungen?

SECOND SLAVE

The gods have heard our prayer. For her safety.

O Dank euch, ihr guten Götter! Ihr habt meine Bitte erhört.

FIRST SLAVE

Haven't I always told you that the day of our revenge would come? So Monostatos will be punished for tormenting us and illtreating the girl.

Sagt ich euch nicht immer, es wird doch ein Tag für uns erscheinen, wo wir gerochen und der schwarze Monostatos bestraft werden wird.**

THIRD SLAVE

She was more cunning than I thought and got away under his very eyes.

FOURTH SLAVE

How was that?

Wieso?

THIRD SLAVE

He tried to rape her but she called out the name of Sarastro. That startled the Moor and he stood as if paralysed. So Pamina ran away to the canal and escaped in a gondola towards the palm grove.

Du kennst ja den üppigen Wanst und seine Weise; das Mädchen aber war klüger, als ich dachte. In dem Augenblick, als er zu siegen glaubte, rief sie Sarastros Namen: das erschütterte den Mohren; er blieb stumm und unbeweglich stehen — indes lief Pamina nach dem Kanal und schiffte von selbst in einer Gondel dem Palmenwäldchen zu.

FIRST SLAVE

[Oh may this timid doe, in mortal terror reach the palace of her beloved mother.]

O wie wird das schüchterne Reh mit Todesangst dem Palast ihrer zärtlichen Mutter zueilen.

Scene Ten. *Monostatos calls from within.*

Footnote cont'd/

FIRST SLAVE

And she got away?

Und sie entkam?

THIRD SLAVE

Certainly. That at least is my dearest wish.

Unfehlbar. Wenigstens ist's mein wahrer Wunsch.

**

SECOND SLAVE

What did the Moor say about this?

Was spricht nun der Mohr zu der Geschichte?

FIRST SLAVE

Has he heard about it yet?

Er weiss doch davon?

THIRD SLAVE

Of course! She escaped right under his nose. According to some of our men, who were working in the garden, and saw and heard everything from a distance, the Moor will not be saved even if Pamina is caught by Sarastro's attendants.

Natürlich! Sie entlief vor seinen Augen. Wie mir einige Brüder erzählten, die in Garten arbeiteten und von weitem sahen und hörten, so ist der Mohr nicht mehr zu retten; auch wenn Pamina von Sarastros Gefolge wieder eingebracht würde.

76

MONOSTATOS

Slaves where are you? Come here to me!   He, Sklaven!

SLAVES

Monostatos!   Monostatos' Stimme!

MONOSTATOS

Bring me chains and fetters!   He, Sklaven! Schafft Fesseln herbei!

SLAVES

[Chains?]   Fesseln?

FIRST SLAVE

[Not for Pamina? Oh ye Gods!]   Doch nicht für Pamina? O ihr Götter!
Look, brothers, the girl has been   Da seht, Brüder, das Mädchen ist
recaptured.   gefangen.

SECOND SLAVE

Pamina! [O wretched sight.]   Pamina! Schrecklicher Anblick!

FIRST SLAVE

The pitiless devil is dragging her back   Seht, wie der unbarmherzige Teufel sie
with him.   bei ihren zarten Händchen fasst – das
[I cannot bear it.]   halt ich nicht aus.

SECOND SLAVE

[Nor I.]   Ich noch weniger.
                                         Exit.

THIRD SLAVE

[To have to see this is a hellish torture.]   So was sehen zu müssen, ist
                                         Höllenmarter.
                                         Exit.

Slaves drag in Pamina. **Scene Eleven.** / *Trio No. 6*

MONOSTATOS [13]
(very quickly)

You won't escape, do what you can!   Du feines Täubchen, nur herein!

PAMINA

You are heartless evil man!   O welche Marter! Welche Pein!

MONOSTATOS

If life is dear, don't taunt me!   Verloren ist dein Leben!

PAMINA

But Death itself can't daunt me!   Der Tod macht mich nicht beben,
Thoughts of my mother pain me,   Nur meine Mutter dauert mich;
So her grieving heart will break I know. Sie stirbt vor Gram ganz sicherlich.

MONOSTATOS

You slaves, now bind and fetter her.   He, Sklaven! Legt ihr Fesseln an!
I'll teach you to disdain me.   Mein Hass soll dich verderben.

PAMINA

I'd rather you had slain me   O lasst mich lieber sterben,
Than lie here helpless in your power.   Weil nichts, Barbar, dich rühren kann!

She falls senseless on the couch.

77

MONOSTATOS
(to the slaves)

Now go. Leave me alone with her.   Nun fort! Lasst mich bei ihr allein.

The slaves leave. Papageno appears at the window, at first without being noticed. **Scene Twelve**

PAPAGENO

Where has he gone? I'm on my own?   Wo bin ich wohl? Wo mag ich sein?
Aha! there's someone sleeping!   Aha, da find ich Leute!
Ah well, I'll go inside —   Gewagt, ich geh hinein.

(Enters)

Dear lady, like a bride   Schön Mädchen, jung und fein,
You lie there white as powder.   Viel weisser noch als Kreide!

Papageno notices Monostatos and both are terrified at the sight of each other.

MONOSTATOS, PAPAGENO

Oo! that must – be Lu – cifer – himself!   Hu! das ist – der Teu – fel si – cherlich!
Have pity! And pardon me!   Hab Mitleid – verschone mich!
Oo! Oo! Oo!   Hu! hu! hu!

Both hide. **Scene Thirteen**

PAMINA
(speaking as if in a dream, then recovering herself and looking around)

Mother, mother, mother! Am I still   Mutter — Mutter — Mutter! Wie?
alive? [Is my heart still not broken?]   Noch schlägt dieses Herz? Noch nicht
Have I woken to new torments? Oh, this   vernichtet? Zu neuen Qualen erwacht?
is cruel, more terrible than death.   O, das ist hart, sehr hart — Mir bitterer
      als der Tod.

Enter Papageno. **Scene Fourteen**

PAPAGENO

What a fool I was to be so frightened.   Bin ich nicht ein Narr, dass ich mich
There are black birds in the world so   schrecken liess? Es gibt ja schwarze
why shouldn't there be black men? The   Vögel in der Welt, warum denn nicht
pretty girl is still there. Greetings,   auch schwarze Menschen? Ah, sieh' da!
daughter of the Queen of Night!   Hier ist das schöne Fräuleinbild noch.
      Du Tochter der nächtlichen Königin!

PAMINA

Who are you?   Wer bist du?

PAPAGENO

A messenger from the Starblazing   Ein Abgesandter der sternflammenden
Queen.   Königin.

PAMINA

From my mother? [Oh joy!] What's your   Meiner Mutter? O Wonne! Dein Name?
name?

PAPAGENO

Papageno.   Papageno.

PAMINA

Papageno? I've often heard of you but   Papageno? Papageno — ich erinnere

78

never seen you.

mich, den Namen oft gehört zu haben, dich selbst aber sah ich nie.

PAPAGENO

Me neither. I mean I haven't seen you before never neither.

Ich dich ebenso wenig.

PAMINA

So you know my kind and gentle mother?

Du kennst also meine gute, zärtliche Mutter?

PAPAGENO

If you're the daughter of the Nocturnal Monarch, yes! . . . Are you her daughter?

Wenn du die Tochter der nächtlichen Königin bist — ja!

PAMINA

Yes, I am!

O, ich bin es.

PAPAGENO
(taking the portrait given to Tamino which hangs on a ribbon around his neck)

I'll just confirm it . . . Hair dark, dark hair. Eyes black, very black. Lips red, very red. Everything correct except for the hands and feet. According to this picture, you haven't got any.

Das will ich gleich erkennen. Schwarze * Haare — schwarze Haare. Die Augen schwarz — richtig, schwarz. Die Lippen rot – richtig rot. Alles trifft ein, bis auf Hand' und Füsse. Nach dem Gemälde zu schliessen, sollst du weder Hände noch Füsse haben; denn hier sind keine angezeigt.

PAMINA

Let me see. Yes, it's really me. But where did you get it?

Erlaube mir — Ja, ich bin's! Wie kam es in deine Hände?

PAPAGENO †

I'll tell you. This morning I was on my way to your mother's palace to hand over my birds as usual, when I came across a man who calls himself a prince. This prince so impressed your mother that she gave him this picture and ordered him to save you. He fell in love with you and agreed at once.

Eben als ich im Begriffe war, meine Vögel abzugeben, sah ich einen Menschen vor mir, der sich Prinz nennen lässt. Dieser Prinz hat deine Mutter so für sich eingenommen, dass sie ihm dein Bildnis schenkte und ihm befahl, dich zu befreien. Sein Entschluss war so schnell, als seine Liebe zu dir.

---

* Some editions have blond for black hair.
† Original dialogue

PAPAGENO

That's too long a story. It passed from hand to hand.

Dir das zu erzählen, wäre zu weitläufig; es kam von Hand zu Hand.

PAMINA

But how did it come into your hand?

Wie aber in die deinige?

PAPAGENO

In a very curious way. I caught it in a trap.

Auf eine wunderbare Art. Ich hab es gefangen.

79

PAMINA
(joyfully)

He fell in love with me? Oh, say that again; I like to hear about love.

Liebe? Er liebt mich also? O, sage mir das noch einmal, ich höre das Wort Liebe gar zu gern.

PAPAGENO

I can easily believe that – you're a very sweet young lady. Where was I?

Das glaub' ich dir, ohne zu schwören du bist ja ein Fräuleinbild. Wo blieb ich denn?

PAMINA

Talking about love.

Bei der Liebe.

PAPAGENO

Ah, yes, love. That's what I call a good memory. Well, to make a long story short, his great love for you set us on our way to tell you a thousand nice things, to clasp you in our arms and hurry you back to your mother's palace.

Richtig, bei der Leibe! Das nenn' ich ein Gedächtnis haben! Die grosse Liebe zu dir war der Peitschenstreich, um unsere Füsse in schnellen Gang zu bringen. Nun sind wir hier, dir tausend schöne und angenehme Sachen zu sagen; dich in unsere Arme zu nehmen, und wenn es möglich ist, ebenso schnell, wo nicht schneller als hierher, in den Palast deiner Mutter zu eilen.

PAMINA

That's very nicely said, but if this unknown prince is so much in love with me, why doesn't he come here himself to set me free?

Das ist alles sehr schön gesagt; aber lieber Freund, wenn der unbekannte Jüngling oder Prinz, wie er sich nennt, Liebe für mich fühlt, warum säumt er so lange, mich von meinen Fesseln zu befreien?

PAPAGENO

That's just the problem: when we said goodbye to your mother's three ladies they told us that three spirits would come to show us where to go and how to behave.

Da steckt eben der Haken. Wie wir von den Jungfrauen Abschied nehmen, so sagten sie uns, drei holde Knaben würden unsere Wegweiser sein, sie würden uns belehren, wie und auf welche Art wir handeln sollen.

PAMINA

What did they say?

Sie lehrten euch?

Footnote cont'd

PAMINA

Caught it in a trap?

Gefangen?

PAPAGENO

I had better tell you all the details This morning, as usual, I arrived at your mother's palace to make my delivery . . .

Ich muss dir das umständlicher erzählen. Ich kam heute früh, wie gewöhnlich, zu deiner Mutter Palast mit meiner Lieferung –

PAMINA

Delivery?

Lieferung?

PAPAGENO

Yes. For many years I have delivered to your mother and her ladies all the beautiful birds in the palace.

Ja, ich liefere deiner Mutter und ihren Jungfrauen schon seit vielen Jahren alle die schönen Vögel in den Palast.

80

Nothing — we haven't been able to find them yet. So the prince sent me on ahead while he goes on looking for them.	Nichts lehrten sie uns, denn wir haben keinen gesehen. Zu Sicherheit also war der Prinz so fein, mich vorauszuschicken, um dir unsere Ankunft anzukündigen.

PAMINA

You've taken a great risk. If Sarastro should find you . . .	Freund, du hast viel gewagt! Wenn Sarastro dich hier erblicken sollte —

PAPAGENO

Don't suppose I'd be making the return journey?	So würde mir meine Rückreise erspart — das kann ich mir denken.

PAMINA*

There's no time to be lost. We must get away at once.	Wohl denn, es sei gewagt!

(As they leave, Pamina stops.)

But supposing this is a trap and you're a malicious sprite sent by Sarastro?	Aber wenn dies ein Fallstrick wäre – wenn dieser nun ein böser Geist von Sarastros Gefolge wäre?

(She looks at him suspiciously.)

PAPAGENO

Me a malicious sprite? [What are you thinking of?] I'm the nicest sprite in the World.	Ich ein böser Geist? Wo denkst du hin? Ich bin der beste Geist von der Welt.

PAMINA**

[Forgive me, forgive me,] I didn't mean to offend you: I can see that you're really	Vergieb, vergieb, wenn ich dich beleidigte! Du hast ein gefühlvolles Herz;

---

* Original dialogue

PAMINA

You would perish in endless torture.	Dein martervoller Tod würde ohne Grenzen sein.

PAPAGENO

To avoid them, let's leave soon!	Um diesem auszuweichen, gehen wir lieber beizeiten.

PAMINA

What hour is it by the sun?	Wie hoch mag wohl die Sonne sein?

PAPAGENO

It's almost midday.	Bald gegen Mittag.

PAMINA

We must not wait a moment. This is the time when Sarastro usually returns from the hunt.	So haben wir keine Minute zu versäumen. Um diese Zeit kommt Sarastro gewöhnlich von der Jagd zurück.

PAPAGENO

So Sarastro is not at home! Hurray! We've won the game! Come lovely picture Princess. Your eyes will pop out when you catch sight of this handsome young man.	Sarastro ist also nicht zu Hause? Pah, da haben wir gewonnenes Spiel! Komm, schönes Fräuleinbild! Du wirst Augen machen, wenn du denn schönen Jüngling erblickst.

** Original dialogue

PAMINA

Oh, no. The picture convinces me that I am not being tricked. It comes from my good mother's hands.	Doch nein; das Bild hier überzeugt mich, dass ich nicht getäuscht bin; es kommt aus den Händen meiner guten Mutter.

very good-natured [from everything about you.]	das sehe ich in jedem deiner Züge.

PAPAGENO

Of course I'm good-natured, but what's the use of that? I sometimes want to pluck out all my feathers one by one when I remember that Papageno has no Papagena.	Ach, freilich habe ich ein gefühlvolles Herz! Aber was nützt mir das Alles? Ich möchte mir oft alle meine Federn ausrupfen, wenn ich bedenke, dass Papageno noch keine Papagena hat.

PAMINA

Poor man, so you have no wife?	Armer Mann! Du hast also noch kein Weib?

PAPAGENO

Not even a girl-friend, let alone a wife! Yes, it's depressing! Yet even we birdcatchers have time off occasionally when it would be nice to enjoy a few minutes of domestic chat.	Noch nicht einmal ein Mädchen, viel weniger ein Weib! Ja, das ist betrübt! Und unsereiner hat doch auch bisweilen seine lustigen Stunden, wo man gern gesellschaftliche Unterhaltung haben möchte.

PAMINA

Have patience Papageno. The gods will send you a wife sooner than you expect.	Geduld, Freund! Der Himmel wird auch für dich sorgen; er wird dir eine Freundin schicken, ehe du dir's vermutest.

PAPAGENO

If they'd only send her quickly.	Wenn er sie nur bald schickte!

Duet No. 7 [14]

PAMINA

The gentle love of man and woman Shows humans are a race apart.	Bei Männern, welche Liebe fühlen, Fehlt auch ein gutes Herze nicht.

PAPAGENO

It is a woman's tender duty To give a man her loving heart.	Die süssen Triebe mitzufühlen, Ist dann der Weiber erste Pflicht.

PAMINA, PAPAGENO

While love is ours, we'll freely give; By love alone we breathe and live.	Wir wollen uns der Liebe freun, Wir leben durch die Lieb' allein.

PAMINA

It's love that sweetens ev'ry sorrow And blesses ev'ry waking hour.	Die Lieb' versüsset jede Plage, Ihr opfert jede Kreatur.

Footnote cont'd

PAPAGENO

Beautiful picture lady, should you have any further wicked doubts, and suspect that I intend to abuse you, you have only to think hard about love and all your dark suspicions will vanish.	Schön's Fräuleinbild, wenn dir wieder ein so böser Verdacht aufsteigen sollte, dass ich dich betrügen wollte, so denke nur fleissig an die Liebe, und jeder böse Argwohn wird schwinden.

PAPAGENO

With love we need not fear the morrow,   Sie würzet unsre Lebenstage,
We feel its Universal power.   Sie wirkt im Kreise der Natur.

PAMINA, PAPAGENO

We know the goal of human life —   Ihr hoher Zweck zeigt deutlich an,
To live in love as man and wife.   Nichts Edlers sei, als Weib und Mann.
Wife and man, and man and wife,   Mann und Weib und Weib und Mann,
Live in Love, for love is life.   Reichen an die Gottheit an.

Both escape. **Transformation.** *The scene changes to a sacred grove. Right at the back is a beautiful temple with the inscription: 'Temple of Wisdom'. Two other temples are joined to this temple by colonnades: the one on the right is inscribed 'Temple of Reason'; the one on the left, 'Temple of Nature'.*
Scene Fifteen. *The Three Boys lead Tamino in, each carrying a silver palm frond.* /
Finale No. 8

THE THREE BOYS [15]

The road you trod has led you here,   Zum Ziele führt dich diese Bahn,
Ask here, you'll find this goal you're   Doch musst du, Jüngling, männlich
   seeking.   siegen.
But you must stand and show no fear.   Drum höre unsre Lehre an:
Be constant, patient and be silent.   Sei standhaft, duldsam und verschwiegen.

TAMINO

But dear young spirits tell me pray   Ihr holden Knaben, sagt mir an,
If my Pamina will be saved.   Ob ich Pamina retten kann?

THE THREE BOYS

We may not say: do what you can.   Dies kundzutun, steht uns nicht an.
Be constant, patient and be silent.   Sei standhaft, duldsam und verschwiegen.
Remember this: you are a man   Bedenke dies; kurz, sei ein Mann,
And you will reach the goal you're   Dann, Jüngling, wirst du männlich
   seeking.   siegen.

TAMINO

I'll heed their wisdom and I'll cherish   Die Weisheitslehre dieser Knaben
Each word of truth until I perish.   Sei ewig mir ins Herz gegraben.
Where am I now? How can I tell?   Wo bin ich nun? Was wird mit mir?
This seems a place for Gods to dwell.   Ist dies der Sitz der Götter hier?
It's written on portals and graven on   Es zeigen die Pforten, es zeigen die
   pillars   Säulen,
That Wisdom, Endeavour and Art here   Dass Klugheit und Arbeit und Künste
   are rulers,   hier weilen;
Where labour is honoured and idleness   Wo Tätigkeit thronet und Müssiggang
   shunned,   weicht,
The hateful corruption of vice can't be   Erhält seine Herrschaft das Laster nicht
   found.   leicht.
And so I'll walk thro' each open door.   Ich wage mich mutig zur Pforte hinein,
My purpose is worthy and honest and   Die Absicht ist edel und lauter und rein.
   fine.
So trembie, cruel sorcerer!   Erzitt're, feiger Bösewicht!
To save Pamina is my vow.   Pamina retten ist mir Pflicht.

Tamino goes to the righthand door and opens it, but a voice from within declares:

A VOICE

Go back!   Zurück!

TAMINO

Go back? I'll try here, come what may! Zurück? So wag ich hier mein Glück!

He approaches the lefthand door, but again a voice proclaims:

A VOICE

Go back! Zurück!

TAMINO

I'm turned away once more. Auch hier ruft man: zurück?
(He looks around.)
I see there's yet one more door. Da seh' ich noch eine Tür,
Perhaps I'll find that way is clear. Vielleicht find ich den Eingang hier.

He knocks at the central door, it opens and an old priest steps forward.

A PRIEST

Intruder, tell me what you seek. Wo willst du, kühner Fremdling, hin?
What makes you tread forbidden Was suchst du hier im Heiligtum?
  ground?

TAMINO

I go where truth and love are found. Der Lieb' und Tugend Eigentum.

A PRIEST

Those words sound fine and brave, I Die Worte sind von hohem Sinn!
  know . . .
But say, how do you hope to find them? Allein, wie willst du diese finden?
For neither love nor truth is found Dich leitet Lieb' und Tugend nicht,
By men whose hate and vengeance blind Weil Tod und Rache dich entzünden.
  them.

TAMINO

I only hate the wicked man. Nur Rache für den Bösewicht.

A PRIEST

You will not find such men within here. Den wirst du wohl bei uns nicht finden.

TAMINO

Sarastro rules and is your leader. Sarastro herrscht in diesen Gründen?

A PRIEST

Oh yes, Sarastro rules us here. Ja, ja! Sarastro herrschet hier!

TAMINO

But not in Wisdom's sacred home? Doch in dem Weisheitstempel nicht?

A PRIEST

He rules in Wisdom's sacred home. Er herrscht im Weisheitstempel hier!

TAMINO
(about to leave)

Then it is all deceit and lies. So ist denn alles Heuchelei!

A PRIEST

So now you wish to go? Willst du schon wieder gehn?

TAMINO

Yes, I shall go, proud and free, Ja, ich will gehn, froh und frei,
Far from these temple walls. Nie euren Tempel sehn.

	A PRIEST
Explain your words to me.	Erklär dich näher mir,
I say you are deceived.	Dich täuschet ein Betrug.
	TAMINO
Sarastro is your Lord.	Sarastro wohnet hier,
You cannot be believed.	Das ist mir schon genug.
	A PRIEST
If you still love your life,	Wenn du dein Leben liebst,
I charge you, stay awhile.	So rede, bleibe da! —
D'you hate Sarastro so?	Sarastro hassest du?
	TAMINO
I hate his very name.	Ich hass ihn ewig! Ja!
	A PRIEST
At least explain your reasoning.	So gib mir deine Gründe an.
	TAMINO
He is inhuman, not a man.	Er ist ein Unmensch, ein Tyrann.
	A PRIEST
And have you proof of all you're saying?	Ist das, was du gesagt, erwiesen?
	TAMINO
There's proof in that unhappy woman	Durch ein unglücklich Weib bewiesen,
Whose life is filled with bitter tears.	Das Gram und Jammer niederdrückt.
	A PRIEST
You take a woman's tears as truth?	Ein Weib hat also dich berückt?
Young man, learn wisdom . . . woman's sighs	Ein Weib tut wenig, plaudert viel.
Are seldom felt and often lies.	Du, Jüngling, glaubst dem Zungenspiel?
Oh, if you know Sarastro well	O, legte doch Sarastro dir
You'd know that ill was not his wish.	Die Absicht seiner Handlung für!
	TAMINO
His wishes are as clear as day.	Die Absicht ist nur allzu klar;
Did he not steal, without compassion,	Riss nicht der Räuber ohn' Erbarmen
Pamina from her mother's arms?	Pamina aus der Mutter Armen?
	A PRIEST
Young man, what you have said is true.	Ja, Jüngling! Was du sagst, ist wahr.
	TAMINO
Where is she, she he stole away?	Wo ist sie, die er uns geraubt?
Oh, has her sacrifice begun?	Man opferte vielleicht sie schon?
	A PRIEST
I cannot tell you now my son,	Dir dies zu sagen, teurer Sohn,
As yet I'm not allowed to say.	Ist jetzt und mir noch nicht erlaubt.
	TAMINO
Explain this myst'ry . . . help me now.	Erklär dies Rätsel, täusch mich nicht.
	A PRIEST
An oath of silence is my vow.	Die Zunge bindet Eid und Pflicht.

When shall this secrecy be broken?   Wann also wird die Decke schwinden?

A PRIEST

When friendship offers you its hand   Sobald dich führt der Freundschaft Hand
And bids you join our holy band.   Ins Heiligtum zum ew'gen Band.

The Priest re-enters the Temple.

TAMINO
(to himself)

Oh, endless night, eternal darkness,   O ewige Nacht! Wann wirst du
    schwinden?
When will the light dispel my blindness?   Wann wird das Licht mein Auge finden?

VOICES
(from within the Temple)

Soon, stranger, you shall see.   Bald, Jüngling, oder nie!

TAMINO

Soon, say if it may be!   Bald, sagt ihr, oder nie?
Mysterious voices, answer me,   Ihr Unsichtbaren, saget mir,
Does my Pamina live?   Lebt denn Pamina noch?

VOICES

Pamina, yes, she lives!   Pamina lebet noch!

TAMINO
(joyfully)

She lives! I need not ask for more.   Sie lebt? Ich danke euch dafür.
Oh, could I find the joyful phrases,   O, wenn ich doch imstande wäre,
Almighty Gods, I'd sing your praises.   Allmächtige, zu eurer Ehre,
This flute shall speak my grateful thanks   Mit jedem Tone meinen Dank
In music; and from here – here it speaks!   Zu schildern, wie er hier, hier entsprang!

Tamino points to his heart. Then he plays on the flute and wild animals and singing birds gather around him. [16]

Ah, now I see your powerful spell, Oh   Wie stark ist nicht dein Zauberton,
    magic flute, —
It is just as strong as I was told   Weil, holde Flöte, durch dein Spielen
Since curious birds and animals come   Selbst wilde Tiere Freude fühlen.
    thronging . . .
Ah, but Pamina does not come.   Doch nur Pamina bleibt davon. —

He plays.

Pamina, hear me.   Pamina! Höre, höre mich!

He plays.

In vain!   Umsonst! —
Where? how can I make you hear?   Wo? Ach, wo find ich dich?

The sound of Tamino's flute is answered by Papageno's pipe. [6]

Ah! That is Papageno's pipe.   Ha, das ist Papagenos Ton!

Papageno again replies on his pipe.

Perhaps he's found Pamina there,   Vielleicht sah er Pamina schon,
Perhaps he's bringing her to me,   Vielleicht eilt sie mit ihm zu mir,
Perhaps, that means my love is near.   Vielleicht führt mich der Ton zu ihr.

Tamino goes off in search of Papageno. Papageno and Pamina enter (without chains). **Scene Thirteen.**

Walk on tip-toe, courage high.	Schnelle Füsse, rascher Mut,
We'll be safe now, you and I.	Schützt vor Feindes List und Wut.
But I hope Tamino's near	Fänden wir Tamino doch,
Or they'll capture us, I fear.	Sonst erwischen sie uns noch!

PAMINA

Oh, Tamino!	Holder Jüngling!

PAPAGENO

Softly, softly, I can lure him.	Stille, stille, ich kann's besser.

He pipes and Tamino's flute is heard in reply.

PAMINA, PAPAGENO

Oh, what joy it is to hear him.	Welche Freude ist wohl grösser?
That's Tamino's flute I know.	Freund Tamino hört uns schon;
Where the flute calls, we must go —	Hierher kam der Flötenton.
Here's an end to care and worry.	Welch ein Glück, wenn ich ihn finde,
Only hurry, only hurry, only hurry!	Nur geschwinde! Nur geschwinde!

Scene Seventeen. *Monostatos surprises them.*

MONOSTATOS

Only hurry, only hurry, only hurry!	Nur geschwinde! Nur geschwinde!
Ha! Now I have caught you both!	Ha, hab ich euch noch erwischt?
I shall clap you both in irons.	Nur herbei mit Stahl und Eisen;
Then I'll feed you to the lions.	Wart, ich will euch Mores weisen.
So you thought that you could cheat me!	Den Monostatos berücken!
It takes more than you to beat me!	Nur herbei mit Band und Stricken,
Ho! You slaves, now bring the ropes.	He, ihr Sklaven, kommt herbei!

Slaves bring chains.

PAMINA, PAPAGENO

Ah! the end of all our hopes.	Ach, nun ist's mit uns vorbei!

PAPAGENO

Do or die, nothing venture, nothing gain.	Wer viel wagt, gewinnt oft viel,
Now, you bells our need is plain,	Komm, du schönes Glockenspiel!
Let me hear your jingle ringle,	Lass die Glöckchen klingen, klingen,
Set their arms and legs a-tingle.	Dass die Ohren ihnen singen.

As Papageno plays the Magic Bells, Monostatos and the Slaves are spell-bound, and begin to dance and sing. [18]

MONOSTATOS, SLAVES

That music enchanting, that music so pure!	Das klinget so herrlich, das klinget so schön!
Larala, larala!	Larala, larala!
I never heard music so fine I am sure.	Nie hab ich so etwas gehört noch gesehn!
Larala, larala!	Larala, larala!

Monostatos and the Slaves dance off.

PAMINA, PAPAGENO [19]

How I wish that ev'ry man	Könnte jeder brave Mann
Could set bells a-ringing,	Solche Glöckchen finden,
Then he'd find that kindness can	Seine Feinde würden dann

Turn all strife to singing.	Ohne Mühe schwinden,
And throughout his life he'd see	Und er lebte ohne sie
Man can live in harmony.	In der besten Harmonie.
Only love and singing,	Nur der Freundschaft Harmonie
Gentle and forgiving,	Mildert die Beschwerden;
Only peace and harmony	Ohne diese Sympathie
Make this life worth living.	Ist kein Glück auf Erden!

The sound of a vigorous march is heard with trumpets and drums.

VOICES
(from within)

All honour Sarastro, Sarastro, hail him!	Es lebe Sarastro, Sarastro lebe!

PAPAGENO

Now what's all this shouting? I'm shiv'ring, I'm quailing.	Wass soll das bedeuten? Ich zittre, ich bebe.

PAMINA

My friend all hope is lost I fear.	O Freund, nun ist's um uns getan!
That sound means that Sarastro's near.	Dies kündigt den Sarastro an.

PAPAGENO

Oh, if I were a mouse,	O, wär ich eine Maus,
I'd vanish down a mousehole!	Wie wollt ich mich verstecken!
Or if I were a tortoise	Wär ich so klein wie Schnecken,
I'd curl up in my house.	So kröch ich in mein Haus.
Oh Lord, deliver us from evil.	Mein Kind, was werden wir nun sprechen?

PAMINA

The Truth will, Truth can shame the devil.	Die Wahrheit, wär sie auch Verbrechen.

Scene Eighteen. *A procession precedes Sarastro, who rides a triumphal chariot, pulled by six lions.*

CHORUS

All honour, Sarastro, Sarastro our leader,	Es lebe Sarastro, Sarastro soll leben!
He rules us with kindness, his service is freedom!	Er ist es, dem wir uns mit Freude ergeben!
Long may he reign over and govern our lives,	Stets mög er des Lebens als Weiser sich freun,
With truth and with justice, all powerful, all wise.	Er ist unser Abgott, dem alle sich weihn.

The chorus continues until Sarastro steps down from his chariot.

PAMINA
(kneeling)

Sir, it is true, I fled from you,	Herr, ich bin zwar Verbrecherin!
And this you well may call a crime.	Ich wollte deiner Macht entfliehn.
But hear, the guilt is not all mine,	Allein die Schuld liegt nicht an mir —
That wicked Moor tried to seduce me	Der böse Mohr verlangte Liebe;
And called it love. I had to fly.	Darum, o Herr, entfloh ich dir.

SARASTRO

Arise and fear no more my dear one.	Steh auf, erheitere dich, o Liebe!
For here we need no inquisition.	Denn ohne erst in dich zu dringen,

I know your heart is true and pure.	Weiss ich von deinem Herzen mehr:
You love another that is sure.	Du liebtest einen andern sehr.
I need not curb this true emotion,	Zur Liebe will ich dich nicht zwingen,
Though I can't grant your freedom yet.	Doch geb ich dir die Freiheit nicht.

PAMINA

But there's a voice I can't forget:	Mich rufet ja die Kindes pflicht,
It is my mother's . . .	Denn meine Mutter . . .

SARASTRO

. . . Whom I shall destroy.	. . . Steht in meiner Macht.
Believe me, she would kill your joy	Du würdest um dein Glück gebracht,
If I should yield and hand you over.	Wenn ich dich ihren Händen liesse.

PAMINA

But yet, I still must love my mother	Mir klingt der Muttername süsse;
For she is . . .	Sie ist es . . .

SARASTRO

. . . She is in my pow'r.	. . . Und ein stolzes Weib.
But now a man must guide and teach you.	Ein Mann muss eure Herzen leiten,
For only he turns womankind	Denn ohne ihn pflegt jedes Weib
From paths of pride to ways of virtue.	Aus seinem Wirkungskreis zu schreiten.

Scene Nineteen. *Monostatos brings in Tamino.*

MONOSTATOS

Now, proud young stranger, come this way;	Nun, stolzer Jüngling, nur hierher,
Hear what Sarastro has to say.	Hier ist Sarastro, unser Herr.

PAMINA

Tamino!	Er ist's!

TAMINO

Pamina!	Sie ist's!

PAMINA

I know it's him.	Ich glaub' es kaum!

TAMINO

Pamina!	Sie ist's!

PAMINA

Tamino!	Er ist's!

TAMINO

It must be true.	Es ist kein Traum!

PAMINA

I'll fold you in my arms my dear.	Es schling' mein Arm sich um ihn her!

TAMINO

I'll fold you in my arms my dear.	Es schling' mein Arm sich um sie her!

PAMINA, TAMINO

And though Death come I'll know no fear.	Und wenn es auch mein Ende wär!

They embrace.

What's this intrusion?   Was soll das heissen?

(to Tamino)
What an impertinence,   Welch eine Dreistigkeit!
Release that woman. You go too far.   Gleich auseinander! Das geht zu weit!
(to Sarastro)
Oh Sir, pronounce your fearful sentence. Dein Sklave liegt zu deinen Füssen,
I bring a sinner to repentance.   Lass den verwegnen Frevler büssen!
Now look upon the evildoer.   Bedenk, wie frech der Knabe ist:
He used this curious birdman's lure   Durch dieses seltnen Vogels List
To steal Pamina from your palace!   Wollt er Pamina dir entführen.
He tried but I have foiled his malice.   Allein ich wusst ihn auszuspüren!
You know me, know my watchful   Du kennst mich! Meine Wachsamkeit —
  eyes . . .

You've earned the just reward of spies,   Verdient, dass man ihr Lorbeer streut.
So for your service I award . . .   He! Gebt dem Ehrenmann sogleich —

Your kindness overwhelms me, Lord!   Schon deine Gnade macht mich reich.

Just give him seventy-seven strokes.   — Nur siebenundsiebzig Sohlenstreich.

Oh Lord, I don't know what to say.   Ach, Herr, den Lohn verhofft ich nicht!

No more, what you have earned, I'll pay. Nicht Dank, es ist ja meine Pflicht!

Monostatos is taken away.

We honour Sarastro, and all men revere   Es lebe Sarastro, der göttliche Weise!
  him,
He'll punish or pardon — We love him   Er lohnet und strafet in ähnlichem
  and fear him.   Kreise.

Now lead these two young strangers in   Führt diese beiden Fremdlinge
And thro' our temple be their guide.   In unseren Prüfungstempel ein;
But first ensure their heads are veiled   Bedecket ihre Häupter dann,
For they must now be purified.   Sie müssen erst gereinigt sein.

*The Speaker and the Second Priest each bring a sort of sack which they place over the heads
of the two strangers.*

When justice and integrity   Wenn Tugend und Gerechtigkeit
Fill ev'ry heart with charity,   Den grossen Pfad mit Ruhm bestreut,
When friendship and when brotherhood   Dann ist die Erd' ein Himmelreich,
Teach ev'ry heart to love the good,   Und Sterbliche den Göttern gleich.
Then ev'ry man shall scorn to lie,
The truth shall live and death shall die.

Act Two

The scene is laid in a palm grove. The trees have silvery trunks and golden leaves. There are 18 seats, covered with golden palm leaves, on each of which a pyramid and a large black horn, bound with gold, have been placed. In the centre are the largest pyramid and the tallest palm trees.
Scene One. *Sarastro and the other priests enter solemnly; each holds a palm frond in his hand. A march for wind instruments accompanies them | No. 9 [20]*

SARASTRO

Fellow servants of the great gods Isis and Osiris, hear me! Today's assembly in the Temple of Wisdom is one of the most important we have ever held. Tamino, a king's son, [twenty years of age] is waiting outside the northern gate of our temple. He seeks to achieve the goal which we can only reach through diligence and suffering. He wishes to throw off the veils which blind him and enter the sanctuary of Light. [It is today one of our most pressing duties to watch over this virtuous man and to offer him the hand of friendship.]

Ihr, in dem Weisheitstempel eingeweihten Diener der grossen Götter Osiris und Isis! Mit reiner Seele erklär' ich euch, dass unsere heutige Versammlung eine der wichtigsten unserer Zeit ist. Tamino, ein Königssohn, zwanzig Jahre seines Alters wandelt an der nördlichen Pforte unseres Tempels und seufzt mit tugendvollem Herzen nach einem Gegenstande, den wir alle mit Mühe und Fleiss erringen müssen. Kurz, dieser Jüngling will seinen nächtlichen Schleier von sich reissen und in's Heiligtum des grössten Lichtes blicken. Diesen Tugendhaften zu bewachen, ihm freundschaftlich die Hand zu bieten sei heute eine unsrer wichtigsten Pflichten.

FIRST PRIEST

Is this man virtuous?

Er besitzt Tugend?

SARASTRO

He is.

Tugend!

SECOND PRIEST

Can he keep silent?

Auch Verschwiegenheit?

SARASTRO

He can.

Verschwiegenheit!

THIRD PRIEST

Is he charitable?

Ist wohltätig?

SARASTRO

Yes. If you consider him worthy, now give the signal.

Wohltätig! – Haltet ihr ihn für würdig, so folgt meinem Beispiele.

First Threefold Chord on the horns | No. 9a

SARASTRO

[Encouraged by the unanimous support of your hearts,] I thank you in the name of humanity. [Prejudice always likes to throw the blame on us, the initiates, but wisdom and reason show up prejudice to be just a spider's web of lies. Prejudice will never shake the pillars of our temple. It will vanish when Tamino has

Menschheit. Mag immer das Vorurteil dankt Sarastro euch im Namen der Menschheit. Mag immer das Vorurteil seinen Tadel über uns Eingeweihte auslassen, Weisheit und Vernunft zerstückt es gleich dem Spinnengewebe. Unsere Säulen erschüttern sie nie. Jedoch das böse Vorurteil soll schwinden, sobald

himself fully mastered the demanding tasks of our art.] The gods have singled out Pamina [the gentle, virtuous maiden] as a bride for Tamino, and for this reason I took her away from her proud mother. That woman [thinks herself powerful. Through deceit and superstition, she hopes to win the people's support and] seeks to destroy our temple but she shall not do so. The noble Tamino shall help us to defend it, [as an initiate,] rewarding virtue and punishing vice.

Tamino selbst die Grösse unserer schweren Kunst besitzen wird. Pamina, das sanfte, tugendhafte Mädchen, haben die Götter dem holden Jünglinge bestimmt; dies ist der Grund, warum ich sie der stolzen Mutter entriss. Das Weib dünkt sich gross zu sein, hofft durch Blendwerk und Aberglauben das Volk zu berücken und unser'n festen Tempelbau zu zerstören. Allein, das soll sie nicht! Tamino, der holde Jüngling selbst, soll ihn mit uns befestigen und als Eingeweihter der Tugend Lohn, dem Laster aber Strafe sein.

Second Threefold Chord

THE SPEAKER
(*standing up*)

Great Sarastro, we well know and wonder at the wisdom of your words but will Tamino endure the heavy trials which await him? [Forgive me for speaking freely and for expressing my doubts. I am afraid for the young man — that he may, depressed by grief, lose his courage and fall in the difficult fight.] He is a prince.

Grosser Sarastro! deine weisheitsvollen Reden erkennen und bewundern wir; allein, wird Tamino auch die harten Prüfungen, so seiner warten, bekämpfen? Verzeih, dass ich so frei bin, dir meinen Zweifel zu eröffnen! Mir bangt es um den Jüngling. Wenn nun, im Schmerz dahingesunken sein Geist ihn verliesse und er dem harten Kampf unterläge? Er ist Prinz.

SARASTRO

More than that, he is a man.

Noch mehr — er ist Mensch!

THE SPEAKER

What if he should perish in the attempt?

Wenn er nun aber in seiner frühen Jugend leblos erblasste?

SARASTRO

Then he will go to join Isis and Osiris and share their happiness before we do.

Dann ist er Osiris und Isis gegeben, und wird der Götter Freuden früher fühlen, als wir.

Third Threefold Chord

SARASTRO

Send Tamino and his companion into the forecourt of the temple. And you, friends, perform your sacred office and teach them their duty as men.

Man führe Tamino mit seinem Reisegefährten in den Vorhof des Tempels ein.

(*to the Speaker who kneels before him*)

[And you, my friend, you whom the gods have chosen as the defender of truth, accomplish your sacred duties. May your wisdom instruct the two profane ones in the duties of man and may it teach them the power of the gods.]

Und du, Freund, den die Götter durch uns zum Verteidiger der Wahrheit bestimmt — vollziehe dein heiliges Amt und lehre durch deine Weisheit beide, was Pflicht der Menschheit sei, lehre sie die Macht der Götter erkennen.

Exeunt the Speaker with one of the two priests.

The priests each hold a palm frond and stand around Sarastro. / Aria with chorus No. 10 [21]

Oh, Isis and Osiris, hear us;
We pray that you will guide this pair.
Oh, grant them strength through all
    temptation,
Help them endure all dangers there.

O, Isis und Osiris, schenket
Der Weisheit Geist dem neuen Paar!
Die ihr der Wandrer Schritte lenket,
Stärkt mit Geduld sie in Gefahr.

CHORUS

Help them endure all dangers there!

Stärkt mit Geduld sie in Gefahr!

SARASTRO

Should they be worthy then acclaim
    them,
But if they fail and Death should claim
    them,
When for these mortals life shall cease
Take them to your abode of peace.

Lasst sie der Prüfung Früchte sehen;
Doch sollten sie zu Grabe gehen,
So lohnt der Tugend kühnen Lauf,
Nehmt sie in euren Wohnsitz auf.

CHORUS

Take them to your abode of peace.

Nehmt sie in euren Wohnsitz auf.

Exit Sarastro, followed by the others.

Transformation. *It is night. Thunder from afar. The scene is a small forecourt of the temple where the remains of sunken columns and pyramids are visible amongst thorn bushes. On both sides stand two high doors in the Egyptian style which represent further buildings at the sides.*
Scene Two. *Tamino and Papageno enter led by the Speaker and the Second Priest, who remove the sacks from their heads and leave them.*

TAMINO

What a fearful night! Papageno, are you
still there?

Eine schreckliche Nacht! Papageno, bist
du noch bei mir?

PAPAGENO

Yes, more's the pity.

I, freilich!

TAMINO

Where do you think we are?

Wo denkst du, dass wir uns nun
befinden?

PAPAGENO

If it wasn't so dark I could see to tell
you.

Oh . . .

Wo? Ja wenn's nicht finster wäre,
wollt' ich dir's sagen – aber so –
(Thunder)
O weh! –

TAMINO

What's the matter now?

Was ist's?

PAPAGENO

This spiritual life is so noisy! [*Lit.* I
would rather not stick to this subject.]

Mir wird nicht wohl bei der Sache!

TAMINO

You're afraid, it seems to me.

Du hast Furcht, wie ich höre.

PAPAGENO

Certainly not. It's just that there's an ice
cold tremor running up and down my
spine.

Furcht eben nicht, nur eiskalt läuft's mir
über den Rücken. O weh!

93

TAMINO

What's happening?	Was soll's?

PAPAGENO*

I think I must have caught a chill.	Ich glaube, ich bekomme ein kleines Fieber.

Enter The Speaker and Second Priest with torches. **Scene Three.**

THE SPEAKER

Strangers, what do you seek here? What brings you within our walls?	Ihr Fremdlinge, was such't oder fordert ihr von uns? Was treibt euch an in unsere Mauern zu dringen?

TAMINO

Friendship and love.	Freundschaft und Liebe.

THE SPEAKER

Are you ready to fight for them [with your life]?	Bist du bereit, sie mit deinem Leben su erkämpfen?

TAMINO

Yes.	Ja!

THE SPEAKER

If necessary with your life?	Auch wenn Tod dein Los wäre?

TAMINO

Yes.	Ja!

THE SPEAKER**

Are you willing to undergo every trial?	Du unterzieh'st dich jeder Prüfung?

TAMINO

I am.	Jeder!

THE SPEAKER

Your hand.	Reiche mir deine Hand!

The Speaker takes Tamino's hand.

SECOND PRIEST

[Before you go on, allow me a few words with this other stranger.]	Ehe du weitersprichst, erlaube mir, ein paar Worte mit diesem Fremdling zu sprechen.

---

*Additional dialogue from the original.

TAMINO

Nonsense, Papageno! Be a man!	Pfui, Papageno! Sei ein Mann!

PAPAGENO

I would rather be a girl!	Ich wollt', ich wär' ein Mädchen!

(violent thunder clap)

Oh woe! My last hour has come!	O! O! O! Das ist mein letzter Augenblick!

** Additional dialogue from the original.

THE SPEAKER

Prince, there is still time to withdraw. One more step and it will be too late.	Prinz, noch ist's Zeit zu weichen — einen Schritt weiter, und es ist zu spät.

TAMINO

May knowledge of wisdom be my achievement and Pamina, the lovely maiden, my reward!	Weisheitslehre sei mein Sieg; Pamina, das holde Mädchen, mein Lohn!

(to Papageno)

And are you ready to fight for the love of wisdom?

Willst auch du dir Weisheitsliebe erkämpfen?

PAPAGENO

Fighting's not my business and I really don't ask for wisdom. I'm [a natural man who's] satisfied with sleep, food and drink — but if I could one day find myself a pretty wife . . .

Kämpfen ist meine Sache nicht. Ich verlange auch im Grund gar keine Weisheit. Ich bin so ein Naturmensch, der sich mit Schlaf, Speise und Trank begnügt; und wenn es ja sein könnte, dass ich mir einmal ein schönes Weibchen fange —

SECOND PRIEST

You'll never find her if you don't undergo our trials.

Die wirst du nie erhalten, wenn du dich nicht unseren Prüfungen unterziehst.

PAPAGENO

But what are these trials?

Worin besteht diese Prüfung?

SECOND PRIEST

To submit to all our laws even if you die in the attempt.

Dich allen unseren Gesetzen zu unterwerfen, selbst den Tod nicht zu scheuen.

PAPAGENO

I'll stay single.

Ich bleibe ledig!

SECOND PRIEST

Even if you could win yourself a virtuous and beautiful wife?

Aber wenn du dir ein tugendhaftes, schönes Mädchen erwerben könntest?

PAPAGENO

I'll stay single.

Ich bleibe ledig.

SECOND PRIEST

But what if Sarastro has a girl waiting for you, and just like you in form and feature?

Wenn nun aber Sarastro dir ein Mädchen aufbewahrt hätte, das an Farbe und Kleidung dir ganz gleich wäre?

PAPAGENO

[Like me?] Is she young?

Mir gleich? — Ist sie jung?

SECOND PRIEST

Young and beautiful.

Jung und schön!

PAPAGENO

What's her name?

Und heisst?

SECOND PRIEST

Papagena.

Papagena.

PAPAGENO

[What? Pa-?]

Wie? Pa-?

SECOND PRIEST

[Papagena!]

Papagena!

PAPAGENO

Papagena? I wouldn't mind seeing her just out of interest.

Papagena? — Die möcht' ich aus blosser Neugierde sehen.

SECOND PRIEST

See her you may . . .

Sehen kannst du sie! —

PAPAGENO

But after I've seen her, *then* must I die?

Aber wenn ich sie gesehen habe, hernach muss ich sterben?

Second Priest shrugs his shoulders.

PAPAGENO

I'll stay single.

Ja? — Ich bleibe ledig!

SECOND PRIEST

You can see her but you mustn't speak to her until the appointed time. Do you think you can resist the temptation and hold your tongue?

Sehen kannst du sie, aber bis zur verlauf'nen Zeit kein Wort mit ihr sprechen. Wird dein Geist so viel Standhaftigkeit besitzen, deine Zunge in Schranken zu halten?

PAPAGENO

Of course.

O ja!

SECOND PRIEST

Your hand. You shall see her.

Deine Hand! Du sollst sie sehen.

THE SPEAKER

You too, prince, must remain silent, otherwise you will both perish. You may see Pamina but not speak to her. This silence is commanded as the first of your trials.

Auch dir, Prinz, legen die Götter ein heilsames Stillschweigen auf; ohne dieses seid ihr Beide verloren. – Du wirst Pamina sehen, aber nicht sie sprechen dürfen; dies ist der Anfang eu'rer Prüfungszeit.

Duet No. 11 [22]

THE SPEAKER AND SECOND PRIEST

Be on your guard for woman's humours —
That is the rule we follow here.
For often Man believes her rumours,
She tricks him, and it costs him dear.
She promises she'll never hurt him,
But mocks his heart, that's true and brave;
At last she'll spurn him and deceive him —
Death and despair was all she gave.

Bewahret euch vor Weibertücken:
Dies ist des Bundes erste Pflicht!
Manch weiser Mann liess sich berücken,
Er fehlte und versah sich's nicht.
Verlassen sah er sich am Ende,
Vergolten seine Treu mit Hohn!

Vergebens rang er seine Hände,

Tod und Verzweiflung war sein Lohn.

Exeunt Priests. **Scene Four**

PAPAGENO

Hey, lights there! Lights! [It's odd] Everytime these people go out, the lights go out as well!

He! He! He! Die Lichter her! Die Lichter her!! — Das ist doch sonderbar: so oft einen diese Herren verlassen, so sieht man mit offenen Augen nichts mehr.

TAMINO

Be quiet and remember what they said.

Ertrag es mit Geduld und denke, es ist der Götter Wille.

96

THE THREE LADIES

So! So! So!	Wie? Wie? Wie?
You are in Sarastro's court?	Ihr an diesem Schreckensort?
Woe! Woe! Woe!	Nie! nie, nie
All your hopes will come to naught!	Kommt ihr wieder glücklich fort!
Tamino, you shall die, you're perjured!	Tamino, dir ist Tod geschworen!
You, Papageno, shall be murdered!	Du, Papageno, bist verloren!

PAPAGENO

No, no, no, I'll die of fright!	Nein, nein, nein! Das wär' zu viel.

TAMINO

Papageno, do be quiet!	Papageno, schweige still!
A promise made cannot be broken,	Willst du dein Gelübde brechen,
But you'll break it once you've spoken.	Nichts mit Weibern hier zu sprechen?

PAPAGENO

You heard that we are both to die.	Du hörst ja, wir sind beide hin.

TAMINO

Just be patient, do be quiet.	Stille, sag ich! Schweige still!

PAPAGENO

Do be quiet and still, be quiet . . .	Immer still und immer still!

THE THREE LADIES

The Queen of Night is now nearby,	Ganz nah ist euch die Königin!
She found a secret way in here.	Sie drang im Tempel heimlich ein?

PAPAGENO

She's what? You say the Queen is near?	Wie? Was? Sie soll im Tempel sein?

TAMINO

Still be silent, quiet I say!	Stille, sag ich! Schweige still!
Must you always chatter,	Wirst du immer so vermessen
Or do promises not matter?	Deiner Eidespflicht vergessen?

THE THREE LADIES

Tamino, you are lost forever,	Tamino, hör! Du bist verloren!
Because you disobey our Queen.	Gedenke an die Königin!
We hear a lot of evil stories	Man zischelt viel sich in die Ohren
About this awful place of sin.	Von dieser Priester falschem Sinn.

TAMINO
(to himself)

The wise man thinks and never fears	Ein Weiser prüft und achtet nicht,
The evil rumours that he hears.	Was der gemeine Pöbel spricht.

THE THREE LADIES

They say that once you join their band,	Man sagt, wer ihrem Bunde schwört,
The Devil drags you down to hell.	Der fährt zur Höll' mit Haut und Haa

PAPAGENO

Now what the Devil, are we damned?	Das wär', beim Teufel, unerhört!
Tell me, Tamino, me as well?	Sag an, Tamino, ist das wahr?

TAMINO

They're only lies old wives repeat,	Geschwätz, von Weibern nachgesagt,
Thought up by those who lie and cheat.	Von Heuchlern aber ausgedacht.

97

They say the Queen is warning you.   Doch sagt es auch die Königin.

TAMINO

She's but a fickle woman too.   Sie ist ein Weib, hat Weibersinn.
Be still, you must believe I'm right;   Sei still, mein Wort sei dir genug,
Just be a man, and don't take fright.   Denk deiner Pflicht und handle klug.

THE THREE LADIES
(to Tamino)

Now why do you behave so rudely?   Warum bist du mit uns so spröde?
Tamino cautiously indicates that he must not speak.
You Papageno too — so cruelly?   Auch Papageno schweigt — so rede!

PAPAGENO

I'd like to answer that . . .   Ich möchte gern — wohl —

TAMINO
(to Papageno)

Hush!   Still!

PAPAGENO
(quietly)

You see I've got to keep . . .   Ihr seht, dass ich nicht soll. —

TAMINO

Hush!   Still!
You find it hard to keep so silent,   Dass du nicht kannst das Plaudern lassen,
But if you talk you'll get the blame.   Ist wahrlich eine Schand für dich!

PAPAGENO

It's really hard to keep so silent,   Dass ich nicht kann das Plaudern lassen,
But if I talk I'll get the blame.   Ist wahrlich eine Schand für mich!

THE THREE LADIES

And now we see they're both defiant   Wir müssen sie mit Scham verlassen,
We'll have to leave them, full of shame.   Es plaudert keiner sicherlich;
For Man is silent and he's strong . . .   Von festem Geiste ist ein Mann,
He knows the time to hold his tongue.   Er denkt, was er sprechen kann.

TAMINO, PAPAGENO

And now they see we're both defiant   Sie müssen uns mit Scham verlassen,
They'll have to leave us, full of shame.   Es plaudert keiner sicherlich;
For Man is silent and he's strong . . .   Von festem Geiste ist ein Mann,
He knows the time to hold his tongue.   Er denkt, was er sprechen kann.

PRIESTS
(from within)

The veil of our silence is broken!   Entweiht ist die heilige Schwelle!
Now banish the women who've spoken!   Hinab mit den Weibern zur Hölle!
A frightening chord resounds: all the instruments, rolls and claps of thunder and lightning; two claps of thunder at once.

THE THREE LADIES

Away! Away! Away!   O weh! O weh! O weh!
They disappear through a trapdoor. Papageno falls to the ground in fear. He sings when the music is silent.

PAPAGENO

Oh dear, oh dear, oh dear!   O weh! O weh! O weh!

The Threefold chord sounds. **Scene Six.** *Enter The Speaker and Second Priest with torches.*

THE SPEAKER

Tamino, we salute you. Your resolute behaviour has passed the first test. You have many more dangerous paths to follow but with the Gods' help you will succeed. [We go forward with a pure heart on our journey.] Follow me!

Heil dir, Jüngling! Dein standhaft männliches Betragen hat gesiegt. Zwar hast du noch manch rauhen und gefährlichen Weg zu wandern, den du aber durch Hilfe der Götter glücklich endigen wirst. Wir wollen also mit reinem Herzen unsere Wanderschaft weiter fortsetzen. So! Nun komm!

He places the sack over Tamino's head.

SECOND PRIEST

What's this, my friend? How are you feeling?

Was seh'ich! Freund, stehe auf! Wie ist dir?

PAPAGENO

Terrible.

Ich lieg' in einer Ohnmacht!

SECOND PRIEST

Stand up. Pull yourself together and be a man.

Auf! Sammle dich und sei ein Mann!

PAPAGENO
(standing up)

Oh well! I'll stand up, pull myself together, and be a man. [Why must I go through all this suffering and all these frights?] But if Papagena is already waiting for me, why do I have to go through so much to win her?

Aber sag't mir nur, meine Herren, warum muss ich denn alle diese Qualen und Schrecken empfinden? — Wenn mir ja die Götter eine Papagena bestimmten, warum denn mit so viel Gefahren sie erringen?

SECOND PRIEST

To prove that you deserve her. [*lit.* Your own intelligence should tell you the answer.] Come, it's my duty to lead you onwards.

Diese neugierige Frage mag deine Vernunft dir beantworten. Komm! Meine Pflicht heischt, dich weiter zu führen.

He places the sack over his head.

PAPAGENO

After so much exercise a man could lose his appetite for love altogether.

Bei so einer ewigen Wanderschaft möcht' einem wohl die Liebe auf immer vergehen!

Exeunt.

Transformation. *The scene changes to a delightful garden. Trees planted in a horseshoe pattern; in the centre stands a bower of flowers and roses, where Pamina is asleep. The moon shines on her face. In front of her is a smooth lawn.* **Scene Seven:** *enter Monostatos, who pauses, then sits down.*

MONOSTATOS

Ah, there she is, the prudish princess [And it is on account of this insignificant creature that they wanted to shred the soles of my feet! I have only the daylight to thank for having escaped with any skin left on them to tread on the ground. Hm! What was my offence anyway? That

Ha, da find'ich ja die spröde Schöne! Und um so einer geringen Pflanze wegen wollte man meine Fusssohlen behämmern? Also bloss dem heutigen Tag hab ich's zu verdanken, dass ich noch mit heiler Haut auf die Erde trete! Hm! Was war denn eigentlich mein

I fell in love with this exotic flower transplanted here from some foreign soil.] Who could not look at her and not be tempted, even if he came from a cooler climate than I do? This girl will drive me mad. The fire smouldering inside me will flare up and consume me. If I could be sure I was alone, I'd take the risk. [What a cursed foolish thing is love!] A surreptitious kiss couldn't do me any harm.

Verbrechen? Dass ich mich in eine Blume vergaffte, die auf fremden Boden versetzt war? Und welcher Mensch, wenn er auch von gelinderem Himmelsstrich daherwanderte, würde bei so einem Anblick kalt und unempfindlich bleiben? Bei allen Sternen, das Mädchen wird mich noch um meinem Verstand bringen! Das Feuer, das in mir glimmt, wird mich noch verzehren. Wenn ich wüsste — dass ich so ganz allein und unbelauscht wäre, ich wagte es noch einmal. Es ist doch eine verdammte närrische Sache um die Liebe! Ein Küsschen, dächte ich, liesse sich entschuldigen.

Aria No. 13 [24]

All enjoy the beds of passion,
Cling, caress and stroke and kiss:
Why should I be out of fashion?
Only I'm denied the bliss.
I am black, that's why I'm hated.
I can love girls just as well.
Life for me without a woman
Is an ever-burning Hell.
I'll deny myself no longer
All the secret joys of love:
Fear is strong but lust is stronger,
Now the hawk desires the dove.
She lies there, and I am lusting —
Now I'll relish fierce desires.
If you find my love disgusting,
You can shut your stupid eyes.

Alles fühlt der Liebe Freuden,
Schnäbelt, tändelt, herzt und küsst;
Und ich sollt' die Liebe meiden,
Weil ein Schwarzer hässlich ist.
Ich bin auch den Mädchen gut!
Bin ich nicht von Fleisch und Blut?
Immer ohne Weibchen leben,
Wäre wahrlich Höllenglut!
Drum so will ich, weil ich lebe,
Schnäbeln, küssen, zärtlich sein!
Lieber guter Mond, vergebe,
Eine Weisse nahm mich ein
Weiss ist schön! Ich muss sie küssen;
Mond, verstecke dich dazu!
Sollt es dich zu sehr verdriessen,
O, so mach die Augen zu!

He creeps slowly and quietly towards Pamina.

Scene Eight. *The Queen of the Night appears, with a thunder clap, from the central trapdoor, so she stands just in front of Pamina.*

QUEEN

Away!   Zurück!

Pamina awakes. *

---

*Additional dialogue

PAMINA

Oh Gods!   Ihr Götter!

MONOSTATOS

(throwing himself into the shadows)

Oh woe! That is, if I am not mistaken, the goddess of the night.

O weh! Das ist — wo ich nicht irre, die Göttin der Nacht.

He stands still.

PAMINA

Mother! Mother! Mother!   Mutter! Mutter! Meine Mutter!

She falls into her arms.

MONOSTATOS

Mother? Hm! I must hear as much as I can of this.

Mutter? Hm! Dass muss man von weitem belauschen.

He hides.

QUEEN

Be thankful to the power which tore   Verdank es der Gewalt, mit der man dich

100

Where is the youth I sent you?	Wo ist der Jüngling, den ich nach dir sandte?

PAMINA

Oh, Mother he has left the world and gone to join Sarastro.	Ach, Mutter, der ist der Welt und den Menschen auf ewig entzogen. Er hat sich den Eingeweihten gewidmet.

QUEEN

[The initiates?] Miserable girl. Now you are lost to me for ever.	Den Eingeweihten? Unglückliche Tochter. Nun bist du auf ewig mir entrissen.

PAMINA

[Lost?] Dearest mother let us escape together; under your protection I'll brave any dangers.	Entrissen? O fliehen wir, liebe Mutter! Unter deinem Schutz trotz ich jeder Gefahr.

QUEEN

Protection! I cannot protect you any longer. I lost all my power when, on his deathbed your father gave the sevenfold circle of the sun to Sarastro and his followers. That all powerful circle Sarastro now wears on his breast.*	Schutz? Liebes Kind, deine Mutter kann dich nicht mehr schützen. Mit deines Vaters Tod ging meine Macht zu Grabe.

Footnote cont'd

you from me that you can still call me mother.	mir entriss, dass ich noch deine Mutter mich nenne.

* Original dialogue

PAMINA

My father . . .	Mein Vater . . .

QUEEN

Gave the sevenfold circle of the sun voluntarily to the Initiates. That powerful circle Sarastro now wears on his breast. When I tried to persuade him to change his mind, he replied with a wrinkled brow, 'Woman, my last hour is upon me — all my treasure is for you and your daughter'. 'The all piercing Circle of the Sun', said I, interrupting him hurriedly. 'That belongs to the Initiates', he answered. 'Sarastro will be the male guardian, just as I have been until now. And now no more; do not try to understand things which are inconceivable to a woman's mind. Your duty must be to commit yourself and your daughter to the authority of these men'.	Übergab freiwillig den siebenfachen Sonnenkreis den Eingeweihten. Diesen mächtigen Sonnenkreis trägt Sarastro auf seiner Brust. Als ich ihn darüber beredete, so sprach er mit gefalteter Stirn: Weib, meine letzte Stunde ist da — alle Schätze, so ich allein besass, sind dein und deiner Tochter. Der alles verzehrende Sonnenkreis — fiel ich ihm hastig in die Rede — Ist den Geweihten bestimmt, antwortete er, Sarastro wird ihn so männlich verwalten wie ich bisher. Und nun kein Wort weiter; forsche nicht nach Wesen, die dem weiblichen Geist unbegreiflich sind. Deine Pflicht ist, dich und deine Tochter der Führung weiser Männer zu überlassen.

PAMINA

O dearly beloved mother! Must this young man also be lost to me forever?	Liebe Mutter, nach alledem zu schliessen, ist wohl auch der Jüngling auf immer für mich verloren?

QUEEN

Lost — unless you can persuade him to escape with you by the underground passages before the sun's rays warm the earth once again. The first light of day	Verloren, wenn du nicht, ehe die Sonne die Erde färbt, ihn durch diese unterirdischen Gemächer zu fliehen beredest. Der erste Schimmer des Tages

101

PAMINA

But my father believed in these good
men and praised their goodness and their
wisdom. May I not continue to love
Tamino now that he has joined them?

QUEEN

You dare to defend those barbarians
and love a man who will join with
them to bring about my ruin?

Do you see this dagger? It was sharpened for Sarastro. Take it, kill him, and bring back the circle of the sun to me.	Siehst du hier diesen Stahl? Er ist für Sarastro geschliffen, und du wirst ihn töten und den mächtigen siebenfachen Sonnenkreis mir überliefern.

PAMINA

But mother . . .	Aber, liebste Mutter! —

QUEEN

Silence!	Kein Wort!

Aria No. 14 [25a, b]

I feel my heart aflame with hate and murder.	Der Hölle Rache kocht in meinem Herzen,
Death and Destruction blaze around my throne.	Tod und Verzweiflung flammet um mich her!
Should you not kill Sarastro as I order,	Fühlt nicht durch dich Sarastro Todesschmerzen,
You are no longer any child of mine, And you shall be neither daughter nor my child.	So bist du meine Tochter nimmermehr —
I'll break our ties forever, renouncing you forever	Verstossen sei auf ewig, verlassen sei auf ewig,
Abandoning forever any mother love or care.	Zertrümmert sei'n auf ewig alle Bande der Natur,
If you won't kill Sarastro as I order,	Wenn nicht durch dich Sarastro wird erblassen!

Footnote cont'd

will decide you fate: either he is yours alone, or he is handed over to be the prisoner of the Initiates.	entscheidet, ob er ganz dir oder den Eigeweihten gegeben ist.

PAMINA

Oh dearly beloved mother! Why can't I love this young man when he is an Initiate as tenderly as I do now? My father himself associated with these wise men? He always spoke of them with joy extolling their excellence, their understanding, their virtue. Sarastro is no less virtuous.	Liebe Mutter, dürft' ich den Jüngling als Eingeweihten denn nicht auch ebenso zärtlich lieben, wie ich ihn jetzt liebe? Mein Vater selbst war ja mit diesen weisen Männern verbunden. Er sprach jederzeit mit Entzücken von ihnen, preise ihre Güte — ihren Verstand — ihre Tugend. Sarastro ist nicht weniger tugendhaft.

QUEEN

What do I hear? You, my own daughter, are able to defend the ignominious principles of these barbarians? Would you love a man in alliance with my mortal enemy who would at any moment send me to my death?	Was hör ich! Du, meine Tochter, könntest die schändlichen Gründe dieser Barbaren verteidigen? So einen Mann lieben, der, mit meinem Todfeind verbunden, mit jedem Augenblick nur meinen Sturz bereiten würde?

Hear, God of Vengeance! Hear a mother's vow.

Hört! Rachegötter! Hört der Mutter Schwur!

She disappears.* Monostatos returns.

PAMINA

She swore to forsake me but how could I kill Sarastro? . . . Monostatos!

MONOSTATOS

I have heard everything. Now both you and your mother are in my power. But if you swear to love me I will be indulgent.

PAMINA

Monostatos, I implore you!

MONOSTATOS

Choose love or death. Your life is at stake!

---

*Original Sequence

Scene Nine.

PAMINA

(the dagger in her hand)

Commit murder! Oh gods! I cannot. I cannot.

Morden soll ich? Götter! Das kann ich nicht — das kann ich nicht.

She stands in thought. **Scene Ten.** *Monostatos approaches fast, furtively and very gleefully.*

MONOSTATOS

So Sarastro's Circle of the Sun has its uses? And to obtain it, the lovely girl must kill him. That serves my purpose.

Sarastros Sonnenkreis hat also auch seine Wirkung? Und diesen zu erhalten, soll das schöne Mädchen ihn mordern. Das ist Salz in meine Suppe.

PAMINA

Didn't my mother swear by all the gods that she would forsake me if I did not use this dagger against Sarastro? O Gods! What should I do?

Aber schwur sie nicht bei allen Göttern, mich zu verstossen, wenn ich den Dolch nicht gegen Sarastro kehre? Götter! Was soll ich tun?

MONOSTATOS

Trust in me!

Dich mir anvertraun.

He takes the dagger from her. Pamina screams.

Why do you tremble? Because I am black or because of your criminal intent?

Warum zitterst du? Vor meiner schwarzen Farbe oder vor dem ausgedachten Mord?

PAMINA

(timidly)

So you know!

Du weiss also?

MONOSTATOS

Everything! I know that your fate, and that of your mother also are in my hands. I have only to say a single word to Sarastro and your mother would be plunged in those vaults of water where the Initiates are, so they say, purified. She would never emerge unharmed from these caverns, unless I so decided. So there is only one way open to you to save yourself and your mother.

Alles. Ich weiss sogar, dass nicht nur dein, sondern auch deiner Mutter Leben in meiner Hand steht. Ein einziges Wort sprech ich zu Sarastro, und deine Mutter wird in diesem Gewölb', in dem Wasser, das die Eingeweihten reinigen soll, wie man sagt, ersäuft. Aus diesem Gewölb' kommt sie nun sicher nicht mehr mit heiler Haut, wenn ich es will. Du hast also nur einen Weg, dich und deine Mutter zu retten.

103

Enter Sarastro

MONOSTATOS

Sir, I am innocent.

Footnote cont'd

PAMINA

And that is? Der wäre?

MONOSTATOS

To love me! Mich zu lieben!

PAMINA
(trembling, to herself)

Oh Gods! Götter!

MONOSTATOS
(happily)

The storm bends the little sapling Das junge Bäumchen jagt der Sturm auf
towards me. Well, maiden, yes or no! meine Seite. Nun, Mädchen, ja oder nein!

PAMINA
(passionately)

No! Nein!

MONOSTATOS
(angrily)

No? And the reason? Because I am the Nein? Und warum? Weil ich die Farbe
colour of a black phantom? No! Ha! You eines schwarzen Gespenstes trage? Nicht?
will die! Ha! So stirb!

He seizes her by the hand.

PAMINA

Monostatos, see me here on my knees — Monostatos, sieh mich hier auf meinen
spare me! Knien — schone meiner!

MONOSTATOS

Love or death! Speak! Your life is at the Liebe oder Tod! Sprich! Dein Leben
point of this blade! steht auf der Spitze.

PAMINA

I have offered my heart to the Prince. Mein Herz hab ich dem Jüngling
geopfert.

MONOSTATOS

What do I care for your 'offer'? — Was kümmert mich dein Opfer —
Speak! sprich!

PAMINA

Never! Nie!

Scene Eleven: *Sarastro enters.*

MONOSTATOS

So, die! So fahre denn hin!

Sarastro pushes him away roughly.

Sir, do not punish me. This is not my Herr, mein Unternehmen ist nicht
plot, I am innocent. They swore to kill strafbar, ich bin unschuldig! Man hat
you, and I wanted to avenge you. deinen Tod geschworen, darum wollte
ich dich rächen.

SARASTRO

I know this only too well. I know your Ich weiss nur allzuviel, weiss, dass deine
soul is as black as your face. And I Seele ebenso schwarz als dein Gesicht ist.
would punish you with the greatest Auch würde ich dies schwarze
severity for this black conspiracy, if I did Unternehmen mit höchster Strenge an
not know that it was a woman, as evil dir bestrafen, wenn nicht ein böses
as her daughter is virtuous, who forged Weib, das zwar eine sehr gute Tochter
the dagger for the murder. Thanks to the hat, den Dolch dazu geschmiedet hätte.
wickedness of this woman's machinations, Verdank es der bösen Handlung des
I will let you go free. Go! Weibes, dass du ungestraft davonziehst.
Geh!

104

SARASTRO

Your soul is as black as your face. Go!

MONOSTATOS

If I can't have the daughter, I'll try my luck with the mother!	Jetzt such'ich die Mutter auf, weil die Tochter mir nicht beschieden ist.

Exit Monostatos. **Scene Twelve**

PAMINA

Sir, do not punish my mother. Her grief at my absence has sent her mad.	Herr, strafe meine Mutter nicht! Der Schmerz über meine Abwesenheit —

SARASTRO

I know everything. She is planning vengeance on me and all humanity. By her own laws she deserves to be punished. But we follow different rules.	Ich weiss Alles.*

Aria No. 15 [26]

To rule by Hate and Vengeance	In diesen heil'gen Hallen
Is not our practice here,	Kennt man die Rache nicht,
And if a man's repentant	Und ist ein Mensch gefallen,
He's saved by love, not fear.	Führt Liebe ihn zur Pflicht.
If he is lost a loving hand	Dann wandelt er an Freundes Hand
Shows him with joy our happy land.	Vergnügt und froh ins bess're Land.
Here Peace and Mercy govern,	In diesen heil'gen Mauern,
By Love alone we live,	Wo Mensch den Menschen liebt,
Though tyrants rage and threaten	Kann kein Verräter lauern,
We love them and forgive.	Weil man dem Feind vergibt.
If man can't learn what love can do	Wen solche Lehren nicht erfreun,
His days on earth are surely few.	Verdienet nicht, ein Mensch zu sein.

Exeunt.

Transformation. *The scene changes to a great hall, in which the flying machine can turn. The flying machine has a door and is decorated with roses and flowers. In the foreground are two grassy platforms.* **Scene Thirteen.** *Tamino and Papageno with their heads uncovered are led in by the two priests.*

THE SPEAKER

We shall leave you both alone here. When the trumpets sound, you must continue in that direction. Farewell Prince, and remember your vow of silence.	Hier seid ihr euch beide allein überlassen. — Sobald die Posaune tönt, dann nehm't ihr euren Weg dahin! — Prinz, leb't wohl! Wir sehen uns, eh' ihr ganz am Ziele seid, Noch einmal vergesst das Wort nicht: Schweigen!

---

*

I know everything. I know that she is wandering in the vaults beneath the temple, conceiving plans of revenge on me and all humanity. You alone will see how I am avenged on your mother. May Heaven give the pleasing young man courage and constancy in his purpose, so that you may share his good fortune. Then your mother will have to retire in disgrace to her palace.	Ich weiss alles. Weiss, dass sie in unterirdischen Gemächern des Tempels herumirrt und Rache über mich und die Menschheit kocht. Allein du sollst sehen, wie ich mich an deiner Mutter räche. Der Himmel schenke nur dem holden Jüngling Mut und Standhaftigkeit in seinem Vorsatz, dann bist du mit ihm glücklich, und deine Mutter soll beschämt nach ihrer Burg zurückkehren.

Exit.

SECOND PRIEST

Papageno, remember, whoever breaks silence in this place will be struck down by thunder and lightning. Farewell.	Papageno! Wer an diesem Ort sein Stillschweigen bricht, den strafen die Götter durch Donner und Blitz. Leb' wohl!

Exit. **Scene Fourteen.** *Tamino sits on a grassy bank.*

PAPAGENO
(after a pause)

Tamino!	Tamino!

TAMINO

Sh!	St!

PAPAGENO

Oh, this is a fine sort of life. Back [in my straw-hut or] in the woods I could at least hear the birds chirrup.	Das ist ein lustiges Leben! — Wär'ich lieber in meiner Strohhütte, oder im Wald, so hört'ich doch manchmal einen Vogel pfeifen!

TAMINO

Sh!	St!

PAPAGENO

Surely I can talk to myself if I want to? [and we two can talk together — we're men.]	Mit mir selbst werd' ich wohl sprechen dürfen; und auch wir zwei können zusammen sprechen — wir sind ja Männer.

TAMINO

Sh!	St!

PAPAGENO
(singing)

LA LA LA . . . They don't even offer you a drop of water in this place, let alone anything stronger!	La la la — la la la! — Nicht einmal einen Tropfen Wasser bekommt man bei diesen Leuten, viel weniger sonst was.

Scene Fifteen. *An ugly old woman enters with a large goblet of water.*

PAPAGENO
(looking at her for a long time)

Hallo! Oh Hallo! Is that for me?	Ist das für mich?

OLD WOMAN

Yes, my angel!	Ja, mein Engel!

PAPAGENO
(looks at her again and drinks)

Thank you.	

OLD WOMAN

No trouble at all.	

PAPAGENO

Ugh . . . water!	Nicht mehr und nicht weniger als Wasser.

106

Thank you kindly.

PAPAGENO

No trouble at all. Tell me, mysterious beauty, do you entertain all strangers like this?	Sag' du mir, du unbekannte Schöne, werden alle fremden Gäste auf diese Art bewirtet?

OLD WOMAN

Certainly, my angel.	Freilich, mein Engel!

PAPAGENO

In that case, I don't suppose you see many visitors?	So, so! — Auf diese Art werden die Fremden auch nicht gar zu häufig kommen.

OLD WOMAN

Very few!	Sehr wenig.

PAPAGENO

I can believe that. Come on, old lady, come and talk to me. I'm bored out of my feathers. Tell me, how old are you?	Kann mir's denken. — Geh', Alte, setze dich her zu mir! mir ist die Zeit verdammt lange. Sag' du mir, wie alt bist du denn?

OLD WOMAN

How old am I?	Wie alt?

PAPAGENO

Yes!	Ja!

OLD WOMAN

Eighteen years and two minutes.	Achtzehn Jahr' und zwei Minuten.

PAPAGENO

[Eighty years and two minutes?]*

OLD WOMAN

[EIGHTEEN years and two minutes!]

PAPAGENO

Ha ha ha! Is that so my little angel? Have you got a boy-friend?	Ha ha ha! — Ei, du junger Engel! Hast du auch einen Geliebten?

OLD WOMAN

Oh, certainly!	I, freilich!

PAPAGENO

Is he as young as you are?	Ist er auch so jung wie du?

OLD WOMAN

Not quite. He is ten years older.	Nicht gar; er ist um zehn Jahre älter.

PAPAGENO

Ten years older? That must be a fiery passion.	Um zehn Jahre, ist er älter als du? Das muss eine Liebe sein!

OLD WOMAN

Oh yes.

---

* A joke traditional in many German productions.

PAPAGENO	
What's your boy-friend called?	Wie nennt sich denn dein Liebhaber?

OLD WOMAN	
Papageno!	Papageno!

PAPAGENO
(screams, then a pause)

Papageno? PAPAGENO? Where is he, this Papageno?	Papageno? — Wo ist er denn, dieser Papageno?

OLD WOMAN	
Standing right here, my angel.	Da steht er, mein Engel.

PAPAGENO	
You mean that I'm your boy-friend?	Ich wär' dein Geliebter?

OLD WOMAN	
Of course, my angel!	Ja, mein Engel!

PAPAGENO
(quickly taking the water and splashing her face with it)

Then, tell me, what's your name?	Sag' du mir, wie heisst du denn?

OLD WOMAN	
My name is . . .	Ich heisse —

A violent thunder clap. The old woman limps hurriedly away. Tamino stands up and reproaches him with his finger.

PAPAGENO	
Oh Gods, forgive me! I won't say another word as long as I live!	O weh! Nun sprech ich kein Wort mehr!

Scene Sixteen. *The Three Boys enter in a flying machine, decorated with roses. In the centre is a beautifully laid table. One of the boys carries the flute; another the music box with the bells.* / *Trio No. 16*

THE THREE BOYS [27]

Twice now we've gladly come to meet you	Seid uns zum zweitenmal willkommen,
Seeking you where Sarastro dwells.	Ihr Männer, in Sarastros Reich.
He bade us find you and, in greeting,	Er schickt, was man euch abgenommen,
Sends you the flute and magic bells.	Die Flöte und die Glöckchen euch.
Now you have suffered thirst and fasting	Wollt ihr die Speisen nicht verschmähen,
He bids you eat and drink your fill.	So esset, trinket froh davon.
We shall return a third and last time,	Wenn wir zum drittenmal uns sehen,
Joy shall reward your steadfast will.	Ist Freude eures Mutes Lohn!
You must be brave and fear no ill.	Tamino, Mut! Nah ist das Ziel.
You Papageno, silence still.	Du Papageno, schweige still!

While the Boys are singing, they put the table on the stage. The Boys fly off. **Scene Seventeen.**

PAPAGENO	
Tamino, aren't you [we] going to eat anything?	Tamino, wollen wir nicht speisen?

Tamino plays the flute

Oh, you whistle on your flute and I'll wet my whistle. Ah, this wine is fit for the Gods. Let's see whether Mr.	Blase du nur fort auf deiner Flöte; ich will meine Brocken blasen! Herr Sarastro führt eine gute Küche. Auf diese Art,

Sarastro's kitchen is as good as his cellar. Mm. The food's wonderful too — even I don't mind keeping quiet when my mouth is full.

ja, da will ich schon schweigen, wenn ich immer solche gute Bissen bekomme — Nun, ich will sehen, ob auch der Keller so gut bestellt ist. Ha! das ist Götterwein!

Scene Eighteen. *Enter Pamino. Tamino stops playing the flute.*

PAMINA
(joyfully)

You're here Tamino. I heard the sound of your flute and hurried to find you. But you look sad. Won't you speak to me?

Du hier? — Gütige Götter! Dank euch, dass ihr mich diesen Weg führtet. Ich hörte deine Flöte — und so lief ich pfeilschnell dem Tone nach — Aber du bist traurig? Sprichst nicht eine Silbe mit deiner Pamina?

Tamino sighs.

[What's this? Must you shun me?] Won't you tell me you still love me?

Wie? Ich soll dich meiden? Liebst du mich nicht mehr?

Tamino sighs and waves her away.

Do you want me to go away without knowing why? Tamino, what have I done? Don't make me suffer. [I look for trust and help from you — and would you make my loving heart suffer still more?]

Ich soll fliehen, ohne zu wissen warum? Tamino! Holder Jüngling! Hab ich dich beleidigt? O kränke mein Herz nicht noch mehr. Bei dir such ich Trost, Hilfe — und du kannst mein liebevolles Herz noch mehr kränken? Liebst du mich nicht mehr?

(Tamino sighs.)

Papageno can you tell me what has happened to Tamino? You too? At least explain your silence to me.

Papageno, sag du mir, was ist mit meinem Freund? Wie? Auch du? Erkläre mir wenigstens die Ursache eures Stillschweigens?

Papageno waves her away with both hands, his mouth full of food.

Oh, this is worse than suffering, worse than death. [Beloved, my only Tamino.]

O, das ist mehr als Kränkung, mehr als Tod! Liebster, einziger Tamino!

Aria No. 17

PAMINA [28]

Ah, I know that all is ended.
Gone forever the joy of love.
Never will those hours of beauty
Come again to fill my heart.
See Tamino, see my weeping tears
That flow for you alone.
Just one word to say you love me,
Or I'll find rest in Death alone.

Ach, ich fühl's, es ist verschwunden,
Ewig hin mein ganzes Glück!
Nimmer kommt ihr, Wonnestunden,
Meinem Herzen mehr zurück!
Sieh, Tamino, diese Tränen
Fliessen, Trauter, dir allein.
Fühlst du nicht der Liebe Sehnen,
So wird Ruh im Tode sein!

Exit Pamino. **Scene Nineteen**

PAPAGENO
(eating greedily)

There, you see, Tamino, I can keep quiet too when it suits me! Yes, when it comes to important things, I'm a man!

Nicht wahr, Tamino, ich kann auch schweigen, wenn's sein muss? — Ja, bei so einem Unternehmen bin ich Mann.

(He drinks.)

I drink to the health of the head cook and the butler!

Der Herr Koch und der Herr Kellermeister sollen leben!

First Threefold Chord. Tamino indicates to Papageno to come along.

109

You go ahead, I'll follow when I've
finished. [It takes more courage to stay!]

Geh' du nur voraus, ich komme schon
nach! Der Stärkere bleibt da!

Tamino warns him and goes out by the opposite side of the stage from which he entered.

Now I can enjoy my supper in peace.
Why should I rush off just when my
taste buds are tingling? Wild animals
couldn't drag me away from this.
[I won't even go if Mr. Sarastro sets his
six lions on me.]

Jetzt will ich mir's erst recht wohl sein
lassen. Da ich in meinem besten Appetit
bin, soll ich gehen? Das lass ich wohl
bleiben. Ich ging' jetzt nicht fort, und
wenn Herr Sarastro seine sechs Löwen an
mich spannte.

The lions appear; Papageno is frightened.

[Oh gods, have pity on me!]
Oh, Tamino, save me, help! help!
[These Mister lions intend to make a
mouthful of me.]

O Barmherzigkeit, ihr gütigen Götter!
Tamino, rette mich! Die Herren Löwen
machen eine Mahlzeit aus mir.

Tamino returns hurriedly and plays his flute. The lions go away; he makes a sign to Papageno.

You and that flute have saved my life.
I promise I'll come with you in future.*

Second Threefold Chord

There they go again! All right, we're
coming! Don't be in such a hurry . . .
I'll just go and have another nibble.

Animals growl

Oh go away and find a mouse to frighten.

Animals growl again. Third Threefold Chord.

Oh. . . !

Papageno screams, exit with table.

Transformation. *The scene changes into the vault of a pyramid. The Speaker and other priests. Two priests carry an illuminated pyramid on their shoulders; other priests hold transparent lamps in the shape of pyramids in their hands.* **Scene Twenty.** *Eighteen priests stand in a triangle, six to each side | Chorus No. 18*

Oh, Isis and Osiris, Gods resplendent!
The darkness fades; the blazing sun's
transcendent.
Soon now this brave young man will find
a new life;
Soon too within these walls he'll find a
true love.

O, Isis und Osiris, welche Wonne!
Die düstre Nacht verscheucht der Glanz
der Sonne.
Bald fühlt der edle Jüngling neues Leben;

Bald ist er unserem Dienste ganz ergeben.

---

* Original Text.

I'm coming. Call me a rascal it I don't
follow you everywhere.

Ich gehe schon! Heiss du mich einen
Schelm, wenn du ich dir nicht in allem folge.

Second Threefold Chord.

There we go again. We're coming soon.
But tell me, Tamino, what will become
of us?

Das geht uns an. Wir kommen schon.
Aber hör einmal, Tamino was wird denn
noch alles mit uns werden?

Tamino points to the heavens.

Must I ask the Gods?

Die Götter soll ich fragen?

Tamino nods.

Ah, yes! The Gods can obviously tell us
more than we know!

Ja, die könnten uns freilich mehr sagen
als wir wissen.

Third Threefold Chord. Tamino drags Papageno away.

What's the hurry? We will only arrive in
good time to be broiled.

Eile nur nicht so, wir kommen noch
immer zeitig genug, um uns braten zu
lassen.

Exeunt.

His heart is chaste, his soul is pure. Sein Geist ist kühn, sein Herz ist rein,
Soon he will join us, cleansed and pure. Bald wird er unser würdig sein.

Scene twenty-one. *Tamino is brought before the assembly.*

SARASTRO

Tamino, so far you have borne yourself Prinz, dein Betragen war bis hierher
with manly composure, but you still have männlich und gelassen; nun hast du noch
two more dangerous paths to follow. If zwei gefährliche Wege zu wandern.
you still love Pamina and wish to rule Schlägt dein Herz noch ebenso warm
as a wise and enlightened sovereign, the für Pamina und wünschest du einst als
gods will go with you. [Your hand!] ein weiser Fürst zu regieren, so mögen
Bring in Pamina. die Götter dich ferner begleiten. Deine
  Hand! Man bringe Pamina!

Silence falls upon the priests. Pamina is brought in. She wears the sack reserved for the
Initiates. Sarastro loosens the thongs which hold on the sack.

PAMINA

[Where am I? What a dreadful silence! Wo bin ich? Welch eine fürchterliche
Sarastro,] Tell me, where is Tamino? Stille! Sarastro, wo ist mein Jüngling?

SARASTRO

He is waiting to take a last farewell. Er wartet deiner, um dir das letzte
  Lebewohl zu sagen.

PAMINA

A last farewell. Oh, where is he? Let me Das letzte Lebewohl? Oh, wo ist er?
see him. Führt mich zu ihm.

SARASTRO

He is here. Hier.

PAMINA

Tamino. Tamino!

TAMINO

Pamina, stay there. Zurück!

Trio No. 19 [30]

PAMINA

My only joy, ah, must we part? Soll ich dich, Teurer, nicht mehr sehn?

SARASTRO

You need not fear, but trust his heart. Ihr werdet froh euch wiedersehn!

PAMINA

I fear the dangers that may harm you. Dein warten tödliche Gefahren!

TAMINO

I trust the truth to guard and arm me. Die Götter mögen mich bewahren!

PAMINA

I fear the dangers that may harm you. Dein warten tödliche Gefahren!

TAMINO, SARASTRO

I}
Now} trust the truth to guard and arm {me.
{him.   Die Götter mögen { ihn
{ mich } bewahren!

111

I hear a dreadful voice of warning	Du wirst dem Tode nicht entgehen,
That makes me long for you to stay.	Mir flüstert dieses Ahnung ein.

TAMINO, SARASTRO

I serve the lovely Gods of Morning —	Der Götter Wille mag geschehen,
Where they command, $\left\{\begin{array}{l}I\\he\end{array}\right\}$ must obey.	Ihr Wink soll $\left\{\begin{array}{l}mir\\ihm\end{array}\right\}$ Gesetze sein!

PAMINA

Oh, if you knew true love's devotion,	O liebtest du, wie ich dich liebe,
You could not stay so firm and calm.	Du würdest nicht so ruhig sein.

TAMINO, SARASTRO

Trust me, $\left\{\begin{array}{l}I\ feel\\he\ feels\end{array}\right\}$ the same emotion,	Glaub mir, $\left\{\begin{array}{l}ich\ fühle\\er\ fühlet\end{array}\right\}$ gleiche Triebe,
And know that love need fear no harm.	Wird ewig dein Getreuer sein!

SARASTRO

The hour has struck, his trials are starting.	Die Stunde schlägt, nun müsst ihr scheiden!

PAMINA, TAMINO

How grievous are the pangs of parting.	Wie bitter sind der Trennung Leiden!

SARASTRO

Tamino now must take his leave.	Tamino muss nun wieder fort.

TAMINO

Pamina, I must really leave.	Pamina, ich muss wirklich fort!

PAMINA

Tamino, must you really leave?	Tamino muss nun wirklich fort?

SARASTRO

Now he must leave.	Nun muss er fort!

TAMINO

Now I must leave.	Nun muss ich fort.

PAMINA

So you must leave?	So musst du fort!

TAMINO

Pamina, fare you well.	Pamina, lebe wohl!

PAMINA

Tamino, fare you well.	Tamino, lebe wohl!

SARASTRO

So leave her now	Nun eile fort.
And keep your vow:	Dich ruft dein Wort.
The hour is come, for you must leave now.	Die Stunde schlägt, wir sehn uns wieder!

PAMINA, TAMINO

Ah, peace of spirit, gone forever!	Ach, goldne Ruhe, kehre wieder!
Fare you well, fare you well!	Lebe wohl! Lebe wohl!

SARASTRO

But not forever!	Wir sehn uns wieder.

They separate. **Scene Twenty-two.**

PAPAGENO
(off stage)

Tamino, Tamino! Don't desert me!	Tamino! Tamino! Willst du mich denn gänzlich verlassen?

(He enters searching for Tamino)

I promise I won't leave you again! [If only I knew where I was! As long as I live I won't leave you again!] Don't leave me alone in the dark.	Wenn ich nur wenigstens wüsste, wo ich wäre! Tamino! Tamino! So lang' ich lebe, bleib' ich nicht mehr von dir! Nur diesmal verlass' mich armen Reisegefährten nicht!

He goes up to the door through which Tamino has just passed.

A VOICE

Go back!	Zurück!

Then, with a clap of thunder, a flame bursts from the door, and there is a loud chord.

PAPAGENO

[Merciful Gods! Where can I turn?] All right, I'm going. If only I knew where I came from. Tamino!	Barmherzige Götter! Wo wend' ich mich hin? Wenn ich nur wüsste, wo ich hereinkam!

He retreats to the door through which he entered.

THE VOICE

Go back!	Zurück!

A thunderclap, flames and chord as before.

PAPAGENO
(crying)

Now they won't let me go forwards or backwards. I suppose they want me to die of starvation. I knew I was wrong to come on this trip.	Nun kann ich weder vorwärts noch zurück! Muss vielleicht am Ende gar verhungern! Schon recht! Warum bin ich mitgereist!

Scene Twenty-three. *Enter the Speaker carrying his pyramid.*

THE SPEAKER

Papageno, you deserve to go wandering in the bowels of the earth for ever. But the gods have taken pity on you though you will now never know true enlightenment.	Mensch! Du hättest verdient, auf immer in finstern Klüften der Erde zu wandern — die gütigen Götter aber entlassen dich der Strafe. Dafür aber wirst du has himmlische Vergnügen der Eingeweihten nie fühlen.

PAPAGENO

Well I shan't be alone in that. There are lots of other folk like me. We prefer wine to wisdom.	Je nun, es gibt noch mehr Leute meinesgleichen! Mir wäre jetzt ein gut Glas Wein das grösste Vergnügen.

THE SPEAKER

Is that all you want from life?	Sonst hast du keinen Wunsch in dieser Welt?

PAPAGENO

Just at the moment, yes. I'll settle for a nice cool drink.	Bis jetzt nicht.

THE SPEAKER

There you are then.	Man wird dich damit bedienen!

Exit the Speaker. A large goblet of red wine appears from the ground.

113

PAPAGENO

That's what I call service. Marvellous! Divine! [Heavenly!] I feel so cheerful I could soar right up to the sun if only I had wings. I'm beginning to feel so happy. But there's something missing . . . something I need. I wonder what it is . . . Ah yes!

Juchhe! da ist er schon! Herrlich! Himmlisch! Göttlich! Ha! ich bin jetzt so vergnügt, dass ich bis zur Sonne fliegen wollte, wenn ich Flügel hätte! Ha! Mir wird ganz wunderlich um's Herz! Ich möchte — ich wünschte — ja, was denn?

Aria No. 20 [31]

PAPAGENO

(while singing, he plays his magic bells)

I'd like a wife to hug me
And keep me warm at night —
A girl who'd really love me
Is Papageno's right, that's Papageno's right.
Then living would give me such pleasure
That Princes would envy my treasure,

I'd know the true meaning of life
If Heaven would find me a wife.
Oh, please find me a wife.

Ein Mädchen oder Weibchen
Wünscht Papageno sich!
O, so ein sanftes Täubchen
Wär' Seligkeit für mich!

[32]

Dann schmekte mir Trinken und Essen,
Dann könnt ich mit Fürsten mich messen,
Des Lebens als Weiser mich freun,
Und wie im Elysium sein.

I'd like a wife to hug me
And keep me warm at night —
A girl who'd really love me
Is Papageno's right, that's Papageno's right.
Oh, am I then really so ugly
That no pretty girl wants to love me?
Unless a young girl shares my bed
I'd really be better off dead.

Ein Mädchen oder Weibchen
Wünscht Papageno sich!
O, so ein sanftes Täubchen
Wär' Seligkeit für mich!
Ach, kann ich denn keiner von allen
Den reizenden Mädchen gefallen?
Helf' eine mir nur aus der Not,
Sonst gräm ich mich wahrlich zu Tod.

I'd like a wife to hug me
And keep me warm at night —
A girl who'd really love me
Is Papageno's right, that's Papageno's right.
If all you young ladies still spurn me,
The fire of my passion will burn me.
But if one will give me a kiss,
My heartache will turn into bliss.

Ein Mädchen oder Weibchen
Wünscht Papageno sich!
O, so ein sanftes Täubchen
Wär' Seligkeit für mich!
Wird keine mir Liebe gewähren,
So muss mich die Flamme verzehren!
Doch küsst mich ein weiblicher Mund,
So bin ich schon wieder gesund!

Scene Twenty-four. *The Old Woman enters dancing and leaning on her stick.*

OLD WOMAN

Here I am, my angel.

Da bin ich schon, mein Engel!

PAPAGENO

So you've decided to take pity on me? That's just my luck!

Du hast dich meiner erbarmt? Das ist mein Glück!

OLD WOMAN

Yes, my angel, and if you promise to be faithful to me, you'll see what a tender little wife I will be.

Ja, mein Engel! Und wenn du mir versprichst, mir ewig treu zu bleiben, dann sollst du sehen, wie zärtlich dein Weibchen dich lieben wird.

114

	PAPAGENO
Oh, you sweet little thing, you.	Ei, du zärtliches Närrchen!

	OLD WOMAN
I'll fondle you and embrace you [and kiss your lips] and press you to my lips [heart].	O, wie will ich dich umarmen, dich liebkosen, dich an mein Herz drücken?

	PAPAGENO
[Only to your heart?]	Auch an's Herz drücken.

	OLD WOMAN
Now give me your hand to seal our bargain.	Komm', reich mir zum Pfand unseres Bundes deine Hand!

	PAPAGENO
Not so fast, my dearest. A decision like that needs some thought.	Nur nicht so hastig, lieber Engel! So ein Bündnis braucht doch auch seine Überlegung.

	OLD WOMAN
Papageno, I advise you not to hesitate. Give me your hand or you'll be locked up here for ever.	Papageno, ich rate dir, zaud're nicht! Deine Hand, oder du bist auf immer hier eingekerkert.

	PAPAGENO
Locked up!	Eingekerkert?

	OLD WOMAN
Bread and water will be your only food. You'll never see either man *or* woman and you'll have to abandon the world for ever.	Wasser und Brot wird deine tägliche Kost sein. Ohne Freund, ohne Freundin musst du leben und der Welt auf immer entsagen.

	PAPAGENO
Only water to drink? Abandon the world? Oh well, better an old girl than no girl at all. Well, there's my hand then, and I promise to be faithful to you . . .	Wasser trinken? Der Welt entsagen? Nein, da will ich doch lieber eine Alte nehmen, als gar keine. Nun, da hast du meine Hand mit der Versicherung, dass ich dir immer getreu bleibe,
(*aside*)	
as long as I don't find anyone prettier.	so lang' ich keine Schönere sehe.

	OLD WOMAN
You promise?	Das schwörst du?

	PAPAGENO
I promise . . .	Ja, das schwör' ich!
The Old Woman turns into Papagena, dressed like Papageno.	
Pa-Pa-Papagena!	Pa-Pa-Papagena!

Papageno goes to embrace her. **Scene Twenty-five.** *The Speaker holds her firmly back.*

	THE SPEAKER
Away with you, young woman. He still is not yet worthy of you!	Fort mit dir, junges Weib! Er ist deiner noch nicht würdig! Zurück! sag' ich, oder zittre!

The Speaker takes her away; Papageno wants to follow them.

115

PAPAGENO

Oooh! Will you kindly stop interfering in
my family affairs. That's a bird I'm
going to catch . . . even if the earth
swallows me up! [Oh Gods!]

Eh' ich mich zurückziehe, soll die Erde
mich verschlingen. O ihr Götter!

Papageno disappears in a hole which has opened at his feet.

Transformation. *The scene changes to a little garden.* **Scene Twenty-six.** / *Finale No. 21*

THE THREE BOYS [33]

The sun arises like a vision	Bald prangt, den Morgen zu verkünden,
And brings a brighter morn;	Die Sonn' auf goldner Bahn!
It ends the reign of superstition —	Bald soll der Aberglaube schwinden,
The day of Truth will dawn.	Bald siegt der weise Mann.
Let no dark evil now affright men.	O holde Ruhe, steig hernieder,
Let Truth now shine here and delight them.	Kehr in der Menschen Herzen wieder;
Then every man shall scorn to lie,	Dann wird die Erd' ein Himmelreich,
Then Truth shall live and Death shall die.	Und Sterbliche den Göttern gleich.

FIRST BOY

But see, some sorrow grieves Pamina!　　　Doch seht, Verzweiflung quält Paminen.

SECOND, THIRD BOYS

What troubles her?　　　Wo ist sie denn?

FIRST BOY

She seems tormented.　　　Sie ist von Sinnen.

THE THREE BOYS

It's love that makes her feel this torture.	Sie quält verschmähter Liebe Leiden.
Let's try to help and reassure her.	Lasst uns der Armen Trost bereiten!
Pamina's pain is our pain too —	Fürwahr, ihr Schicksal geht uns nah!
Though we but guess what Love can do.	O wäre nur ihr Jüngling da! —
She comes; let's wait in hiding here	Sie kommt, lasst uns beiseite gehn,
Until her purpose is more clear.	Damit wir, was sie mache, sehn.

Scene Twenty-seven. *Pamina enters, as if she has lost her wits, with a dagger in her hand. They hide.* [34]

PAMINA

And so a knife must wed me now?	Du also bist mein Bräutigam?
Embracing you, I keep my vow.	Durch dich vollend' ich meinen Gram!

THE THREE BOYS
(aside)

What were those fearful words she said?	Welch dunkle Worte sprach sie da?
I fear her love has made her mad.	Die Arme ist dem Wahnsinn nah.

PAMINA

Ah see, my love, I'll be your bride,	Geduld mein Trauter, ich bin dein,
Our wedding knot will soon be tied.	Bald werden wir vermählet sein.

THE THREE BOYS

Madness leads her to destruction —	Wahnsinn tobt ihr im Gehirne;
Suicide's her sure intention!	Selbstmord steht auf ihrer Stirne. —

(to Pamina)

Sweet young lady — See us here!　　　Holdes Mädchen, sieh uns an!

I will die now, since Tamino,	Sterben will ich, weil der Mann,
Who said he'd always love me,	Den ich nimmermehr kann hassen,
Means to break the vow he gave me.	Seine Traute kann verlassen.

(showing the dagger)

See, my mother gave this knife!	Dies gab meine Mutter mir.

THE THREE BOYS

Don't forget. God gave you life!	Selbstmord strafet Gott an dir.

PAMINA

Better far to end this anguish	Lieber durch dies Eisen sterben,
Than to live alone and languish.	Als durch Liebesgram verderben.
Mother, Mother! Your curse makes me wild,	Mutter, durch dich leide ich,
And your knife destroys your child.	Und dein Fluch verfolget mich.

THE THREE BOYS

Wait though! Wait and come with us!	Mädchen, willst du mit uns gehn?

PAMINA

Ah! my cup of grief is full —	Ha, des Jammers Mass ist voll!
False Tamino fare you well.	Falscher Jüngling, lebe wohl!
See Pamina will not lie:	Sieh, Pamina stirbt durch dich:
Love's forsworn, I swear I'll die!	Dieses Eisen töte mich.

She raises the dagger to stab herself.

THE THREE BOYS
(preventing her)

Wait, unhappy girl, oh wait!	Ha, Unglückliche! Halt ein!
If you kill yourself through sorrow	Sollte dies dein Jüngling sehen,
Then your love will die tomorrow,	Würde er vor Gram vergehn;
For his grief will be so great!	Denn er liebet dich allein.

PAMINA
(recovering herself)

What! You say that he adores me,	Was? Er fühlte Gegenliebe?
Tho' he scorns me and ignores me,	Und verbarg mir seine Triebe,
And pretends he has not heard?	Wandte sein Gesicht von mir?
Why then can't he speak a word?	Warum sprach er nicht mit mir?

THE THREE BOYS

We can't tell you, but believe us,	Dieses müssen wir verschweigen,
And we'll gladly take you with us,	Doch, wir wollen dir ihn zeigen!
You will see we don't deceive,	Und du wirst mit Staunen sehn,
For your lover still is true —	Dass er dir sein Herz geweiht,
He will dare to die for you.	Und den Tod für dich nicht scheut.

PAMINA

Lead me there, I long to see him.	Führt mich hin, ich möcht ihn sehen.

THE THREE BOYS

Come with us and do not grieve.	Komm, wir wollen zu ihm gehen.

PAMINA, THE THREE BOYS

Two loving hearts that beat together	Zwei Herzen, die von Liebe brennen,
Are safe from earthly woes forever.	Kann Menschenohnmacht niemals trennen.

They need not fear the fires of Hell;   Verloren ist der Feinde Müh';
The Gods themselves will guard them   Die Götter selbst beschützen sie.
well.

Exeunt.

Transformation. Scene Twenty-eight. *Two high mountains. From one mountain, the rushing and roaring of a waterfall may be heard; the other spits out fire. Through a grill in each mountain, the fire and water can be seen — where the fire burns the horizon should be red as hell, while a thick mist lies on the water. There are rocks all over the stage, which is divided into two separate parts, each enclosed within an iron gate. Tamino is lightly clothed, without sandals. Two men in black armour accompany Tamino; on their helmets, flames burn. They read him the inscription, illuminated from within, on a pyramid high up in the centre, above the grills.*

THE ARMED MEN [35]

Man that is born of woman walks thro'   Der, welcher wandert, diese Strasse voll
     life in shadow,   Beschwerden,
Yet light and truth may pierce   Wird rein durch Feuer, Wasser, Luft
     thro' pain and sorrow.   und Erden;
Man must brave Death, the dread that   [36] Wenn er des Todes Schrecken über-
     haunts him from his birth —   winden kann,
Then he shall find his heaven here on   Schwingt er sich aus der Erde himmelan.
     earth.
Enlightened Man will see truth pure and   Erleuchtet wird er dann imstande sein,
     whole,
And, finding truth, he shall find his   Sich den Mysterien der Isis ganz zu
     immortal soul.   weihn.

TAMINO

I'll not fear Death, no man is braver.   Mich schreckt kein Tod, als Mann zu
     handeln,
In seeking Truth, I'll never waver.   Den Weg der Tugend fortzuwandeln.
So fling the gates of terror wide: Schliesst mir die Schreckenspforten auf,
I'll gladly bear the trials inside.   Ich wage froh den kühnen Lauf.

PAMINA
(from within)

Tamino, wait, oh, wait for me.   Tamino, halt! Ich muss dich sehn.

TAMINO

What was that? Pamina calling?   Was hör ich? Paminens Stimme?

THE ARMED MEN

Yes, yes, you heard Pamina calling.   Ja, ja, das ist Paminens Stimme.

TAMINO, THE ARMED MEN

Thank God, {now / for} she may {come / go} with {me / you}   Wohl {mir / dir}; nun kann sie mit {mir / dir} gehn,

And so as one {we'll / you'll} meet {our / your} fate,   Nun trennet {uns / euch} kein Schicksal mehr,

Though even Death may lie in wait.   Wenn {gleich / auch} der Tod beschieden wär!

TAMINO

And now, am I allowed to greet her?   Ist mir erlaubt, mit ihr zu sprechen?

THE ARMED MEN

Yes, now you are allowed to greet her.   Dir ist erlaubt, mit ihr zu sprechen!

118

What joy to see $\left\{\begin{array}{l}\text{my}\\\text{your}\end{array}\right\}$ love again.

With her, $\left\{\begin{array}{l}\text{I'll}\\\text{you'll}\end{array}\right\}$ feel no other pain.

A girl who'll brave death by $\left\{\begin{array}{l}\text{my}\\\text{his}\end{array}\right\}$ side.

May surely fill a man with pride.

Welch Glück, wenn wir $\left\{\begin{array}{l}\text{uns}\\\text{euch}\end{array}\right\}$ wiedersehn,

Froh Hand in Hand in Tempel gehn.

Ein Weib, das Nacht und Tod nicht scheut,

Ist würdig und wird eingeweiht.

The door opens; Tamino and Pamina embrace. [37]

PAMINA

Tamino mine! Oh what great joy!

Tamino mein! O welch ein Glück!

TAMINO

Pamina mine! Oh what great joy!
See here the dreaded doorway
Where pain and death may lie.

Pamina mein! O welch ein Glück!
Hier sind die Schreckenspforten,
Die Not und Tod mir dräun.

PAMINA

Our love will find a sure way,
With you I'll live or die.
I'll stay here by your side
And Love shall be our guide.

Ich werde aller Orten
An deiner Seite sein,
Ich selbsten führe dich,
Die Liebe leitet mich.

She takes him by the hand.

Beside our road the wild thorn grows,
But midst the thorn there is a rose.
So take the magic flute and play.
Its sound will guard us on our way.
'Twas carved by Father, in an hour of enchantment
In the deepest forests,
From root and wood of ancient oak —
While lightning carved it, storm clouds broke.
So take the magic flute and play.
Its sound will guard us on our way.

Sie mag den Weg mit Rosen streun,
Weil Rosen stets bei Dornen sein.
Spiel du die Zauberflöte an,
Sie schütze uns auf unsrer Bahn.
Es schnitt in einer Zauberstunde

Mein Vater sie aus tiefstem Grunde
Der tausendhähr'gen Eiche aus,
Bei Blitz und Donner, Sturm und Braus.

Nun komm und spiel die Flöte an,
Sie leite uns auf grauser Bahn.

TAMINO, PAMINA, THE ARMED MEN [38]

$\left.\begin{array}{l}\text{We'll}\\\text{They'll}\end{array}\right\}$ walk unharmed, thro' music's power

Thro' deepest night and Death's dark hour.

$\left.\begin{array}{l}\text{Wir}\\\text{Ihr}\end{array}\right\}$ wandeln durch des Tones Macht,

Froh durch des Todes düstre Nacht!

The doors close behind them. Tamino and Pamina can be seen advancing. The spitting of fire and howling of wind can be heard; at times also the muffled sound of thunder and the rushing of water. Tamino plays his flute [39]. Drums softly sound. As soon as they emerge from the mountain of fire, they embrace and take up a position in the centre of the stage.

TAMINO AND PAMINA

We walked unharmed thro' flames of passion,
The temper of our souls was true.
Oh flute, now guard us in this fashion,
Whatever floods of grief may do.

Wir wandelten durch Feuergluten,
Bekämpften mutig die Gefahr.
Dein Ton sei Schutz in Wasserfluten,
So wie er es im Feuer war.

Tamino plays. They are seen to descend and shortly afterwards to come up again. Then a door opens, through which a brilliantly lit temple may be seen. Solemn silence. This vision must be of the utmost splendour. The chorus, accompanied by trumpets and drums, begin to sing.

Oh Gods, we see a blessed sight.	Ihr Götter! Welch ein Augenblick!
Now man's dark world is filled with light.	Gewähret ist uns Isis Glück.

Rejoice, rejoice, you noble pair.	Triumph! Triumph! Du edles Paar!
Your hearts were true, your courage rare!	Besieget hast du die Gefahr,
The prize of virtue now is yours.	Der Isis Weihe ist nun dein,
Come, see the temple's open doors.	Kommt, tretet in den Tempel ein!

Exeunt

Scene Twenty-nine. *The scene changes to the garden again. Enter Papageno.*

PAPAGENO
(having played a little on his pipes [6]*)* [40]

Papagena! Papagena! Papagena!	Papagena, Papagena, Papagena!
Sweetheart, hear me — are you hiding?	Weibchen, Täubchen, meine Schöne!
It's useless! Ah, she's gone forever.	Vergebens! Ach, sie ist verloren!
I should have tried to be more clever.	Ich bin zum Unglück schon geboren.
I had to talk, *had* to talk, I'd not be taught.	Ich plauderte — und das war schlecht,
I must admit it was my fault.	Darum geschieht es mir schon recht.
Since I first drank that lovely wine,	Seit ich gekostet diesen Wein,
Since I first saw that lovely girl,	Seit ich das schöne Weibchen sah,
I cannot rest till she is mine.	So brennt's im Herzenskämmerlein,
My heart's on fire, my heads awhirl.	So zwickt es hier, so zwickt es da.
Papagena! I adore you!	Papagena, Herzensweibchen!
Papagena! I implore you!	Papagena, liebes Täubchen!
It's no use, she cannot hear me;	's ist umsonst, es ist vergebens!
Now my life is cold and dreary!	Müde bin ich meines Lebens!
Papageno, save your breath —	Sterben macht der Lieb ein End,
Farewell, Life and welcome, Death!	Wenn's im Herzen noch so brennt.
I shall hang here on the gibbet	Diesen Baum da will ich zieren,
With a rope around my gizzard.	Mir an ihm den Hals zuschnüren,
Tired of life and crossed in love,	Weil das Leben mir missfällt;
Farewell, World, I'm off above.	Gute Nacht, du schwarze Welt.
While I lived the girls ignored me:	Weil du böse an mir handelst,
Now I'm martyred, they'll adore me.	Mir kein schönes Kind zubandelst:
That's enough, I'm going to die —	So ist's aus, so sterbe ich,
Lovely ladies do not cry.	Schöne Mädchen, denkt an mich.
But if one of you will have me,	Will sich eine um mich Armen,
Well, you've one more chance to save me,	Eh' ich hänge, noch erbarmen,
Tell me quick, or else I'll go —	Wohl, so lass ich's diesmal sein!
Don't be shy, say yes or no?	Rufet nur, ja — oder nein. —
No one answers: what a silence.	Keine hört mich, alles stille!
No one, no one loves me.	Also ist es euer Wille?
Not a single lady loves me.	Papageno, frisch hinauf!
Papageno, give up hope —	Ende deinen Lebenslauf.
You must dangle from a rope.	Nun, ich warte noch, es sei,
No. I'll wait a bit, maybe . . .	Bis man zählet, eins, zwei, drei.
'Till I've counted one, two, three . . .	

(he pipes)

One!	Eins!

(he pipes)

Two! [Two is already gone!]	Zwei! Zwei ist schon vorbei.

(he pipes)

Three!	Drei!

120

Ah, well, that's the end of me.   Nun wohlan, es bleibt dabei!
Since I cannot find my love,   Weil mich nichts zurücke hält!
Cruel world, I'm off above.   Gute Nacht, du falsche Welt.

He prepares to hang himself.

THE THREE BOYS
(descending from above)

Oh, wait, oh, Papageno, that's no way.   Halt ein, o Papageno, und sei klug;
You've only one life, live it while you   Man lebt nur einmal, dies sei dir genug.
     may.

PAPAGENO

That's very true and nicely spoken,   Ihr habt gut reden, habt gut scherzen.
But don't you see my heart is broken?   Doch brennt es euch wie mich im
     Herzen,
One day you too will want a wife.   Ihr würdet auch nach Mädchen gehn.

THE THREE BOYS

Well, why not ring the bells you carry?   So lasse deine Glöckchen klingen,
They'll bring the girl you want to marry.   Dies wird dein Weibchen zu dir bringen.

PAPAGENO

I'm such a fool to be so tragic.   Ich Narr vergass der Zauberdinge!
Come on you bells, let's hear your magic.   Erklinge, Glöckenspiel, erklinge!
I long to see my girl again.   Ich muss mein liebes Mädchen sehn.

As he plays the bells, the Three Boys run to their flying machine and help Papagena to dismount. [41]

Now bells, let your music   Klinget, Glöckchen, klinget,
Bring my sweetheart here: Schafft mein Mädchen her!
Sweet bells, sound your music   Klinget, Glöckchen, klinget,
Make my loved one hear.   Bringt mein Weibchen her!
Now bells, with your music,   *(repeat)*
If my dear girl's near,
Sweet bells sound your music,
Make my dear wife hear.
With your magic music,
Make my sweetheart hear.
If she's near,
Oh bring her here,
My dearest dear!

THE THREE BOYS

Now Papageno, turn around!   Nun, Papageno, sieh dich um!

Papageno looks around. Then each plays a comic routine. [42]

PAPAGENO

Pa-Pa-Pa-Pa-Pa-Pa-Papagena!   Pa-Pa-Pa-Pa-Pa-Pa-Papagena!

PAPAGENA

Pa-Pa-Pa-Pa-Pa-Pa-Papageno.   Pa-Pa-Pa-Pa-Pa-Pa-Papageno!

TOGETHER

Pa-Pa-Pa-Pa-Pa-Pa{Papagena!   Pa-Pa-Pa-Pa-Pa-Pa{Papagena!
              {Papageno!   {Papageno!

PAPAGENO

Ah, now shall we live together?   Bist du mir nun ganz gegeben?

121

	PAPAGENA
Yes, we'll always live together.	Nun bin ich dir ganz gegeben.

	PAPAGENO
Then you'll be my wife for ever?	Nun, so sei mein liebes Weibchen!

	PAPAGENA
Yes, I'll share your life forever.	Nun, so sei mein Herzenstäubchen!

	TOGETHER
We'll live together, in love forever.	(repeat)

Oh, what happiness and joy	Welche Freude wird das sein,
If the kindly gods will maybe	Wenn die Götter uns bedenken,
Bless our marriage with a baby,	Unsrer Liebe Kinder schenken,
A little girl or little boy . . .	So liebe kleine Kinderlein!

	PAPAGENO
First send a little Papageno.	Erst einen kleinen Papageno!

	PAPAGENA
Then send a little Papagena.	Dann eine kleine Papagena!

	PAPAGENO
We'll have another Papageno.	Dann wieder einen Papageno!

	PAPAGENA
Then have another Papagena.	Dann wieder eine Papagena!

	PAPAGENO
Papageno, Papageno, Papageno, Papageno.	Papageno, Papageno, Papageno, Papageno.

	PAPAGENA
Papagena, Papagena, Papagena, Papagena.	Papagena, Papagena, Papagena, Papagena.

	TOGETHER
It is the sweetest human pleasure	Es ist das höchste der Gefühle,
To have a dear young	Wenn viele, viele, viele, viele
⎰ Pa-Pa-Pa-Pa-geno	⎰ Pa-Pa-Pa-Pa-geno
⎱ Pa-Pa-Pa-Pa-gena	⎱ Pa-Pa-Pa-Pa-gena
To comfort their old parents' lives.	Der Eltern Segen werden sein.

They hurry off.

Scene Thirty. *Monostatos, the Three Ladies and the Queen of the Night enter stealthily, carrying flaming black torches.* [43]

	MONOSTATOS
We must be silent, silent, silent.	Nur stille, stille, stille, stille!
We're near the inner temple now.	Bald dringen wir im Tempel ein.

	THE QUEEN, THREE LADIES
We must be silent, silent, silent.	Nur stille, stille, stille, stille!
We're near the inner temple now.	Bald dringen wir im Tempel ein.

	MONOSTATOS
But Highness, keep your word. You promised	Doch Fürstin, halte Wort! Erfülle —
I'd have your daughter as my wife.	Dein Kind muss meine Gattin sein.

THE QUEEN

I'll keep my word. As I have promised	Ich halte Wort; es ist mein Wille.
You'll have my daughter as your wife.	Mein Kind soll deine Gattin sein.

THE THREE LADIES

Her child shall be your wife.	Ihr Kind soll deine Gattin sein.

Sounds of thunder and rushing water.

MONOSTATOS

But now I hear a fearful thunder	Doch still! Ich höre schrecklich Rauschen
Of roaring flames and surging waves.	Wie Donnerton und Wasserfall.

THE QUEEN, THREE LADIES

Yes, sound of wind and crashing thunder —	Ja, fürchterlich ist dieses Rauschen
How it re-echoes thro' these caves.	Wie fernen Donners Widerhall.

MONOSTATOS

Now they are met in solemn counsel.	Nun sind sie in des Tempels Hallen.

THE QUEEN, THREE LADIES, MONOSTATOS

Then it is there we'll fall upon them,	Dort wollen wir sie überfallen —
And while they worship their false Lord	Die Frömmler tilgen von der Erd'
We'll rise and put them to the sword.	Mit Feuersglut und mächt'gem Schwert.

THREE LADIES, MONOSTATOS

Thou blazing Queen who rules in might,	Dir, grosse Königin der Nacht,
Now see us take the vengeance of Night.	Sei unsrer Rache Opfer gebracht.

With a very violent chord, thunder and lightning, the scene changes so that the whole stage represents a sun. Sarastro stands on high; Tamino and Pamina are both in priestly robes. On either side of them are the Egyptian priests. The Three Boys hold flowers in their hands.

THE QUEEN, THREE LADIES, MONOSTATOS

Ah God, we're cast down and our glory departs,	Zerschmettert, zernichtet ist unsere Macht,
The bright light of Truth drives its sword thro' our hearts.	Wir alle gestürzet in ewige Nacht.

They sink into the ground.

SARASTRO

The grandeur and glory of truth sheds its light,	Die Strahlen der Sonne vertreiben die Nacht,
Destroyed are the sinful, destroyed is the night.	Zernichten der Heuchler erschlichene Macht.

CHORUS [44]

Hail the Two who triumphed!	Heil sei euch Geweihten!
They dared all for Truth!	Ihr dranget durch Nacht.
Praise the God of Wisdom!	Dank sei dir, Osiris,
See the Truth shining bright!	Dank dir, Isis, gebracht!
For Truth is all-powerful,	[45]Es siegte die Stärke
And Love is his Lord,	Und krönet zum Lohn
And Beauty and Wisdom	Die Schönheit und Weisheit
Shall earn their reward!	Mit ewiger Kron'!

THE END

Discography

In order of UK release. All recordings are in stereo, unless asterisked ⋆, and in German.

Conductor / Company/Orchestra	Karajan / Vienna Singverein / Vienna PO	Böhm / Vienna Opera & PO	Fricsay / RIAS Choir Berlin SO	Klemperer / Philharmonia	Böhm / Berlin PO	Solti / Vienna Opera & PO
Tamino	A. Dermota	L. Simoneau	E. Haefliger	N. Gedda	F. Wunderlich	S. Burrows
Pamina	I. Seefried	H. Gueden	M. Stader	G. Janowitz	E. Lear	P. Lorengar
Sarastro	L. Weber	K. Bohme	J. Greindl	G. Frick	F. Crass	M. Talvela
Queen of the Night	W. Lipp	W. Lipp	R. Streich	L. Popp	R. Peters	C. Deutekom
Papageno	E. Kunz	W. Berry	D. Fischer-Dieskau	W. Berry	D. Fischer-Dieskau	H. Prey
Ladies	S. Jurinac	J. Hellwig	M. Schech	E. Schwarzkopf	H. Hillebrecht	H. van Bork
	F. Riegler	C. Ludwig	L. Losch	C. Ludwig	C. Ahlin	Y. Minton
	E. Schurhof	H. Rossl-Majdan	M. Klose	M. Hoffgen	S. Wagner	H. Phimacher
Monostatos	P. Klein	A. Jaresch	M. Vantin	G. Unger	F. Lenz	G. Stolze
Speaker	G. London	P. Schoeffler	K. Borg	F. Crass	H. Hotter	D. Fischer-Dieskau
Priest	E. Majkut	E. Majkut	H. Vandenburg	G. Unger	M. Vantin	K. Equiluz
Papagena	E. Loose	E. Loose	L. Otto	R.M. Pütz	L. Otto	R. Holm
Disc UK Number	SLS 5062 ⋆	GOS501 - 3	2701 015	SLS912	2709 017	SET 479 - 81
Tape Number					3371 - 002	K2A4
Excerpts (Disc)		SDD218			1316440	SET 527
Excerpts (Tape)		SDD218			922 - 014	KSET 527
Disc US Number		SRS63507		S-3651	DG 2709017	LON-1397
Tape Number				—	3371 - 002	—
Excerpts (Disc)				S 36315	DG 136440	LON 26257
Excerpts (Tape)				8X514-XS - 36315	922014	

The essay by Peter Branscombe on *Die Zauberflöte* in *Opera on Record* (edited by Alan Blyth, Hutchinson, 1979) is an exhaustive and stimulating review of the recordings made of this opera.

	Beecham (recorded 1937/8)	*Ericson* (Swedish TV sound track)
Conductor		
Company/Orchestra	**Berlin PO**	**Swedish Radio Chorus & Orchestra**
Tamino	H. Roswaenge	J. Kostlinger
Pamina	T. Lemnitz	I. Urrilla
Sarastro	W. Streinz	U. Cold
Queen of the Night	E. Berger	B. Nordin
Papageno	G. Husch	H. Hagegard
Ladies	—	—
	—	—
	—	—
Monostatos	H. Jessmer	R. Ulfung
Speaker	W. Grossman	E. Saeden
Priest	E. Fabbry	—
Papagena	I. Beilke	E. Eriksson
Disc UK Number	SH158 - 60 ★	**BBC REK 223**
Disc US Number	—	A & M 4577
Tape Number	—	CS - 4577

Excerpts

Number	Artists	UK Numbers only Disc Number	Tape
Overture	Vienna Haydn Orch/Kertesz	SET 548-9	
	LPO/Boult		ZCCOB730 (Cassette) Y8COB730 (Cartridge)
	Columbia SO/Walter	61022	
	Berlin PO/Böhm	2532 229	3335 229
	BBC SO/Davis	6580 048	
	Hallé/Barbirolli	GH508	ZCG H 508 (Cassette) Y8GH 508 (Cartridge)
	BBC SO/Davis	6833 154	
Der Vogelfänger	D. Fischer-Dieskau (also *Ein Mädchen oder Weibchen*)	135008	
	G. Evans	SXL6262	

Dies Bildnis ist bezaubernd schön	P. Anders	AJ6 42232*	
	N. Gedda	ASD 2364	
	S. Burrows	DSL 013	
	(also *Zum Ziele führt dich*)		
O zittre nicht	J. Sutherland	SET 268	
		SDB 317	
		D65D3	
O Isis und Osiris/	A. Kipnis	SH280 *	
In diesen heil'gen Hallen	O. Brannigan (in English)	ESD7059	TC-ESD7059
Ach, ich fühls	H. Gueden	ECS557	
	I. Cotrubas	76521	
Also *O zittre nicht* and	M. André (trumpet)	STU 71132	
Der holle Rache			

Bibliography

A very selective list of books in English for further reading.

Albert Einstein's *Mozart, his character — his work*, translated by Albert Mendel and Nathan Broder (Cassell 1969, Panther Books 1971) is an indispensable companion to the study of Mozart's compositions. *Mozart's Letters* (translated by Emily Anderson, ed. Hyatt-King & Carolan, Macmillan 1966) are a source of constant interest, as is Otto Erich Deutsch's *Mozart: A documentary biography* (Black, 1965). *Mozart's Operas* E.J. Dent, Oxford University Press, 1947), *Three Mozart Operas* (R. Moberley, Gollancz, 1967) and *The Operas of Mozart* (William Mann, Cassell 1977) each contain illuminating chapters about the opera, its composition, appreciation and background. Joseph Kerman's *Opera as Drama* (Vintage Books, New York, 1959) also includes a monograph on this opera. *The Magic Flute, Masonic Opera* by Jacques Chailley (Gollancz, 1972) is the most comprehensive study of the Masonic symbolism of the opera, and is illustrated with plates of exceptional interest. On the symbolism generally, see 'A New Metaphor for Mozart's *Magic Flute*' (in European Studies Review, vol. 5, no. 3, July 1975) by Dorothy Koenigsberger.

The controversial preface to and translation of *The Magic Flute* by W.H. Auden and Chester Kallman (Faber, 1957) is of interest to English-speakers suggesting, inter alia, a rearrangement of the scenes in Act Two.

Finally as a useful French compendium of information about the opera *L'Avant-Scène (Opera)* no. 1 (Jan - Feb 1976) may be highly recommended.

The full score is published by Eulenberg.

Books consulted in researching 'A Public for Mozart's Last Opera' include Benjamin Lumley's 'Reminiscences of the Opera' (1860); *Die Zauberflöte Zweiter Teil* by Goethe in the edition by Wilhelm Zentner (Philipp Reclam Jun. Stuttgart, 1978); Otto Erich Deutsch's 'Documentary Biography of Mozart' (Black, 1965); G.B. Shaw's 'Music in London' (1932); E.M. Battley's 'A Preface to *The Magic Flute*' (Dobson, 1969) and 'Schriftung zur Musik (Nachlese)' (1963) by E.T.A. Hoffmann.

English
National
Opera
Guide

4

Fidelio
Beethoven

English National Opera
receives financial
assistance from the Arts
Council of Great Britain
and the Greater London
Council.

Nineteenth century set design for 'Fidelio' Act Two, scene one (Theater Museum, Munich)

Preface

English National Opera Guides are intended to be companions to opera in performance. They contain articles and illustrations relevant to any production and not only those mounted by English National Opera. Of general interest, also, is the inclusion of the complete original libretto of the opera, side by side with an English translation. There are many reasons why sung words may not be clearly distinguishable, whatever the language and however excellent the performance. The composer may have set several lines of text together, for instance, or he may have demanded an orchestral sound through which no voice can clearly articulate. ENO Guides supply English readers with an opportunity to know a libretto in advance and so greatly increase their understanding and enjoyment of performances whether live, broadcast or recorded.

ENO is very grateful to National Westminster Bank for sponsoring this *Fidelio* Guide, as well as a new production, in its wide ranging programme of community service. Such sponsorship is an indication of a steadily growing public interest in opera, and we hope the Guides will prove useful to new and experienced opera-lovers alike. An audience which knows what to look and listen for — one that demands a high standard of performance and recognises it when it is achieved — is our best support and, of course, an assurance for the future of opera in the English-speaking world.

Nicholas John
Editor

Fidelio

Ludwig van Beethoven

English National Opera Guides Series Editor:
Nicholas John

This Guide is sponsored by
National Westminster Bank.

John Calder ● London
Riverrun Press ● New York

First published in Great Britain, 1980, by
John Calder (Publishers) Ltd.,
18 Brewer Street,
London W1R 4AS
and
in the U.S.A., 1980, by
Riverrun Press Inc.,
175 Fifth Avenue,
New York, NY 10010

ISBN 0 7145 3823   Paperback edition

BRITISH LIBRARY CATALOGUING DATA

Sonnleithner, Joseph Ferdinand
　Fidelio. — (English National Opera guides; 4).
　1. Operas — Librettos
　I. Title   II. John, Nicholas   III. Hammond, Tom
　IV. Blumer, Rodney   V. Beethoven, Ludwig van
　VI. Series
　782.1'2　　　　　ML50.B422

Typeset in Plantin by Alan Sutton Publishing Limited, Gloucester.
Printed by Whitstable Litho Limited in Great Britain.

Contents

List of Illustrations

Introduction

Elizabeth Forbes

Fidelio, because it is Beethoven's only opera, and because of the sublimity of the music and the nobility of its theme, has become a work unique in the operatic repertory, one to be approached with special reverence by audiences and performers alike. Yet Beethoven spent the last twenty years of his life searching for a suitable text for *Fidelio's* successor, while the opera itself was only one, and at the time by no means the most popular, of a category developed in France after the Revolution, and which spread to Italy, Germany and Austria — the 'Rescue' opera. Today, apart from *Fidelio* itself, the best known opera in this genre is Cherubini's *Les Deux Journées*, or *The Water Carrier* as it is usually called in English, which was first produced in Paris in January 1800. The text of *Les Deux Journées* was by Jean-Nicolas Bouilly, who two years previously had supplied the libretto for an opera by Pierre Gaveaux, performed at the Théâtre Feydeau, Paris, on February 19, 1798, and entitled *Léonore, ou l'amour conjugal*.

According to the author, this story of a wife who rescued her husband by dressing as a boy and taking a job in the prison where he was incarcerated, was based on an actual incident that took place during the Terror at Tours, where Bouilly then held an official position. He thought it prudent, in case of possible repercussions, to transfer the setting of the action from France to Spain. Two Italian versions of *Léonore*, much altered from the original, appeared during the next few years — Ferdinand Paer's *Eleonora ossia l'amore conjugale*, which was produced at Dresden in October 1804, and Simon Mayr's *L'amor conjugale*, first performed at Padua the following spring. In the latter work the setting was moved yet again, this time to Poland.

Meanwhile in Vienna the 34-year-old Beethoven had nearly finished composing a German version of the Bouilly libretto. Early in 1803 he had been engaged by Emanuel Schikaneder as resident composer at the recently opened Theater an der Wien, successor to the Theater auf den Wieden where *The Magic Flute* had first been performed a dozen years previously — a post which carried free accommodation in the theatre. The first rumours of an opera from Beethoven, the virtuoso pianist, were published in March. On April 5 he gave a concert in the Theater an der Wien whose programme included his First and Second Symphonies, the Piano Concerto in C Minor (No. 3) played by the composer himself, and the first performance of an oratorio, *Christ on The Mount of Olives*, which was criticised as being over-dramatic in style.

He was already suffering from the deafness that was to plague him for the rest of his life, becoming progressively worse year by year until the loss of hearing was complete. In his notebook for that year, among the preliminary sketches for his third symphony — the *Eroica* — is a trio for soprano, tenor and bass, the finale to an opera on the subject of Alexander the Great in India. This fragment probably represented an exercise in operatic writing, and was in any case not wasted, as will be seen. Then, in August, he was reported to be working on a libretto by Schikaneder — *Vestas Feuer* or *The Fire of Vesta* — but after composing some sketches for the first scene, he became disenchanted, both with the text and with its author. 'I have finally broken with Schikaneder', wrote Beethoven early in

7

Josef Sonnleithner 1766-1835, platinotype by J. Lowy (Historisches Museum der Stadt Wien)

January 1804, when returning a libretto on a theme 'connected with magic' to Johann Friedrich Rochlitz in Leipzig. 'Just picture to yourself a Roman subject (of which I had not been told either the scheme or anything else whatever) and language and verses such as could proceed only out of the mouths of Viennese *apple-women* — Well I have quickly had an old French libretto adapted and am now beginning to work on it'.

The 'old French libretto' was of course Bouilly's *Léonore*, translated and adapted by Joseph Sonnleithner, an official of the Vienna Court Theatres. At first Beethoven spoke hopefully of completing his opera by June 1804 but the following spring he had still not finished it. In the autumn he wrote to Sonnleithner, 'I am quite ready now — and am waiting for the last *four verses* — for which I have already thought out the theme provisionally — It is my *definite purpose* to write the overture during the rehearsals and not until then'. Sonnleithner kept close to Bouilly's original text but, by expanding the work from two to three acts, he fatally weakened its dramatic structure. Beethoven took immense trouble over his score; as his notebooks show, he rewrote the quartet in the first scene about a dozen times, and the aria for Florestan almost as frequently, while the theme of the trio-excerpt from the Alexander opera was used for the rapturous reunion between Leonora and Florestan in the latter's dungeon.

Fidelio, preceded by the overture now known as *Leonora No. 2*, was finally produced at the Theater an den Wien on November 20, 1805. Unfortunately for Beethoven and his opera, French troops had occupied Vienna exactly one week earlier, while Napoleon took up residence at the Palace of Schönbrunn two days after that. The inhabitants of the city were in no mood to give their attention to a new opera, not even — or more especially not — one devoted to the subject of freedom, and *Fidelio* was only repeated twice after the first performance, before being withdrawn.

8

Realising that the opera had failed chiefly because of the dramatic deficiencies of the libretto, and feeling strongly that so much wonderful music should not be allowed to disappear, Beethoven's friends urged him to revise his score. After a fiercely-fought, six-hour-long battle at the house of Prince Karl Lichnowsky, a patron of Beethoven's since the composer had first arrived in Vienna from Bonn, he agreed to make some cuts. The rearrangement of the three acts into two, and other alterations to the text, were made by Stephan von Breuning. Sonnleithner, perhaps luckily, was busy with the production of Cherubini's *Faniska*, an opera for which he had provided the libretto.

The revised *Fidelio* was given at the Theater an der Wien on March 29, 1806, preceded by a newly composed overture, *Leonora No. 3*. Beethoven was not at all pleased with the orchestral playing — 'the murdering of my music' as he put it — and after one more performance he quarrelled with Baron Peter von Braun (who had taken over the Theater an der Wien early in 1804) and withdrew his score. These first two versions of *Fidelio* are now generally entitled *Leonore*, as indeed the composer originally intended that they should be, though the theatre management at the time insisted on *Fidelio*, to avoid confusion with Paer's opera on the same subject.

During the next eight years Beethoven's thoughts were frequently turned towards opera. In October 1806, when the direction of the Court Theatres in Vienna passed into the hands of a group of noblemen, he applied for a permanent position as Court composer, offering to supply one opera and one lighter stage piece each year. His request was refused. Two years later he discussed the setting of *Macbeth* by Heinrich von Collin, author of the tragedy *Coriolan* for which Beethoven had composed an overture. He also briefly considered *Bradamante*, another work by the same writer. After Collin's death in 1811, Beethoven turned to Georg Friedrich Treitschke — of whom more will be heard — and toyed with the idea of a collaboration on *The Ruins of Babylon*. The following year he asked August von Kotzebue, for whose dramas *The Ruins of Athens* and *King Stephen*, specially written for the opening of the theatre in Pest, he had composed incidental music, to provide him with a libretto 'on a big historical subject, preferably from the Dark Ages, for example, about Attila . . .'. In 1813 he discussed *The Return of Ulysses* as a possible operatic theme with the poet Theodor Körner. Nothing came of any of these projects.

Then, in the New Year of 1814, three singers engaged at the Court theatre in Vienna, who were entitled to a benefit performance, broached the idea of a revival of *Fidelio* to its composer. Beethoven was by now an immensely distinguished figure in Viennese musical circles. His popularity had been augmented, late in 1813, by *Wellington's Victory*, or the Battle Symphony, which, originally conceived for performance in England, proved immensely successful in Vienna. The singers no doubt calculated that public interest in the opera, unheard for so long, would have greatly increased. There was, too, an excellent role in it for each of them. Johann Michael Vogl, the baritone who first interpreted so many of Schubert's songs, was to sing Pizarro, Karl Friedrich Weinmüller, a bass, would play Rocco and Herr Saal would take the part of Don Fernando. Beethoven had apparently mislaid his own score of *Fidelio*, and late in January or early in February he wrote to Count Moritz Lichnowsky (younger brother of his patron Prince Karl) to ask if he might borrow his copy. At the composer's

G F Treitschke in 1830 (1776 - 1842), lithograph by J. Kriehuber (Historisches Museum der Stadt Wien)

own request, the revision of the text, far more drastic than that of 1806 by Breuning, was to be undertaken by Treitschke, who was official poet as well as stage director at the Kärntnertor Theatre.

Treitschke's theatrical experience was backed by an innate sense of drama which ensured that this time Beethoven's opera would be thoroughly stageworthy. The composer's share of the revision was also more fundamental than before and every number in the score, apart from the March in the first act, underwent at least some musical rewriting. As usual, the work took much longer than Beethoven at first envisaged. There were also other distractions. He composed a song, *Germania*, for bass and chorus, to serve as finale to a *Singspiel* by Treitschke, *Die güte Nachtricht*, produced at the Kärntnertor Theatre on April 11, with Weinmüller as bass soloist. Before that, on February 27, he gave a concert in the Redoutensaal of the Hofburg, at which the Seventh Symphony, first performed the previous December, was repeated and the Eighth given its first performance.

'That accursed concert', complained Beethoven to Treitschke, 'has put me back in regard to the opera . . . Now, of course, everything has to be done at once and I could have composed something new far more quickly than patch up the old with something new, as I am now doing . . . Meanwhile the first act will be finished in a few days — But there is still much to be done to the second act and I have to compose a new overture as well . . . Before my concert I had just made a few sketches here and there — In short I assure you dear T., that this opera will win for me the martyr's crown. Had you not taken so much trouble with it and revised everything so satisfactorily, for which I shall ever be grateful to you, I would hardly bring myself to do my share — But by your work you have salvaged a few good bits of a ship that was wrecked and stranded'.

The stranded ship was relaunched on May 23, 1814 at the Kärntnertor Theatre. The new overture was not ready in time, and tradition has it that the overture to *The Ruins of Athens* was played instead. Treitschke himself says, in his memoirs, that the overture to the ballet *Prometheus* was used. A third alternative stems from Anton Schindler, who mentions 'an overture to *Leonore*', which could be construed as meaning the *Leonora No. 1*, thought by some, though not all, Beethoven scholars to have been composed for a projected performance of the second version at Prague in 1808 — a performance that did not materialise. At the second hearing of the third version, on May 25, 1814, the new overture, known ever since as the *Fidelio* overture, was definitely played.

One of the numbers cut in the 1806 revision of the opera had been the jailer Rocco's 'Gold' aria. At the seventh repeat of the third version, on July 18, 1814, which was a benefit performance for Beethoven, this aria, suitably revised by Treitschke and the composer, was reinstated for Weinmüller. There was also a new singer in the role of Pizarro. Vogl was ill and Beethoven gave the part to Anton Forti, a twenty-four-year-old bass whose voice, according to the composer, was better suited to the music than Vogl's. The change of cast meant extra rehearsals, of great advantage to the standard of performance.

In its new form, *Fidelio* was quickly taken up by theatres outside Vienna. Weber conducted the opera in Prague on November 27, 1814. The following year there were productions at Leipzig, Dresden and Berlin, where Leonora was sung at some of the performances by Anna Milder-

Anna Milder-Hauptmann (1785 - 1838), copper engraving by D. Weiss, from a drawing by Sigmund Perger. She created the role of Leonora at the age of nineteen in 1805. Haydn said, 'My dear girl, you have a voice the size of a house!'

Carolina Unger (Opera Rara Collection) and Henriette Sontag (Opera Rara Collection), two beautiful singers famous for their interpretations of his music. On one unfortunate visit to Beethoven, they drank some wine which did not agree with them and were both ill.

Hauptmann, the famous Austrian-born soprano who at the age of nineteen had created the role in the first (1805) version of the opera, at the Theater an der Wien. *Fidelio* reached St Petersburg in 1819, Amsterdam in 1824, Paris in 1829, London in 1832 and New York in 1839, by which time it had become one of the most popular and admired operas in the German repertory, a position which it has never subsequently lost. For the centenary of the first performance, in 1905, Richard Strauss conducted a revival of the original version at the Court Opera in Berlin, and the two hundredth anniversary of the composer's birth, in 1970, inspired other revivals of *Leonore*, including one by the Sadler's Wells Opera, as it then was, at the London Coliseum.

After the success of the third version of *Fidelio*, which Beethoven recognised was in large measure due to Treitschke, composer and poet planned

Wilhelmine Schröder-Devrient (1804 - 1860) in a pastel by E.B. Kietz (Beethoven-Haus, Bonn) and a lithograph by W. Santer (National Library, Vienna). She made her debut as Leonora in 1822 and became famous all over Europe for her interpretation of the part. Berlioz remembered how her arm shook from convulsive laughter as she stretched it out towards Pizarro.

Maria Malibran in the prison scene of 'Fidelio' in London 1836 (Theatre Museum)

an opera on the subject of Romulus and Remus. In January 1815, Beethoven wrote to Treitschke, 'I am composing *Romulus*! and shall begin to write it down one of these days'. But practical and financial difficulties intervened, and the following September he was complaining to his librettist that the Directors of the Court Opera were only willing to pay him the takings for one night for the proposed opera, 'and although I have so willingly offered, and still offer, many sacrifices to my art, yet by accepting such a condition I should lose far too much . . . I have asked the Theatrical Directors to pay me for *Romulus* 200 gold ducats and the takings for one night'.

The idea of an opera on the twin founders of Rome was not dropped for two or three years. Meanwhile, in January 1816, Beethoven wrote to Anna Milder-Hauptmann in Berlin to congratulate her. 'How I should like to be able to contribute in person to the enthusiasm of the Berliners which your performance in *Fidelio* has aroused . . . If you would ask Baron de la Motte Fouqué on my behalf to think out a subject for a grand opera which would also be suitable for *you*, then you would win great honour for me and for Germany's theatre. Moreover, I should like to set it to music solely for the *Berlin theatre*, for with these niggardly Directors in Vienna I shall never contrive to come to an arrangement for a new opera'. Nothing came of this idea either, and it is particularly ironic that Beethoven should have considered a collaboration with de la Motte Fouqué, as his last serious opera project was a poem by the distinguished poet and playwright Franz Grillparzer on the subject of *Melusine*. Grillparzer sent this libretto to Beethoven in 1823 but it had to be abandoned some three years later, because its theme was too close to that of *Undine*, the libretto which de la Motte Fouqué had adapted from his own story for E.T.A. Hoffmann's opera in 1816.

So *Fidelio* was destined to remain Beethoven's sole and glorious contribution to the operatic stage. When, in the aftermath of the Second World War, the many theatres in German-speaking countries destroyed by bombs, shells or fire re-opened their doors again, a large number of them did so with *Fidelio*, whose contemporary relevance was once more as vital and direct as in the years following the French Revolution. The extraordinary reception accorded to the work at the opening of the rebuilt Vienna State Opera in November 1955, a few weeks after the occupying powers had moved out of the city, bore witness to *Fidelio's* continuing and tremendous emotional impact.

'Fidelio': an operatic marriage
Basil Deane

Although Beethoven's early career as a composer was devoted above all to instrumental music, an artist with his innate dramatic sense was bound to be drawn to the stage. Moreover, success in the theatre was generally regarded as the pinnacle of achievement for a composer of the time. He was attracted by the most grandiose subjects from history and legend but in the event his only opera was based on an obscure incident that occurred within his own lifetime in provincial France. And for this the contemporary state of Viennese opera was largely responsible. By 1800 opera in Vienna was due for a renewal. The Italian forms of *opera seria* and *opera buffa* had outlived their attraction in the German-speaking capital. The German form of comic opera, the *Singspiel*, with its mixture of singing and spoken dialogue, its tendency towards exotic, magical or fantastic plots, had its limitations — limitations triumphantly transcended by Mozart in *The Magic Flute*, certainly. *The Magic Flute* was, however, inimitable and, in any case, Beethoven, much as he admired its high moral tone, was out of sympathy with its 'magical' elements. So the season of imported French opera, which took place in Vienna during 1803, was an eye-opener. Here, in such dramas as *Lodoïska* and *Les Deux Journées (The Water Carrier)* by Cherubini, Beethoven discovered an operatic path to follow. They were 'Rescue' operas, set, it is true, in some distant land or time but none the less relevant to the life and thought of the early 19th century. They exalted the ideals of marital love, of simple fidelity, of devoted heroism, and proclaimed the triumph of good over evil, of freedom over tyranny. Beethoven was overwhelmed. Ever afterwards Cherubini was for him the greatest of living composers, to be spoken of and listened to with deference. And he turned at once to the French writers in his search for a libretto. Bouilly was an obvious choice. He was a competent writer — indeed, his libretto for *The Water Carrier* was acknowledged by no less an authority than Goethe to be a masterpiece of its kind. But there were certain aspects of the French Revolutionary operatic libretto, arising out of its origins in the earlier 18th century *opéra comique*, that imposed restrictions and other problems for a composer attempting an elevated heroic style. The constant switch between spoken dialogue and music easily broke the musical continuity and the dramatic tension. Little provision was made for ensembles, or for extended finales. There was often an unresolved juxtaposition of the trivial and the portentous, the comic and the serious, the domestic and the stately. There was incident in plenty but little systematic working-out of dramatic relationships or character development. In short, the texts were primarily intended for musicians who were essentially short-winded and undemanding. And if these descriptions were inappropriate to the best French composers, such as Cherubini and Méhul, they certainly did not apply to Beethoven. So *Fidelio* is the offspring of the union of two very different artistic worlds: those of the French librettist and the German composer, of literary naivety and musical profundity, of nearsightedness and far-ranging vision. What the two artists shared, and what ultimately makes for the supreme greatness of the opera, is a common idealism, a belief in the essential goodness of man, a conviction that right, in the end, will triumph. Yet the birth was not an easy one, as Beethoven

15

confessed to Schindler: 'Of all the children of my spirit, this one is dearest to me, because it was the most difficult to bring into the world'. The story of Beethoven's travails, and of the contributions made by his three Viennese librettists to the adaptation of the text, is a fascinating one. But here we shall look at the final revision of 1814, which is, of course, the form in which the work is most commonly presented.

Overture

Beethoven's problems began with the overture. Theorists of his day were much exercised by the role and nature of the overture to an opera. Should it prepare the spectators for the opening scene? Or should it rather foreshadow the end of the opera? Should it express the range of emotions to be experienced in the course of the drama? Should it even (as one writer suggested) attempt to indicate the earlier events leading up to the forthcoming action? Should it use themes from the opera, or not? There was no common consensus. But French composers sometimes anticipated later themes in their overtures, and the story of the three versions of the *Leonora* overture is the story of Beethoven's attempt to reconcile thematic reference, and the formal freedom of the French musicians, with his own superb sense of musical structure. Although *Leonora No. 3* is the most complete and satisfying version, it *does* anticipate the whole course of action and on that account is, in purely dramatic terms, unsuitable as a curtain raiser. (The custom of playing it in the course of the opera is open to the same objection.) So, however much we may justly admire the earlier overtures, the *Fidelio* overture undoubtedly makes the most suitable prelude to the opera. It is formally coherent, and dramatic, without pre-empting the ensuing action. Two of the principal sentiments of the work, heroic energy and romantic tenderness, are adumbrated in the opening bars of the introduction, as the confidently rising fanfare is answered by a soft horn call [1]. On its second appearance the horn call takes us into mysterious harmonic regions, but a crescendo and an insistent drum stroke compel a return in preparation for the Allegro. Here the main theme derives its initial shape from the fanfare, and its colour from the horn. The vigorous exposition is followed by a quiet, delicately shaded passage, in which the woodwind play with the main theme. This leads unobtrusively into the recapitulation, which in turn reintroduces the opening bars of the overture. The horn call is now enhanced with triplet arabesques of Schubertian grace. But a final Presto, taking up the dotted rhythm and adding the weight of the trombones to the orchestral forces, concludes the overture on a burst of jubilant energy.

Act One

No.1 Duet: MARCELLINA, JACQUINO

The opening scene of the opera presents a domestic situation of the type frequently encountered in French opera at the time. It is set in the courtyard of a state prison, not far from Seville. In the first two versions of the opera the action started with Marcellina's solo, now No.2, with the duet placed second. By reversing this order in the later version, Beethoven begins with the A major duet, which follows appropriately on the E major of the overture. Marcellina, the daughter of the jailer, Rocco, is engaged in her domestic duties. Jacquino, the porter, is attempting to propose to her, despite repeated interruptions from callers at the gate. She deftly evades his

Elizabeth Schwarzkopf (Marcellina) and Dennis Stephenson (Jacquino) at Covent Garden in 1948 (photo: Edward Mandinian; by courtesy of the Archives of the Royal Opera House)

importunate questioning and, when his back is turned, expresses her love for Fidelio, her father's young assistant. The music contrasts Jacquino's impatience with Marcellina's daydreaming. The opening motive [2], with its concise rhythmic shape, reappears in various guises, and Jacquino's first phrase [3] epitomises both the general Mozartian style and, in the rather angular triplets of the third bar, Beethoven's individual touch.

Jacquino, increasingly frustrated, is called away by Rocco, and Marcellina, at last able to relax, turns her thoughts again to Fidelio. She thinks he is well disposed to her, but what of her father?

17

No.2 Aria: MARCELLINA

Marcellina is essentially a simple soul, and her one aria defines her personality. As her thoughts develop from almost timid reflection upon her present situation of undeclared love to hope of future bliss, so the music changes from a hesitant minor to a confident major, the major section itself being a variation of the preceding one [4 and 5]. The orchestral accompaniment underlines the change, and its palpitations foreshadow Florestan's great aria. Although the vocal line remains the same in each of the two verses, Beethoven embellishes the accompaniment in the second, and concludes the aria with a characteristically bright C major coda.

Rocco, followed by Jacquino, appears, and asks if Fidelio has not returned with dispatches for the Governor. The disguised Leonora arrives, laden with chains and provisions. Rocco praises his assistant's economical purchasing, and promises a reward, hinting that he can see into Fidelio's heart.

No.3 Quartet: MARCELLINA, LEONORA, JACQUINO, ROCCO

Up until this point in the action Beethoven and his collaborators kept closely to the French libretto, and consequently the implied range of the drama hardly exceeds that of an 18th century domestic comedy. Now the opera takes on a wholly new dimension. There is no precedent in Bouilly's text for the quartet, which was included in the work from the first version onwards. No doubt Beethoven and his original librettist, Sonnleithner, felt the need to expand Bouilly's framework by introducing an element which would further define the relationships of the characters already presented, and would at the same time provide a concerted number of substantial proportions at this point in the opera. All four characters react to the situation in different ways. Marcellina is delighted; Leonora is apprehensive; Jacquino is jealous; Rocco is benevolent. Yet Beethoven, paradoxically, chooses for his setting the musical form that, above all others, seems to preclude differentiation of emotion — the canon, in which each voice in turn follows faithfully the course of its predecessor. It is the mark of his supreme genius that the pathos of this situation is enriched, not diminished, by his adherence to the strict form. And this is because the sheer beauty and tenderness of the music gives an emotional depth to the movement which embraces all the individual reactions. Here, for the first time in the opera, Leonora herself is presented in music. And it is *her* love, *her* nobility, the root causes of the deception which has, in spite of herself, led to this situation, that determine the musical essence of the quartet, in the quiet string harmonies of the introduction [6] and the ensuing melodic phrase [7]. The subtlety of colouring in the orchestral accompaniment looks forward to the music of the composer's last period. In the final version of the opera Beethoven shortened the musical numbers in almost every case: the quartet remained virtually unaltered.

Rocco promises to speed the betrothal, but warns that something besides love is essential for domestic contentment . . .

No.4 Aria: ROCCO

. . . Gold. Gold brings love and authority. It fulfils desires, and invites the benevolence of Fortune. Rocco is portrayed as a bluff, forthright character with a keen sense of financial advantage, as his earlier approbation of Fidelio showed. With this return to the original source, we are brought back again to the realms of comic opera, and the aria belongs to a familiar *buffo* type, with alternating sections, contrasted in tempo and metre [8 and 9]. In his first version of the aria Beethoven included trumpets and drums. His later decision to reduce the scoring gives Rocco a less bombastic appearance.

Leonora is torn by conflicting impulses. The talk of a marriage is inevitably distressing. She is, however, dependent on Rocco's continued goodwill to gain access to the prisoners and to seek out her husband. She temporises. She acknowledges that the union of two loving hearts is the source of true happiness but, in addition, she needs something else — his trust. She presses the point, and begs to be allowed to assist him with his duties among the prisoners. Rocco is persuaded to ask the Governor's permission to allow Fidelio to go with him into the dungeons — although there is one dungeon where she may never penetrate. The prisoner has been immured there for over two years. Leonora reacts at once. 'Two years? He must be a dangerous criminal'. 'Or he must have dangerous enemies', Rocco replies. The prisoner's rations, on the orders of the Governor, are being reduced to starvation level, and he will soon die. He has neither light, nor straw bedding. Marcellina begs her father not to let Fidelio see this distressing sight. Leonora, flaring up, exclaims, 'Why not? I have strength, and courage'.

No.5 Trio: MARCELLINA, LEONORA, ROCCO

Now the opera abruptly moves on to a new plane of dramatic intensity, one that it is not to leave before the final resolution. The 'domestic' action involving the relationship of Marcellina and Jacquino becomes irrelevant. From the preceding dialogue Leonora derives both hope and fear. She believes she may have found her husband. Yet if so, he is in deadly danger, and only she can save him. She is a prey to various emotions. She is resolute, and will pay whatever price is demanded. She prays that hope will bring release from her bitter tears. The comforting sentiments of her two companions, who are of course ignorant of her true situation, merely underline her predicament. The emotional tension is established by the staccato strings and stabbing chords of the opening. There are certain key words in the opera, here as elsewhere, which evoke a graphic response from the composer. Leonora's comparison of love (Liebe) and sorrows (Leiden) provokes a sudden switch from major to minor, and a florid elaboration of the phrase [10]. The reference to the healing power of hope is set to a phrase of melting tenderness [11]. And tears — bitter for Leonora, sweet for Marcellina — inspire a poignant falling motive [12], followed by a chain of descending thirds. All this detail takes its place in the overall sweep of the music. The two hundred bars of the trio establish a new musical dimension in the opera, and indeed the ensemble served as the Finale of the first act in Beethoven's original version.

Rocco announces that he will ask the Governor for his consent to the projected marriage, and to the proposal that Fidelio should have access to all the prisoners. Distant music is heard.

19

No.6 March

During the march, which, despite its brevity, is one of Beethoven's most attractive essays in the genre, the Governor, Don Pizarro, enters with his retinue. He issues some orders, takes his dispatches, and opens a letter, which he reads aloud after dismissing the prison staff (Leonora, however, contrives to remain). Pizarro is warned by the writer that the Minister has heard that some prisoners are being unlawfully detained, and intends to pay a surprise visit the next day. He reflects that the discovery of Florestan in chains would ruin him; but he sees a way out — one bold deed will settle the matter.

No.7 Aria with Chorus: PIZARRO

The treatment of Pizarro underlines the gulf between Beethoven and his sources. He is of course central to the drama, yet in Bouilly's libretto Pizarro was a spoken role, a situation which deprived any intending composer of a major musical dimension, as Beethoven and Sonnleithner realised.

The villain in early 19th century drama is an unqualified one, and Beethoven had no occasion to modify the depth of his dye. But mere parody would not be enough. Pizarro *is* a real man of flesh-and-blood, a terrifying figure in a context of absolute power. As this century has cause to know, the most fearful tyrant is the psychopath whose vindictiveness is thinly disguised, whose self-control is fragile, whose outbursts are unpredictable. Thus Pizarro. His inner agitation is expressed, in the time honoured way, by the orchestra: the ominous drum roll; the twisting string figure [13], which seems like a perversion of Leonora's 'tear' motive [12]; the stabbing accents; the blaring brass. His own line begins with the angular interval of B flat — C sharp [14], and it is characterized throughout by short phrases whose irregular outlines and leaps seem to be intent on breaking the bounds of normal musical restraint. The transition from minor to major as he gloats in anticipation of his revenge is a travesty of the meaning the progression generally conveys in Beethoven's music. And the cowed murmurings of the chorus serve to emphasise his invulnerability.

After the aria Pizarro commands, with appropriate threats, that a watch shall be kept, and a trumpet sounded when any escorted carriage shall be seen approaching from Seville. Then he summons Rocco.

No.8 Duet: PIZARRO, ROCCO

Pizarro needs Rocco's complicity, in order to carry out his design. He begins, shrewdly enough, by attacking the jailer's weak point, and promises to make him rich. He flatters Rocco by praising his courage, developed through long service, before revealing to his impatient servant what the jailer must do — 'Murder'. The word is given its full horror by the *mezza voce* drop in pitch [15]. Rocco, aghast, can only stammer at first, then pulls himself together, and points out that murder is not part of his statutory duties. Pizarro, no doubt anticipating this refusal, undertakes to do the deed himself and identifies his victim as the dying prisoner. Rocco's task is merely to dig the grave. Rocco, relieved, eases his conscience by reflecting that the poor man would in any case be better off dead. The continuity of the music is unbroken by the recitative in which Pizarro announces the detail of his plan.

No.9 Recitative and Aria: LEONORA

Leonora, now left alone, is deeply suspicious of Pizarro's intentions. She expresses her horror at his cruelty but hope consoles her and she renews

Gwyneth Jones as Leonora at Covent Garden (photo: Alfredo Evan; by courtesy of the Archives of the Royal Opera House)

her determination to follow the course, strengthened by the devotion of true married love. Although in his final version Beethoven shortened the aria, he entirely rewrote the recitative, greatly increasing its importance. In its colour, its dramatic changes of mood from anger to tenderness, it belongs to Beethoven's full maturity. The aria itself takes its character from its unusual scoring for strings and obligato accompaniment of three horns and bassoon. The voice begins with one of Beethoven's most serenely beautiful melodies [16] and flowers into delicate ornamentation, entwining with the accompanying instruments. In the concluding quick section, wide-ranging agility on the part of singer and instrumentalists expresses Leonora's fixity of purpose.

Marcellina and Jacquino return, still quarrelling about Fidelio. Leonora, anxious to inspect the prisoners, begs Rocco to allow them out into the courtyard. He gives permission but, to her disappointment, only for the prisoners in the upper cells.

The treatment of this incident illustrates the tightening of the dramatic motivation by successive librettists. In the French original, which Sonnleithner followed, the prisoners are allowed a daily exercise period, and Marcellina releases them on the orders of the Governor. Breuning devolved this action to Leonora. Treitschke went further, and attributed their release to an act of grace in defiance of the Governor, instigated by Leonora herself.

21

The prisoners' chorus at Her Majesty's Theatre, 1851 (BBC Hulton Picture Library)

No.10 Finale Act One

Leonora and Jacquino unbar the prisoners' doors, and one by one the captives emerge into the sunlight, against a quiet string texture, which expands and then contracts again. This shape foreshadows the ensuing scene. The prisoners begin their chorus hesitantly, as they breathe in the life-giving air, and compare it to the grave-like dungeons [17]. The key changes from B flat to a bright G major, and one of them steps forward and proclaims that with God's help they will find once again freedom and peace — the rest respond with an outburst of joy [18]. Then they realise that they are overheard by the guards, and they take up the opening chorus, this time in a whisper, and fall silent. No moment in opera is more profoundly moving, none has more universal meaning than the emergence of these anonymous prisoners from darkness into light.

Rocco returns from an interview with the Governor, and tells Leonora that his two requests have been granted, and that she may accompany him into the dungeons this very day. She is at first delighted, then dismayed to learn that their task is to dig a grave for the Governor's victim. With ominous solemnity Rocco describes where they shall dig the grave [19]. He would like to spare her the unpleasant duty but, apprehensive though she now is, she insists on going with the jailer.

Jacquino and Marcellina arrive, breathless, with dramatic news. The Governor has heard that the prisoners have been allowed out and is in a fury [20]. Pizarro himself appears and rages at Rocco, demanding to know why he disobeyed orders [21]. Rocco, after the initial shock, recovers his composure and placates his master, by saying that it is the King's name day, and that moreover a death will soon take place. The prisoners, their hopes of freedom dashed, are shepherded back to their cells, bidding a lingering farewell to the light of day [22], while Pizarro urges Rocco to hasten to his grisly task.

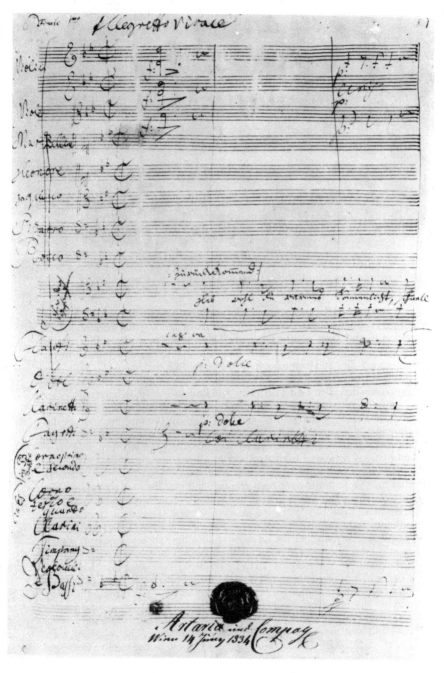

The autograph score of 'Leb wohl, du warmes Sonnenlicht' (Bildarchiv Preussischer Kulturbesitz, Berlin)

Julius Patzak as Florestan at the 1949 Salzburg Festival. His performance is described by Lord Harewood in 'Opera on Record' as of extraordinary quality — 'the uncannily evocative diction, the sensitive, even serene vocal line, the constant intensity' (photo: Ernst Hausknost)

Act Two

No.11 Introduction and Aria: FLORESTAN

The orchestral introduction in F minor sets a mood of sombre foreboding. It is a masterpiece of orchestral colouring, in which each section of the orchestra plays a distinctive part in the texture — not the least remarkable is that of the drums, tuned, most unusually, to A and E flat, a diminished fifth, the interval which medieval musicians regarded as 'diabolical'. A momentary gleam of light after a major cadence is overwhelmed by the prevailing gloom. And, in this respect, the music matches the scene revealed by the rising curtain — Florestan's dungeon, illumined only by a flicker of light. From the desolate figure comes a great cry, 'God! what darkness here!' [23]. Nothing else lives in the solitude. But God's will is best, and His the reckoning. The remarkable harmonies supporting the recitative [24] lead into the A flat aria, whose theme, announced by clarinets, bassoons and horns, appears in each of the Leonora overtures [25]. In music whose expressive beauty equals that of Leonora's aria, Florestan reflects on his unjust fate and finds consolation in the knowledge that he has done his duty. Then he rises in ecstasy as he sees a vision of his beloved wife Leonora leading him to freedom [26]. The vision fades, he sinks back exhausted, and the music dies away. This F major section, with its oboe obbligato, was written for the final version of the opera, and provides a much more dramatically effective conclusion to the scene than did the earlier F minor section it replaced.

No.12 Melodrama and Duet: LEONORA, ROCCO

Rocco and Leonora enter Florestan's dungeon. Leonora tries in vain to discern the prisoner's features before they begin their task of preparing the grave. Melodrama, the declamation of speech against an instrumental background, was a familiar feature of contemporary French opera, applied at moments of high dramatic tension in the dialogue. Beethoven uses it effectively here to create the atmosphere for the following duet, directed to be performed softly throughout. It is a remarkably evocative piece. The quietly repeated chords on low muted strings and woodwind create a sense of urgency, while the rumbling figure in the bass [27] imbues the music with sinister meaning. The dialogue between the two protagonists is hushed and to the point, until Leonora, distracted by her thoughts of Florestan, allows her attention to wander, and is recalled to her duties by Rocco.

Florestan awakes, and is recognised by Leonora, who, despite her overwhelming emotions, must continue to conceal her identity. He learns that he has been imprisoned by Don Pizarro, whose crimes he exposed. He asks for a drink, and Leonora gives him some wine.

No.13 Trio: LEONORA, FLORESTAN, ROCCO

Florestan expresses his gratitude in music of lyrical warmth [28], and the others respond. Leonora persuades the reluctant Rocco to allow her to give the starving prisoner a piece of bread she is carrying in her pocket. The opening phrase returns, and Florestan again thanks his unknown benefactor. Leonora finds the situation more than she can bear, and Rocco

25

reflects that the prisoner will soon be dead.

Pizarro enters, intent on accomplishing his purpose, and draws a dagger.

No.14 Quartet: LEONORA, FLORESTAN, PIZARRO, ROCCO

Against a turbulent orchestral background Pizarro gloats over his victim. He reveals his identity in a phrase of characteristically chromatic outline [29]. Then the chromaticism gives place to a triumphant D major as he moves to the kill. He is prevented by Leonora, whose turn it now is to

Lotte Lehmann
as Leonora

disclose her own identity, in an utterance of soaring defiance, 'First kill his wife!' [30]. Pizarro renews his attempt on Florestan, but is halted by a trumpet call from the tower [31]. There is a moment of stunned silence as the protagonists register the significance of the interruption, and then follows a phrase of ethereal calm, incorporated also into the third Leonora overture [32]. The trumpet sounds again. Jacquino announces the arrival of the Minister, and the quartet ends in a tumult of excitement. Pizarro rushes out, the others leave, and Leonora and Florestan are left alone.

In the earlier versions, the lovers were still in suspense as to their ultimate Fate. Would Rocco cover up for his master? But in the final revision, the clouds are lifted. Rocco demonstrates his goodwill to them before following Pizarro. Leonora reassures Florestan that all will be well.

No.15 Duet: LEONORA, FLORESTAN

Throughout the opera the love between Leonora and Florestan has been the mainspring of the action. Now it is expressed in music of ecstatic happiness. All the frustrations and terrors of separation and the unknown are resolved in this brilliant, surging G major duet [33].

One of Rex Whistler's designs for 'Fidelio' at Covent Garden in 1934 (photo: Edward Mandinian; by courtesy of the Archives of the Royal Opera House)

No.16 Finale

The scene is the parade ground of the castle. The Minister, Don Fernando, is surrounded by his officers. Pizarro is also present. Jacquino and Marcellina lead in the prisoners. The introduction takes the form of one of Beethoven's massive crescendos on tonic and dominant, in the triumphal key of C major. The crowd burst into jubilation. Don Fernando, in broad stately phrases [34], proclaims the King's dedication to justice for all. Rocco produces Leonora, and Florestan, still in chains. Their case is explained to the astonished Minister by Rocco. The crowd demand that Pizarro should be punished, and he is taken away by the guards. Don Fernando invites Leonora to remove Florestan's fetters. Here the mood changes, as Beethoven introduces into his score an extract from his early *Cantata on the Death of Joseph II*. In the cantata Joseph is praised for having overcome Fanaticism, a monster from Hell who spread darkness over the earth. The music is taken from the aria, 'Mankind rose up to the light, and the sun warmed the earth with the rays of the Godhead.' The parallelism is clear, and this F major section with its beautiful melodic curve [35] provides a moment of general reflection on the mystery of God's mercy and justice. Then all is celebration as the chorus lead off with a line from Schiller's *Ode to Joy* : 'Let him who has won a fair wife join in our rejoicing'.

Death is swallowed up in victory; captivity is led captive; the light shines in the darkness; love conquers all. 'Music' declared Beethoven, 'is a higher revelation than all your wisdom and philosophy.' As the curtain comes down on *Fidelio*, who will be the first to contradict him?

An extract from 'Beethoven the Creator'

Romain Rolland
translated by Ernest Newman

Romain Rolland's study of 'Beethoven, Les Grandes époques créatrices' was published in French between 1928 and 1957. The first volume entitled 'De l'Héroïque à l'Apassionata' (1928) contains a chapter devoted to 'Leonore'. Since the whole work is at present out of print in Britain, an extract from Newman's translation is given here as a short example of this remarkable piece of critical appreciation.

What then is this work that kept its place in Beethoven's affections until the last, and of which three successive versions and four (if not five) overtures were insufficient to satisfy his *Sehnsucht*, his passionate desire to realise it? Note the fact that the overtures, with the exception of the fourth, are not simply introductions to the work but separate and independent attempts at the solution of the same problem, fresh desperate efforts to convey the idea of the work by purely symphonic means! Why this pertinacity? Did he see a dramatic-musical problem to resolve? Assuredly, as we shall see, Beethoven brought into the opera house a new form, and his instinct must have made him aware of its difficulties and of the insufficiency of certain realisations of it. But would it not have been simpler, and more consonant with his nature, that took more pleasure in inventing than in re-touching, to approach the problem afresh in a new work instead of obstinately working again and again over the old one? What was there in this work that bound him to it so? What was the unique nature of it? Was it perhaps the subject?

Before examining it more closely, one detail ought to put us on our guard. At the end of the libretto, — which is virtually a translation from the French — Beethoven introduces into the final chorus — *maestoso* for four voices, then *tutti* — these words of Schiller:—

'*Wer ein holdes Weib errungen, stimm' in unseren Jubel ein!*' ('Let him who has won him a dear wife, join us in our joy!')

Twenty years later he will use these same words again in the hymn to Joy at the end of the Ninth Symphony, so much did the thought mean for him!

That life-long dream of his, that it was never given to him to realise! That idealisation of women and of conjugal fidelity, in which, in spite of all deceptions, he has never ceased to believe! I am not speaking now of the refusals he received, but of the bitter revelations life brought him with regard to the women he had loved, and that made him say to Nanni Giannatasio del Rio in 1817:—

'I have never known a marriage in which, after a time, one or other of the pair has not regretted the false step. And of the few women the possession of whom would formerly have seemed to me supreme happiness, I have lived to see that it was a good thing that not one of them became my wife. Ah! How fortunate it is that often the vows of mortals are not accomplished!'

No matter! He is never an apostate to his religious ideal of the betrothed, the wife. He will render her in public a solemn homage, in his two greatest works, the one dramatic, the other choral.

In the same way Goethe, who no doubt had less apparent reason to think himself unfortunate in love, but who, in reality, having known it better had also more reason to know its insufficiency and its bitterness, Goethe, who could not find or keep a companion worthy of him, cannot make his exit from life before he has sung, in the Epilogue to *Faust* his credo in woman.

Possibly thoughts of this kind seem, to our aesthetes of to-day, to lie outside the circle of art. But since the emperor of art, Goethe, has sealed his greatest work with them, I have some right to note their secret importance in the mind of Beethoven, and the part they played in the enduring attraction that the theme of *Fidelio* had for him.

☆

Let us return to this theme.

It has been much disparaged. The general opinion rather looks down on it, and the wretched performances the work has had during a whole century have confirmed this verdict. It must be confessed that until our time *Fidelio* was played in a way that misrepresented it.

Let us study it more closely. Anyone who has had the good fortune, as I had, to see the centenary performances at Vienna must make his *mea culpa* for the misunderstanding of a century; and one feels the need to share the discovery with others, — the newly-revealed splendour, dramatic and musical, of the entire second act, that unique masterpiece that had no forerunner and has had no successor in the musical theatre. And without a shadow of doubt the grandeur of it is wholly the work of the genius of the musician. Yet the poem has not served him ill; this libretto is a sturdy horse that does not stumble under the weight of its rider. Beethoven did it justice: he maintained *mordicus* that the subject was an excellent one. In 1823, when he was chatting with Weber and joking about the libretti of his younger colleague, and expressing himself scathingly on the incurable mediocrity of the German librettists, he paid the French a compliment and recalled the fact that his *Fidelio* came to him from them.

☆

What came to him from them, in *Leonora*, was not merely an anecdote more or less well told but an atmosphere of tragic reality: it was the Revolution.

But the French themselves, — as happens to those who, absorbed in an event, their nose to the detail of the daily round, cannot see the great eternal lines — had been unconscious of the Æschylean breath that came from their tale. Just as in the *Eroica* Beethoven had been the Homer of the Empire, so now, in *Leonora*, he was the Æschylus of the Revolution.

Everyone knows the story of *Leonora* is taken from Bouilly, who himself was not its inventor, for he had known the heroine of it — a woman of Touraine. He has given an account of her in his memoirs; but Beethoven knew nothing of these, for they did not appear until after his death; and *Leonora* came to him in the Spanish costume in which Bouilly, for prudential reasons, had disguised it. There is no Spanish local colour in his music, however; and his intuition, that pierces to the eternal depths, seems to have divined the proximity of the terrible period he was describing — at no more than ten years' distance from the real drama, and when the actual heroine was still alive.

There is no need for me to tell again the story of the drama, which, in its

30

broad lines, depicts the horrors of a State prison and the devotion of a woman who entered it in diguise to save her husband. The critics have in general insisted only on the improbabilities and incongruities of the libretto, or on the difficulty that Beethoven's symphonic genius had in adapting itself to the dramatic necessities of opera. We are entitled to assume that they have not perceived the true essence either of the poem that Beethoven was setting or of the dramatic Ode he wished to make of it.

To the first of these points some effective answers have recently been made. Hermann W. von Waltershausen* has undertaken the defence of the French libretto. He shows that the mixture of styles, that has been so freely criticised — the bourgeois opening that hardly prepares us for the high tragedy that is to come — comes from a view of the subject that is as veracious as it is striking. At the height of the Terror, even in the darkness of this prison in which, it would seem, those who have entered have left all hope behind, the tranquil life of the bourgeois goes on just the same, with its pots of geranium in the window, the young girl's love-dreams, the old gaoler's simple and affectionate calculations of self-interest, his quiproquos and his comic vexations. But the art is in the lightness of the touches, in the imperceptible oncoming of the tragic shadow, that at first just touches these scenes of egoistic tranquillity with the tip of its wing, then reaches further, and at last envelops the whole stage. The French librettist has indicated this. It is not without interest for us that these *poetae minores* (the word poet is a big one!) of the French bourgeois comedy and opéra-comique did much, according to the German historians, to form that atmosphere of chiaroscuro and mysterious terror in which German musical romanticism found its nourishment. From these *crescendi* of inexplicable anguish and terror, Weber, in *Der Freischütz*, drew effects till then unknown. Our poor French librettists were far enough from these; no doubt these agitations would have frightened them; they had undergone too many of them in the life of the time not to tone them down in their comedies. In the same way some of our writers of to-day who witnessed and were wounded in the bloody catastrophe of the Europe they knew, fly from the representation of it in their art; but in spite of them their aesthetic diversions bear the agitated imprint of it. The obscure source of the tragic perturbation that was so much to the liking of romanticism was the social agitation, — the terror during the Terror — of the preceding generation. What that generation had been able only to stammer forth, a Beethoven expresses in its naked truth, without any beating about the bush, out of the plenitude of a great heart and with the mastery of genius. His *Leonora* is a monument of the anguish of the period, of the oppressed soul and its appeal to liberty, — a formidable *crescendo* swelling from suffering to joy, traversing the road of hope and combat — an ascent from the abyss to the clear sky.

This filiation between a robust junior and the elder members of a noble race — these, however, a trifle debilitated and overborne by the rigours of the time, — is not confined merely to vague moral resemblances. It is clearly marked in the music, with a precision that permits of no doubt. The symphonic style of *Leonora* derives in essentials from that of Méhul and Cherubini. Here again it has been able to ripen the rather green and dry

* Neues Beethoven —— Jahrbuch, 1924: zur Dramaturgie des *Fidelio*

fruit, to press out the whole of the juice of it where they were content with a few drops.

We have to remember that in the *Leonora* period Beethoven, who could still hear, enjoyed the French operas that were the delight of Vienna; and for him no living master could compare with Cherubini. Among the *Fidelio* sketches we find, in Beethoven's writing, passages from *The Water Carrier*. Seyfried and Schindler bear testimony to his unceasing admiration for the composer of *Medea*; and we know that Beethoven himself, at the height of his genius (in 1823), wrote to Cherubini paying humble homage to this work.

It is not surprising, then, that traces of this influence should be found in his own music. Even during his lifetime E.T.A. Hoffmann, who always saw more deeply than his contemporaries, had been struck by the community of race between Cherubini's overtures and the *Coriolan*. Since that time Wagner and the German critics of our own day have pointed out several resemblances between them. The question has recently been elucidated, so far as the Beethoven overtures are concerned, by Arnold Schmitz (1925).* The examples he gives, the similarities he notes, show clearly that Beethoven derived a good deal from the French composers of the Revolution; but they prove also the magnificent use he made of his booty. If some of the analogues may be explained on the theory of a common source — Gluck (for example, the mighty unisons with which all Beethoven's tragic overtures open) — the majority of the others bear witness to the moral contagion of the France that has as yet barely emerged from the Revolution and still felt the shock of it; a whole family of characteristic effects or motives in the operas of Méhul and Cherubini exhibits the nervous fever, the uneasy agitation, the painful excess of excitement of which I spoke a moment ago in connection with the poems; the composers may not have been clearly conscious of it, but for long enough afterwards it ran shuddering beneath their skin, like the periodic attacks of an old malaria. Schmitz has drawn up a remarkable inventory of them: the obstinate use of certain stereotyped formulae for effect, such as the boil and swirl of the unison strings in the coda of the *Leonora No. 3*, the source of which is Cherubini's *Elisa* overture; 'alarm' effects; brusque repetitive figures that seem to keep clashing with each other between two walls; sequences of syncopated chords (here the resemblance is striking) employed at the same moment and in the same place in the coda of the *Leonora No. 2* and in that of *Elisa*; unquestionable analogies of complementary rhythms in the *Leonora No. 1*, the *Fidelio No. 4*, the *Coriolan* on the one hand and Cherubini's *Elisa* and Méhul's *Stratonice* on the other; resemblances between certain themes in Méhul's overtures and in those of Beethoven; and so on. Lastly, the idea of the tremendous trumpet fanfare in the *Leonora No. 2* and *Leonora No. 3* came from Méhul's overture to *Hélène!*

But here we become more than ever conscious of the magic power of genius. It is nothing to have ideas: the thing is to realise them. And for the realisation of them neither intelligence, nor a fine sense of art, nor skill in form, necessary as all these are, is enough; these are only the portico. Enter the building and erect the vault! Each of the really remarkable suggestions

* Neues Beethoven — Jahrbuch, 1925: Cherubinis Einfluss auf Beethovens Ouvertüren

32

of Méhul or Cherubini is merely the invitation to proceed along a certain path; they draw back at the first step, but Beethoven presses on. Passion does not merely suggest; it demands the complete embrace! Cherubini recoils; he is too intelligent not to know what he is letting slip from his grasp, but he doubts his own strength; he turns away from the lovely form, and is satisfied to sketch a noble intellectual portrait of it. His themes lack blood, his melodies are abstract: he has formulated the rules of the game clearly enough, but he will not risk the hazard of it. Beethoven throws the whole of himself into it. And into this inferno of the soul — passions, combats, sufferings — that the musicians of the Revolution have indeed known but have not dared to enter, Beethoven, following in their track, boldly penetrates, and, leaving them on the threshold, descends to the depths.

☆

The descent into the abyss and the subsequent ascent out of the night into full sunlight: this is the dominant impression produced by *Leonora*. The tragic contrast and the *crescendo* of light are realised with perfect mastery, however, only in the second part of the first act — after Leonora's famous aria. Until then Beethoven has been hesitating, searching; as yet he has caught only a glimpse of his true subject and when suddenly it dawns upon him: '*Ach! brich noch nicht, du mattes Herz!*' he is overwhelmed, transported into a completely different world of music. It is too late now to re-establish the transition from Singspiel to opera, from the comedy of everyday life to high tragedy! Certainly that task was not an easy one: but it was not above the capacity of a Beethoven. Mozart had accomplished it, and even Gluck, whose *Iphigenia in Aulis* and *Orfeo* are a harmonious blend of the highest lyrical forms and the simplest, the most popular.

But *Leonora* was for Beethoven a first essay; when he began it he was entering a *terra ignota*. And his natural mistake was that, for lack of power to take in the whole of this new continent with one of those eagle glances that, in the *Eroica* or the C minor, survey the whole field of battle, he prudently set himself to begin at the beginning. He followed the order of the 'numbers' with exemplary patience and unexampled tenacity, constraining his herculean muscles to turn the spinning-wheel of the little Marcellina, to copy Mozart in the familiar domestic scenes, to array his giant music in the hoods of the puppets of the little song-plays of Leipzig or Paris.

It goes without saying that a labour of this kind cannot be absolutely in vain in the case of a Beethoven; and these introductory numbers are distinguished by some fine details of orchestration, some delicate expressions of feeling. Particularly successful are the quartet in canon, — the vocalised evolution of which was not lost on the young Berlioz of *Benvenuto Cellini* — and the duet between Marcellina and Leonora, with its innocent tenderness and its charming orchestral ornamentation.

But it is evident that Beethoven's heart is not in his work as yet, that he is writing like a pupil of the Singspiel elegants. The whole of this first part of the first act, this half-way house in which Mozart was thoroughly at home, is cold, and imitative not of nature but of books. Even in the second half of the act the scenes and characters that do not lie close to the thoughts and passions of Beethoven are only half-successful. Pizarro is a traitor of melodrama, not lacking in savage grandeur (Weber did not forget him), but with a touch of the ridiculous about him. And in the first version of the end of the first act (Pizarro, Rocco, Leonora: Pizarro and his bodyguard) some fairly new and moving pages are combined with the heavy conventions of pompous declamatory opera, — a sort of Meyerbeer *avant la lettre*. It is the revenge, we might almost say the punishment, of sincerity. Beethoven cannot lie: an artistic nature like his is completely unable to simulate emotions it has not experienced. By the very nature of his being he must love, hate, believe, take fire. Nothing by halves: everything in extremes.

He might have made a frank plunge into the very centre of the drama with Leonora's aria and the Prisoners' scene; but to do that he would have needed the support of some great librettist formed in the school of Gluck. He had around him none but mediocrities, hangers-on of the theatre, who were nowhere so much at their ease as in the insipid conventions that had been manipulated a thousand times already. Being a newcomer in the theatre, he lacked the authority to assail them as Gluck would have done. Still less had he Gluck's robust health, his weight of manner, that would have made it possible for him to ascend the stage and give battle with fist and tongue to this crew of routineers and liars, the actors, the singers, the chorus, the instrumentalists, the librettist, the producer! He was a sick man; he heard only half of what was going on; he ran the risk of having it said, 'Why do you interfere? You are deaf.' And so he accepted what was given him; he began with the established conventions.

But what we have to consider is not the point of departure but the point of arrival. These conventions that he so meekly and unwillingly endorses, this formal frock-coat in which his great chest suffocates during the first ten numbers — see him burst them and tear them in pieces with a single stroke!

Thematic Guide

Many of the themes from the opera have been identified in the preceding articles by numbers in square brackets, which refer to the themes on these pages. The original numbers of the musical items in the full score have been noted in italics, and should not be confused with the numbers of the thematic guide. The numbers in square brackets also appear at relevant moments in the libretto so that the words can be related to the musical examples in the thematic guide.

|1| OVERTURE

|2|

|3| JACQUINO

Now, sweetheart as no-one is near, let's talk for a while here in priv-ate.

Jetzt, Schätzchen, wir können vertraulich nun plau-dern.
jetzt sind wir all-ein,

|4| MARCELLINA

Andante con moto

Oh were I now al- rea- dy wed that hus-band I might call you

O wär' ich schon mit dir—ver-eint und dür-fte Mann dich nen-nen!

|5| MARCELLINA

Poco più Allegro

No words can tell the pure de-light, that hope al-rea-dy brings in sight,

Die Hoffnung füllt die Brust mit un-aus-sprechlich süs-ser Lust,
schon er–

35

Andante sostenuto

sempre ***p***

MARCELLINA
Andante sostenuto

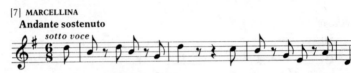

sotto voce

Such strange de-light is here, my heart now weeps for me

Mir ist so wun - der - bar, es engt das Herz mir ein.

[8] **ROCCO**
Allegro moderato

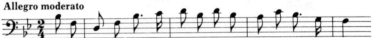

If you lack for gold, my children then your home is full of care,

Hat man nicht auch Gold bei - ne - ben, kann man nicht ganz glücklich sein;

[9] **ROCCO**
Allegro

But when in your pockets you jin-gle your gold

Doch wenn's in den Taschen fein klin-gelt und rollt

[10] **LEONORA**
Allegro ma non troppo

True love's pre - pared to suf - fer tor - ture, suf——————— fer

Kann Lie - be schon auch ho - he Lei - den, ho——————— he

end————less tor——————— ture.

Lei————den tra——————— gen.

[11] **LEONORA**
Allegro ma non troppo

Now hope at — last brings com - fort brings com——fort here —

Du, Hoff - nung reichst mir La - bung, mir La——bung dar,

36

[12] LEONORA, MARCELLINA
Allegro molto

L {
Though bit-ter, bit-ter — tears — were — flowing.
Es kos-tet bitt'-re, bitt' — re — Tränen.
}

M {
Tho' joy-ous tears— be— flow-(ing)
O süs-se, süs—— se — Trän-(en)
}

[13]
Allegro agitato

pp

[14] PIZARRO
Allegro agitato

Now, now, now, now the time has come my vengeance shall be sa-ted
Ha, ha, ha, welch ein Au-gen-blick! Die Rache werd ich küh-len!

[15] PIZARRO
Allegro con brio
mezza voce

Mur————der!
Mor————den!

[16] LEONORA
Adagio

Sweet hope, oh ne-ver let your star, your last faint star of com-fort be de-nied - me
Komm Hoff-nung, lass den letzten Stern, den letzten Stern der Müden er -blei – chen!
nicht

Oh what de-light
O wel-che Lust

[17]
Allegro ma non troppo

O what de-light
O wel-che Lust

Oh what de-light to breathe the air,
O wel-che Lust in frei er Luft

Oh what de-light — Oh what de light to breathe the air,
O wel-che Lust — in frei-er Luft, in frei-er Luft

37

[18] **A PRISONER** (*tenor solo*)
Allegro ma non troppo

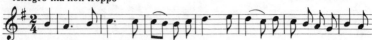

We trust for our de - liv'rance in Hea - ven's help - in Heaven's
help and guidance
Wir woll - en mit ver - trau - en auf Gott - es Hi - lfe, auf Gottes Hilfe bauen!

[19] **ROCCO**
Andante con moto

No time to waste, we must get ready. I'll need your help, keep calm and steady.
Wir müssen gleich zu Werke schreiten, du musst mir helf - en, mich be - glei-ten.

[20] **MARCELLINA**
Allegro molto

Oh fa —————— ther, father dear.
Ach, Va —————— ter, Vater, eilt!

[21] **PIZARRO**
Allegro molto

Pre - sump ——— tuous scoundrel
do you dare com - mit such an out - rage as I see?
Ver - weg ——— ner Alte welche Rech - te legst du dir frevelnd selber bei?

[22] **PRISONERS**
Allegretto vivace

Fare - well to spring and heaven's light, joys all too soon de - nied us
Leb wohl, du war - mes Son - nen - licht, schnell schwindest du uns wie - der

[23] **FLORESTAN**
Recit.

God! what end—less night!
Gott! Welch Dun-kel hier!

38

FLORESTAN
Poco Allegro　　　　**Adagio**

I'll not com-plain. I must suf —————— fer,　lies with Thee.

Ich mur-re nicht! Dass Mass der Lei —————— den　steht bei dir.

|25| FLORESTAN
Adagio

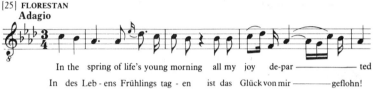

In the spring of life's young morning all my joy de-par ————— ted

In des Leb-ens Frühlings tag - en ist das Glück von mir ————— geflohn!

|26| FLORESTAN
Poco Allegro

What gen-tle, soft breezes a-round me now play? What brightens my grave with such splendour?

Und spür ich nicht linde, sanft säuseln - de Luft? Und ist nicht mein Grab mir er hellet?

|27|
Andante con moto

|28| FLORESTAN
Moderato

Some bet - ter world, one day — re — ward you

Euch wer - de Lohn in be — ssern — Welten,

|29| PIZARRO
Allegro

Pi - zarro, whom you would have ruined　Pi - zarro

Pi - zarro, den du stür-zen wolltest,　Pi - zarro

|30| LEONORA
Allegro

First kill his wife! —————

Töt erst sein weib! —————

[31] FANFARE

Un poco sostenuto

[32]

Un poco sostenuto

cresc.   p   cresc.   p

[33] LEONORA

Allegro vivace

Oh   sweet de - light   beyond   all   telling!

O   na - men,   na - menlo - se   Freude!

[34] FERNANDO

Un poco maestoso

Our sov'reign   the King has   to seek out those who've suf- fered here
liege,   charged me

Des besten Kö———nigs Wink und   führt mich zu euch, ihr Ar—men, her,
Wil - le

[35]

Sostenuto assai

40

Alberto Remedios as Florestan at ENO (photo: Andrew March)

Josephine Barstow as Leonora at ENO (photo: Andrew March)

Fidelio

Opera in two acts

Music by Ludwig van Beethoven
Libretto after Jean-Nicolas Bouilly
by Josef Sonnleithner, Stefan von Breuning
and Georg Friedrich Treitschke
English version: Lyrics Tom Hammond
Dialogue Rodney Blumer

This text of *Fidelio* is the authentic libretto for the final (1814) version of the opera. It is written in an old-fashioned German style which sounds distinctly melodramatic to the modern reader. It includes much dialogue which is very rarely (if ever) now performed and original stage directions which do not necessarily describe the ENO or any other modern production. For the new ENO production in May 1980, the English version of the lyrics was especially revised and the entire dialogue was freshly translated (for performance in a shortened form). The translation of the complete dialogue of Fidelio was, however, undertaken especially for this Guide and it was never intended for performance. This almost literal translation provided the basis for the performing version used by ENO, which was also the product of many revisions in the course of rehearsal. Alterations were, inevitably, also made to the lyrics in that period as well, of which as many as possible have been incorporated.

The musical numbers which follow the stage directions after an oblique are those in the full score. The numbers in square brackets refer to the Thematic Guide.

Fidelio was first performed at the Theater an der Wien, Vienna on November 20, 1805. The first version was then revised and produced in a second edition on March 29, 1806. A third and final version was made for a revival on May 23, 1814. That version was first performed in England at the King's Theatre, Haymarket on May 18, 1832 and in the USA at the Park Theatre, New York on September 9, 1839. *Fidelio* was first given by Sadler's Wells Opera in 1937. *Leonora* (the first version) was given at the London Coliseum in 1970.

THE CHARACTERS

Don Fernando *Minister*	bass-baritone
Don Pizarro *Governor of a State prison*	baritone
Florestan *a prisoner*	tenor
Leonora (Leonore) *his wife, using the name of 'Fidelio'*	soprano
Rocco	bass
Marcellina (Marzelline) *his daughter*	soprano
Jacquino (Jaquino) *porter*	tenor
First Prisoner	tenor
Second Prisoner	bass

Captain of the Watch, Officers, Soldiers, State-prisoners, People

Fidelio

The action takes place in a State Prison, some miles from Seville, in the eighteenth century.

Act One

The courtyard of the State Prison. In the background the main gate and a high wall with ramparts over which trees are visible. In the gate itself, which is shut, there is a little wicket which is opened for occasional visitors on foot. Near the gate is the porter's lodge. The wings on the left represent the prisoners' cells; all the windows are barred and the doors, which are numbered, are reinforced with iron and shuttered with heavy bolts. In the forwardmost wing is the door to the gaoler's quarters. On the right there are trees protected by iron railings, and these, with a garden gate, show the entrance to the castle gardens.

Scene One. *Marcellina is ironing laundry in front of her door; at her side is a brazier on which she warms the iron. Jacquino stands close to his lodge; he opens the door to various people who hand him parcels, which he puts in his lodge. | Duet No. 1 [2]*

JACQUINO
(ardently rubbing his hands)

Now, sweetheart, as no-one is near,	[3] Jetzt, Schätzchen, jetzt sind wir allein,
Let's talk for a while here in private.	Wir können vertraulich nun plaudern.

MARCELLINA
(continuing her work)

No time to be serious, I fear,	Es wird wohl nichts Wichtiges sein,
I daren't stop my work for a moment.	Ich darf bei der Arbeit nicht zaudern.

JACQUINO

Well listen, you obstinate girl!	Ein Wörtchen, du Trotzige, du!

MARCELLINA

Speak up then, I'm list'ning you'll find.	So sprich nur, ich höre ja zu.

JACQUINO

If you'll not be friendlier towards me	Wenn du mir nicht freundlicher blickest,
Then I cannot think what to say.	So bring ich kein Wörtchen hervor.

MARCELLINA

If you dislike my demeanour	Wenn du dich nicht in mich schickest,
I'll stop up my ears right away!	Verstopf ich mir vollends das Ohr.
You'll give me no peace, I can see,	So hab' ich denn nimmermehr Ruh;
Let's hear what you're longing to say!	So rede, so rede nur zu.

JACQUINO

Oh spare me a moment, I pray,	Ein Weilchen nur höre mir zu,
And then I will go right away.	Dann lass ich dich wieder in Ruh.
I've . . . I've chosen . . .	Ich, ich habe,
I've chosen to make you my wedded wife,	Ich habe zum Weib dich gewählt,
You follow?	Verstehst du?

MARCELLINA

That's all very clear.	Das ist ja doch klar.

JACQUINO

If you say you're willing to take me	Und, und wenn mir dein Jawort nicht fehlet,

45

Then we'd make . . . | Was meinst du?

MARCELLINA

A fine loving pair. | So sind wir ein Paar.

JACQUINO

A month then and we could be married . . . | Wir könnten in wenigen Wochen . . .

MARCELLINA

Bravo, so you've settled the day! | Recht schön, du bestimmst schon die Zeit!
(knocking is heard)

JACQUINO
(to himself)

Oh curse them they never stop knocking, | Zum Henker das ewige Pochen!
And just when success seemed so near, | Da war ich so herrlich im Gang,
That always evades me I fear. | Und immer entwischt mir der Fang.

MARCELLINA
(to herself)

At last he will leave me in peace! | So bin ich doch endlich befreit!
I'm bored by his passion, I fear | Wie macht seine Liebe mir bang,
How tedious his signs now appear! | Und wie werden die Stunden mir lang.

Jacquino opens the wicket, takes a parcel and places it in his lodge; meanwhile Marcellina works on.

MARCELLINA

I know all the lad must be suff'ring | Ich weiss, dass der Arme sich quälet,
I pity, yes pity his sighs, alas! | Es tut mir so leid auch um ihn!
Fidelio now I have chosen | Fidelio hab' ich gewählet,
His love is the treasure I prize. | Ihn lieben ist süsser Gewinn.

JACQUINO
(coming back)

Where was I? She won't look my way. | Wo war ich? Sie sieht mich nicht an!

MARCELLINA
(aside)

He's back, then – he'll start up again! | Da is er – er fängt wieder an!

JACQUINO
(aside)

Now when will you give me your answer? | Wann wirst du das Jawort mir geben?
It could be this morning you know. | Es könnte ja heute noch sein.

MARCELLINA
(aside)

Oh God, I shall soon lose my temper! | O weh! er verbittert mein Leben!
(aloud)
This morning, tomorrow and always my answer is no, no. | Jetzt, morgen und immer nein, nein!

JACQUINO

You must have a heart made of stone, | Du bist doch wahrhaftig von Stein,
No love or compassion you show. | Kein Wünschen, kein Bitten geht ein.

MARCELLINA
(aside)

I'm forced to be hard, that I know, | Ich muss ja so hart mit ihn sein,
He builds on the slightest of hopes. | Er hofft bei dem mindesten Schein.

46

JACQUINO

So you're firm in this sudden decision?   So wirst du dich nimmer bekehren?
Come, tell me!   Was meinst du?

MARCELLINA

When will you be gone?   Du könntest nun gehn.

JACQUINO

What?   Wie?
Just watching you, is that forbidden,   Dich anzusehen willst du mir wehren?
What that too?   Auch das noch?

MARCELLINA

Oh stay and have done.   So bleibe hier stehn.

JACQUINO

You know that you frequently   Du hast mir so oft doch versprochen . . .
  promised . . .

MARCELLINA

I promised? Now you go too far!   Versprochen? Nein, das geht zu weit!
(knocking is heard)

JACQUINO
(to himself)

Damnation! They never stop knocking!   Zum Henker das ewige Pochen!

MARCELLINA
(to herself)

At last I'll be left here in peace   So bin ich doch endlich befreit!
That sound is most welcome to hear.   Das ist ein wilkommener Klang,
I really was frightened to death, then,   Es wurde zu Tode mir bang.
  I fear.

JACQUINO

I've really surprised her that's clear,   Es ward ihr im Ernste schon bang,
Who knows, success might have been   Wer weiss, ob es mir nicht gelang.
  near.

Another parcel is delivered.

JACQUINO

If I haven't opened that door two hundred   Wenn ich diese Tür heute nicht schon
times already today then my name's not   zweihundertmal aufgemacht habe, so will
Caspar Eustace Jacquino.   ich nicht Kaspar Eustach Jaquino heissen.

(to Marcellina)

Now at last I can talk again.   Endlich kann ich doch wieder einmal
                                          plaudern.
(knocking is heard)
Damnation! Not again!   Zum Wetter! schon wieder!
He goes to open the door.

MARCELLINA
(downstage)

How can I help it if I don't like him as   Was kann ich dafür, dass ich ihn nicht
much as I used to?   mehr so gern wie sonst haben kann?

JACQUINO
(to the person who knocked, as he quickly shuts the door)
I'll take care of it, right away.   Ich werde es besorgen. Schon recht!

<table>
<tr><td colspan="2" align="center">(going up to Marcellina)</td></tr>
<tr><td>Now I won't let anyone disturb us.</td><td>So! – Nun, hoffe ich, soll niemand mehr
uns stören.</td></tr>
</table>

ROCCO
(calling from the garden)

Jacquino! Jacquino!	Jaquino! Jaquino!

MARCELLINA

Don't you hear? Father's calling.	Hörst du? Der Vater ruft!

JACQUINO

Let him wait a little. I mean . . . about our love . . .	Lassen wir ihn ein wenig warten. Also, auf unsere Liebe zu kommen –

MARCELLINA

Go to him. Father will be wanting news of Fidelio.	So geh doch. Der Vater wird sich nach Fidelio erkundigen wollen.

JACQUINO
(jealously)

Oh well, of course then, no one can move fast enough . . .	Ei freilich, da kann man nicht schnell genug sein.

ROCCO
(calling again)

Jacquino! Don't you hear?	Jaquino, hörst du nicht?

JACQUINO
(calling)

I'm coming.	Ich komme schon!

(to Marcellina)

Just wait here, I'll be back with you in two minutes.	Bleib fein hier, in zwei Minuten sind wir weider beisammen.

Exit to the garden through the open door. Scene Two. Marcellina alone.

MARCELLINA

Poor Jacquino – I'm almost sorry for him. But can I do anything about it? I *was* quite fond of him, but then Fidelio came to live with us and since then every- thing's changed.	Der arme Jaquino dauert mich beinahe. Kann ich es aber ändern? Ich war ihm sonst recht gut, da kam Fidelio in unser Haus, und seit der Zeit ist alles in mir und um mich verändert. Ach!

She heaves a heavy sigh.

And just through feeling sorry for Jacquino I see now how fond I am of Fidelio. I think he's fond of me too, and if only I knew what my father thought, then perhaps my happiness would be complete.	Aus dem Mitleiden, das ich mit Jaquino habe, merke ich erst, wie sehr gut ich Fidelio bin. Ich glaube auch, dass Fidelio mir recht gut ist, und wenn ich die Gesinnungen des Vaters wüsste, so könnte vielleicht mein Glück bald vollkommen werden.

Aria No. 2

MARCELLINA [4]

Oh, were I now already wed, That husband I might call you. A girl may only half confess The secret of her feelings. Then I would never blush to own The kiss that makes you mine alone	O wär ich schon mit dir vereint Und dürfte Mann dich nennen! Ein Mädchen darf ja, was es meint, Zur Hälfte nur bekennen. Doch wenn ich nicht erröten muss, Ob einem warmen Herzenskuss

48

And tears were left behind me!	Wenn nichts uns stört auf Erden —
No words can tell the pure delight	[5] Die Hoffnung schon erfüllt die Brust,
That hope already brings in sight,	Mit unaussprechlich süsser Lust,
How happy love would find me.	Wie glücklich will ich werden!
Throughout our simple daily life,	In Ruhe stiller Häuslichkeit
With joy I'd face each morrow.	Erwach ich jeden Morgen,
For then the smiles of man and wife	Wir grüssen uns mit Zärtlichkeit,
Would banish ev'ry sorrow.	Der Fleiss verscheucht die Sorgen.
When all the work of day is done,	Und ist die Arbeit abgetan,
And night has veiled the setting sun	Dann schleicht die holde Nacht heran,
And he was close beside me,	Dann ruhn wir von Beschwerden.
No words can tell the pure delight	Die Hoffnung schon erfüllt die Brust
That hope already brings in sight	Mit unaussprechlich süsser Lust,
How happy love would find me.	Wie glücklich will ich werden!

Scene Three. *Marcellina, Rocco, Jacquino. Rocco comes out of the garden. Behind him Jacquino carries gardening tools, which he takes into Rocco's house.*

ROCCO

Good morning Marcellina. Is Fidelio not back yet?	Guten Tag, Marzelline. Ist Fidelio noch nicht zurückgekommen?

MARCELLINA

No, father.	Nein, Vater.

ROCCO

The time's coming for me to take to the governor the despatches that Fidelio's supposed to be bringing. I await him with impatience.	Die Stunde naht, wo ich dem Gouverneur die Briefschaften bringen muss, welche Fidelio abholen sollte. Ich erwarte ihn mit Ungeduld.

During these last words there was a knocking at the door.

JACQUINO
(coming out of Rocco's house)

I'm coming.	Ich komme schon!

(he runs officiously to open it)

MARCELLINA

He'll have had to wait such a long time at the blacksmith's.	Er wird gewiss so lange bei dem Schmied haben warten müssen.

Meanwhile she has seen Leonora come through the door. Gaily.

There he is!	Da ist er!

Scene Four. *The same, Leonora. Enter Leonora. She wears a dark jerkin, a red waistcoat, dark breeches, short boots, a broad belt of black leather with a copper buckle: her hair is worn in a net cap. On her back, she carries a box of provisions and in her arms are chains which she leaves at the porter's lodge as she enters; at her side hangs a metal tin on a cord.*

MARCELLINA
(running up to Leonora)

How he's loaded down! Dear God! The sweat's running down his brow.	Wie er belastet ist. Lieber Gott! Der Schweiss läuft ihm von der Stirn.

She takes her handkerchief and tries to wipe Leonora's brow.

ROCCO

Wait, wait.	Warte! Warte!

He helps Marcellina to take the box off Leonora's back and place it in the lefthand arcade.

JACQUINO
(aside, downstage)

Well, that was worth the bother of opening up so quickly to let the 'young master' in.	Es war auch der Mühe wert, so schnell aufzumachen, um den Patron da hereinzulassen.

He goes into his lodge but soon comes out as though about his business, yet really trying to keep an eye on Marcellina, Leonora and Rocco.

ROCCO
(to Leonora)

Poor Fidelio, this time you've loaded yourself up too much.	Armer Fidelio, diesmal hast du dir zuviel aufgeladen.

LEONORA
(coming forward and wiping her face)

I must confess I am a little tired. The smith took so long mending the fetters that I thought he'd never be done.	Ich muss gestehen, ich bin ein wenig ermüdet. Der Schmied hatte an den Ketten so lange auszubessern, dass ich glaubte, er würde nicht damit fertig werden.

ROCCO

Has he done them properly?	Sind sie jetzt gut gemacht?

LEONORA

Oh yes, they're good and strong. None of the prisoners will be able to break them now.	O gewiss, recht gut and stark. Keiner der Gefangenen wird sie zerbrechen.

ROCCO

And how much did all th ; cost?	Wieviel kostet alles zusammen?

LEONORA

About twelve piastres. Here is the detailed account.	Zwölf Piaster ungefähr. Hier ist die genaue Berechnung.

ROCCO
(checking the bill)

Good. Well done. Good heavens, there are things here we'll be able to get twice as much back on. You're a clever boy. I can't even understand how you do your reckoning. You buy everything more cheaply than I. In the six months since I've put you in charge of the stores you've made more than ever I did in a whole year.	Gut, brav! Zum Wetter! Da gibt's Artikel, auf denen wir wenigstens das Doppelte gewinnen können. Du bist ein kluger Junge! Ich kann gar nicht begreifen, wie du deine Rechnungen machst. Du kaufst alles wohlfeiler als ich. In den sechs Monaten, seit ich dir die Anschaffung der Lebensmittel übertrug, hast du mehr gewonnen als ich vorher in einem ganzen Jahr.

(aside)

The rascal's obviously going to all this trouble on account of my Marcellina.	Der Schelm gibt sich alle diese Mühe offenbar meiner Marzelline wegen.

LEONORA

I try to do what I can.	Ich suche zu tun, was mir möglich ist.

ROCCO

Yes, yes, you're a good lad, you couldn't be more zealous or prudent. I grow to like you more every day that passes and	Ja, ja, du bist brav, man kann nicht eifriger, nicht verständiger sein. Ich habe dich aber auch mit jedem Tage

– rest assured, your reward will not be slow.	lieber und — sei versichert, dein Lohn soll nicht ausbleiben.

During the last words, he glances from Leonora to Marcellina.

LEONORA
(disconcerted)

Don't think I do my duty just for reward . . .	O glaubt nicht, dass ich meine Schuldigkeit nur des Lohnes wegen —

ROCCO

Hush now!	Still!

(looking at them as before)

D'you think I can't see into your heart?	Meinst du, ich könnte dir nicht ins Herz sehen?

He appears to take pleasure in Leonora's increasing embarrassment and then goes to one side to examine the chains. / Quartet No. 3 [6]

MARCELLINA
(while Rocco considers Leonora approvingly, Marcellina watches and sings to herself)

Such strange delight is here,	[7] Mir ist so wunderbar,
My heart now weeps for me.	Es engt das Herz mir ein.
He loves me that is clear,	Er liebt mich, es ist klar,
How happy I shall be.	Ich werde glücklich sein.

LEONORA
(aside)

How great the danger here.	Wie gross ist die Gefahr,
Faint hope is left for me.	Wie schwach der Hoffnung Schein.
She loves me, that is clear,	Sie liebt mich, es ist klar,
How harsh and cruel fate can be.	O namenlose Pein!

ROCCO
(during the foregoing, Rocco comes downstage and sings to himself)

She loves him, that is clear,	Sie liebt ihn, es ist klar,
Her husband he shall be.	Ja Mädchen, er wird dein.
They'll make a handsome pair,	Ein gutes, junges Paar,
How happy they will be.	Sie werden glücklich sein.

JACQUINO
(watching them and moving closer and closer to the side, a little behind the others)

My heart is numb with fear,	Mir sträubt sich schon das Haar,
Her father's choice I see,	Der Vater willigt ein,
To me she's ever dear,	Mir wird so wunderbar;
What chance remains for me?	Mir fällt kein Mittel ein.

Jacquino returns to his lodge.

ROCCO

Listen Fidelio, even though I don't know where you come from or who your father was, I know what I'll do, I'm going to take you as my son-in-law.	Höre, Fidelio, wenn ich auch nicht weiss, wie und wo du auf die Welt gekommen bist, und wenn du auch gar keinen Vater gehabt hättest, so weiss ich doch, was ich tue - ich - ich mache dich zu meinem Tochtermann.

MARCELLINA
(quickly)

And will you do it soon, dear father?	Wirst du es bald tun, lieber Vater?

51

(laughing)

Ay ay, how eager!	Ei, ei, wie eilfertig!

(more seriously)

When the governor's gone to Seville we'll have more time. You know he has to go every month to give account of everything that happens in the prison. In a few days he'll be off again, and the day after his departure I'll see you married. You can eount on that.	Sobald der Gouverneur nach Sevilla gereist sein wird, dann haben wir mehr Musse. Ihr wisst ja, dass er alle Monate hingeht, um über alles, was hier in dem Staatsgefängnis vorfällt, Rechenschaft zu geben. In einigen Tagen muss er wieder fort, und den Tag nach seiner Abreise gebe ich euch zusammen. Darauf könnt ihr rechnen.

MARCELLINA

The day after his departure? That's very sensible, dear father.	Den Tag nach seiner Abreise? Das machst du vernünftig, lieber Vater.

LEONORA
(disconcerted, then cheerfully)

The day after his departure?	Den Tag nach seiner Abreise?

(aside)

Yet another complication!	O welche neue Verlegenheit!

ROCCO

So, my children, you really are in love with each other, aren't you? But that's not everything that's needed for a really solid and happy household; you also need . . .	Nun, meine Kinder, ihr habt euch doch recht herzlich lieb, nicht wahr? Aber das ist noch nicht alles, was zu einer guten, vergnügten Haushaltung gehört; man braucht auch –

He makes the gesture of counting money.| Aria No. 4

ROCCO

If you lack for gold, my children,	[8] Hat man nicht auch Gold beineben,
Then your home is full of care,	Kann man nicht ganz glücklich sein;
You will find that life is cheerless,	Traurig schleppt sich fort das Leben,
Gloomy days you both must share.	Mancher Kummer stellt sich ein.
But when in your pockets you jingle your gold,	Doch wenn's in den Taschen fein
You'll find what a fortune you're making,	[9] klingelt und rollt,
Then love and power and pleasure untold,	Da hält man das Schicksal gefangen,
Will always be yours for the taking!	Und Macht und Liebe verschafft dir das Gold
Good luck's a slave that's bought and sold,	Und stillet das kühnste Verlangen.
Oh what a glorious thing is gold.	Das Glück dient wie ein Knecht für Sold,
	Es ist ein schönes Ding, das Gold.
If your purse is always empty,	Wenn sich Nichts mit Nichts verbindet,
Then you'll never pay your way.	Ist und bleibt die Summe klein;
What's the use of love in plenty,	Wer bei Tisch nur Liebe findet,
When you're hungry ev'ry day?	Wird nach Tische hungrig sein.
May smiling good fortune its favours unfold,	Drum lächle der Zufall euch gnädig und hold,
And prosper your ev'ry endeavour,	Und segne und lenk' euer Streben;
Your sweetheart beside you, your purse full of gold,	Das Liebchen im Arme, im Beutel das Gold,
Then you could be happy for ever.	So mögt ihr viel Jahre durchleben.
Good luck's a slave that's bought and sold,	Das Glück dient wie ein Knecht für Sold,

Oh what a glorious thing is gold.

Es ist ein mächtig Ding, das Gold.

LEONORA

That's easily said, master Rocco, but I, I believe that the union of two hearts that feel alike is the source of true happiness.

Ihr könnt das leicht sagen, Meister Rocco, aber ich, ich behaupte, dass die Vereinigung zweier gleichgestimmter Herzen die Quelle des wahren ehelichen Glückes ist.

(warmly)

That happiness must be the greatest joy on earth!

O dieses Glück muss der grösste Schatz auf Erden sein!

(catching herself, and restraining herself)

Though I must admit there is something that would be hardly less precious to me, though I'm sad that in spite of all my efforts I am not going to win it.

Freilich gibt es noch etwas, was mir nicht weniger kostbar sein würde, aber mit Kummer sehe ich, dass ich es durch alle meine Bemühungen nicht erhalten werde.

ROCCO

And what might that be?

Und was wäre denn das?

LEONORA

Your trust! Forgive me this little reproach, but how often have I seen you coming up from the underground vaults of this fortress out of breath and exhausted. Why won't you let me go with you? I would like so much to help you with your work and be able to share your burden.

Euer Vertrauen! Verzeiht mir diesen kleinen Vorwurf, aber oft sehe ich Euch aus den unterirdischen Gewölben dieses Schlosses ganz ausser Atem und ermattet zurück kommen. Warum erlaubt Ihr mir nicht, Euch dahin zu begleiten? Es wäre mir so lieb, wenn ich Euch bei Eurer Arbeit helfen und Eure Beschwerden teilen könnte.

ROCCO

You know quite well I'm under strictest orders to let no one, whoever they may be, near the prisoners of state.

Du weisst doch, dass ich den strengsten Befehl habe, niemanden, wer es auch sein mag, zu den Staatsgefangenen zu lassen.

MARCELLINA

But there are far too many of them in this fortress. You're working yourself to death, father dear.

Es sind ihrer aber gar zu viele in dieser Festung. Du arbeitest dich ja zu Tode, lieber Vater.

LEONORA

She is right, master Rocco. Duty must be done;

Sie hat recht, Meister Rocco. Man soll allerdings seine Schuldigkeit tun;

(affectionately)

but sometimes we are allowed to think, surely, of sparing ourselves a little for those who love us and depend on us.

aber es ist doch auch erlaubt, mein ich, zuweilen daran zu denken, wie man sich für die, die uns angehören und lieben, ein bisschen schonen kann.

She presses his hand into hers.

MARCELLINA

(pressing Rocco's other hand to her breast)

Everyone has a duty to keep well for the sake of their children.

Man muss sich für seine Kinder zu erhalten suchen.

53

ROCCO
(looking at them both with emotion)

You're right, in the end this heavy task will be too much for me. However strict the Governor may be, he must let me take you with me to the secret dungeons.

Ja, ihr habt recht, diese schwere Arbeit würde mir doch endlich zuviel werden. Der Gouverneur ist zwar sehr streng, er muss mir aber doch erlauben, dich in die geheimen Kerker mit mir zu nehmen.

Leonora makes a violent gesture of joy.

And yet, there's *one* vault I'll never be allowed to show you, even though I can rely on you completely.

Indessen gibt es ein Gewölbe, in das ich dich wohl nie werde führen dürfen, obschon ich mich ganz auf dich verlassen kann.

MARCELLINA

That must be the one with the prisoner you've told us about so often?

Vermutlich, wo der Gefangene sitzt, von dem du schon einige Male gesprochen hast?

ROCCO

You have guessed.

Du hast's erraten.

LEONORA
(enquiring)

I suppose he's been imprisoned for a long time?

Ich glaube, es ist schon lange her, dass er gefangen ist?

ROCCO

More than two years.

Es ist schon über zwei Jahre.

LEONORA
(vehemently)

Two years, d'you say?

Zwei Jahre, sagt Ihr?

(catching herself)

He must be a dangerous criminal.

Er muss ein grosser Verbrecher sein.

ROCCO

Or he must have dangerous enemies. It comes to much the same thing.

Oder er muss grosse Feinde haben, das kommt ungefähr auf eins heraus.

MARCELLINA

Hasn't anyone been able to find out where he comes from or who he is?

So hat man denn nie erfahren können, woher er ist und wie er heisst?

ROCCO

He's often tried to talk about it.

O wie oft hat er mit mir von alledem reden wollen.

LEONORA

And?

Nun?

ROCCO

For people like us it's best to know as few secrets as possible. So I've never listened to him. I might have blabbered it out, and that wouldn't have helped him anyway.

Für unsereinen ist's aber am besten, so wenig Geheimnisse als möglich zu wissen, darum hab ich ihn auch nie angehört. Ich hätte mich verplappern können, und ihm hätte ich doch, nicht genützt.

(confidentially)

But he won't be a burden to me much longer. It can't last long now.

Nun, er wird mich nicht lange mehr quälen. Es kann nicht mehr lange mit ihm dauern.

54

(aside)

Oh God!   Grosser Gott!

MARCELLINA

Dear heaven, how can he have deserved   Lieber Himmel! Wie hat er denn eine so
so heavy a punishment?   schwere Strafe verdient?

ROCCO
(even more confidentially)

For a month now on Don Pizarro's   Seit einem Monat schon muss ich auf
orders I've been steadily reducing his   Pizarros Befehl seine Portion immer
rations. Now he has no more than two   kleiner machen. Jetzt hat er binnen
ounces of bread and a half measure of   vierundzwanzig Stunden nicht mehr als
water every twenty-four hours. No light   zwei Unzen schwarzes Brot und ein halb
save for a lamp, no straw, nothing . . . Mass Wasser; kein Licht als den Schein
                                          einer Lampe – kein Stroh mehr – nichts –

MARCELLINA

Father, don't take Fidelio down there, he   O lieber Vater, führe Fidelio ja nicht zu
couldn't bear the sight!   ihm! Diesen Anblick könnte er nicht
                                            ertragen.

LEONORA

Why not? I have both the strength and   Warum denn nicht? Ich habe Mut and
the courage!   Stärke!

ROCCO
(patting her on the shoulder)

Well spoken my boy, well spoken. I   Brav, mein Sohn, brav! Wenn ich dir
could tell you how I had to wrestle with erzählen wollte, wie ich anfangs in
my conscience when I started this job.   meinem Stande mit meinem Herzen zu
And I was quite a different sort of fellow kämpfen hatte! – Und ich war doch ein
from you, with your smooth skin and   ganz anderer Kerl als du mit deiner
your soft hands.   feinen Haut und deinen weichen Händen .

Trio No. 5

ROCCO

Well said, young man,   Gut, Söhnchen, gut,
But keep your head,   Hab' immer Mut,
In all that lies before you,   Dann wird dir's auch gelingen;
And steel your heart   Das Herz wird hart
When you are faced with sights   Durch Gegenwart
That may appall you.   Bei fürchterlichen Dingen.

LEONORA
(vigorously)

I'm brave and strong,   Ich habe Mut!
Without a qualm.   Mit kaltem Blut
I'll venture down below there,   Will ich hinab mich wagen;
For rich reward,   Für hohen Lohn
True love's prepared   [10] Kann Liebe schon
To suffer any torture.   Auch hohe Leiden tragen.

MARCELLINA
(affectionately)

Your kindly heart   Dein gutes Herz
May feel distressed   Wird manchen Schmerz
By what you there discover;   In diesen Grüften leiden;
But here above,   Dann kehrt zurück

Return to love
And all your joy recover!

Der liebe Glück
Und unnennbare Freuden.

ROCCO

Your dearest hopes will soon be granted.

Du wirst dein Glück ganz sicher bauen.

LEONORA

My trust in God and right is planted.

Ich hab auf Gott und Recht Vertrauen.

MARCELLINA

I know your heart will not be daunted,
The pow'r of Love is strong and sure.
Yes, a love that's strong and sure
Brings us joy for evermore.

Du darfst mir auch in's Auge schauen;
Der Liebe Macht ist auch nicht klein.
Ja, wir werden glücklich sein.

LEONORA

Yes, and yet may bring me joy.

Ja, ich kann noch glücklich sein.

ROCCO

Yes, a love that's strong and sure,
Brings us joy for evermore.
My lord himself today must tell me
That you may share my work with me.

Ja, ihr werdet glücklich sein.

Der Gouverneur soll heut' erlauben,
Dass du mit mir die Arbeit teilst.

LEONORA

Of peace of mind you will deprive me
If one more day's delay there be!

Du wirst mir alle Ruhe rauben,
Wenn du bis morgen nur verweilst.

MARCELLINA

Yes, father ask this very morning
Then we can wed without delay!

Ja, guter Vater, bitt' ihn heute,
In kurzem sind wir dann ein Paar.

ROCCO

I fear my strength at last is failing,
I need some help, yes, that is clear.

Ich bin ja bald des Grabes Beute,
Ich brauche Hilf', es ist ja wahr.

LEONORA
(aside)

For long I've borne this bitter torment. . .
Now Hope at last brings comfort here.

Wie lang bin ich des Kummers Beute!
[11] Du, Hoffnung, reichst mir Labung dar.

MARCELLINA
(affectionately to Rocco)

Beloved father, what's this you say?
You'll stay beside us for many a day.

Ach, lieber Vater, was fällt euch ein?
Lang Freund und Rater müsst ihr uns
sein.

ROCCO

If we take care, all will go well,
And fears to joy will soon be turning.

Nur auf der Hut, dann geht es gut,
Gestillt wird euer Sehnen.

MARCELLINA

Have no fear, when love is here,
What deep, mysterious yearning!

O habe Mut, o welche Glut!
O welch' ein tiefes Sehnen!

LEONORA

Kind words I hear, they calm my fear
And all my fevered yearning.

Ihr seid so gut, ihr macht mir Mut,
Gestillt wird bald mein Sehnen!

56

ROCCO

Come join your hands at love's

Command, tho' joyous tears be flowing.

Gebt euch die Hand, und schliesst das
Band
In süssen Freudentränen.

LEONORA
(aside)

I gave my hand at love's command
Tho' bitter tears were flowing.

Ich gab die Hand zum süssen Band,
[12] Es kostet bitt're Tränen.

MARCELLINA

A lasting bond with heart and hand
Tho' joyous tears be flowing!

Ein festes Band mit Herz und Hand!
O süsse, süsse Tränen!

ROCCO

Now it's time for me to take the despatches to the Governor.

Aber nun ist es Zeit, dass ich dem
Gouverneur die Briefschaften überbringe.

March No. 6
ROCCO

Ha! He's coming here himself!

Ah! Er kommt selbst hierher!

(to Leonora)

Give them to me Fidelio, and go.

Gib sie, Fidelio, und dann entfernt euch!

Leonora takes the tin box, gives it to Rocco, and goes into the house with Marcellina. During the march the main gate is opened from the outside by a sentry. Enter officers with a detachment, then Pizarro. The gate is shut behind him. **Scene Five.** *Pizarro. Officers. Watch.*

PIZARRO
(to the officers)

Three sentries to the ramparts, six
guards day and night on the drawbridge,
and as many by the postern. Anyone
seen approaching the moat to be brought
straight to me.

Drei Schildwachen auf den Wall! Sechs
Mann Tag und Nacht an die Zugbrücke,
ebenso viele gegen den Garten zu, und
jedermann, der sich dem Graben der
Festung nähert, werde sogleich vor mich
gebracht!

(to Rocco)

Any news?

Ist etwas Neues vorgefallen?

ROCCO

No sir.

Nein, Herr.

PIZARRO

Despatches?

Wo sind die Depeschen?

ROCCO
(takes the letters from the tin box)

Here they are.

Hier sind sie.

PIZARRO
(opens the papers and goes through them)

Character references, complaints. If I
took any notice of all this I'd never be
finished.

Immer Empfehlungen oder Vorwürfe.
Wenn ich auf alles das achten wollte,
würde ich nie damit zu Ende kommen.

(stopping at one letter)

What's this? I seem to know this hand

Was seh'ich? Mich dünkt, ich kenne diese
Schrift.

(opening the letter, and coming forward. Rocco and the Watch step back. He reads.)

'I herewith inform you that it has been

'Ich gebe Ihnen Nachricht, dass der

brought to the Minister's notice that in the State Prisons in your charge there are several victims of arbitrary exercise of power. He is setting out tomorrow for a surprise inspection. Be on your guard and see yourself safe.'

(disconcerted)

If he should discover that I have this Florestan lying in chains, him he thinks long since dead, this Florestan who sought to expose me to him, rob me of his favour . . . There is one remedy.

(briskly)

Decisive action can dispel all anxiety.

Minister in Erfahrung gebracht hat, dass die Staatsgefängnisse, denen Sie vorstehen, mehrere Opfer willkürlicher Gewalt enthalten. Er reist morgen ab, um Sie mit einer Untersuchung zu überraschen. Seien Sie auf Ihrer Hut und suchen Sie sich sicherzustellen.'

Ah, wenn er entdeckte, dass ich diesen Florestan in Ketten liegen habe, den er längst tot glaubt, ihn, der so oft meine Rache reizte, der mich vor dem Minister enthüllen und mir seine Gunst entziehen wollte. – Doch, es gibt ein Mittel!

Eine kühne Tat kann alle Besorgnisse zerstreuen!

Aria with Chorus No. 7 [13]

PIZARRO

Now, now the time has come,
My vengeance shall be sated.
Yes, fate demands his life,
I'll watch him die before me.
I'll stand no more delay,
Oh glorious, glorious day!
Remember how once he made me
The sport of men who hate me,
And then he brought me to disgrace,
Yet, here in chains he's languished,
The victor I have vanquished.
And in his dying torment
While he still writhes before me,
I'll shout into his ear
That I now triumph here.

[14] Ha! Welch' ein Augenblick!
Die Rache werd' ich kühlen,
Dich rufet dein Geschick!
In seinem Herzen wühlen,
O Wonne, grosses Glück!

Schon war ich nah' im Staube,
Dem lauten Spott zum Raube,
Dahin gestreckt zu sein.
Nun ist es mir geworden,
Den Mörder selbst zu morden.
In seiner letzten Stunde,
Den Stahl in seiner Wunde,
Ihm noch ins Ohr zu schrei'n:
Triumph! Der Sieg ist mein!

SENTRIES' CHORUS
(under their breath)

His mood portends some danger,
Our rounds we'd best continue,
Be careful, here's some affair of state.
His mood portends some danger,
Our rounds we'd best continue.
Here's some affair of state.
Be careful, watch out.

Er spricht von Tod und Wunde!
Nun fort auf uns're Runde!
Wie wichtig muss es sein!
Er spricht von Tod und Wunde!
Wacht scharf auf eurer Runde!
Wie wichtig muss es sein!

PIZARRO

Not a moment can I delay in making preparations for my plan. The Minister is expected today. Only the greatest care and speed can save me.

Ich darf keinen Augenblick säumen, alle Anstalten zu meinem Vorhaben zu treffen. Heute soll der Minister ankommen. Nur die grösste Vorsicht und Eile können mich retten.

(to the officer)

Captain! Listen.

Hauptmann! Hören Sie.

(leading him forward and speaking softly to him)

You are to climb tne tower with the trumpeter at once. Watch the road from Seville with the utmost vigilance. As soon as you see a coach with outriders

Besteigen Sie mit einem Trompeter sogleich den Turm. Sehen Sie unablässig und mit der grössten Achtsamkeit auf die Strasse von Sevilla. Sobald Sie einen

approaching, have the signal sounded immediately. D'you understand? Immediately. I expect complete obedience. You will answer for it with your head.

Wagen von Reitern begleitet erblicken, lassen Sie augenblicklich ein Zeichen geben. Verstehn Sie, augenblicklich! Ich erwarte die grösste Pünktlichkeit. Sie haften mir mit Ihrem Kopf dafür.

(The officer leaves. Pizarro addresses the soldiers on watch.)

Away to your posts.

Fort auf eure Posten!

(The soldiers leave. Pizarro to Rocco.)

Old man!

Alter!

ROCCO

Sir.

Herr!

PIZARRO

(to himself, as he examines Rocco closely)

I must try to win him to me. Without his help I cannot see it through.

Ich muss ihn zu gewinnen suchen. Ohne seine Hilfe kann ich es nicht ausführen.

(aloud)

Come here.

Komm näher!

Duet No. 8

PIZARRO

Now Rocco! This matter's urgent,
And fortune smiles upon you,
You'll be a wealthy man.

Jetzt, Alter, hat es Eile!
Dir wird ein Glück zu teile,
Du wirst ein reicher Mann;

(throwing him a purse)

I'll give you that for now.

Das geb' ich nur daran.

ROCCO

But, tell me, if you please sir,
What service must be done?

So sagt doch nur in Eile,
Womit ich dienen kann.

PIZARRO

A man like you is wanted
Your heart is still undaunted,
Time's harden'd you still further.

Du bist von kalten Blute,
Von unverzagtem Mute
Durch langen Dienst geworden.

ROCCO

My task sir, tell me.

Was soll ich? Redet!

PIZARRO

Murder!

[15]   Morden!

ROCCO

Sir?

Wie?

PIZARRO

Listen to my plan.
What's this? Are you a man?
This cannot wait till later,
The State itself may fall,
A plot we must forestall,
And kill a worthless traitor.

Höre mich nur an!
Du bebst? Bist du ein Mann?
Wir durfen gar nicht säumen;
Dem Staate liegt daran,
Den bösen Untertan
Schnell aus dem Weg zu räumen.

ROCCO

My lord!

O Herr!

PIZARRO

You understand?

Du stehst noch an?

(aside)

While Florestan is living	Er darf nicht länger leben,
My danger's all too plain	Sonst ist's um mich geschehn.
Pizarro dare you falter?	Pizarro sollte beben?
He dies and I remain.	Du fällst – ich werde stehn.

ROCCO

My hands are cold and trembling.	Die Glieder fühl' ich beben,
What fever wracks my brain?	Wie könnt ich das bestehn?
I will not kill this pris'ner,	Ich nehm' ihm nicht das Leben,
So come what may, that's plain.	Mag, was da will, geschehn.
To take a life, your lordship,	Nein, Herr, das Leben nehmen,
Is not my duty here.	Das ist nicht meine Pflicht.

PIZARRO

I'll see to that myself then	Ich will mich selbst bequemen,
If your own courage fails;	Wenn dir's an Mut gebricht;
Go down, delay no longer,	Nun eile rasch und munter
To him who lies below there,	Zu jenem Mann hinunter,
You know . . .	Du weisst . . .

ROCCO

. . . You mean to him	. . . Der kaum mehr lebt
Who lives a ling'ring death?	Und wie ein Schatten schwebt?

PIZARRO

(grimly)

To him! Go down to him,	Zu dem, zu dem hinab!
I'll wait there at a distance.	Ich wart' in kleiner Ferne,
Whilst down in that old cistern	Du gräbst in der Zisterne
You dig his grave.	Sehr schnell ein Grab.

ROCCO

And then? And then?	Und dann? Und dann?

PIZARRO

Then, hidden in my cloak,	Dann werd' ich selbst, vermummt,
I'll steal into the dungeon.	Mich in den Kerker schleichen:
One thrust . . .	Ein Stoss . . .

(he shows the dagger)

. . . and he's no more!	. . . und er verstummt!

ROCCO

(aside)

Both starved and bound in fetters,	Verhungernd in den Ketten
For long he's known such pain,	Ertrug er lange Pein,
That knife will surely save him,	Ihn toten, heisst ihn retten,
And set him free again.	Der Dolch wird ihn befrei'n.

PIZARRO

(aside)

He'll die where he lies fettered,	Er sterb' in seinen Ketten,
Too short was all his pain,	Zu kurz war seine Pein!
Until he's dead and buried,	Sein Tod nur kann mich retten,
My peace I'll never gain.	Dann werd' ich ruhig sein.

Now, Rocco, this matter's urgent!	Jetzt, Alter, jetzt hat es Eile!
Do you understand me?	Hast du mich verstanden?
You'll give a signal	Du gibst ein Zeichen!
Then, hidden in my cloak	Dann werd ich selbst, vermummt,

| I'll steal into the dungeon. | Mich in den Kerker schleichen; |
| One thrust and he's no more! | Ein Stoss – und er verstummt! |

ROCCO

Both starved and bound in fetters	Verhungernd in den Ketten
For long he's known such pain,	Ertrug er lange Pein,
The knife would surely save him,	Ihn töten, heisst ihn retten,
And set him free again.	Der Dolch wird ihn befrei'n.

PIZARRO

He dies where he lies fettered,	Er sterb' in seinen Ketten,
Too short was all his pain,	Zu kurz war seine Pein!
Until he's dead and buried	Sein Tod nur kann mich retten,
My peace I'll never gain.	Dann werd' ich ruhig sein.

Exit to garden. Rocco follows him. **Scene Six.** */Recitative and Aria No. 9*

LEONORA

(in a state of violent emotion)

Perfidious wretch! Where do you haste?	Abscheulicher! Wo eilst du hin?
What evil plan now stirs within you?	Was hast du vor in wildem Grimme?
Compassion's voice, or human feelings	Des Mitleids Ruf, der Menschheit Stimme,
Can nothing move your tiger's heart?	Rührt nichts mehr deinen Tigersinn?

Yet though the storm of anger rages	Doch toben auch wie Meereswogen
Deep in that savage breast of yours,	Dir in der Seele Zorn und Wut,
For me a distant rainbow shimmers,	So leuchtet mir ein Farbenbogen,
Serene against the stormy flood.	Der hell auf dunklen Wolken ruht:
It brings me peace, my fears are banished,	Der blickt so still, so friedlich nieder,
It wakens memories long vanished,	Der spiegelt alte Zeiten wieder,
And calmer flows my fevered blood.	Und neu besänftigt wallt mein Blut.

Sweet hope, oh never let your star,	[16] Komm, Hoffnung, lass den letzten Stern
Your last faint star of comfort be denied me.	Der Müden nicht erbleichen!
Oh come, shine forth and light my path, tho'it be long and far,	Erhell mein Ziel, sei's noch so fern,
For love will surely guide me.	Die Liebe wird's erreichen.

Some inner voice now calls me.	Ich folg' dem innern Triebe,
I'll show no fear,	Ich wanke nicht,
My path lies here,	Mich stärkt die Pflicht
My faithful heart shall guide me.	Der treuen Gattenliebe!

Oh you for whom I've borne the past,	O du, für den ich alles trug,
Could I but come to find you.	Könnt' ich zur Stelle dringen,
Where savage hate still chains you fast,	Wo Bosheit dich in Fesseln schlug,
Some word of hope to bring you!	Und süssen Trost dir bringen!

Some inner voice now calls me.	Ich folg' dem innern Triebe,
I'll show no fear,	Ich wanke nicht,
My path lies here,	Mich stärkt die Pflicht
My faithful heart shall guide me.	Der treuen Gattenliebe!

Exit to garden. **Scene Seven.** *Marcellina comes out of the house. Jacquino follows her.*

JACQUINO

| But Marcellina . . . | Aber, Marzelline – |

61

MARCELLINA

Not a word, not a syllable. I won't have any more of your silly sighs, and that's that.

Kein Wort, keine Silbe. Ich will nichts mehr von deinen albernen Liebesseufzern hören, und dabei bleibt es.

JACQUINO

Who could have foretold that when I decided to fall in love with you? In those days, yes, I was the good, kind Jacquino, here, there and everywhere, the one who had to put your iron on the stove, fold the linen for you, take parcels to the prisoners, in short do everything that a respectable girl could require of a respectable boy. But since this Fidelio . . .

Wer mir das vorher gesagt hätte, als ich mir vornahm, mich recht ordentlich in dich zu verlieben. Damals, ja da war ich der gute, der liebe Jaquino an allen Orten und Ecken. Ich musste dir das Eisen in den Ofen legen, Wäsche in Falten schlagen, Päckchen zu den Gefangenen bringen, kurz alles tun, was ein ehrbares Mädchen einem ehrbaren Junggesellen erlauben kann. Aber seit dieser Fidelio –

MARCELLINA
(quickly breaking in)

I won't deny that I was fond of you, but look, I'll be honest with you, that wasn't love. Fidelio attracts me much more, and between him and me I feel a much greater understanding.

Ich leugne nicht, ich war dir gut, aber sieh, ich bin offenherzig, das war keine Liebe. Fidelio zieht mich weit mehr an, zwischen ihm und mir fühle ich eine weit grössere Übereinstimmung.

JACQUINO

What? Understanding with some vagrant boy from God knows where, who your father found at the gate and took in out of sheer pity, who . . . who . . .

Was? Übereinstimmung mit einem solchen hergelaufenen Jungen, der Gott weiss woher ist, den der Vater aus blossem Mitleid am Tor dort aufgenommen hat, der – der –

MARCELLINA
(irritably)

Who's poor and abandoned . . . and who I'm going to marry.

Der arm and verlassen ist – und den ich doch heirate.

JACQUINO

D'you think I'm going to allow that? To stop that happening under my eyes, watch out that I don't cause trouble!

Glaubst du, dass ich das leiden werde? He, däss es ja nicht in meiner Gegenwart geschieht, ich möchte euch einen gewaltigen Streich spielen!

Scene Eight. *The same. Rocco, Leonora come from the garden.*

ROCCO

What are you two quarrelling about?

Was habt ihr denn beide wieder zu zanken?

MARCELLINA

Oh father, he's always nagging at me.

Ach, Vater, er verfolgt mich immer.

ROCCO

Why's that?

Warum denn?

MARCELLINA

He wants me to love him, says I've got to marry him.

Er will, dass ich ihn lieben, dass ich ihn heiraten soll.

JACQUINO

Yes, yes, she must love me, must at least

Ja, ja, sie soll mich lieben, sie soll mich

marry me, and I . . .   wenigstens heiraten, und ich –

ROCCO

What? Have I cared so well for my only   Was? Ich sollte eine einzige Tochter so
daughter,   gut gepflegt
(patting Marcellina on the cheek)
gone to so much trouble raising her 'til   mit so viel Mühe bis in ihr sechzehntes
she's sixteen, all that for the gentleman   Jahr erzogen haben, und das alles für
there?   den Herrn da?
(looking laughingly at Jacquino)
No Jacquino, marriage with you is out of   Nein, Jaquino, von deiner Heirat ist jetzt
the question; my mind is occupied with   keine Rede, mich beschäftigen andere,
other, more propitious prospects.   klügere Absichten.

MARCELLINA

I understand, father.   Ich verstehe, Vater.
(tenderly and softly)
Fidelio!   Fidelio!

LEONORA

Enough of that for now. Rocco, you   Brechen wir davon ab. – Rocco, ich
know I've asked you before to allow the   ersuchte Euch schon einige Male, die
poor prisoners who live at ground level   armen Gefangenen, die hier über der
out into the castle garden. You've always   Erde wohnen, in unsern Festungsgarten
promised but then put it off. Today the   zu lassen. Ihr verspracht und verschobt
weather is so fine, and the Governor   es immer. Heute ist das Wetter so
doesn't come here at this time.   schön, der Gouverneur kommt um diese
                                             Zeit nicht hierher.

MARCELLINA

Oh yes, I agree with him.   O ja! Ich bitte mit ihm!

ROCCO

Children, without the Governor's   Kinder, ohne Erlaubnis des
permission?   Gouverneurs?

MARCELLINA

He spoke with you for such a long time.   Aber er sprach so lange mit Euch.
Perhaps he had some special request for   Vielleicht sollt Ihr ihm einen Gefallen
you, and so he won't be so strict.   tun, und dann wird er es so genau nicht
                                             nehmen.

ROCCO

A special request? You're right   Einen Gefallen? Du hast recht,
Marcellina, because of that I can risk it.   Marzelline. Auf diese Gefahr hin kann
Right then, Jacquino and Fidelio, open   ich es wagen. Wohl denn, Jaquino and
the upper cells. Meanwhile I'll go to   Fidelio, öffnet die leichteren Gefängnisse.
Pizarro and occupy him, while I   Ich aber gehe zu Pizarro und halte ihn
                                             zurück, indem ich
(to Marcellina)
speak to him on your behalf.   für dein Bestes rede.

MARCELLINA
(presses his hand)
That's right, father.   So recht, Vater.

Rocco goes into the garden. Leonora and Jacquino open the heavily-secured cell doors and withdraw with Marcellina into the background to watch sympathetically as the prisoners gradually emerge. **Scene Nine.** *Finale No. 10 | During the prelude, the prisoners gradually fill the stage.*

63

Oh what delight! To breathe the air,	O welche Lust! in freier Luft
The open air around us.	Den Atem leicht zu heben!
Here light still comes to greet us;	Nur hier, nur hier ist Leben,
This dungeon is a tomb.	Der Kerker eine Gruft.

A PRISONER [18]

We trust for our deliv'rance	Wir wollen mit Vertrauen
In Heaven's help and guidance,	Auf Gottes Hilfe bauen.
The voice of hope still whispers here	Die Hoffnung flüstert sanft mir zu:
We shall be freed, we shall find peace.	Wir werden frei, wir finden Ruh!

THE OTHERS

Deliv'rance! Rescue! Glorious dream!	O Himmel! Rettung! Welch' ein Glück!
Oh freedom, will you be ours once again?	O Freiheit! Kehrest du zuruck?

An officer appears on the wall and then withdraws.

SECOND PRISONER

Speak softly, guard your ev'ry word	Sprecht leise! haltet euch zuruck!
For we're both watch'd and overheard.	Wir sind belauscht mit Ohr und Blick.

CHORUS

(Speak softly) guard your ev'ry word (Have a care),	Sprecht leise, haltet euch zurück!
For we're both watch'd and overheard.	Wir sind belauscht mit Ohr und Blick.
Oh what delight! To breathe the air	Sprecht leise, ja leise!
The open air around us.	O welche Lust! In freier Luft
Here life still comes to greet us.	Den Atem leicht zu heben! O welche Lust!
	Nur hier, nur hier ist Leben.
(Speak softly) guard your ev'ry word (Have a care),	Sprecht leise, haltet euch zurück!
For we're both watch'd and overheard.	Wir sind belauscht mit Ohr und Blick.

Before the Chorus has quite finished, Rocco enters at the back of the stage and talks urgently to Leonora. The prisoners move away into the garden. Marcellina and Jacquino follow them. Rocco and Leonora come forward. **Scene Ten.**/*Recitative*

LEONORA

Tell me, what news?	Nun sprecht, wie ging's?

ROCCO

So far, so good.	Recht gut, recht gut!
I tried to do the best I could,	Zusammen rafft' ich meinen Mut
I told him of our plans,	Und trug ihm alles vor;
And all we'd hoped for,	Und sollt'st du's glauben,
And you shall hear what he replied.	Was er zur Antwort mir gab?
Your marriage was quickly approved and from this morning,	Die Heirat und dass du mir hilfst, will er erlauben,
You'll come to help me in the dungeons by my side.	Noch heute führ ich in die Kerker dich hinab.

Duet

LEONORA

This morning? this morning?	Noch heute, noch heute?
Oh happy day, what glorious tidings.	O welch ein Glück, o welche Wonne!

ROCCO

I see that gives you pleasure,	Ich sehe deine Freude;
In just a moment now,	Nur noch ein Augenblick,
We'll both go down together.	dann gehen wir schon beide –

64

LEONORA

Go down, to where? Wohin?

ROCCO

Down to that man below, Zu jenem Mann hinab,
For many weeks I've starved him Dem ich seit vielen Wochen
And giv'n him less to eat each day. Stets weniger zu essen gab.

LEONORA

Ah! Have they now reprieved him? Ha! Wird er losgesprochen?

ROCCO

Oh no! O nein!

LEONORA

What then? Come say! So sprich!

ROCCO

Alas, no, no! O nein!
(mysteriously)
We'll set him free, but how? Take care . . . Wir müssen ihn, doch wie? – befrei'n.
In just an hour, no longer, Er muss in einer Stunde –
(No word of this remember) Den Finger auf dem Munde –
We must inter him there! Von uns begraben sein.

LEONORA

Then he is dead? So ist er tot?

ROCCO

Not yet, not yet! Noch nicht, noch nicht!

LEONORA
(recoiling)
And then to kill him, is your task? Ist ihn zu töten deine Pflicht?

ROCCO

No. My good lad, you need not fear, Nein, guter Junge, zittre nicht!
For murder's not for Rocco here. Zum Morden dingt sich Rocco nicht.
My lord himself will be at hand; Der Gouverneur kommt selbst hinab;
We do but dig the grave, he's planned. Wir beide graben nur das Grab.

LEONORA
(aside)
Perhaps the grave of my own husband, Vielleicht das Grab des Gatten graben?
What more frightful could there be? O was kann fürchterlicher sein!

ROCCO

I could not give him food or water. Ich darf ihn nicht mit Speise laben,
The grave at least will bring him peace. Ihm wird im Grabe besser sein!
No time to waste, we must get ready, [19] Wir müssen gleich zum Werke schreiten;
I'll need your help, keep calm and steady, Du musst mir helfen, mich begleiten;
Hard is the jailer's gloomy task. Hart ist des Kerkersmeisters Brot.

LEONORA

I'll follow you, do all you ask. Ich folge dir, wär's in den Tod.

ROCCO

The ruined well will serve our purpose In der zerfallenen Zisterne
It won't take long as you will see. Bereiten wir die Grube leicht.
Believe me, I don't like this bus'ness Ich tu'es, glaube mir, nicht gerne

| You are too troubled, seems to me! | Auch dir ist schaurig, wie mich deucht. |

LEONORA

| I've not done work like this before. | Ich bin es nur noch nicht gewohnt. |

ROCCO

I would have spared you this, be sure,	Ich hätte gerne dich verschont,
But it's too much for me alone	Doch wird es mir allein zu schwer,
My lord's impatient to be done.	Und gar so streng ist unser Herr.

LEONORA
(aside)

| My heart will break – | O welch ein Schmerz! |

ROCCO
(aside)

| I fear he's weeping. | Mir scheint, er weint. |

(aloud)

| No, you stay here, I shall not need you. | Nein, du bleibst hier, ich geh alleine, |
| I'll go alone. | ich geh allein. |

LEONORA
(earnestly pressing herself upon him)

No, let me go,	O nein, O nein!
For I must see that pris'ner	Ich muss ihn seh'n, den Armen sehen.
(Although my life should be in danger,	Und müsst' ich selbst zu Grunde gehn!
Tho' I myself should die down there.)	

ROCCO AND LEONORA

| No more delay, what may befall | O säumen wir nun länger nicht, |
| We'll answer duty's fearful call. | Wir folgen unserer strengen Pflicht. |

Scene Eleven. *Jacquino and Marcellina hurry in breathlessly.*

MARCELLINA [20]

| Oh father dear! | Ach! Vater, eilt! |

ROCCO

| Now what is wrong? | Was hast du denn? |

JACQUINO

| Do not delay! | Nicht länger weilt! |

ROCCO

| What's gone amiss? | Was ist geschehn? |

MARCELLINA

| Pizarro's coming round this way. | Voll Zorn folgt mir Pizarro nach! |
| He's threat'ning you! | Er drohet dir! |

JACQUINO

| Do not delay! | Nicht länger weilt! |

ROCCO

| Be calm, be calm! | Gemach! gemach! |

LEONORA

| Get out of sight! | So eilet fort! |

ROCCO

| Just let me know, | Nur noch dies Wort: |
| Say has he heard? | Sprich, weiss er schon? |

66

JACQUINO

Yes, of course he's heard.	Ja, er weiss es schon.

MARCELLINA

Somebody said to him that we'd	Der Offizier sagt' ihm, was wir
Let all the prisoners come out of here.	Jetzt den Gefangenen gewähren.

ROCCO

Well, let them all go back at once, then!	Lasst alle schnell zurücke kehren!

Exit Jacquino to garden.

MARCELLINA

Remember how he rages,	Ihr wisst ja, wie er tobet,
You know his angry mood.	Und kennet seine Wut.

She goes after Jacquino.

LEONORA
(aside)

My heart within me rages	Wie mir's im Innern tobet!
And will not be subdued!	Emporet ist mein Blut!

ROCCO
(aside)

My conscience reassures me,	Mein Herz hat mich gelobet,
Despite the tyrant's mood.	Sei der Tyrann in Wut!

Scene Twelve. *Enter Pizarro.*

PIZARRO [21]

Presumptuous scoundrel, do you dare commit	Verwegner Alter, welche Rechte
Such an outrage as I see?	Legst du dir frevelnd selber bei?
What servant ever had permission	Und ziemt es dem gedungnen Knechte,
To let the prisoners go free?	Zu geben die Gefangenen frei?

ROCCO
(in confusion)

Good sir.	O Herr!

PIZARRO

Speak up!	Wohlan!

ROCCO
(looking for an excuse)

The sun is shining	Des Frühlings Kommen,
The Spring begins to smile again,	Das heitre warme Sonnenlicht,
And . . .	Dann . . .

(composing himself)

. . . Have you realised what further	. . . Habt ihr wohl in Acht genommen,
Speaks in my favour here today?	Was sonst zu meinem Vorteil spricht?

(taking his cap off)

Our Sov'reign's name-day, we are keeping,	Des Königs Namensfest ist heute,
We honour him like this each year.	Das feiern wir auf solche Art.

(quietly to Pizarro)

Death waits below, so let these others here,	Der unten stirbt – doch lasst die andern
Take the air a moment longer.	Jetzt fröhlich hin und wieder wandern;
Let all your anger fall on him.	Fur *jenen* sei der Zorn gespart!

67

PIZARRO
(softly)

Go dig his grave, your task is urgent,	So eile, ihm sein Grab zu graben,
Here I will have both peace and quiet.	Hier will ich stille Ruhe haben.
Back to their cells with all these men.	Schliess die Gefangenen wieder ein,
Never dare disobey again.	Mögst du nie mehr verwegen sein!

THE PRISONERS
(coming back from the garden) [22]

Farewell to spring and heaven's light,	Leb wohl, du warmes Sonnenlicht,
Joys all too soon denied us.	Schnell schwindest du uns wieder!
Once more the gloom will hide us,	Schon sinkt die Nacht hernieder,
Our days are but eternal night.	Aus der so bald kein Morgen bricht.

MARCELLINA
(watching the prisoners)

We led them forth to heaven's light,	Wie eilten sie zum Sonnenlicht,
And now they all must leave us.	Und scheiden traurig wieder!

(aside)

Here danger hovers round us	Die Andern murmeln nieder,
And joy gives way to cheerless night.	Hier wohnt die Lust, die Freude nicht!

LEONORA
(to the prisoners)

No more delay, you heard aright	Ihr hört das Wort, drum zögert nicht,
Go back into your dungeons!	Kehrt in den Kerker wieder!

(aside)

Where can we look for justice	Angst rinnt durch meine Glieder.
To shame this tyrant in men's sight?	Ereilt den Frevler kein Gericht?

JACQUINO
(to the prisoners)

No more delay, you heard aright,	Ihr hört das Wort, drum zögert nicht,
Go back into your dungeons.	Kehrt in den Kerker wieder.

(aside, watching Rocco and Leonora)

They're plotting something serious,	Sie sinnen auf und nieder!
I'd like to know what it's about!	Könnt' ich verstehn, was jeder spricht!

PIZARRO

Now Rocco, quick get out of sight	Nun, Rocco, zögre länger nicht,
You know what lies before us!	Steig in den Kerker nieder.

(softly)

You must not dare come back here,	Nicht eher kehrst du wieder,
Stay down there, until I've put this wrong to right.	Bis ich vollzogen das Gericht.

ROCCO

My lord, I'll work with all my might,	Nein, Herr, ich zögre länger nicht,
Yes, I'll obey your orders.	Ich steige eilend nieder.

(aside)

Hard is the task before us,	Mir beben meine Glieder;
My limbs are cold and numb with fright.	O unglückselig harte Pflicht!

The prisoners return to their cells, which Leonora and Jacquino lock behind them.

Engraving of the Second Act of 'Fidelio' by V.R. Grüner, from the 'Wiener Hoftheater-Taschenbuch' of 1815. (National Library, Vienna) Below: the same scene in the ENO production with Neil Howlett (Pizarro), Josephine Barstow (Leonora) and Alberto Remedios (Florestan) (photo: Andrew March)

Act Two

A dark subterranean dungeon. Left, a well covered with stones and rubble. In the background are several openings in the wall, covered by grilles, through which a flight of steps leading upwards is visible. On the right is the last step and the door to the cell. A lamp is burning.

Scene One. *Florestan sits on a stone, his body chained by a long fetter to the wall. | Orchestral prelude and Aria No. 11*

FLORESTAN [23]

God! What endless night! What grim, foreboding silence!	Gott! welch' Dunkel hier! O grauenvolle Stille.
Naught stirs within these walls. Naught lives down here but me.	Od' ist es um mich her: nichts lebet ausser mir.
How harsh this trial! Yet Thy will, oh God, is righteous.	O schwere Prüfung! – Doch gerecht ist Gottes Wille!
I'll not complain. What I must suffer, [24] lies with Thee.	Ich murre nicht! Das Mass der Leiden steht bei dir.

In the Spring of life's young morning [25]	In des Lebens Frühlingstagen
All my joy departed!	Ist das Glück von mir geflohn!
Words of truth I bravely uttered,	Wahrheit wagt' ich kühn zu sagen,
And these chains are my reward.	Und die Ketten sind mein Lohn.
I will bear my grief with patience	Willig duld' ich alle Schmerzen,
Die in shame when my course has run.	Ende schmählich meine Bahn;
Yet my heart can still find solace,	Süsser Trost in meinem Herzen:
For my duty I have done.	Meine Pflicht hab' ich getan!

(in rapture, bordering on delirium) [26]

What gentle soft breezes around me now play?	Und spür' ich nicht linde, sanft säuselnde Luft?
What brightens my grave with such splendour?	Und ist nicht mein Grab mir erhellet?
I see there an angel in roseate array,	Ich seh', wie ein Engel im rosigen Duft
Her glances are gentle and tender . . .	Sich tröstend zur Seite mir stellet,
An angel who resembles Leonora, the wife whom I love,	Ein Engel, Leonoren, der Gattin, so gleich,
Who leads me to freedom in heaven above.	Der führt mich zur Freiheit ins himmlische Reich.

He drops, exhausted, on the boulder, covering his face in his hands.

Scene Two. *Rocco and Leonora are seen climbing down the steps by the light of a lantern, carrying a jug and digging tools for the grave. The door at the back opens, and the stage is partly lit. | Melodrama and Duet No. 12*

Melodrama
LEONORA
(sotto voce)

How cold it is in this underground vault.	Wie kalt ist es in diesem unterirdischen Gewölbe!

ROCCO

Of course it is – it's so deep.	Das ist natürlich, es ist ja so tief.

LEONORA
(glancing uneasily around)

I thought we'd never even find the entrance.	Ich glaubte schon, wir würden den Eingang gar nicht finden.

70

ROCCO
(hurrying towards Florestan)

There he is.	Da ist er.

LEONORA
(haltingly, trying to recognise the prisoner)

He doesn't even seem to move . . .	Er scheint ganz ohne Bewegung.

ROCCO

Perhaps he's dead.	Vielleicht ist er tot.

LEONORA
(shuddering)

D'you think so?	Ihr meint es?

Florestan moves.

ROCCO

No, no he's asleep. We must take advantage of that. There's no time to lose.	Nein, nein, er schläft. – Das müssen wir benutzen und gleich ans Werk gehen; wir haben keine Zeit zu verlieren.

LEONORA
(aside)

I can't see his face. God stand by me if it is him.	Es ist unmöglich, seine Züge zu unterscheiden. – Gott steh' mir bei, wenn er es ist!

ROCCO
(puts his lamp down on the rubble)

Here, under this rubble, is the cistern I told you about. We won't need to dig much to find the opening. Give me a pick-axe, and stand there.	Hier, unter diesen Trümmern ist die Zisterne, von der ich dir gesagt habe. – Wir brauchen nicht viel zu graben, um an die Öffnung zu kommen. Gib mir eine Haue, und du, stelle dich hierher.

He climbs into the hole up to his waist, sets down the jug and places his bunch of keys beside him. Leonora stands on the edge and hands him the pick.

You're trembling. Are you afraid?	Du zitterst, fürchtest du dich?

LEONORA
(speaking firmly)

No, it's just that it's so cold.	O nein, es ist nur so kalt.

ROCCO
(briskly)

Get on with it then, the work will warm you up.	So mache fort, im Arbeiten wird dir schon warm werden.

As the duet begins, Rocco starts digging; when he bends down Leonora watches the prisoner. The duet is sung sotto voce throughout. / Duet [27]

ROCCO
(under his breath, as he works)

We must be quick, don't waste a moment.	Nur hurtig fort, nur frisch gegraben,
My lord himself will soon be here.	Es währt nicht lang, er kommt herein.

LEONORA
(also working)

You'll have no reason for complaining I'll do my best, so have no fear.	Ihr sollt ja nicht zu klagen haben, Ihr sollt gewiss zufrieden sein.

ROCCO

(jacking up a large stone)

Come on. Let's see if we can shift it.	Komm, hilf doch diesen Stein mir heben!
Take care. Take care. It's no light weight.	Hab Acht! Hab Acht! Er hat Gewicht.

LEONORA

(helping to lift it)

I'll take this end, keep it straight,	Ich helfe schon, sorgt Euch nicht;
I'll hold it fast so you can lift it.	Ich will mir alle Mühe geben.

ROCCO

A fraction more!	Ein wenig noch!

LEONORA

Hold on!	Geduld!

ROCCO

It's moved!	Er weicht!

LEONORA

We'll make quite sure!	Nur etwas noch!
It's free at last.	

ROCCO

It's no light weight!	Er ist nicht leicht!

They let the stone roll over the rubble while they catch their breath.

ROCCO

(returning to work)

We must be quick, don't waste a moment,	Nur hurtig fort, nur frisch gegraben,
My lord himself will soon be here.	Es währt nicht lang, er kommt herein.

LEONORA

(also beginning to work again)

Let me but gather strength I beg you.	Lasst mich nur wieder Kräfte haben,
We'll soon be done, the end is near.	Wir werden bald zu Ende sein.

(trying to watch the prisoner; aside)

Who you may be, I'm here to save you,	Wer du auch seist, ich will dich retten,
I vow you shall not perish here!	Bei Gott, du sollst kein Opfer sein!
No more shall cruel chains enslave you,	Gewiss, ich löse deine Ketten,
You shall be rescued, that I swear.	Ich will, du Armer, dich befrei'n.

ROCCO

(suddenly straightening up)

Why this delay, what's this I see?	Was zauderst du in deiner Pflicht?

LEONORA

(setting to work again)

No, father, no, I'll not delay, come bear with me.	Nein, Vater, nein, ich zaudre nicht.

ROCCO

Come waste no more time, take care,	Nur hurtig fort, nur frisch gegraben,
My lord himself will soon be here.	Es währt nicht lang, so kommt er her.

LEONORA

You'll have no reason for complaining.	Ihr sollt ja nicht zu klagen haben,
Let me but gather strength, I beg you.	Lasst mich nur wieder Kräfte haben,
No work will be too hard for me	Denn mir wird keine Arbeit schwer.
Father, I'll not fail you, have no fear!	

Rocco drinks. Florestan comes round and raises his head without turning towards Leonora.

LEONORA

He's waking!

Er erwacht!

ROCCO
(suddenly stopping drinking)

Waking, is he?

Er erwacht, sagst du?

LEONORA
(in great confusion, looking at Florestan)

Yes, he's just raised his head.

Ja, er hat eben den Kopf in die Höhe
gehoben.

ROCCO

No doubt he'll start asking all those
questions again. I must speak with him
at once. He'll soon be dead.

Ohne Zweifel wird er wieder tausend
Fragen an mich stellen. Ich muss allein
mit ihm reden. Nun hat er es bald
überstanden.

He climbs out of the grave.

You get down there instead and clear as
much away as we need to find the
opening to the cistern.

Steig du statt meiner hinab und räume
noch so viel weg, dass man die Zisterne
öffnen kann.

LEONORA
(goes down a few steps, shivering)

There are no words for what is going
through my mind.

Was in mir vorgeht, ist unaussprechlich!

ROCCO
(pauses slightly, then to Florestan)

Well, have you rested a little?

Nun, Ihr habt wieder einige Augenblicke
geruht?

FLORESTAN

Rested? How could I find rest?

Geruht? Wie fände ich Ruhe?

LEONORA
(aside)

That voice! If only I could see his face,
just for an instant.

Diese Stimme! – Wenn ich nur einen
Augenblick sein Gesicht sehen könnte.

FLORESTAN

Will you always be deaf to my pleas, you
heartless man?

Werdet Ihr immer bei meinen Klagen
taub sein, grausamer Mann?

(looking towards Leonora as he speaks the last words)

LEONORA
(aside)

God! It is him.

Gott! Er ist's!

She falls unconscious on the edge of the grave.

ROCCO

What do you want of me? I carry out the
orders I get. That is my job and my
duty.

Was verlangt Ihr denn von mir? Ich
vollziehe die Befehle, die man mir gibt;
das ist mein Amt, meine Pflicht.

FLORESTAN

Tell me at least, who is the Governor of
this prison?

Sagt mir endlich einmal, wer ist
Gouverneur dieses Gefängnisses?

73

(aside)

It can't do any harm now.　　　　　　　Jetzt kann ich ihm ja ohne Gefahr
　　　　　　　　　　　　　　　　　　genugtun.

(to Florestan)

The Governor of this prison is Don　　Der Gouverneur diese Gefängnisses ist
Pizarro.　　　　　　　　　　　　　　Don Pizarro.

FLORESTAN

Pizarro!　　　　　　　　　　　　　Pizarro!

LEONORA
(recovering gradually)

Monster! Your cruelty restores my　　O Barbar! Deine Grausamkeit gibt mir
strength.　　　　　　　　　　　　　meine Kräfte wieder.

FLORESTAN

Send as soon as possible to Seville, ask　　O schickt so bald als möglich nach Sevilla,
for Leonora Florestan . . .　　　　　　fragt nach Leonore Florestan –

LEONORA

Dear God! He has no idea that even now　　Gott! Er ahnt nicht, dass sie jetzt sein
she is digging his grave!　　　　　　Grab gräbt!

FLORESTAN

Let her know that I am lying here in　　Sagt ihr, dass ich hier in Ketten liege.
chains.

ROCCO

That's not possible, I tell you. I'd　　Es ist unmöglich, sag ich Euch. Ich
destroy myself without having helped you.　　würde mich ins Verderben stürzen, ohne
　　　　　　　　　　　　　　　　　　Euch genützt zu haben.

FLORESTAN

Then if I'm fated to end my life here, at　　Wenn ich denn verdammt bin, hier mein
least don't let me waste slowly away.　　Leben zu enden, o so lasst mich nicht
　　　　　　　　　　　　　　　　　　langsam verschmachten.

LEONORA
(jumping up and leaning against the wall)

Oh God, how am I to bear this?　　　O Gott! Wer kann das ertragen?

FLORESTAN

Out of pity give me a little water. That's　　Aus Barmherzigkeit, gib mir nur einen
not asking much.　　　　　　　　　Tropfen Wasser. Das ist ja so wenig.

ROCCO
(aside)

Against my will I'm touched.　　　　Es geht mir wider meinen Willen zu
　　　　　　　　　　　　　　　　　　Herzen.

LEONORA

He seems to be giving in.　　　　　Er scheint sich zu erweichen.

FLORESTAN

You give me no answer?　　　　　　Du gibst mir keine Antwort?

ROCCO

I can't get you what you ask for. All I　　Ich kann Euch nicht verschaffen, was Ihr can give you is what's left of some wine in my jug. Fidelio!

verlangt. Alles, was ich Euch anbieten kann, ist ein Restchen Wein, das ich in meinem Kruge habe. – Fidelio!

LEONORA
(quickly bringing the jug)

Here it is, here it is!

Da ist er! Da ist er!

FLORESTAN
(looking at Leonora)

Who is that?

Wer ist das?

ROCCO

My turnkey and soon to be my son-in-law.

Mein Schliesser und in wenigen Tagen mein Eidam.

(gives Florestan the jug)

Drink. It's only a little wine but I give it you gladly.

Trinkt! Es ist freilich nur wenig Wein, aber ich gebe ihn Euch gern.

(to Leonora)

You, why, you seem strangely moved?

Du bist ja ganz in Bewegung?

LEONORA
(confused)

Who wouldn't be? You too, Master Rocco . . .

Wer sollte es nicht sein? Ihr selbst, Meister Rocco –

ROCCO

It's true. The man has such a voice . . .

Es ist wahr, der Mensch hat so eine Stimme . . .

LEONORA

Yes. It strikes to the very depth of the soul.

Jawohl, sie dringt in die Tiefe des Herzens.

Trio No. 13

FLORESTAN [28]

Some better world, one day, reward you,
Kind heaven has guided you here,
My thanks, your help to me is dear,
Though for your kindness I cannot
recompense you.

Euch werde Lohn in bessern Welten,
Der Himmel hat euch mir geschickt.
O Dank! Ihr habt mich süss erquickt;
Ich kann die Wohltat nicht vergelten.

ROCCO
(softly to Leonora, whom he draws to his side)

I gladly help one such as he,
He's not much longer left to live.

Ich labt' ihn gern, den armen Mann,
Es ist ja bald um ihn getan.

LEONORA
(aside)

My heart is racing past belief!
It beats with joy and bitter grief.

Wie heftig pochet dieses Herz!
Es wogt in Freud' und scharfem
Schmerz!

FLORESTAN
(aside)

The lad seems moved I'm bound to say.
The man himself was kind to me.

Bewegt seh' ich den Jüngling hier,
Und Rührung zeigt auch dieser Mann,

Oh God, you send me hope today
That I may win their loyalty.

O Gott, du sendest Hoffnung mir,
Dass ich sie noch gewinnen kann.

LEONORA
(aside)

The fearful hour at last is near,
That brings me death or rescue here.

Die hehre, bange Stunde winkt,
Die Tod mir oder Rettung bringt.

ROCCO
(aside)

My duty thus commanded me,
Tho' I still hate such cruelty.

Ich tu', was meine Pflicht gebeut,
Doch hass' ich alle Grausamkeit.

LEONORA
(softly to Rocco, taking a piece of bread from the satchel)

This piece of bread, that I have with me,
I've kept it here since yesterday.

Dies Stückchen Brot, ja seit zwei Tagen
Trag' ich es immer schon bei mir.

ROCCO

A kindly thought, I'm bound to say,
But now we simply dare not risk it.

Ich möchte gern, doch sag' ich dir,
Das hiesse wirklich zu viel wagen.

LEONORA
(coaxing him)

Yet,
You freely gave him wine just now.

Ach!
Ihr labtet gern den armen Mann.

ROCCO

But here's a thing I can't allow.

Das geht nicht an, das geht nicht an.

LEONORA
(as before)

He's not much longer left to live!

Es ist ja bald um ihn getan!

ROCCO

All right then, yes all right, well you
may risk it.

So sei es, ja, du kannst es wagen!

LEONORA
(with deep emotion, giving the bread to Florestan)

Come take this bread, unhappy man.

Da nimm das Brot, du armer Mann!

FLORESTAN
(grasping Leonora's hand and pressing it to him)

My grateful thanks, my thanks, my
thanks!
May some better world one day reward
you
For heav'n itself has sent you here.
My thanks! Your help to me is dear.
Such kindness I cannot repay.

O, Dank dir, Dank! O Dank!

Euch werde Lohn in bessern Welten,

Der Himmel hat euch mir geschickt.
O Dank! Ihr habt mich süss erquickt.

LEONORA

May heaven send you rescue here
For then will my reward be near.
You gave him comfort here just now,
Poor, lonely, man!

Der Himmel schicke Rettung dir,
Dann wird mir hoher Lohn gewährt.

ROCCO

Though deeply moved by all your grief	Mich rührte oft dein Leiden hier,
To help you, I was not allowed.	Doch Hilfe war mir streng verwehrt.

(aside)

I'm glad to comfort such as he,	Ich labt' ihn gern, den armen Mann,
The end is near as you can see,	Es ist ja bald um ihn getan.
Soon death will come to seek him here!	
Unhappy, lonely man!	

LEONORA

Oh this is more than I can bear!	O mehr, als ich ertragen kann!

FLORESTAN

For such good deeds could I reward you!	O dass ich Euch nicht lohnen kann!

Florestan eats the bread.

ROCCO
(to Leonora, after a moment's silence)

Everything's ready. I'll give the signal.	Alles ist bereit. Ich gehe, das Signal zu geben.

(going to the back of the stage)

LEONORA

Oh God, give me strength and courage.	O Gott, gib mir Mut und Stärke!

FLORESTAN
(to Leonora, as Rocco goes to open the doors)

Where is he going?	Wo geht er hin?

Rocco opens the doors and gives the signal with a sharp whistle.

Is that the harbinger of my death?	Ist das der Vorbote meines Todes?

LEONORA
(deeply moved)

No, no! Be calm, dear prisoner!	Nein, nein! Beruhige dich, lieber Gefangener.

FLORESTAN

My Leonora . . . am I then never to see you again?	O meine Leonore! So soll ich dich nie wieder sehen?

LEONORA
(drawn to Florestan but attempting to master the impulse)

How my heart draws me to him!	Mein ganzes Herz reisst mich zu ihm hin!

(to Florestan)

Be calm, I say. Don't forget, whatever you may see or hear, that a divine providence watches over all of us! Yes, there *is* a divine providence.	Sei ruhig, sag ich dir! Vergiss nicht, was du auch hören und sehen magst, dass überall eine Vorsehung ist. – Ja, ja, es gibt eine Vorsehung!

Leonora moves away towards the well. **Scene Three.** *The same. Pizarro, muffled in a cloak.*

PIZARRO
(to Rocco, disguising his voice)

Everything ready?	Ist alles bereit?

ROCCO

Yes, we only need to open the cistern.	Ja, die Zisterne braucht nur geöffnet zu werden.

PIZARRO

Good. Get rid of the boy.	Gut, der Junge soll sich entfernen.

ROCCO
(to Leonora)

Go. Be off.	Geh, entferne dich!

LEONORA
(very confused)

Who? Me? But you . . .	Wer? – Ich? – Und Ihr?

ROCCO

Haven't I still to take the prisoner's chains off? Go, go!	Muss ich nicht dem Gefangenen die Eisen abnehmen? Geh, geh!

Leonora goes to the back of the stage and gradually approaches Florestan in the shadows, keeping her eyes on Pizarro.

PIZARRO
(aside, glancing at Rocco and Leonora)

I must dispose of these two today to make sure that everything's kept under cover.	Die muss ich mir noch heute beide vom Halse schaffen, damit alles verborgen bleibt.

ROCCO
(to Pizarro)

Shall I take off his fetters?	Soll ich ihm die Ketten abnehmen?

PIZARRO

No. Just free him from the stone.	Nein, aber schliesse ihn von dem Stein los.

(aside)

Time presses.	Die Zeit ist dringend.

He draws a dagger. | Quartet No. 14

PIZARRO

It's time now. Yes, but first I'll tell him Whose blade shall pierce his righteous heart.	Er sterbe! Doch er soll erst wissen, Wer ihm sein stolzes Herz zerfleischt.
No more I'll hide my secret from him, Look here! I was not tricked by you!	Der Rache Dunkel sei zerrissen, Sieh her! Du hast mich nicht getäuscht!

(he throws off his cloak)

Pizarro, whom you would have ruined. [29] Pizarro, whom you should have dreaded, Now claims his vengeance here!	Pizarro, den du stürzen wolltest, Pizarro, den du fürchten solltest, Steht nun als Rächer hier.

FLORESTAN
(calmly)

A murd'rer, here I see.	Ein Mörder steht vor mir!

PIZARRO

Once more let me recall The wrong you've done to me. And so without delay This blade of mine . . .	Noch einmal ruf' ich dir, Was du getan, zurück; Nur noch ein Augenblick, Und dieser Dolch –

He is about to stab Florestan. Leonora hurls herself forward with a piercing cry and shields Florestan with her body.

LEONORA

Stand back!	Zurück!

FLORESTAN

Oh God!	O Gott!

ROCCO

What's this?   Was soll?

LEONORA

Your dagger   Durchbohren
Must pierce my own heart first.   Musst du erst diese Brust.
May death soon be your sentence   Der Tod sei dir geschworen
For all your evil crimes.   Für deine Mörderlust.

PIZARRO
(*pushing her away*)
You maniac!   Wahnsinniger!

ROCCO
(*to Leonora*)
Stand back!   Halt ein!

PIZARRO

I'll make you pay for this.   Er soll bestraft sein!

LEONORA
(*once more shielding her husband*)
First, kill his wife!   [30] Töt' erst sein Weib!

ROCCO AND PIZARRO

His wife?   Sein Weib?

FLORESTAN

My wife!   Mein Weib!

LEONORA
(*to Florestan*)
Yes, I am Leonora!   Ja, sieh hier Leonoren!

FLORESTAN

Leonora!   Leonore!

LEONORA
(*to the others*)
I am his wife, I swore   Ich bin sein Weib, geschworen
I would rescue him and ruin you. Hab' ich ihm Trost, Verderben dir!

PIZARRO
(*aside*)
What an audacious deed!   Welch' unerhörter Mut!

FLORESTAN
(*to Leonora*)
My heart beats high with joy.   Vor Freude starrt mein Blut!

ROCCO
(*aside*)
My blood runs cold with fear.   Mir starrt vor Angst mein Blut!

LEONORA
(*aside*)
His anger I defy, yes!   Ich trotze seiner Wut!

PIZARRO

Must I give way before a woman? Soll ich vor einem Weibe beben?

79

LEONORA

May death soon be your sentence!   Der Tod sei dir geschworen!

PIZARRO

My victims both of them shall be!   So opfr' ich beide meinem Grimm.

He rushes at Leonora and Florestan.

LEONORA

Your dagger must pierce my own heart   Durchbohren musst du erst diese Brust!
first.

PIZARRO

You shared your life with that poor   Geteilt hast du mit ihm das Leben,
madman,
So die with him and share his fate!   So teile nun den Tod mit ihm.

LEONORA
(quickly pointing a pistol at him)

Say but a word and you shall die!   Noch einen Laut – und du bist tot!

The sound of the trumpet call from the tower is heard. [31, 32]

LEONORA
(embracing Florestan)

Ah! That brings salvation! God be   Ach, du bist gerettet! Grosser Gott!
praised!

FLORESTAN

Ah! That brings salvation! God be   Ach, ich bin gerettet! Grosser Gott!
praised!

PIZARRO
(stunned)

Ah! Don Fernando! Cursed fate!   Ha, der Minister! Höll' und Tod!

ROCCO
(stunned)

Ah! What's this I hear? Oh, righteous   O was ist das, gerechter Gott!
God!

The trumpet sounds again, louder.[31]

Scene Four. *The same. Jacquino. Soldiers appear with torches at the uppermost grille on the staircase.*

JACQUINO
(speaking)

Father Rocco! The Minister is arriving,   Vater Rocco! Der Herr Minister kommt
his party's at the gate!   an. Sein Gefolge ist schon vor dem
                    Schlosstor.

ROCCO
(aside, startled and happily)

God be praised!   Gelobt sei Gott!

(very loudly to Jacquino)

We're coming, yes we're coming straight-   Wir kommen – ja, wir kommen
away. Men with torches, summon them   augenblicklich. Und diese Leute mit
to accompany the Governor up!   Fackeln sollen heruntersteigen und den
                    Herrn Gouverneur hinaufbegleiten.

The soldiers come down to the door. Exit Jacquino.

LEONORA AND FLORESTAN

The hour of retribution!   Es schlägt der Rache Stunde!

(Your) (My) danger now is past.	(Du) (Ich) sollst gerettet sein!
(For) (Your) courage and devotion	Die Liebe wird im Bunde
Will set (you) (me) free at last.	Mit Mute (dich) (mich) befrein!

PIZARRO

They mock me in derision,	Verflucht sei diese Stunde!
This hour shall be accursed.	Die Heuchler spotten mein;
Despairing frenzy drives me,	Verzweiflung wird im Bunde
I'll have revenge at last.	Mit meiner Rache sein.

ROCCO

I'm lost in this confusion,	O fürchterliche Stunde!
What now will come to pass?	O Gott, was wartet mein?
No longer will I serve him	Ich will nicht mehr im Bunde
The tyrant stands unmasked.	Mit diesem Wütrich sein.

Pizarro rushes out. Rocco gives Leonora a reassuring gesture as he leaves. Soldiers with torches precede them. **Scene Five.** *Leonora. Florestan.*

FLORESTAN

My Leonora! Dearest wife! Angel miraculously sent by God to save me, come to my heart!	Meine Leonore! Geliebtes Weib! Engel, den Gott wie ein Wunder zu meiner Rettung mir gesendet, lass an dies Herz dich drücken.

(embracing her)

Can we still hope?	Aber dürfen wir noch hoffen?

LEONORA

We can. The arrival of the Minister, whom we know, Pizarro's confusion and, above all, Father Rocco's consoling gestures are grounds enough for me to believe that our sufferings are at an end and the hour of good fortune is at hand.	Wir dürfen es. Die Ankunft des Ministers, den wir kennen, Pizarros Verwirrung und vor allem Vater Roccos tröstende Zeichen sind mir ebenso viele Gründe, zu glauben, unser Leiden sei am Ziele und die Zeit unseres Gluckes wolle beginnen.

FLORESTAN

Tell me, how did you come here?	Sprich, wie kamst du hierher?

LEONORA
(quickly)

I left Seville, came on foot and in man's clothes, the gaoler took me into his service, and your persecutor himself made me his turnkey.	Ich verliess Sevilla, ich kam zu fuss in Manneskleidern, der Kerkermeister nahm mich in seine Dienste, dein Verfolger selbst machte mich zum Schliesser.

FLORESTAN

Faithful wife! Woman without equal! What have you suffered on my account?	Treues Weib! Frau ohnegleichen! Was hast du meinetwegen erduldet?

LEONORA

Nothing, my Florestan! I was with you in spirit; how could my body not have been strong when it was fighting for its better self?	Nichts, mein Florestan! Meine Seele war mit dir; wie hätte der Körper sich nicht stark gefühlt, indem er für sein besseres Selbst kämpfte?

LEONORA

Oh sweet delight beyond all telling!	O namenlose Freude!
By my dear husband's side.	Mein Mann an meiner Brust!

FLORESTAN

O sweet delight beyond all telling!	O namenlose Freude!
By Leonora's side.	An Leonorens Brust!

BOTH

Our grief is now forgotten	Nach unnennbarem Leide
And joy returns at last.	So übergrosse Lust!

LEONORA

With you once more I stand united!	Du wieder nun in meinen Armen!

FLORESTAN

Kind heav'n at last our faith requited.	O Gott! Wie gross ist dein Erbarmen!

BOTH

Give thanks to God, our friend and guide,	O Dank dir, Gott für diese Lust!
My love, my life is at my side.	Mein $\binom{\text{Mann}}{\text{Weib}}$, mein $\binom{\text{Mann}}{\text{Weib}}$ an meiner Brust!

FLORESTAN

My life!	Du bist's!

LEONORA

My love!	Ich bin's!

FLORESTAN

What heav'n descended pleasure!	O himmlisches Entzücken!
Leonora!	Leonore!

LEONORA

Florestan!	Florestan!

BOTH

Oh sweeet delight beyond all telling,	O namenlose Freude!
Our grief is now forgotten	Nach unnennbarem Leide
And joy returns at last.	So übergrosse Lust!
$\binom{\text{My love, my life}}{\text{My wife, my wife}}$ to me restored	
Thanks be to God for this reward.	

Scene Six. *The same. Rocco.*

ROCCO
(bursting in)

Good news, you poor suffering creatures! His Excellency the Minister has brought a list of all the prisoners with him, and all of them are to be presented to him. Jacquino is already opening the upper cells.	Gute Botschaft, ihr armen Leidenden! Der Herr Minister hat eine Liste aller Gefangenen mit sich; alle sollen ihm vorgeführt werden. Jacquino öffnet die oberen Gefängnisse.

(to Florestan)

You alone are not mentioned on the list. Your imprisonment here was a personal act on the part of the Governor. Come,	Ihr allein seid nicht erwähnt. Euer Aufenthalt hier ist eine Eigenmächtigkeit des Gouverneurs. Kommt, folgt mir hin-

follow me. And you, too, dear lady! And if God grants power to my words, and if he rewards the heroic action of this most noble wife, then you will be set free, and your good fortune is the result of my efforts!

auf. Auch Ihr, gnädige Frau. Und gibt Gott meinen Worten Kraft und lohnt er die Heldentat der edelsten Gattin, so werdet Ihr frei, und Euer Glück ist mein Werk.

FLORESTAN

Leonora!   Leonora!

LEONORA

By what miracle!   Durch welche Wunder!

ROCCO

Come, don't delay! Up above you will learn everything. And keep those fetters on; God grant that they act as a plea for mercy, and will be put instead on the monster who caused you such suffering.

Fort, zögert nicht! Oben werdet ihr alles erfahren. Auch diese Fesseln behaltet noch. Gott gebe, dass sie Euch Mitleid erflehen und dem Grausamen angelegt werden, der Euch so viele Leiden bereitet.

Exeunt.

Scene change: *The parade ground of the castle, with a statue of the king.*

Scene Seven. *The castle guard march in and form an open square. Then from one side enters the Minister, Don Fernando, accompanied by Pizarro and officers. A crowd surges forward. From the other side, Jacquino and Marcellina lead in the state prisoners, who kneel before Don Fernando. | Finale No. 16*

CHORUS
(of Prisoners and People)

Hail glorious day, day of deliv'rance,   Heil sei dem Tag, Heil sei der Stunde,
So long desired, so long denied,   Die lang ersehnt, doch unvermeint,
Here clemency unites with justice,   Gerechtigkeit mit Huld im Bunde
Before the gates that guard our tomb   Vor unseres Grabes Tor erscheint!
The gloomy gates now opened wide!

FERNANDO [34]

Our sov'reign liege, the King, has charged me   Des besten Königs Wink und Wille
To seek out those who've suffered here.   Führt mich zu euch, ihr Armen, her,
That I may lift this veil of evil   Dass ich der Frevel Nacht enthülle,
Shrouding you all in gloom and fear.   Die All' umfangen schwarz und schwer.
No! No longer kneel like slaves before me,   Nein, nicht länger knieet sklavisch nieder,

The prisoners stand up.

No tyrant here you'll find in me.   Tyrannenstrenge sei mir fern!
A brother comes to seek his brothers,   Es sucht der Bruder seine Brüder,
If he can help, he gladly will.   Und kann er helfen, hilft er gern.

CHORUS

Hail glorious day! Day of deliv'rance.   Heil sei dem Tag, Heil sei der Stunde!

FERNANDO

A brother comes to seek his brothers   Es sucht der Bruder seine Brüder,
If he can help, he gladly will.   Und kann er helfen, hilft er gern.

Scene Eight. *Rocco pushes his way through the guard, followed by Leonora and Florestan.*

ROCCO

My lord then show this pair your mercy.   Wohlan, so helfet! Helft den Armen!

83

PIZARRO

What's this I see? Ha! Was seh' ich? Ha!

ROCCO
(to Pizarro)

This moves you then? Bewegt es dich?

PIZARRO
(to Rocco)

Go back! Fort, fort!

FERNANDO
(to Rocco)

Continue! Nein rede!

ROCCO

Oh, have pity, All' Erbarmen,
These two poor suff'rers need your aid. Vereine diesem Paare sich!

Florestan comes forward.

Don Florestan . . . Don Florestan . . .

FERNANDO
(amazed)

I thought he'd perished, Der Totgeglaubte,
That noble soul who fought for truth? Der Edle, der für Wahrheit stritt?

ROCCO

For that he suffered endless grief. Und Qualen ohne Zahl erlitt.

FERNANDO

The friend, the friend, I thought had Mein Freund! Mein Freund! Der
   perished?   Totgeglaubte?
In fetters, pale and wracked with pain. Gefesselt, bleich steht er vor mir.

ROCCO AND LEONORA

Yes, Florestan returns again. Ja, Florestan, ihr seht ihn hier.

ROCCO
(Leonora comes forward)

And Leonora . . . Und Leonore . . .

FERNANDO
(still more astonished)

Leonora? Leonore!

ROCCO

The pearl of women, here you see, Der Frauen Zierde führ' ich vor;
She came to me . . . Sie kam hierher –

PIZARRO

My lord, one moment. Zwei Worte sagen . . .

FERNANDO

Stand back! *Kein* Wort!
(to Rocco)

She came? Sie kam –

84

. . . Here to my door . . .   . . .dort an mein Tor
Dressed as a youth she joined my service,   Und trat als Knecht in meine Dienste
Working so well, that I decided   Und tat so brave, treue Dienste,
She'd be my future son-in-law.   Dass ich zum Eidam sie erkor.

MARCELLINA

What tidings! Heavens! What is this   O weh mir, was vernimmt mein Ohr!
I hear?

ROCCO

Pizarro at this very hour,   Der Unmensch wollt' in dieser Stunde
Had come down to put this man to   Vollziehn an Florestan den Mord.
death!

PIZARRO
(in the utmost rage)

With *their* connivance!   Vollziehn, *mit* ihm! –

ROCCO
(indicating himself and Leonora)

Yes, *our* connivance!   Mit *uns* im Bunde!
(to Fernando)
But your arrival stayed his hand.   Nur euer Kommen rief ihn fort.

CHORUS
(with great animation)

This tyrant here shall pay for this,   Bestrafet sei der Bösewicht,
Let justice wield her sword,   Der Unschuld unterdrückt.
For all these harsh and cruel deeds,   Gerechtigkeit hält zum Gericht
He'll reap a just reward.   Der Rache Schwert Gezückt.
At a sign from Fernando, Pizarro is taken away.

FERNANDO
(to Rocco)

You opened up his grave today,   Du schlossest auf des Edlen Grab,
Now go and take his chains away.   Jetzt nimm ihm seine Ketten ab –
No, wait. You, you his noble wife,   Doch halt! Euch, edle Frau, allein,
Yes, you alone shall set him free.   Euch ziemt es ganz ihn zu befrein.

LEONORA
(taking the key, she releases Florestan with great emotion from his fetters; he falls into her arms)
Oh God! Oh what happiness!   [35] O Gott! – Welch' ein Augenblick!

FLORESTAN
Oh joy that words could not express!   O unaussprechlich süsses Glück!

FERNANDO
Your judgement, Lord, is right and just,   Gerecht, O Gott, ist dein Gericht!
withal.
MARCELLINA AND ROCCO
You try us, yet you guard us all.   Du prüfest, du verlässt uns nicht.

ALL
Oh God! What blessed happiness!   O Gott! welch' ein Augenblick!
Oh joy that words could not express!   O unaussprechlich süsses Glück!
Your judgement, Lord, is just withal.   Gerecht, O Gott, ist dein Gericht,
You try us, yet you guard us all!   Du prüfest, du verlässt uns nicht!

CHORUS

Let all join in our rejoicing
For the prize of such a wife,
Ne'er can this be praised too highly
Thus to save a husband's life.

Wer ein holdes Weib errungen,
Stimm'in unsern Jubel ein!
Nie wird es zu hoch besungen,
Retterin des Gatten sein.

FLORESTAN

By your love I was protected,
Faith and virtue triumph here!

Deine Treu' erhielt mein Leben,
Tugend schreckt den Bösewicht.

LEONORA

Love alone my path directed,
True devotion knows no fear!

Liebe führte mein Bestreben,
Wahre Liebe fürchtet nicht.

CHORUS

Praise her courage and acclaim
Leonora's noble name!

Preist mit hoher Freude Glut
Leonorens edlen Mut!

FLORESTAN
(stepping forward and indicating Leonora)

Let all join in our rejoicing
For the prize of such a wife,
Ne'er can this be praised too highly
Thus to save a husband's life.

Wer ein solches Weib errungen,
Stimm' in unsern Jubel ein!
Nie wird es zu hoch besungen,
Retterin des Gatten sein.

LEONORA
(embracing him)

Love alone released you from your
    bondage,
Love has broken ev'ry chain,
Joyful hearts sing out your message,
Florestan is mine again.

Liebend ist er mir gelungen,

Dich aus Ketten zu befrein.
Liebend sei es hoch besungen,
Florestan ist wieder mein!

CHORUS

Let all join in our rejoicing
For the prize of such a wife,
Ne'er can this be praised too highly,
Thus to save a husband's life.

Wer ein holdes Weib errungen
Stimm' in unsern Jubel ein!
Nie wird es zu hoch besungen,
Rettern des Gatten sein.

LEONORA

Love released you from your bondage,
Florestan returns to life.

Liebend sei es hoch besungen:
Florestan ist wieder mein!

ALL THE OTHERS

Ne'er can this be praised too highly
Thus to save her husband's life.

Nie wird es zu hoch besungen,
Retterin des Gatten sein.

THE END

The final scene in the ENO production by Joachim Herz, designed by Reinhart Zimmermann, with costumes by Eleonore Kleiber (photo: Andrew March,

A fresco by Moritz von Schwind from the Vienna State Opera showing a scene from 'Fidelio'. (reproduced by permission of the Trustees of the British Museum)

Bibliography

A very selective list from the many books about Beethoven available in English.

The biography of Beethoven by Thayer, an American whose work was published in the last century (in German) remains the basic text about the composer's life; this is now available in English (edited and revised by Elliot Forbes, Princeton 1970). The account of Beethoven left by his pupil, Schindler, (*Beethoven as I knew him*, edited by MacArdle, translated by C S Jolly, London 1966) is invaluable, if prejudiced. The essay by Grove (London, 1951) on Beethoven is illuminating. Almost all of Beethoven's letters were translated by Emily Anderson (3 vols., London 1961) and a selection, edited by Alan Tyson, is available (*Selected Letters of Beethoven*, Macmillan, 1967). *Beethoven: A Documentary Study*, compiled by H Robbins London (Thames & Hudson, 1970) contains beautiful illustrations and a vast number of translated documents written by Beethoven's contemporaries.

Discography In order of UK release. All performances are in stereo unless asterisked* and in German.

Conductor Company/Chorus	*Fricsay* Bavarian State Opera	*Klemperer* Philharmonia Orch. & Chorus	*Maazel* VPO/Vienna State Opera Chorus
Don Fernando	K. Engen	F. Crass	H. Prey
Don Pizarro	D. Fisher-Dieskau	W. Berry	T. Krause
Florestan	E. Haefliger	J. Vickers	J. McCracken
Leonore	L. Rysanek	C. Ludwig	B. Nilsson
Rocco	G. Frick	G. Frick	K. Böhme
Marzelline	I. Seefried	I. Hallstein	G. Sciutti
Jacquino	F. Lenz	G. Unger	D. Grobe
1st Prisoner	—	K. Wehofshitz	K. Equiluz
2nd Prisoner	—	R. Wolansky	G. Adam
Disc UK number	DG 2705-073	SLS 5006	SET 272-3
Tape UK number	—	TC-SLS 5006	—
Excerpts (Disc)	—	—	SXL 6276
Excerpts (Tape)	—	—	—
Disc US number	—	3-Ang S-3625	2-Lon 1259
Tape US Number	—	—	—
—			

Karajan **Berlin PO/ German Opera Chorus**	*Böhm* **Dresden State OP. Orch & Chorus**	Bernstein **VPO/Vienna State Opera Chorus**	Blomstedt **Dresden Staatskapelle/Leipzig Radio Chorus**
J. van Dam	M. Talvela	D. Fischer-Dieskau	H.-C. Polster
Z. Keleman	T. Adam	H. Sotin	T. Adam
J. Vickers	J. King	R. Kollo	R. Cassilly
H. Dernesch	G. Jones	G. Janowitz	E. Moser
K. Ridderbusch	F. Crass	M. Jungwirth	K. Ridderbusch
H. Donath	E. Mathis	L. Popp	H. Donath
H. Laubenthal	P. Schreier	A. Dallapozza	E. Buchner
W. Hollweg	E. Buchner	A. Sramek	—
S. Rudolf	G. Leib	K. Terkal	—
SLS 954	**2721 136**	**2709 082**	**SLS 999**
—	3378 054	3371 039	—
—	—	2537 048	—
—	—	3305 048	—
3-Ang S-3773	3-DG 2709031	3-DG 2709082	—
—	—	3371 039	—

The essay by Lord Harewood in *Opera on
Record* (edited by Alan Blyth, Hutchinson,
1979) vividly introduces us to the many interpretations on record.

Excerpts

Number	Artists	UK Numbers only Disc Number ** Tap
O wär ich schon	P. Lorengar	SXL6525
Mir ist so wunderbar	Robson/Jones/Kelly/Dobson	
	Covent Garden/Solti	SET 392 - 3
Ha! Welch ein' Augenblick	G. Evans	SXL6262
Abscheulicher	B. Nilsson	SXL6077
Excerpts (arr. Sedlak)	London Wind Soloists/	
	Brymer	SDD 485